SCHOOL-BASED BEHAVIORAL INTERVENTION CASE STUDIES

School-Based Behavioral Intervention Case Studies translates principles of behavior into best practices for school psychologists, teachers, and other educational professionals, both in training and in practice. Using detailed case studies illustrating evidence-based interventions, each chapter describes all the necessary elements of effective behavior intervention plans including rich descriptions of target behaviors, detailed intervention protocols, data collection and analysis methods, and tips for ensuring social acceptability and treatment integrity. Addressing a wide array of common behavior problems, this unique and invaluable resource offers real-world examples of intervention and assessment strategies.

Michael I. Axelrod is Director of the Human Development Center and Professor of Psychology at the University of Wisconsin, Eau Claire, USA. His primary clinical and research interests include helping parents and schools solve problems involving academic, behavioral, and social/emotional functioning.

Melissa Coolong-Chaffin is Associate Professor of Psychology and Co-Director of the Academic Intervention Clinic in the Human Development Center at the University of Wisconsin, Eau Claire, USA. Her research and clinical work focuses on reading and social behavioral interventions in home and school settings.

Renee O. Hawkins is the Director of the School of Human Services and Professor of School Psychology at the University of Cincinnati, USA. Her research focuses on identifying effective school-based interventions to promote positive academic and social emotional outcomes for children, with a specific focus on children with emotional and behavioral disorders.

SCHOOL-BASED BEHAVIORAL INTERVENTION CASE STUDIES

Effective Problem Solving for School Psychologists

Edited By Michael I. Axelrod, Melissa Coolong-Chaffin, and Renee O. Hawkins

NEW YORK AND LONDON

First published 2021
by Routledge
52 Vanderbilt Avenue, New York, NY 10017

and by Routledge
2 Park Square, Milton Park, Abingdon, Oxon, OX14 4RN

Routledge is an imprint of the Taylor & Francis Group, an informa business

© 2021 Taylor & Francis

The right of Michael I. Axelrod, Melissa Coolong-Chaffin, and Renee O. Hawkins to be identified as the authors of the editorial material, and of the authors for their individual chapters, has been asserted in accordance with sections 77 and 78 of the Copyright, Designs and Patents Act 1988.

All rights reserved. No part of this book may be reprinted or reproduced or utilized in any form or by any electronic, mechanical, or other means, now known or hereafter invented, including photocopying and recording, or in any information storage or retrieval system, without permission in writing from the publishers.

Trademark notice: Product or corporate names may be trademarks or registered trademarks, and are used only for identification and explanation without intent to infringe.

Library of Congress Cataloging-in-Publication Data
A catalog record for this title has been requested

ISBN: 978-0-367-26070-5 (hbk)
ISBN: 978-0-367-26069-9 (pbk)
ISBN: 978-0-429-29131-9 (ebk)

Typeset in Bembo
by SPi Global, India

This book is dedicated to school psychologists everywhere for their invaluable work supporting students and teachers.

To my parents, Bill and Mary Pat Axelrod (M.I.A.)

To my parents, Frank and Janie Coolong, and to Dave and Will Chaffin (M.C.C.)

To my children, Jack, Luke, and Tyler (R.O.H.)

CONTENTS

List of Figures   xi
List of Tables   xiii
Contributors   xv
Acknowledgments   xix

1 Introduction   1
  Michael I. Axelrod, Melissa Coolong-Chaffin, and Renee O. Hawkins

2 Differential Reinforcement   15
  Tai A. Collins, Christa L. Newman, Bryn Endres, and Julia N. Villarreal

3 Token Economy   30
  Denise A. Soares, Judith R. Harrison, and Lauren E. Puente

4 Time-Out   48
  Anna C.J. Long, Jessie A.G. Munson, and Catherine R. Lark

5 Premack's Principle and Visual Schedules   62
  Susan Rattan and Mahri Wrightington

6	Video Modeling *Scott Bellini and Olivia Heck*	76
7	Behavioral Skills Training and Positive Practice *Clayton R. Cook and Shawn N. Girtler*	93
8	Behavioral Momentum *Michael I. Axelrod, Melissa Coolong-Chaffin, and Renee O. Hawkins*	111
9	Response Effort and Overcorrection *Todd Haydon, Cara Dillon, Alana M. Kennedy, and Tina Stanton-Chapman*	129
10	Response Cost Raffle and Mystery Motivator *Gina Coffee and Sally Whitelock*	142
11	Self-Monitoring *Faith G. Miller and Alexandria C. Muldrew*	161
12	Cognitive Behavioral Therapy *Michael Handwerk and Jessamine Manack*	175
13	Exposure Therapy *Rachel E. Mathews, Michael L. Sulkowski, and Cary Jordan*	198
14	Behavioral Activation *Laura Nabors, Christina Klein, and Myia Graves*	214
15	Good Behavior Game *Evan H. Dart, Keith C. Radley, Christley McGirt, Jordyn Martin, Talia Shuman, and Rachael Hite*	229
16	Timely Transitions Game *Elizabeth McCallum, Ara J. Schmitt, and Brittany Evans*	243
17	Positive Peer Reporting *Christine E. Neddenriep*	257

18	Color Wheel *Kathleen Aspiranti*	275
19	Check-In Check-Out/Behavior Report Card *Daniel D. Drevon, Michael D. Hixson, Amy Campbell,* *Allison M. Brown, and Alexander M. Rigney*	290
20	Social Stories™ *Frank J. Sansosti*	302
21	Functional Analysis *Ajamu Nkosi and Michael M. Mueller*	317
	Index	*331*

FIGURES

2.1	Information collected from the Functional Assessment Checklist for Teachers and Staff	18
2.2	Sylvia's DBR data	21
3.1	Interventions in the BIP	35
3.2	Steps in teaching the replacement behavior	36
3.3	Steps to develop a token economy	36
3.4	Noncompliance with reading during baseline and intervention phases	39
3.5	ODRs for physical aggression during baseline and intervention phases	39
4.1	Daily frequency of aggressive behaviors	55
4.2	Weekly points earned	55
5.1	Data collection form	67
5.2	Average estimates of percentage of written work completed by subject area during baseline	68
5.3	Intervention fidelity checklist	70
5.4	Average estimates of percentage of written work completed for all classes across baseline and intervention phases	72
6.1	Social validity and treatment fidelity form	83
6.2	Percentage of unprompted social engagement and frequency of ineffective and problematic behaviors before, during, and after VSM intervention	85
7.1	Behavior and skills to teach through behavioral skills training	96
7.2	Progress monitoring graphs for on-task and disruptive behavior	107
7.3	Data-based decision-making grid	108
8.1	Casey's percentage compliance with low-probability instructions	119
8.2	Goal attainment scale for percentage compliance with low-probability instructions	121

xii Figures

9.1	Instances of aggression per hour	137
9.2	Rate of appropriate card use in one hour	138
10.1	Off-task verbal behaviors	150
10.2	On-task verbal behaviors	150
10.3	Assignment completion	152
11.1	Self-monitoring form	166
11.2	Percentage of time of AEBs across baseline, self-monitoring, and self-monitoring with reinforcement conditions	169
11.3	Proportion of items completed on in-class worksheets	170
12.1	School days with full and partial attendance	189
12.2	Average hours at school per week	189
12.3	SUDS ratings for CBT sessions	190
13.1	Number of days attending school per week during baseline and intervention phases	205
13.2	Number of hours per week Anna spent in school during baseline and intervention phases	206
13.3	Number of times Anna attempted to leave school per week during baseline and intervention phases	207
14.1	Asia's average weekly average for daily mood ratings, number of daily activities, and number of daily positive statements during baseline and intervention phases	223
15.1	Academic engagement during baseline and intervention phases as measured by Planned Activity Checks (PAC) and Daily Behavior Ratings (DBR)	232
15.2	Good Behavior Game fidelity data	237
16.1	Timely Transitions Game procedural checklist	250
16.2	Transition time in seconds across baseline (BL) and intervention (TTG or Timely Transitions Game) phases	251
17.1	Effects of PPR on Meagan's level of social involvement during small-group work with peer comparison	265
17.2	Effects of PPR on Meagan's level of social involvement during recess with peer comparison	266
17.3	Effects of PPR on class-wide direct behavior rating of positive peer interactions during small-group work	267
18.1	Percentage of intervals with inappropriate noises during no-CWS and CWS phases	282
18.2	Percentage of intervals in transition time during no-CWS and CWS phases	283
19.1	Percent of points earned on the BRC across consecutive school days for Timothy	295
20.1	Minutes of time engaged (Academic Engaged Time) during selected instructional activity	312
21.1	Functional analysis results for Cody	324
21.2	Responses per minute during the treatment evaluation for Cody	326

TABLES

2.1	Results of Mr. Snow's IRP-15	22
2.2	Results of Sylvia's CIRP	22
4.1	A-B-C Data for Direct Observation of Ramona's Problem Behaviors	51
4.2	School-Home Note for Ramona's Problem Behaviors	52
4.3	Frequency Chart for Direct Observation of Ramona's Problem Behaviors	53
5.1	A-B-C Data	66
5.2	Baseline Data	67
5.3	Baseline and Intervention Data: Average Estimates of Percentage of Written Work Completed	71
7.1	Goal Statements for Billie's Disruptive and On-Task Behavior	101
7.2	Baseline Data for Disruptive Behavior (Frequency) and On-Task Behavior (Duration)	102
7.3	Intervention Target Behavior and Skills	104
7.4	Intervention Fidelity Data for BST and Positive Practice	105
8.1	Summary of A-B-C Data Collected during Classroom Observations	114
8.2	Casey's Percentage Compliance with Instructions Identified as High-Probability	115
8.3	Goal Attainment Scale	116
8.4	Behavioral Momentum Procedural Checklist for 3:1 Condition	118
8.5	Frequency of Escalations of Behavior by Condition	120
9.1	A-B-C Recording Data from Classroom Observations	134
9.2	Social Validity Scale: Intervention Rating Scale Profile-15	139
10.1	Example Data from A-B-C Narrative Observations	146

12.1	Karla's Anxiety Hierarchy with SUDS Ratings from the First CBT Session	180
12.2	Therapeutic Alliance & Outcome Questionnaire (TAOQ) Ratings	188
14.1	Common Behavioral Activation Elements Used With Adolescents	216
14.2	Daily Journal	220
14.3	Asia's Ratings on the PROMIS Scale and Discussion Items With for Therapy	224
18.1	CWS Color Rules and Situations for Each Color Use	279
20.1	Following Directions Social Story (each bullet corresponded with a page)	310
20.2	Mean Rates of Felipe's Following Instructions and Inappropriate Behaviors Across Phases	311
21.1	A-B-C Observation Results for Cody	322

CONTRIBUTORS

Kathleen Aspiranti, Ph.D.
University of Kentucky, USA

Michael I. Axelrod, Ph.D.
University of Wisconsin – Eau Claire, USA

Scott Bellini, Ph.D.
Indiana University – Bloomington, USA

Allison M. Brown, B.A.
Central Michigan University, USA

Amy Campbell, Ph.D.
Grand Valley State University, USA

Gina Coffee, Ph.D.
Denver Public Schools, USA

Tai A. Collins, Ph.D.
University of Cincinnati, USA

Clayton R. Cook, Ph.D.
University of Minnesota-Twin Cities, USA

Melissa Coolong-Chaffin, Ph.D.
University of Wisconsin – Eau Claire, USA

Evan H. Dart, Ph.D.
University of South Florida, USA

Cara Dillon, M.Ed.
University of Cincinnati, USA

Daniel D. Drevon, Ph.D.
Central Michigan University, USA

Bryn Endres, M.Ed.
University of Cincinnati, USA

Brittany Evans, M.S.Ed.
Duquesne University, USA

Shawn N. Girtler, M.S.
University of Minnesota, USA

Myia Graves, Ph.D.
Southeastern Louisiana University, USA

Michael Handwerk, Ph.D.
Streamwood Behavioral Healthcare, USA

Judith R. Harrison, Ph.D.
Rutgers, The State University of New Jersey, USA

Renee O. Hawkins, Ph.D.
University of Cincinnati, USA

Todd Haydon, Ph.D.
University of Cincinnati, USA

Olivia Heck, B.A.
Indiana University – Bloomington, USA

Rachael Hite, B.S.
University of South Florida, USA

Michael D. Hixson, Ph.D.
Central Michigan University, USA

Cary Jordan, Ph.D.
University of Arizona, USA

Alana M. Kennedy, Ed.S.
University of Cincinnati, USA

Christina Klein, MPH.
University of Cincinnati, USA

Catherine R. Lark, Ph.D.
Jefferson Neurobehavioral Group, USA

Anna C.J. Long, Ph.D.
Louisiana State University, USA

Jessamine Manack, B.S.
Arizona State University, USA

Jordyn Martin, B.A.
University of South Florida, USA

Rachel E. Mathews, Ed.S.
Kent State University, USA

Elizabeth McCallum, Ph.D.
Duquesne University, USA

Christley McGirt, B.A.
University of South Florida, USA

Faith G. Miller, Ph.D.
University of Minnesota – Twin Cities, USA

Michael M. Mueller, Ph.D.
Southern Behavioral Group, USA

Alexandria C. Muldrew, M.A.
University of Minnesota – Twin Cities, USA

Jessie A.G. Munson, M.S.
Louisiana State University, USA

Laura Nabors, Ph.D.
University of Cincinnati, USA

Christine E. Neddenriep, Ph.D.
University of Wisconsin – Whitewater, USA

Christa L. Newman, M.Ed.
University of Cincinnati, USA

Ajamu Nkosi, Ph.D.
Southern Behavioral Group, USA

Lauren E. Puente, M.Ed.
Grimes County Special Education Cooperative, USA

Keith C. Radley, Ph.D.
University of Utah, USA

Susan Rattan, Ph.D.
Duquesne University, USA

Alexander M. Rigney, M.Ed.
Central Michigan University, USA

Frank J. Sansosti, Ph.D.
Kent State University, USA

Ara J. Schmitt, Ph.D.
Duquesne University, USA

Talia Shuman, B.A.
University of South Florida, USA

Denise A. Soares, Ph.D.
University of Mississippi, USA

Tina Stanton-Chapman, Ph.D.
University of Cincinnati, USA

Michael L. Sulkowski, Ph.D.
University of Arizona, USA

Julia N. Villarreal, M.Ed.
University of Cincinnati, USA

Sally Whitelock, M.A.
Denver Public Schools, USA

Mahri Wrightington, Ph.D.
PD Monster, LLC, USA

ACKNOWLEDGMENTS

As with any book, *School-Based Behavioral Intervention Case Studies: Effective Problem Solving for School Psychologists* is the product of the hard work of a number of individuals, to whom we would like to give credit. We would like to extend our gratitude to Daniel Schwartz and Olivia Powers from Routledge/Taylor & Francis. Their assistance, encouragement, and support during all stages of this book were invaluable. We are also appreciative of our colleagues, especially Dr. Mary Beth Tusing (UW – Eau Claire) and Dr. Tai A. Collins (University of Cincinnati), for sharing their knowledge and providing guidance and friendship over the years. We would also like to thank Toni Volbrecht for taking on added responsibilities while we completed this book and Michaela Clement for the many hours she committed to supporting our work. Finally, this work would not have been possible without the inspiration from the countless educators, students, and families with whom we have worked throughout the years.

1
INTRODUCTION

Michael I. Axelrod, Melissa Coolong-Chaffin, and Renee O. Hawkins

Introduction

Schools across the nation are implementing Multi-Tiered Systems of Support (MTSS) as a way to address the academic and behavioral needs of all students. These systems have broad support from many educational leaders and organizations (e.g., Batsche et al., 2005; Council for Exceptional Children, 2008; National Association of School Psychologists, 2009). The purpose of these systems is to use a data-driven process to efficiently and effectively deliver resources according to student need (CRTI, n.d.). This process is designed to be efficient in that more intensive resources (e.g., small-group instruction, individualized interventions) are reserved for students for whom objective data identify a need. The process is designed to be effective, as it rests on practices with theoretical and empirical support (e.g., high-quality core instruction, reliable and valid assessment procedures, evidence-based interventions) (CRTI, n.d.).

Positive Behavioral Interventions and Supports (PBIS) is the application of MTSS principles to support the development of academic, behavioral, and social skills in schools. Implementation of PBIS has been associated with improved outcomes for students and schools, such as increased academic performance, increased social-emotional competence, decreased bullying behaviors, decreased disciplinary actions (i.e., office disciplinary referrals, suspensions, and expulsions), and increased perceptions of school climate and safety (see Noltemeyer, Palmer, James, & Wiechman, 2019). PBIS encompasses a three-tiered model in which coordinated school systems collect relevant outcome data to inform universal practices for all students (i.e., Tier 1); targeted practices for students whose behavior indicates a need for more support (i.e., Tier 2); and intensive practices for students who have not responded adequately to lower-level supports and thus require individualized interventions (i.e., Tier 3). Recommendations for successful implementation of intensive services include conducting function-based assessments, providing wraparound supports across school and home environments, and carefully considering cultural and contextual fit.

One approach that can inform the process of developing successful interventions and supports within a PBIS framework comes from the tradition of applied behavior analysis. Applied behavior analysis uses principles of learning theory to guide the selection, implementation, and evaluation of interventions designed to impact socially significant behaviors (Baer, Wolf, & Risley, 1968). Behaviors targeted for intervention may be social or academic in nature. An important consideration in the development of effective behavioral interventions is matching the intervention to the function the behavior serves for the student. Fundamental to this process is the premise that students (and indeed, all living organisms) engage in behaviors for a reason and that behaviors persist because of the reinforcement contingencies established through experience. Behavior is generally reinforced by access to social attention, access to preferred tangible items or activities, avoiding or escaping demands or situations, and, in some scenarios, sensory stimulation. Effective behavioral interventions seek to increase desired behaviors and/or decrease undesired behaviors by understanding these variables that maintain problem behavior. With this in mind, educators can design interventions that allow students to access something pleasant or avoid/escape something unpleasant through appropriate rather than inappropriate behavior. Students are then empowered with skills to get their wants and needs met without causing harm or damaging relationships.

Guided by hypotheses regarding the function the behavior serves for the student, interventions may focus on stimuli or conditions that occur or exist prior to the behavior (i.e., antecedents) or stimuli or conditions that happen after the behavior occurs (i.e., consequences). Antecedent variables include type of demand (e.g., level of difficulty of the material, duration of the activity, social partner), modeling of the behavior, prompting (i.e., physical, verbal, visual), pacing of instruction, size and composition of the instructional or social group, and opportunities to respond. Consequences include error correction, contingent incentives for academic or behavioral performance, praise or acknowledgment, access to or removal of tangible items or desired activities, and removal of stimuli. Importantly, all of the aforementioned variables can be manipulated by educators to change student behavior. Intervention packages including multiple variables can be developed and the effects of those packages on individual student performance can be evaluated. Readers are referred elsewhere for more detailed information about the behavioral principles that guide this approach (see Alberto & Troutman, 2013; Cooper, Heron, & Heward, 2007).

Perhaps obvious, but often overlooked, is the fact that the identification and implementation of effective interventions does not happen in a vacuum.

Ecological theory posits that since children develop in a variety of interconnected systems (e.g., family, peer group, classroom, school, neighborhood, culture), careful consideration of these contexts and the interactions between them is essential to understanding problems and developing solutions (Bronfenbrenner, 1977). Effective interventions are ones that will actually be implemented correctly and as intended, and therefore the understanding of variables such as the beliefs, values, knowledge, motivation, skills, and resources of the multiple stakeholders involved is critical. Consequently, the development of interventions through collaboration with key stakeholders is essential. The achievement gap between white and minority children is a persistent and well-documented problem in this country. It is tempting to conclude that the different outcomes experienced by members of different groups indicates different learning needs are present and thus different intervention strategies are required. However, in the same way that attempting to develop interventions based on aptitude by treatment interactions has failed to result in better outcomes (Burns et al., 2016), research has not shown that matching interventions to students based on their cultural background is effective (see Kane & Boan, 2005 for a review). Fortunately, many strategies are generally effective for learners across backgrounds, and engaging in collaborative problem-solving is an effective way to ensure the intervention fits the context.

Essential Elements of Effective Behavior Intervention Plans

The interventions in this text were selected because of their documented evidence of effectiveness for improving the behaviors they were intended to change. School psychologists and others (e.g., teachers, administrators) charged with addressing students' problem behavior are compelled to identify interventions that have strong empirical support. However, the successful implementation of school-based interventions requires more than simply identifying practices that are labeled "evidence-based." Broad factors involving a school's ethos supporting intervention efforts, the service delivery process (e.g., MTSS), and availability of human and material resources influence an intervention plan's effectiveness. More specifically, important features of an intervention plan can greatly affect its success.

Comprehensive intervention plans are developed through systematic problem-solving generated by careful consideration of data. Best practices in data-based problem-solving rely on a paradigm consistent with the scientific method (Christ & Arañas, 2014). This method conceptually guides school psychologists and others to identify and analyze the problem, develop and implement the plan, and assess the plan's effects. There are four fundamental questions forming the basis of the problem-solving model: (1) What is the problem? (problem identification), (2) Why is it occurring? (problem analysis), (3) What should be done about it? (intervention plan development and implementation), and (4) Did it work? (intervention plan evaluation). This section describes several key elements of the problem-solving model nested within these questions and intended to guide intervention planning. These same characteristics are highlighted in each of the book's chapters.

Problem Identification

Intervention Targets and Operational Definitions

Defining a student's problem is an inherent feature of all school-based intervention service delivery models and is the first step in the problem-solving model (Bender & Shores, 2007; Pluymert, 2014). Problem identification begins with the collaborative process of selecting intervention targets. Team members (e.g., school psychologists, teachers, administrators, parents) can prioritize problems and collectively identify behaviors that are most concerning (e.g., behaviors that are frequent, longstanding, and pose a danger to others; Axelrod, 2017). In addition, problem identification may include selecting target behaviors that are relatively easy to change, likely to lead to generalization, are part of larger response chains, and are important for student success (Cooper et al., 2007; Nelson & Hayes, 1979). Finally, considering behavioral cusps (i.e., behaviors that when changed can have far-reaching positive consequences for the student) when identifying problems can lead to favorable outcomes across other behaviors and domains. For example, sharing with peers might be a behavioral cusp, as mastery could lead to naturally occurring positively reinforcing consequences that shape other adaptive social behaviors. Behavioral cusps can also involve foundational behaviors necessary to learn more complex skills or include behaviors that are needed to adapt to different contexts or settings (Rosales-Ruiz & Baer, 1997).

The next step involves clearly defining the problem. A well-defined problem describes the behavior's structure or topography (i.e., what the behavior looks like). Developing operational definitions that communicate action verbs labeling the problem assists in ensuring precision when explaining the target behavior to and gaining agreement among team members on specific behaviors to target (Alberto & Troutman, 2013). Moreover, operational definitions allow for accurate and reliable observations of target behaviors (Bicard, Bicard, & the IRIS Center, 2012). Refinement of an operational definition includes determining the strength of the problem's behavioral description. Morris (1985) suggested posing the following questions when developing an operational definition:

- Can the behavior be seen by an observer?
- Can the behavior be measured? Can its frequency be counted? Can the length of time the behavior is exhibited be computed?
- Can a person unfamiliar with the student accurately identify the target behavior when given the definition?

Description of Contextual Variables

Identifying relevant contextual factors allows for a more thorough appreciation of the problem. An ecological analysis involves understanding student, peer group, classroom and teacher, curricular and instructional, and home variables (Burns, Riley-Tillman, & Rathvon, 2017). For example, setting events or routines that occur in the relatively distant past can sometimes set circumstances for the later display of problem behavior (Iovannone, Anderson, & Scott, 2017). Setting events must happen long before the problem behavior, occur sometimes and not at other times, and have properties that allow for the event or routine to change. Common examples include hunger or sleep deprivation, cancellation of a rewarding activity, losing privileges at home, not taking a medication, fighting with a peer before school, and quality of a relationship with a teacher. Non-examples include the presence of a diagnosis (e.g., autism, Attention Deficit/Hyperactivity Disorder), parental divorce, moving to a new town, and getting a new teacher. Also considered temporally distant events, motivating operations are environmental circumstances that temporarily change the reinforcing value of a stimulus (Nosik & Carr, 2015). Practically speaking, motivating operations influence the occurrence of behavior by momentarily altering the value of reinforcing consequences. Infrequent teacher attention could be conceptualized as a motivating operation when it increases the value of attention as a reinforcer. Similarly, aversive academic tasks can be considered a motivating operation when it increases the value of escape as a reinforcer. While setting events are generally defined based on their descriptive nature relative to the problem behavior, motivating operations are more closely aligned with a functional understanding of behavior. In other words, motivating operations cause changes to the value of reinforcement and the behavior being reinforced (Michael, 1982).

Identifying antecedent and consequent conditions also assists in understanding the problem and contributes to the development of functionally-driven hypotheses about the target behavior (Axelrod, 2017). Assessing events that precede or follow the problem offer the team a comprehensive picture of the behavior including influential contextual and causal variables. Antecedents influence later responding through their relationships with reinforcement (Wacker, Berg, Harding, & Cooper-Brown, 2011). This is done either by establishing a stimulus as a signal for reinforcement (discriminative stimulus; Cooper et al., 2007) or momentarily changing the value of reinforcement (motivating operation; Michael, 1982). Consequences determine the contingencies that establish reinforcers and punishers (Axelrod, 2017). Specifically, reinforcement increases the behavior it follows and punishment decreases the behavior it follows. Identifying contextual variables that are related to an increase or decrease of the targeted behavior is a primary goal of the problem-solving process.

Assessing Present Levels of Performance

There are several important reasons for collecting baseline data on students' preintervention performance levels. First, assessing current levels of performance helps answer the question, "is there a problem?" The problem might actually represent someone's perception of or experience with the stated concern (Pluymert, 2014). Second, assessing discrepancies between students' current and expected levels of performance clarifies the magnitude of the problem (Axelrod, 2017). Baseline data help determine the degree to which present and desired performance levels differ. Finally, comparisons between baseline and intervention performance levels are necessary when evaluating intervention effects (Riley-Tillman & Burns, 2009).

Problem Analysis

The problem analysis phase features data-driven hypothesis development with the consideration that interventions are most effective when developed based on specific student need. Considering the identified problem and its context, teams use data to identify if concerns represent a class-wide problem requiring changes in behavior management approaches (Tier 1), a broader problem involving behavioral or social skill deficits (Tier 2), or a narrowly defined problem where specific causal variables are involved (Tier 3; see Burns et al., 2017). Accordingly, problem analysis focuses on answering several fundamental questions that facilitate hypothesis generation supporting intervention plan development.

Is It a Skill Deficit or Performance Problem?

Teams might initially ask whether the student's problem represents a skill deficit (i.e., "can't do") or performance problem (i.e., "won't do"). A skill deficit implies the student does not know how to perform the behavior or skill, or does not know how to apply the behavior or skill to new or more complex tasks. A performance problem suggests that the student knows how to perform the behavior or skill, but does not engage in the behavior or use the skill consistently.

What Alterable Contextual Variables Maintain the Problem?

Problems most often develop through the complex transaction of variables between the environment and student. However, alterable variables are typically contextual (e.g., instructional pace, frequency of positive reinforcement for appropriate behavior) and not within the student (e.g., learning disability). The problem analysis process involves generating hypotheses concerning the alterable variables that likely initiate or maintain a problem (Christ & Arañas, 2014). Teams consider setting events, motivating operations, and specific antecedents and consequences when positing possible contextual variables that influence the initiation or maintenance of the problem.

What Is the Problem's Function?

Decades of research have demonstrated that behavior is shaped by its probabilistic relationship with consequences (Axelrod & Santagata, 2020). By definition, reinforcement increases the behavior it follows and here it is applied to students' problem behavior. Desired attention and access to preferred activities or items can positively reinforce problem behavior, while avoidance of or escape from unpleasant activities or interactions can negatively reinforce problem behavior. Recognizing the functional relationship between a consequence and the behavior it predictably follows provides important contextual clues about the problem and helps the team develop functionally-driven hypotheses that can inform intervention development.

Functionally-Driven Hypotheses

Traditional intervention selection models are often based on the hypothesis that the problem is a result of the student's disability category. Interventions become "packages" that involve an array of components (e.g., individual and family therapy, behavioral contracting, time-out) considered appropriate for a specific cluster of problems (Watson & Steege, 2003). Put differently, teams often select interventions that have been previously implemented with students with similar problems. Despite similarities in the topography of the behavior, the function may be vastly different for each student and circumstance (Axelrod, 2017). Functionally driven hypotheses are derived from assessments that consider the variables that initiate or maintain the problem behavior and use that information to develop individualized interventions.

Intervention Plan Development

Progress Monitoring Data Collection Plan

Progress monitoring and data-based decision-making are interconnected components of any MTSS. Universally (i.e., Tier 1), progress monitoring data allow teams to identify discrepancies between current and expected levels of performance (Stoiber, 2014). As service delivery intensifies, progress monitoring serves to assess how individual students are responding to interventions, if individual students require more concentrated intervention, and what long-term goals are appropriate for individual students (Stecker, Fuchs, & Fuchs, 2008). While a description of how to design a school-wide progress monitoring program is beyond the scope of this chapter or book, there are several key features relevant to intervention plan development. First, progress monitoring should involve those behaviors targeted for intervention. Operational definitions assist in ensuring reliable measurement of relevant outcome variables. Second, repeated measurement of the target behavior should be sufficient enough for the team to draw valid conclusions from the data (Axelrod, 2017). Specifically, multiple observations of a behavior or skill across varying conditions (e.g., baseline, intervention, follow-up) allow for patterns to be identified and enhances the data's predictive qualities. Third, progress monitoring plans should be relatively easy to implement, and teams should consider balancing the need to collect quality data with available resources. Moreover, collaborating with teachers on data collection communicates regard for their perspective and confirms them as active contributors in providing evidence for students' improvements (Burns et al., 2017). Finally, school psychologists should be prepared to train, observe, and provide feedback to those collecting progress monitoring data. In some instances, school psychologists might be collecting some of the data themselves.

Specification of Intervention Goals

In order to fairly evaluate student progress, teams must establish valid goals. Goals should be ambitious yet reasonable so that judgments about the effectiveness of an intervention are a reflection of student behavior and not poorly selected goals. For example, an intervention that does not meaningfully impact student behavior may be judged to be effective if goals are set too low. Conversely, goals that are too challenging may lead teams to decide that a potentially effective intervention is not working because the goal is not achieved (Hosp, Howell, & Hosp, 2003).

Several different sources of information should be considered when establishing behavior goals. First, it is important to consider the local context for behavior. Local norms based on peer behavior in the same classroom and under the same learning conditions can clarify the extent of the problem and offer insight as to what behaviors are considered acceptable versus unacceptable in the setting (Habedank, 1995). Local norms provide a direct point of comparison that is socially valid and culturally relevant. However, local norms may not necessarily reflect desired levels of behavior and should be interpreted along with other data sources. Second, teams may consider national norms, which compare the behavior of students to their same age/grade peers nationally. National norms are available for some behavioral assessment tools, such as published rating scales and checklists (O'Shaughnessy, Lane, Gresham, & Beebe-Frankenberger, 2003). Teams should be cautious because, unlike local norms, national norms may not be reflective of the student population and context of a particular school. Criterion-referenced measures or empirically derived benchmarks indicate levels of performance/behavior that are predictive of future success and represent another source of data for goal-setting. There are published criterion-referenced behavioral assessments (O'Shaughnessy et al., 2003), and research provides guidelines for levels of academic engagement that are linked to learning (Finn & Zimmer, 2012). Finally, teams should consider input from all key stakeholders involved, including teachers, parents, and, when appropriate, students to ensure the goals selected are socially valid (Spear, Strickland-Cohen, Romer, & Albin, 2013).

Decision Rules

Decision rules are clear guidelines for decision-making that are established by problem-solving teams prior to intervention implementation (Kratochwill, Altschaefl, & Brice-Urbach, 2014). The use of decision rules adds objectivity and accountability to the problem-solving process. Rather than taking a wait-and-see approach to making decisions regarding student progress, teams should establish decision rules to ensure timely and data-based decision-making. Decision rules can be based on time, trend estimation, or a combination of both. An example of a time-based decision rule would be, "If the goal is not met in two weeks, the intervention plan will be modified." Trend estimation involves the use of an aim line drawn from the average or median of baseline data to the goal. Student progress is then compared to this aim line for decision-making. An example of a decision rule based on trend estimation is, "If three progress-monitoring points fall below (or above depending on the target behavior) the aim line, the intervention will be modified." Finally, an example of a decision rule based on time and trend estimation is, "If after three weeks of intervention implementation, three or more progress-monitoring points are below the aim line, the intervention will be adjusted."

Detailed Intervention Plans

To support strong implementation and to allow for informed problem-solving, teams should carefully develop clear and detailed intervention plans. The intervention plan should operationalize each step of the procedures, providing a step-by-step script for the individual(s) responsible for implementation. The use of detailed intervention scripts can increase the accuracy of implementation and the acceptability of procedures (Ehrhardt, Barnett, Lentz, Stollar, & Reifin, 1996). Further, collaboratively developed intervention plans can help ensure that all members of the team have the same understanding of the supports being provided to students.

Plans for Monitoring Intervention Adherence

Intervention adherence, also referred to as treatment integrity or fidelity, refers to the degree to which intervention plans are implemented as designed. The validity of decisions that are made regarding the effectiveness of an intervention are linked to information about intervention adherence (Barnett, Hawkins, & Lentz, 2011). Without evidence that an intervention has been implemented with high levels of adherence, problem-solving teams cannot confidently attribute improvements in behavior to the intervention, nor can they infer that an intervention was ineffective when desired improvements are not achieved. During intervention planning, problem-solving teams should establish a plan for monitoring adherence so they will have this information when evaluating intervention effects. Methods for monitoring and documenting adherence include direct observation, self-report by the individual responsible for implementation using an adherence checklist, and permanent products (e.g., sticker chart, self-monitoring form, daily behavior report card; Barnett et al., 2014).

There are no clear standards regarding how often adherence should be evaluated in practice; however, researchers suggest matching the intensity of the assessment of adherence to the intensity of the problem and the resources involved (Barnett et al., 2011). For example, for a class-wide, low-intensity behavior management system, it may be acceptable to collect adherence data once a month. In the case of a more intense Tier 2 small-group social skills intervention that occurs three times a week, teams may decide to collect data once every other week (16.67% of sessions). For the most intense individualized Tier 3 interventions that involve significant resources and high-stake decisions, including decisions around special education eligibility, teams should consider a thicker assessment schedule. With more adherence data, teams can be more confident in their evaluation of intervention effects and decisions about the continued use of valuable resources that are often limited in schools (e.g., staff to implement the intervention, time, intervention materials). For Tier 3 problem-solving, teams may look to research guidelines and consider assessing adherence for at least 20% of intervention sessions, with a goal of 25–33% of intervention sessions (Cooper et al., 2007; Kennedy, 2005).

Plans for Monitoring Interobserver Agreement

Interobserver or interrater agreement (IOA) is used to establish the reliability of the assessments used to evaluate student behavior. Teams can have increased confidence in decisions they make based on data that is proven to be reliable through agreement checks. IOA is determined by having two observers independently observe and record behavior. As examples, a teacher and teacher assistant may both complete a direct behavior rating for the same student, or two professionals may observe a class using systematic direct observation and compare ratings at the end of the session. Research indicates that IOA should be assessed for approximately 25% of data collected with a commonly cited criterion of 80% agreement. In practice, teams may consider collecting more reliability data early in the problem-solving process to make sure that operational definitions are clear and data-collection methods are feasible. Also, as with the collection of adherence data, the frequency of IOA data collection may increase with increasing intensity of problem behavior. Teams may require more data quickly for efficient problem-solving with high-intensity, challenging behavior.

Assessment of Intervention Acceptability

Intervention acceptability refers to the degree to which goals and procedures are judged to be appropriate and reasonable, as well as the degree to which the outcomes satisfy key stakeholders (Wolf, 1978). Throughout intervention planning, teams should be seeking feedback on the acceptability of procedures, particularly those who will be most directly involved in implementing the intervention. Some research has identified a positive correlation between acceptability and adherence (Dart, Cook, Collins, Gresham, & Chenier, 2012), although more research is needed in the area (Silva, Collier-Meek, Codding, & DeFouw, 2019). Acceptability data can be collected through a variety of methods including interviews, questionnaires, and rating scales. These can be developed by teams, or there are several published tools available (Silva et al., 2019).

Evaluation of Intervention Effects

Intervention effects should be continuously monitored throughout implementation for timely problem-solving. Data presented in time-series graphs that include goals lines, aim lines, and phase changes can aid teams in evaluating student progress. Further, decision rules create accountability for making changes to intervention plans when needed. A-B accountability designs are often used in practice to compare student performance before and after intervention; however, it is important to note that these designs do not allow for causal inferences. When using A-B designs, teams must carefully consider other changes in the student's environment that may have led to changes in behavior, especially if these changes occurred around the time the intervention was implemented. While the use of A-B designs is appropriate in many practice contexts, there are occasions when problem-solving teams may want to know, with confidence, that an intervention led to the observed change in student performance.

Internally valid, single-case designs can establish cause–effect functional relationships between interventions and student behavior (Cooper et al., 2007). By systematically introducing the intervention and allowing for repeated demonstration of intervention effects, single-case designs can rule out other extraneous, environmental variables as being the cause of changes in student performance. For example, alternating treatment designs can be used to systematically compare two intervention options with the team continuing to implement the more effective procedure based on data. As another example, the implementation of an intervention can be staggered over time across multiple target behaviors, establishing a multiple-baseline design for causal evaluations of treatment effects. Withdrawal, or A-B-A-B, designs can be applied by simply withdrawing an intervention once desired effects are observed, continuing to monitor behavior, and reintroducing the intervention when the behavior worsens again. The use of single-case designs to draw causal conclusions regarding intervention effects may be especially important for teams addressing high-intensity, dangerous problem behavior, when an intervention requires significant resources to implement, or when high-stakes cases are involved.

Conclusion

With these ideas in mind, the purpose of this book is to provide school psychologists and other educational professionals (e.g., special education teachers, school counselors) with practical, real-world examples of how to implement best-practice principles of behavior to solve common student problems. This resource goes beyond descriptions of behavioral theory by providing step-by-step examples of how to actually apply those principles in school settings. Each chapter describes a case study involving the use of an evidence-based behavioral intervention to solve common student problems presented in school settings. Case studies include detailed information about the targeted student(s), educator(s), and setting(s). The problem behavior is operationally defined in the context of relevant contextual variables, such as when and where the problem behavior occurs. Present levels of performance are described in terms of pertinent characteristics (e.g., frequency, duration, intensity). Data regarding problem behaviors are analyzed with respect to perceived functions. Interventions are described in detail, including information about theoretical and empirical bases for the intervention and potentially targeted populations. Intervention plans detail step-by-step protocols, articulation of goals, data-collection systems and progress-monitoring strategies, tactics for monitoring implementation integrity and fidelity of data collection, and ideas for ensuring and measuring intervention acceptability. Finally, data are analyzed and interpreted relative to intervention goals. This book also includes forms and templates for data collection for a variety of behaviors, intervention plans, and assessment of social acceptability and treatment integrity.

References

Alberto, P. A., & Troutman, A. C. (2013). *Applied behavior analysis for teachers* (9th ed.). Upper Saddle River, NJ: Pearson.

Axelrod, M. I. (2017). *Behavior analysis for school psychologists*. New York: Routledge. doi:10.4324/9781315650913

Axelrod, M. I., & Santagata, M. L. (2020). Behavioral parent training. In A. Maragakis, T. Waltz, & C. Drossel (Eds.), *Applications of behavior analysis to healthcare and beyond*. New York: Springer.

Baer, D. M., Wolf, M. M., & Risley, T. R. (1968). Some current dimensions of applied behavior analysis. *Journal of Applied Behavior Analysis*, 1, 91–97. doi:10.1901/jaba.1968.1-91

Barnett, D., Hawkins, R., & Lentz, F. E. (2011). Intervention adherence for research and practice: Necessity or triage outcome? *Journal of Educational and Psychological Consultation*, 21(3), 175–190. doi:10.1080/10474412.2011.595162

Barnett, D. W., Hawkins, R. O., Wahl, E., Shier, A., Denune, H., McCoy, D., & Kimener, L. (2014). Methods used to document procedural fidelity in school-based intervention research. *Journal of Behavioral Education*, 23, 89–107. doi:10.1007/s10864-013-9188-y

Batsche, G., Elliott, J., Graden, J. L., Grimes, J., Kovaleski, J. F., Prasse, D., et al. (2005). *Response to intervention: Policy considerations and implementation*. Alexandria, VA: National Association of State Directors of Special Education, Inc.

Bender, W. N., & Shores, C. (2007). *Response to intervention: A practical guide for every teacher.* Thousand Oaks, CA: Corwin Press.

Bicard, S. C., Bicard, D. F., & the IRIS Center. (2012). Defining behavior. Retrieved November 1, 2019 from http://iris.peabody.vanderbilt.edu/case_studies/ICS-015.pdf

Burns, M. K., Riley-Tillman, T. C., & Rathvon, N. (2017). *Effective school interventions: Evidence-based strategies for improving student outcomes* (3rd ed.). New York: Guilford.

Burns, M. K., Petersen-Brown, S., Haegele, K., Rodriguez, M., Schmitt, B., Cooper, M. et al. (2016). Meta-analysis of academic interventions derived from neuropsychological data. *School Psychology Quarterly,* 31, 28–42. doi:10.1037/spq0000117

Bronfenbrenner, U. (1977). Toward an experimental ecology of human development. *American Psychologist,* 32(7), 513–531. doi:10.1037/0003-066X.32.7.513

Center on Response to Intervention. (n.d.). Essential components of MTSS. Retrieved June 1, 2020, from https://rti4success.org/

Christ, T. J., & Arañas, Y. A. (2014). Best practices in problem analysis. In P. L. Harrison & A. Thomas (Eds.), *Best practices in school psychology: Data-based and collaborative decision making* (pp. 87–97). Bethesda, MD: National Association of School Psychologists.

Cooper, J., Heron, T., & Heward, W. (2007). *Applied behavior analysis* (2nd ed.). Upper Saddle River, NJ: Merrill/Pearson Education.

Council for Exceptional Children. (2008). *CEC's position on Response to Intervention (RTI): The Unique role of special education and special educators.* Arlington, VA: Author.

Dart, E. H., Cook, C. R., Collins, T. A., Gresham, F. M., & Chenier, J. S. (2012). Test driving interventions to increase treatment integrity and student outcomes. *School Psychology Review,* 41, 467–481.

Ehrhardt, K. E., Barnett, D. W., Lentz, F. E., Stollar, S. A., & Reifin, L. H. (1996). Innovative methodology in ecological consultation: Use of scripts to promote treatment acceptability and integrity. *School Psychology Quarterly,* 11, 149–168. doi:10.1037/h0088926

Finn, J. D., & Zimmer, K. S. (2012). Student engagement: What is it? Why does it matter? In S. L. Christenson, A. L. Reschly, & C. Wylie (Eds.), *Handbook of research on student engagement* (pp. 97–131). New York: Springer. doi:10.1007/978-1-4614-2018-7_5

Habedank, L. (1995). Best practices in developing local norms for problem solving in the schools. In A. Thomas & J. Grimes (Eds.), *Best practice in school psychology* (3rd ed., pp. 701–715). Washington, DC: National Association of School Psychologists.

Hosp, J. L., Howell, K. W., & Hosp, M. K. (2003). Characteristics of behavior rating scales: Implications for practice in assessment and behavioral support. *Journal of Positive Behavior Interventions,* 5, 201–208. doi:10.1177/10983007030050040301

Iovannone, R., Anderson, C., & Scott, T. (2017). Understanding setting events: What they are and how to identify them. *Beyond Behavior,* 26, 105–112. doi:10.1177/1074295617729795

Kane, H., & Boan, C. H. (2005). A review and critique of multicultural learning styles. In C. L. Frisby & C. R. Reynolds (Eds.), *Comprehensive handbook of multicultural school psychology.* Hoboken, NJ: John Wiley & Sons, Inc.

Kennedy, C. H. (2005). *Single-case designs for educational research.* Boston, MA: Allyn and Bacon.

Kratochwill, T. R., Altschaefl, M. R., & Brice-Urbach, B. (2014). Best practices in school-based problem solving consultation: Applications in prevention and intervention systems. In P. L. Harrison & A. Thomas (Eds.), *Best practices in school psychology: Data-based and collaborative decision making* (pp. 468–472). Bethesda, MD: National Association of School Psychologists.

Michael, J. (1982). Distinguishing between discriminative and motivational functions of stimuli. *Journal of the Experimental Analysis of Behavior*, 37, 149–155. doi:10.1901/jeab.1982.37-149

Morris, R. J. (1985). *Behavior modification with exceptional children: Principles and practices*. Glenview, IL: Scott Foresman.

National Association of School Psychologists. (2009). Appropriate academic supports to meet the needs of all students (Position Statement). Bethesda, MD: Author.

Nelson, R. O., & Hayes, S. C. (1979). Some current dimensions of behavioral assessment. *Behavioral Assessment*, 1, 1–16.

Noltemeyer, A., Palmer, K., James, A. G., & Wiechman, S. (2019). School-Wide Positive Behavioral Interventions and Supports (SWPBIS): A synthesis of existing research. *International Journal of School & Educational Psychology*, 7, 253–262.

Nosik, M. R., & Carr, J. E. (2015). On the distinction between the motivating operation and setting even concepts. *Behavior Analyst*, 38, 219–223. doi:10.1007/s40614-015-0042-5

O'Shaughnessy, T. E., Lane, K. L., Gresham, F. M., & Beebe-Frankenberger, M. E. (2003). Children placed at risk for learning and behavioral difficulties: Implementing a school-wide system of early identification and intervention. *Remedial and Special Education*, 24, 27–35. doi:10.1177/074193250302400103

Pluymert, K. (2014). Problem-solving foundations for school psychological services. In P. L. Harrison & A. Thomas (Eds.), *Best practices in school psychology: Data-based and collaborative decision making* (pp. 25–39). Bethesda, MD: National Association of School Psychologists.

Riley-Tillman, T. C., & Burns, M. K. (2009). *Evaluating educational interventions: Single-case designs for measuring response to intervention*. New York: Guilford.

Rosales Ruiz, J., & Baer, D. M. (1997). Behavioral cusps: A developmental and programmatic concept for behavior analysis. *Journal of Applied Behavior Analysis*, 30, 533–544. doi:10.1901/jaba.1997.30-533

Silva, M. R., Collier-Meek, M. A., Codding, R. S., & DeFouw, E. R. (2019). Acceptability assessment of school psychology interventions from 2005 to 2017. *Psychology in the Schools*, 57, 62–77. doi:10.1002/pits.22306

Spear, C. F., Strickland-Cohen, M. K., Romer, N., & Albin, R. W. (2013) An examination of social validity within single-case research with students with emotional and behavioral disorders. *Remedial and Special Education*, 34, 357–370.

Stecker, P. M., Fuchs, D., & Fuchs, L. S. (2008). Progress monitoring as essential practice within response to intervention. *Rural Special Education Quarterly*, 27, 10–17. doi:10.1177/875687050802700403

Stoiber, K. C. (2014). A comprehensive framework for multitiered systems of support in school psychology. In P. L. Harrison & A. Thomas (Eds.), *Best practices in school psychology: Data-based and collaborative decision making* (pp. 41–70). Bethesda, MD: National Association of School Psychologists.

Wacker, D. P., Berg, W. K., Harding, J. W., & Cooper-Brown, L. J. (2011). Functional and structural approaches to behavioral assessment of problem behavior. In W. W. Fisher, C. C. Piazza, & H. S. Roane (Eds.), *Handbook of applied behavior analysis* (pp. 165–181). New York: Guilford.

Watson, T. S., & Steege, M. W. (2003). *Conducting school-based functional behavioral assessments: A practitioner's guide*. New York: Guilford.

Wolf, M. M. (1978). Social validity: The case for subjective measurement or how applied behavior analysis is finding its heart. *Journal of Applied Behavior Analysis*, 11, 203–214. doi:10.1901/jaba.1978.11-203s

2

DIFFERENTIAL REINFORCEMENT

Tai A. Collins, Christa L. Newman, Bryn Endres, and Julia N. Villarreal

Introduction

Disruptive behaviors are problematic in schools because they have negative effects on the students, teachers, and other staff in the classroom. Off-task and disruptive behaviors make it difficult for teachers to focus on efficiently and effectively delivering academic content (Theodore, Bray, & Kehle, 2004). Instead, valuable instructional time is lost due to the management and prevention of problem behaviors (Cook et al., 2014). Disruptive behaviors are associated with both immediate and long-term consequences, including impacts on the academic engagement and achievement of both the target students and their peers (Cook et al., 2014; Stage & Quiroz, 1997).

Out-of-seat behavior is a particular type of off-task or disruptive behavior, typically described as a student being out of their designated area without permission. Out-of-seat behavior can vary in its disruptiveness, as students may sometimes wander around the classroom or engage in specific behaviors (e.g., sharpening their pencil without permission), or they may actively disrupt other students (Patterson, 2009). There are also potential safety concerns with students being away from their assigned areas without permission and/or oversight. School staff often need strategies to establish orderly, predictable, and productive school environments with limited disruptive behaviors such as out-of-seat behaviors. As such, school psychologists may be called upon to support teachers and other school staff in promoting appropriate behaviors and reducing disruptive behaviors so that a positive and safe school environment is maintained (Stage & Quiroz, 1997).

Differential Reinforcement

A variety of strategies, including group contingencies (e.g., Stage and Quiroz, 1997; Theodore et al., 2004) and antecedent interventions (e.g., Patterson, 2009) have been used to reduce disruptive behaviors in schools. Many of these interventions utilize differential reinforcement, which involves reinforcing one class of behaviors (i.e., appropriate behaviors) and withholding reinforcement for another class of behaviors (i.e., inappropriate behaviors; Cooper, Heron, & Heward, 2007). For example, a teacher might choose to ignore a student's out-of-seat behavior and praise remaining in their assigned area. Procedural variations of differential reinforcement include Differential Reinforcement of Alternative or Incompatible behaviors (DRA/I), Differential Reinforcement of Other behaviors (DRO), and Differential Reinforcement of High Rates (DRH) or Low Rates (DRL) of behaviors.

Differential Reinforcement of Low Rates (DRL) interventions are commonly used when the goal is to reduce but not totally eliminate a behavior, such as when a behavior is problematic but not dangerous. When implementing a DRL intervention, teachers allow access to rewards if students engage in a number of behaviors below a criterion (Stage & Quiroz, 1997). As such, teachers set a limit for the number of behaviors a student may exhibit and reinforce staying under the limit (Cooper et al., 2007). An advantage of DRL is that it may reduce problem behaviors while avoiding the use of punishment techniques, which are often invasive, improperly used, and associated with many negative side effects (Cooper et al., 2007). DRL interventions have high social validity, as teachers have rated the interventions as effective and easy to implement (e.g., Stage & Quiroz, 1997).

Class Pass Intervention (CPI)

The Class Pass Intervention (CPI; Cook et al., 2014) is an example of an intervention utilizing differential reinforcement to reduce disruptive behaviors and increase appropriate behaviors in schools. CPI was developed as a function-based intervention for escape-maintained problem behavior, as it allows for students to appropriately request breaks rather than engaging in inappropriate behaviors such as getting out of one's seat (Cook et al., 2014). With CPI, students are taught a functionally equivalent replacement behavior, as they are instructed how to use a break card (i.e., a class pass) to request a time-limited break (Cook et al., 2014). This may be advantageous over an intervention such as escape extinction, as it may be difficult or impossible to prevent students' escape-maintained behavior (Cook et al., 2014). CPI also includes a DRL component, as students may exchange remaining class passes for a highly preferred reward (Cook et al., 2014). As such, students are incentivized to hold on to one or more of their class passes rather than using all of them.

Two studies have examined the use of the CPI to manage disruptive behaviors and promote appropriate behaviors in schools. Cook et al. (2014) conducted the first examination of the CPI, finding that the intervention was effective for three elementary-aged students with hypothesized escape-maintained problem behavior in an urban school. Collins et al. (2016) replicated the original Cook et al. (2014) study, demonstrating the CPI was effective in reducing disruptive behaviors and increasing academic engaged time for four high school students. In both studies, the DRL component of the intervention was intended to reduce the amount of instructional time lost due to breaks, promote teachers' acceptability of the intervention (i.e., so that students would not be allowed unlimited breaks), and allow for fading, as some of the participants' available class passes were systematically reduced. As such, the CPI shows promise as a strategy to reduce escape-maintained behavior by teaching a replacement behavior and utilizing differential reinforcement to incentivize the limited use of class passes.

Case Study

Background Information

Mr. Snow, a 2nd Grade teacher at Elysian Fields Elementary School, contacted the school psychologist for behavioral support for a 7-year old Latinx student, Sylvia. Mr. Snow indicated that Sylvia engaged in disruptive out-of-seat behavior during math class. Specifically, Sylvia often wandered around the classroom without permission, and she sometimes distracted other students when they were expected to work independently. Sylvia spoke Spanish and English fluently and her parents primarily spoke Spanish. Sylvia did not receive special education supports and she earned satisfactory grades across all subjects excluding math, during which time she engage in problem behavior. Tier I behavior supports included praise, redirection, and school bucks consistent with Elysian Fields' School-Wide Positive Behavior Interventions and Supports (SWPBIS) system. Mr. Snow indicated that the Tier I supports were not effective and he sought support from the school psychologist and her practicum student to address the problem behavior.

Description of the Problem Behavior

Mr. Snow indicated that Sylvia had the skills to complete the math work according to the school's math screening; however, she engaged in out-of-seat behavior almost immediately after math class started each day.

Problem Analysis

The school psychologist conducted a one-on-one interview with Mr. Snow using a semi-structured interview form-the Functional Assessment Checklist for Teachers and Staff (FACTS) (March et al., 2000). This interview tool was formulated to be used with teachers and staff to identify a student's problem behaviors, routines, and maintaining variables. Figure 2.1 provides a summary of the information gathered using the FACTS.

(FACTS)

Student: Sylvia M.   **Date of Interview:** 10/14/19

Student Strengths: Sylvia is a very friendly child who cares for her peers in the classroom. Additionally, she is very organized. Finally, Sylvia helps others when they are in need.

Problem Behaviors: Withdrawn, work not done, often out of seat -Sylvia has difficulty staying on task, and exhibits out of seat behaviors that impede on instruction comprehension.

Where, When and With Whom Problem Behaviors are Most Likely: Math (independent seatwork–out of seat and off-task behavior.

Additional Details:

Description of behavior: Out of seat, wandering-quiet and not disruptive, but allows for escape from task.

Frequency of the problem behavior: During math class when students must complete work individually.

Duration of the problem behavior: The problem bx lasts for the duration of the assignment or until the child is removed from the classroom for not working on the math worksheet.

Intensity and/or level of danger of the problem behavior(s): While there is a high frequency of the behavior, the intensity level of danger is low. The student's bx is not harming themselves or others.

Setting Events	Problem Behavior(s)	Maintaining Consequences
Math Class Difficult task Individual work time	Off-task Out of seat	Escape from task demand Reprimand

Attempted methods to address problem behavior: reprimands, removal from class

FIGURE 2.1 Information collected from the Functional Assessment Checklist for Teachers and Staff

Mr. Snow stated that the problem behaviors were primarily occurring during independent work assignments in math class. Mr. Snow noted that typical consequences for Sylvia's behavior included escape from task demands, verbal reprimands, and infrequent removal from class. As a result, Mr. Snow and the school psychologist hypothesized that Sylvia's behaviors were being maintained by escape from task demands. After completing the FACTS interview with Mr. Snow, the school psychologist and her practicum student conducted direct observations of Sylvia throughout a typical school day. The observations substantiated Mr. Snow's hypothesis because Sylvia only exhibited the problem behaviors during math class when students were assigned to complete worksheets individually. Additionally, the school psychologist noted that Sylvia's problem behaviors permitted her to escape the task demand of completing the math worksheet.

Intervention Goals

The team decided to target academically engaged behavior (AEB) and out-of-seat behavior using the CPI. With regard to goals, Mr. Snow indicated that he would like to have Sylvia consistently be engaged in her math work for over 80% of the time with zero instances of out-of-seat behavior. The team also made a plan for fading the class passes (see below), as Mr. Snow did not want Sylvia to continue to miss valuable instructional time.

Measurement of Target Behaviors, Data Collection Strategies, and Progress Monitoring

The team decided to use an adaptation of Direct Behavior Ratings (DBR; Chafouleas, Riley-Tillman, & Christ, 2009; see Appendix A) to assess the target behaviors of AEB and out-of-seat behavior. The DBR was written in both English and Spanish so that the completed forms could be sent home each week to Sylvia's parents. This also provided more opportunities for reinforcement because the parents were encouraged to provide praise for Sylvia's AEB during math. On the DBR, Mr. Snow estimated the percentage of time that Sylvia was academically engaged (defined as having her eyes oriented toward her teacher or task, sitting quietly while completing the assigned task, asking for help when needed, and working with peers on the task if appropriate) and tallied the number of instances of out-of-seat behavior (defined as Sylvia's body being out of her assigned seat without permission). Out-of-seat behavior was not tallied during breaks when Sylvia used a class pass. Mr. Snow completed the DBR each day following math class and the practicum student picked up the forms at the end of each week.

Intervention Plan

Baseline data were collected during math instruction over the course of six days. Toward the end of baseline, the practicum student met with Mr. Snow to review the intervention materials and script (Appendix B). Mr. Snow taught Sylvia how to appropriately request a 5-min break using a personalized class pass (Appendix C) during a 30-min training session. During this training, Mr. Snow modeled how to use the class pass, gave Sylvia opportunities to practice using the class pass, and provided feedback until Sylvia demonstrated mastery for three consecutive attempts. Mr. Snow also instructed Sylvia to draw herself as a superhero so that she could personalize her class pass. In doing this, Sylvia was able to play a role in crafting her own culturally relevant intervention. Finally, Mr. Snow taught Sylvia how to exchange remaining class passes for preferred items or activities identified from a reinforcer menu (Appendix D). This DRL contingency encouraged Sylvia to refrain from using all of her class passes each day.

The intervention was delivered every day during math instruction. Decision rules for intervention fading were determined through consultation with Mr. Snow based on the number of occurrences of the problem behavior. When the intervention was first implemented, Sylvia was given three class passes to use during math. Once Sylvia had three consecutive days with two or fewer inappropriate out of seat behaviors, the team decided to reduce the amount of class passes available to Sylvia to two. Once Sylvia demonstrated one or fewer problem behaviors for three consecutive days, the team faded to one card. Finally, once Sylvia engaged in zero out-of-seat behaviors for three consecutive days, the team removed the class passes and continued to monitor her behavior.

Intervention Fidelity and Interobserver Agreement Plans

The practicum student collected adherence data weekly via direct observation. The adherence checklist (Appendix E) included: (1) Mr. Snow gave Sylvia the appropriate number of class passes; (2) Mr. Snow reminded Sylvia how to use her class passes; (3) Sylvia was allowed a 5-min break when she appropriately used a class pass; and (4) a preferred item or activity was exchanged for any remaining class passes, or withheld if Sylvia used all of her class passes. Adherence data were represented as the percent of components implemented across implementation occasions. Adherence data were collected on 20% of the implementation occasions, evenly distributed across CPI phases. The average adherence was 90% (range: 80%–100%). Mr. Snow skipped the script on a few occasions, which accounted for the lower scores; however, he otherwise implemented the intervention using all of the correct steps. During the weekly adherence observation, the practicum student also collected interobserver agreement data (IOA), as she also tallied Sylvia's of out-of-seat behaviors. IOA between Mr. Snow and the practicum student was 97% (range: 90%–100%).

Intervention Outcome Data

Intervention outcome data are included in Figure 2.2. During baseline, Sylvia averaged 28.33% AEB and 7.33 instances of out-of-seat behavior during math instruction. When CPI was implemented with three class passes, Sylvia's AEB increased immediately and an increasing trend was observed (M = 58%). Similarly, she engaged in fewer instances of out-of-seat behavior, with a decreasing trend (M = 2.4). When the intervention was faded to the use of a maximum of two class passes, Sylvia engaged in a higher percentage of AEB (M = 75%) and fewer out-of-seat behaviors (M = 1.5). Similar results were seen when CPI was faded to one class pass per session (M_{AEB} = 86.66%; $M_{out\text{-}of\text{-}seat}$ = 1). When the intervention was removed, Sylvia's average AEB was 87.5% and she engaged in an average of 0.5 out-of-seat behaviors during math class.

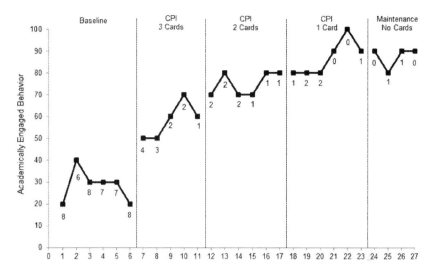

FIGURE 2.2 Sylvia's DBR data. The data line represents DBR data for AEB. The numbers under the data line represent the tallies of inappropriate behavior during math class each day

Intervention Acceptability

To evaluate the social validity of the intervention, Mr. Snow completed the Intervention Rating Profile (IRP-15; Martens, Witt, Elliott, & Darveaux, 1985) following the implementation of CPI. The IRP document contains 15 questions, each of which are evaluated on a six-point Likert scale (e.g., Strongly Disagree to Strongly Agree). As can be seen in Table 2.1, Mr. Snow indicated high overall acceptability of the CPI intervention. Mr. Snow provided feedback that some teachers might find allowing frequent breaks during math class difficult to implement, but he found the intervention to be acceptable.

Sylvia completed the Children's Intervention Rating Profile (CIRP; Witt & Elliott, 1985) to assess her acceptability of the CPI. Results of the Sylvia's social validity questionnaire are depicted in Table 2.2. Overall, Sylvia enjoyed participating in the CPI and found that it helped her thrive in the classroom.

Intervention Considerations

This case study illustrates the use of a culturally relevant, function-based intervention targeting inappropriate behaviors in a classroom. In this example, the school psychologist and her practicum student consulted with Mr. Snow to design an intervention that would allow Sylvia to appropriately request breaks during math. Additionally, the team built in a strong fading component using DRL, such that Sylvia was encouraged to limit her use of class passes and maintain her academically

TABLE 2.1 Results of Mr. Snow's IRP-15

Statement	Mr. Snow's Response
This would be an acceptable intervention for the child's problem behavior.	Strongly Agree
Most teachers would find this intervention appropriate for behavior problems in addition to the one described.	Agree
This intervention should prove effective in changing the child's problem behavior.	Agree
I would suggest the use of this intervention to other teachers.	Agree
The child's behavior problem is severe enough to warrant use of this intervention.	Strongly Agree
Most teachers would find this intervention suitable for the behavior problem described.	Disagree
I would be willing to use this intervention in the classroom setting.	Agree
This intervention would *not* result in negative side effects for the child.	Agree
This intervention would be appropriate for a variety of children.	Agree
This intervention is consistent with those I have used in classroom settings.	Disagree
The intervention was a fair way to handle the child's problem behavior.	Agree
This intervention is reasonable for the behavior problem described.	Agree
I liked the procedures used in this intervention.	Agree
This intervention was a good way to handle the child's behavior problem.	Agree
Overall, this intervention would be beneficial for the child.	Strongly Agree

TABLE 2.2 Results of Sylvia's CIRP

Statement	Sylvia's Response
The program we used was fair.	Agree
I think my teacher was too harsh on me.	Disagree
Being in this program caused problems with my friends.	Disagree
There are better ways to teach me.	Disagree
This program helped other kids too.	Agree
I liked being in this program.	Strongly Agree
Being in this program helped me do better in school.	Agree

engaged behavior. As such, this case study demonstrates how differential reinforcement can be strategically used as an intervention component. As seen with previous CPI studies (Collins et al., 2016; Cook et al., 2014), the use of the DRL component allowed for the intervention to be systematically faded, resulting in a socially valid intervention that would be feasible for use in a variety of school contexts.

The culturally relevant components included in this case study are a particular strength, as we demonstrated how a team can personalize function-based interventions. Sylvia was allowed to draw herself when designing her own class pass, which likely improved her engagement with the intervention. She was also allowed to choose from a menu of high-quality reinforcers, which also increases the personalization and cultural relevance of interventions. Finally, the DBR includes both English and Spanish, which facilitates home-school connection and limits systemic barriers to the engagement of parents who do not speak the primary language spoken in the school. Each of these elements were intended to limit any barriers to engagement and participation, resulting in an intervention that Sylvia found to be socially valid.

Conclusion

School psychologists are often called upon to support teachers in the development of behavior intervention plans targeting increases in appropriate behaviors and decreases in inappropriate behaviors. Differential reinforcement is a common and effective component of reinforcement-based interventions. This case study demonstrates how school psychologists can consult with teachers to design effective, function-based interventions utilizing differential reinforcement, and practical ways to infuse culturally appropriate elements into interventions to address the needs of an increasingly diverse student population.

References

Chafouleas, S. M., Riley-Tillman, T. C., & Christ, T. J. (2009). Direct behavior rating (DBR): An emerging method for assessing social behavior within a tiered intervention system. *Assessment for Effective Intervention*, 34(4), 195–200. doi:10.1177/1534508409340391

Collins, T. A., Cook, C. R., Dart, E. H., Socie, D. G., Renshaw, T. L., & Long, A. C. (2016). Improving classroom engagement among high school students with disruptive behavior: Evaluation of the class pass intervention. *Psychology in the Schools*, 53(2), 204–219. doi:10.1002/pits.21893

Cook, C. R., Collins, T., Dart, E., Vance, M. J., McIntosh, K., Grady, E., Vance, M., & DeCano, P. (2014). Evaluation of the class pass intervention for typically developing students with hypothesized escape-motivated disruptive classroom behavior. *Psychology in the Schools*, 51(2), 107–125. doi:10.1002/pits.21742

Cooper, J. O., Heron, T. E., & Heward, W. L. (2007). *Applied behavior analysis* (2nd ed.). Upper Saddle River, NJ: Pearson.

March, R. E., Horner, R. H., Lewis-Palmer, T., Brown, D., Crone, D. A., Todd, A. W. et al. (2000). *Functional assessment checklist for teachers and staff (FACTS)*. Eugene, OR: University of Oregon.

Martens, B. K., Witt, J. C., Elliott, S. N., & Darveaux, D. X. (1985). Teacher judgments concerning the acceptability of school-based interventions. *Professional Psychology: Research and Practice*, 16(2), 191.

Patterson, S. T. (2009). The effects of teacher-student small talk on out-of-seat behavior. *Education and Treatment of Children*, 32, 167–174.

Stage, S. A., & Quiroz, D. R. (1997). A meta-analysis of interventions to decrease disruptive classroom behavior in public education settings. *School Psychology Review*, 26, 339–368.

Theodore, L. A., Bray, M. A., & Kehle, T. J. (2004). A comparative study of group contingencies and randomized reinforcers to reduce disruptive classroom behavior. *School Psychology Quarterly*, 19(3), 253–271. doi:10.1521/scpq.19.3.253.40280

Witt, J. C., & Elliott, S. N. (1985). Acceptability of classroom intervention strategies. In T. R. Kratochwill (Ed.), *Advances in school psychology* (Vol. 4, pp. 251–288). Hillsdale, NJ: Lawrence Erlbaum Associates.

Appendix A: DBR

Student name/Nombre de Estudiante:
Teacher name/Nombre de Maestro:
Date/Fecha:

Daily Behavior Rating for Academically Engaged Behavior

1. Academically engaged behavior: the student will have academically engaged behavior when they a.) have eyes oriented toward the teacher b.) are in their seat actively working on the assigned task c.) raise their hand to ask questions d.) work with peers upon teacher request to complete a task. The student will not be demonstrating academically engaged behavior when they are out of their seat, calling out, or asleep at their desk.

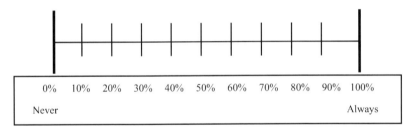

Conducta Académica Tomada por el estudiante: El estudiante demuestra conducta académica cuando: a.) tienen su vista orientada hacia el profesor b.) están en sus asientos y participando activamente en su asignación c.) levantan la mano para hacer preguntas d.) trabajan con sus compañeros para completar su asignación. El estudiante no está demostrando conducta académica cuando está afuera de su asiento, hablando en tiempos inapropiados, gritando en clase, durmiendo en su asiento, o jugando con su celular.
% of Time

2. How many times did Sylvia get out of seat without permission?/ ¿Cuantas veces se paró Sylvia sin permiso de su asiento en clase?
Tally/Cuenta:

Form adapted from "Direct Behavior Rating (DBR): An Emerging Method for Assessing Social Behavior within a Tiered Intervention System," by S.M. Chafouleas, T.C. Riley-Tillman, and T.J. Christ, 2009, *Assessment for Effective Intervention, 34*, 195-200.

Appendix B: Intervention Scripts

Class Pass Intervention Scripts

A Teacher Training

Materials
Intervention

- Class Passes
- Sample Reinforcer Menu
- Paper and pencil for break frequency count

Progress Monitoring

- Direct Behavior Rating (DBR) form
- Pencil

Intervention Script
Frequency

- Teacher training: 1 session, 25 mins

Teacher Training Script

- School psychologist and practicum student describe the intervention:
  - *This intervention will address Sylvia's escape-maintained out-of-seat behavior during math class. Using class passes in part designed by your student, you will encourage your student how to appropriately ask for breaks when needed. These passes will be exchanged for a 5 minute break. In order to decrease the need for the passes, there will be opportunities to earn rewards when the student uses fewer than a certain number of passes.*
- The school psychologist and practicum student show the passes and describe that the student will be able to personalize them. They also discuss potential reinforcers that the teacher is comfortable with.
- The school psychologist and practicum student show the teacher a sample reinforcer menu and explain that this will be personalized to the student and used when the student uses fewer than the required number of cards.
- Then, they model how the script would sound when the teacher speaks to the student using the Student Training and Daily Break Card Intervention Script.
- Time is provided for role-play to practice the student training and potential daily intervention scenarios.

- The teacher is provided with the written script describing the intervention components.
- The teacher is also provided with the physical passes that have a blank space for the student to draw a picture to personalize them.

B Student Training and Daily Break Card Intervention

Materials
Intervention

- Class Passes
- Reinforcer Menu
- Any tangible reinforcers
- Paper and pencil for break frequency count

Progress Monitoring

- Direct Behavior Rating (DBR) form
- Pencil

Adherence

- Adherence Checklist
- Pencil

Intervention Script
Frequency

- Student training: 1 session, 30 mins
- Break Card Intervention: Every day during math class
- DBR form: Every day
- Adherence: Once per week

Student Training

- Teacher greets student and says:
  - *Today we will be talking about the things you like and what we can do to best support you and help you succeed in math class.*
- Teacher conducts an informal preference assessment asking the student what they would be willing to work for. This will be used to create a reinforcer menu.
- The teacher places the blank break card in front of the student and says:
  - *I want you to draw yourself as a superhero, because that is how I see you! These passes will be used during math class and I will explain how they are to be used in a bit.*

- The teacher then begins to explain the intervention:
  - *I have noticed that you have been out of your seat during math class. We all need breaks sometimes, but it is important to ask for them.*
- Pointing to the pass, the teacher says:
  - *You will have 3 passes to use during math class. Whenever you need a break, raise your hand and let me know by saying, "I need a break, please." and then hand me one of your passes. When you give me a pass, you can have a 5-minute break. However, there is actually a game we can play with these passes!. If you do not use all of your cards and you have at least one left, I will bring you your menu of cool rewards that you get to pick. You may choose a reward from the menu at the end of class, but only if you have at least one pass at the end of class.*
- Then, the teacher role plays with the student. They practice appropriate requests for breaks and choosing rewards when at least one pass remains. Role play with the student for at least 3 scenarios to demonstrate mastery.
- The practicum student creates a reinforcer menu based off of the informal preference assessment and gives it to the teacher.

Daily Intervention Script

- Teacher greets the student at the beginning of class and says:
  - *Remember, you have 3 class passes today. If you need a 5-minute break, ask for one in the manner we practiced and give me a pass. If you have at least one pass left at the end of the class period, you may choose a reward from your menu.*
- If the student has at least one pass left at the end of the class period, present the reinforcer menu and allow the student to choose a reward.
- If the student does not have cards left, but used the cards to request breaks, give the student a high five and say:
  - *Great work asking for breaks today. You raised your hand and used your cards! Remember, if you do not use all of your passes tomorrow, you get to pick a prize!*
- If the student takes breaks without using the pass, say:
  - *Remember, when you need a break during class, you need to ask and exchange one of your passes. We will try using the cards again tomorrow.*
  - If necessary, select some of the training activities and practice using the cards with the student.

Class Pass Rules

- Begin by giving the student 3 passes to use, but encourage them to use 2 or fewer in order to earn a reward.
- Once the student has three consecutive days with two or fewer inappropriate out-of-seat behaviors, reduce the amount of passes available to two cards. Say:
  - *You are becoming a master of this game! I think you are up for a new challenge...* And explain the new rules.

- Once they demonstrate one or fewer problem behaviors for three consecutive days, reduce the passes available to one card.
- Once they engage in zero behaviors for three consecutive days, remove the class passes altogether.

Progress Monitoring

- The teacher will fill out the DBR form every day following math class. Inappropriate out-of-seat behaviors will be tallied during math class.
- The practicum student will pick up at the predetermined drop spot at the end of the week.

Adherence/IOA

- The practicum student will collect adherence and IOA once per week using the adherence checklist to ensure the intervention is being implemented as intended and a reliable tally of out-of-seat behaviors is collected.

Appendix C: Sylvia's Class Pass

Appendix D: Reinforcer Menu

SYLVIA'S REINFORCER MENU

CANDY	COMPUTER
SIT BY FRIEND FOR A CLASS PERIOD	READ FOR 10 MINUTES
LISTEN TO MUSIC	IPAD
TREASURE BOX	STICKER
10 MINUTES DRAWING TIME	LINE LEADER

Appendix E: Adherence Checklist

Date:

Class Pass Checklist

1. Mr. Snow gave Sylvia the appropriate number of class passes ____
2. Mr. Snow prompted Sylvia to use class passes at the beginning of the class ____
3. When Sylvia appropriately used the class pass, she received a 5-min break ____
4. Sylvia traded any remaining class passes for a preferred item/activity; If no class passes remained, no reward was given ____

____/4 steps completed.

3
TOKEN ECONOMY

Denise A. Soares, Judith R. Harrison, and Lauren E. Puente

Introduction

Effective classroom management strategies, such as Token Economies (TE), can help teachers reduce disruptive behavior and increase academic performance (Soares, Harrison, Vannest, & McClelland, 2016). In this chapter, we begin with an overview of TE, followed by a case study of a fourth-grade student, Ryan, who received special education services as a student with an Emotional and Behavioral Disorder (EBD). Our use of TE with Ryan depicts its application in an authentic classroom setting with a step-by-step example of establishing a behavior plan. The plan includes a TE to address the function of challenging behaviors (i.e., noncompliance, physical aggression) with behavioral goals while utilizing a Daily Behavior Report (DBR) to collect and analyze the effectiveness. In addition, we describe methods of measuring fidelity, social acceptability, outcomes, and intervention considerations.

TE is a secondary reinforcement system (Alberto & Troutman, 2009) based on operant conditioning that has been used for many years prior to the study of operant behavior and the Industrial Revolution (Ivy, Meindl, Overley, & Robson, 2017). In a TE, students earn tokens for predetermined desired behaviors that they can exchange for a backup reinforcer. TE is appropriate for a range of educational settings (e.g., self-contained, content mastery, resource rooms, etc.), is compatible with teaching, and fits well in inclusive settings and multi-tiered systems of support (Soares et al., 2016).

TEs consist of multiple procedures implemented by teachers and/or school psychologists, a majority of which are completed prior to the implementation with the student. Specifically, the teacher/school psychologist defines the desired behavior, assessment methodology and time frame, primary and secondary reinforcers, the type of token, the exchange rate based on the behaviors demonstrated by the student, and procedures for dispensing the secondary reinforcers. In addition, the teacher/school psychologist administers a reinforcement survey to the student to determine the desired reinforcers that are then placed on the reinforcement menu for selection as backup reinforcers. After these procedures have been established, the TE is implemented with the student.

TEs have sufficient empirical evidence to be deemed a research-based (Simonsen, Fairbanks, Briesch, Myers, & Sugai, 2008) or at least a preliminarily evidence-based strategy (Soares et al., 2016), depending on the criteria used with research conducted, for over a century. Within the last several decades, TEs have been found effective in classrooms with students with challenging behavior (including those with and at risk of EBD), with cognitive impairment, with behavioral disorders, and with autism. As such, TEs are very applicable in school settings.

While many interventions including TEs are considered evidence-based for use in schools, few are actually implemented in classrooms with fidelity. Experts contend this lack of fidelity may contribute to limited intervention success for students with EBD, and thus may led to low treatment acceptability and reduced trust in educational research. Fortunately, this is not the case with TE, which is one strategy actually used by teachers and recommended by school psychologists. TE, when used with fidelity, is a highly acceptable intervention.

Further, there are many advantages to TE systems. It is highly portable across conditions or settings, bridges the gap between a target response and the secondary reinforcer, maintains performance over an extended period of time until the secondary reinforcer can be delivered, allows behavior to be reinforced at any time, and is customizable to deliver within a multi-tiered systems of support (MTSS) framework to a whole group (Tier 1), small group (Tier 2), or individual (Tier 3). TEs are also less likely to be affected by satiation than other interventions and can provide a visual reminder of the progress or lack of progress the student has made (Kazdin & Bootzin, 1972). As such, TEs can be a powerful behavioral intervention for improving school behavior.

Case Study

Background Information

Ryan was a fourth-grade student at River Rock Elementary School who received special education services as a student with EBD. River Rock Elementary School had an established Positive Behavioral Interventions and Supports (PBIS) plan with school-wide expectations that were represented with the acronym PRIDE: **p**repare for success, **r**espect everyone, **i**nclude others, **d**o what is right, and **e**xpect great things. The PBIS system was used as a Response to Intervention (RTI) model for behavior. Prior to special education eligibility, Ryan progressed through Tiers 1 and 2 and did not respond to any evidence-based interventions implemented with fidelity at each tier.

When Ryan was in kindergarten, Tier 1 interventions included school-wide prevention strategies implemented with all students, including a schoolwide TE, in which all students earned Bobcat Bucks (tokens) for following schoolwide expectations in common areas, such as the playground, lunch table, bus lines, and restrooms. Check-In/Check-Out (CICO; Crone, Hawken, & Horner, 2010), was developed through collaboration with the Student Success Team (SST), Ryan's family, and Mr. Kade (teacher). Unfortunately, although he enjoyed CICO with Coach Bryce (his mentor), his problem behaviors continued to increase, especially after long breaks from school or when there was a break in his routine. In addition, Ryan's behavior diverted teacher time from instruction and caused a disruption in the classroom. As such, he was found eligible for special education as a student with EBD and was placed in a self-contained classroom.

Four years later, as a fourth-grade student, Ryan continued to receive instruction in a self-contained class and struggled behaviorally. In addition, his aggressive and noncompliant behaviors increased in frequency and intensity. His teachers and school psychologist requested an updated Functional Behavior Assessment (FBA) and Behavior Intervention Plan (BIP). The Individualized Education Program (IEP) team met to conduct an FBA, which consisted of a collection of background information from school records, parent interviews, teacher interviews, and an interview with Ryan, as well as three direct observations by the school psychologist.

Description of the Problem Behavior

A review of school records indicated that academically, Ryan was reading at his grade level (fourth grade). Discipline records indicated that Ryan had been referred to the principal's office 22 times for verbally and nonverbally refusing to follow teacher directions (i.e., noncompliant behavior) and seven times for being physically aggressive towards peers and teachers. Prior to the request for the new FBA/BIP, Ryan had gone to an identified "cool off space" and kicked the window, making it shatter. Ryan had been removed from his classroom and placed in in-school-suspension (ISS) for 10 days and out-of-school suspension (OSS) for 7 days. He continued to receive school-wide positive behavioral interventions and supports and Tier 2 CICO.

Interviews with Ryan's father and mother revealed recent changes and problem behaviors at home. Ryan's father reported that he and Ryan's mother were recently divorced and that Ryan was spending the majority of his time at his father's house. Ryan was allowed to see his mother only when his grandmother was present for supervised visitation. Ryan's father reported working long hours and often nights. Ryan's father and mother reported that he had little structure at home and that his father's neighbors tried to supervise Ryan when his parents were not available. However, when Ryan became aggressive, they would send him home. Ryan's parents reported that he had thrown ceramic dishes at a window when he was asked to take the trash out and had broken his favorite game by impulsively throwing it on the ground when the game was not working correctly. Ryan's parents reported that he took Risperdal™ for bipolar disorder and Paxil™ for anxiety and depression. Ryan's father reported that Ryan often refused to take the medication and/or pretended that he took it and spit it out when no one was looking.

Interviews with two of Ryan's teachers revealed that Ryan refused to comply with requests and responded with physical aggression. Teachers reported other students stated they did not like Ryan and did not want to sit next to him. Teachers reported that Ryan's disruptive and aggressive behavior was out of control, they had tried everything, and they did not know what else to do. They reported that when Ryan was angry, he would hit other classmates and had threatened to destroy the classroom. Ryan had been sent to the office on many occasions and received ISS and OSS on multiple occasions but continued to engage in these behaviors. Teachers reported feeling frustrated because Ryan's behavior had affected the overall atmosphere in the classroom and disrupted the learning of his peers.

The interview with Ryan indicated that he felt angry when asked to complete reading tasks. He reported that he "hated to read the social studies and science chapters and answer questions, because that was just a stupid boring thing to do." Further, Ryan hated when he had to participate in reciprocal teaching groups. He stated that he did not want to participate in group discussions because his peers thought that he "was stupid and couldn't read and did not understand what was read." He reported that they tried to bully him, but that he "beat them up," so they do not do that anymore. Ryan stated that teachers also tried to push him around and thought he was not as smart as other students. He reported that he was physically restrained for assaulting a teacher in the second grade and that he was physically injured. Ryan reported similar thoughts about his behavior at home. When asked about homework, he stated that he did not have to do homework and was only required "to watch television and be quiet." He said that he could "watch what he wanted when [he] wanted" and that he "said what's on [his] mind, all the time."

The school psychologist, Mr. Davis, observed Ryan's behavior on three occasions using an A-B-C Observation Form (see Appendix A). The first was during a reciprocal teaching reading activity. The class read a short story and met to discuss the story. Ryan was given the role of the "questioner." Ryan put his head down and refused to make eye contact with the group. As the group discussed the story, Ryan did not participate. When encouraged to ask a question by his teacher, he threw his pencil across the room and ran to the principal's office. The second observation occurred during math class. The teacher taught a class and instructed the class to complete a worksheet. Ryan completed the worksheet quietly.

The third observation was during social studies class. The class read a story together. Ryan sat with his head down and did not participate. When it was his turn to read, he verbally refused. The student sitting behind him stated, "Mr. Kade, you know that Ryan won't read. Why do you keep asking him to read?" at which point, Ryan turned and hit him. The teacher sent Ryan out of the class to the principal's office.

Problem Analysis

With the information gathered from the interviews and observations, the teachers met with the school psychologist and developed an A-B-C summary statement (see Appendix B). The team defined the problem behaviors as noncompliance and physical aggression. Noncompliance was defined as failure or refusal to engage in or follow teacher directions when asked to read within 15 seconds. Physical aggression was defined as throwing items, hitting, shoving, and pushing peers or teachers. The team identified being asked to read as the antecedent to the problem behavior and leaving or being sent out of the classroom as the maintaining consequence for the behavior. The team identified the setting event, which increased the likelihood that the behavior would occur, was when he transitioned from one parent to the other. From this information, the team hypothesized that the function of the behavior was to escape reading tasks. As such, the summary statement to be analyzed was:

> When asked to read aloud or participate in a reciprocal teaching group, Ryan displayed noncompliance and physical aggression and was sent out of the classroom and not required to read. The behaviors were more likely to occur when he had transitioned between parents the night before. The team hypothesized that the function of the behavior was to escape the reading task.

To test this hypothesis, the team agreed to measure noncompliant and aggressive behavior when the demand to read aloud was removed. The observer measured frequency (e.g., how often) and intensity (e.g., the level of how dangerousness or disruptiveness) of the noncompliant and aggressive behaviors and found that the behaviors did not occur when the task demand was removed. As such, the team verified that the function of the behavior was to escape reading tasks.

Intervention Goals

Mr. Davis, the school psychologist, worked with the teachers and selected the replacement behavior as requesting not to read by displaying a red index card on his desk. A token economy system was developed to reinforce the use of the replacement behavior, compliance with requests to read or utilizing his red card as a request not to read.

Mr. Davis met with Ryan's teacher to collaborate and identify goals related to the target behaviors (i.e., noncompliance, physical aggression). The team arrived at the following goals:

1. Given a request to read, Ryan would either read or place the red card on the corner of his desk, three out of five opportunities.
2. Given five requests to read in one week, Ryan would verbally refuse two or fewer times in five opportunities as reported on his weekly DBR.
3. Given five requests to read, Ryan would demonstrate zero instances of physical aggression.

To monitor Ryan's progress, the school psychologist met with Ryan's teachers weekly and reviewed the weekly DBR (described below) and ODRs. If all goals were met, the teachers continued with the intervention. If any goal was not met, the intervention was modified. The team developed the following intervention plan.

Intervention Plan and Measurement of the Target Behavior

To achieve the goals for Ryan, multiple components (i.e., teach the replacement behavior [read or skip reading], CICO, DBR, TE) were selected for Ryan's behavior intervention plan (see Figure 3.1).

First, the teachers and Coach Bryce, the CICO mentor, taught Ryan the replacement behavior (see Figure 3.2).

Second, they developed a TE. Third, the TE was implemented with daily data collection and discussion with the Coach Bryce. To teach Ryan to make a

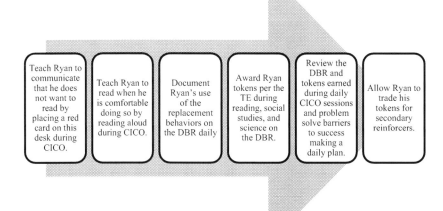

FIGURE 3.1 Interventions in the BIP

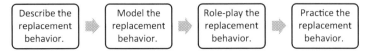

FIGURE 3.2 Steps in teaching the replacement behavior

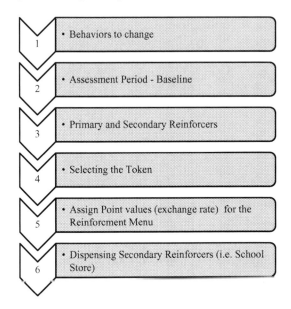

FIGURE 3.3 Steps to develop a token economy

decision to either read or use the red card to "skip" his turn to read, Coach Bryce met with Ryan each day for one week. On the first day, he described the replacement behavior and modeled either reading or using the card. He talked to Ryan about how to determine if he was willing to read or if he wanted to use the card. After describing the process, Coach Bryce demonstrated his thoughts through a think-aloud procedure, stating his problem-solving thoughts verbally for Ryan to hear. On the second day, Coach Bryce role-played the procedures with Ryan, demonstrating the behaviors. On the third day, Ryan practiced the procedures with Coach Bryce. Finally, Coach Bryce demonstrated the use of reinforcement through earning tokens when Ryan either read aloud or used the red card to skip his turn. Coach Bryce met with Ryan before and after school daily to review his DBR and tokens earned.

Next, the team developed the TE following 6 steps (see Figure 3.3).

The team reviewed the FBA data to establish the target behaviors (Step 1) and baseline rates (Step 2) of verbal/nonverbal noncompliance (e.g., refusing to follow directions) and physical aggression (the problem behaviors) that were used to determine the frequency at which the behaviors were occurring (i.e., 22 instances of refusing to follow directions, seven instances of physical aggression towards peers).

As part of the TE intervention (Step 3), Mr. Kade conducted a reinforcement survey (see Appendix C), where it was evident that Ryan liked snacks such as Taki Chips, Sour Patch Kids, and Dr. Pepper. He also enjoyed YouTube videos of football games that recently occurred and enjoyed playing video games. Additionally, the reinforcement survey revealed that there were several people in the school that Ryan enjoyed spending time with including his Kindergarten teacher, Ms. Ainsworth, and his PE coach and CICO mentor, Coach Bryce. Ryan also communicated that when he did a good job, he liked the principal and assistant principals to know, as he sometimes was in trouble with them. In addition, he stated that he wished the teachers would call/text his dad when he had a successful day at school. Ryan revealed that he wished the teachers would stop correcting him in front of his friends and that he was OK with a teacher correcting him, just not in front of his peers. Mr. Kade asked Ryan what he would do if he was given $10 and Ryan mentioned that he would use the money to go to the local trampoline park for the "ALL YOU CAN JUMP PASS" on Friday nights with his friends.

Mr. Kade used the information listed on the reinforcer survey along with the identified behaviors of concern to construct Ryan's token economy system. The team decided to use Quality Quarters as the token (i.e., primary reinforcer; Step 4). Quality Quarters were given for demonstrating the replacement behavior on the DBR during the school day. One quality quarter equaled 1 point. Ryan had the opportunity to earn 0 to 2 quarters during his reading, science, and social studies classes. Mr. Kade created a menu of secondary reinforcers with "prices" for each based on Ryan's responses on the reinforcer survey (Step 5). The team determined that secondary reinforcers (Step 6) would be exchanged for Quality Quarters once weekly. Each morning, Ryan picked up a DBR (see Appendix D) sheet from Coach Bryce, his CICO mentor, where the two had a goal-setting conference (CICO) in the morning. During this CICO meeting, Coach Bryce praised Ryan for progress and reviewed his CICO sheets with Ryan to identify barriers to Ryan's success. Together, they identified barriers and made a plan to overcome those barriers. After the meeting, Ryan went to class, and throughout the day, each of Ryan's teachers selected a rating of two quarters, one quarter, or no quarters at the end of the class period and documented that on Ryan's DBR. In the afternoon prior to going home, Ryan met with Coach Bryce and the two graphed his points for the day on a spreadsheet and reviewed points needed to earn his weekly reinforcer. At the end of the week, Ryan was allowed trade his Quality Quarters for his selected secondary reinforcer (Step 6).

Intervention Fidelity and Interobserver Agreement

The team acknowledged that for the BIP and the TE to be successful, the plan had to be followed by all involved with a high degree of fidelity (Fixsen, Blase, Metz, & Van Dyke, 2013) and that the behaviors had to be measured accurately and consistently across days (Hartmann, Barrios, & Wood, 2004). Intervention fidelity is the degree to which the intervention is implemented as designed (Gersten et al., 2005). As such, fidelity of the plan was documented using a checklist (see Appendix E), daily for the first two weeks and once weekly the following weeks. During the first week, Mr. Davis and the teacher documented fidelity during reading instruction to check simple agreement on the sheet. Mr. Davis rated fidelity as 69% and Mr. Kade as 100%. The rate was different as Mr. Kade was unaware that Ryan did not meet with the Coach Bryce in the afternoon, meaning that 5 of the 11 steps were not followed. The team changed the sheet to be completed by everyone involved instead of relying on Mr. Kade to communicate with Coach Bryce to assess fidelity of the entire plan.

To assure that the behaviors were operationally defined for consistent measurement, Mr. Davis and Mr. Kade completed DBRs simultaneously and calculated simple agreement on five occasions during the first and second weeks and once each following week. During the first week, the agreement was 80%. The disagreements were related to giving one or two tokens. The team met to clarify the criteria for earning two tokens and decided that two tokens would be given if Ryan read or used his red card without any teacher prompting. They agreed that he would receive one token if the teacher prompted him one or more times and he was compliant.

Intervention Outcome Data and Summary of Intervention Effects

Results from the DBR and TE indicated the multicomponent intervention was effective at increasing Ryan reading aloud for reading, social studies, and science (see Figures 3.4 and 3.5).

In summary, the TE was effective at decreasing the frequency that Ryan refused to read (see graph) and the frequency of ODRs. Specifically, the mean refusals decreased from 93.8% (range from 75% to 100%) to 15.6% (range of 0% to 50%) during intervention. Similarly, the mean ODRs for physical aggression decreased from 1.75 average incidents to 0.25 average incidents with a range of 1-2 during baseline and 0-1 during intervention.

Intervention Acceptability

To determine the social validity of the TE, Coach Bryce, Mr. Kade, and Ryan completed a School Intervention Rating Scale (SIRF; Kern & Gresham, 2002; see Appendix F) adapted for this intervention during the first week of implementation. Social validity is defined as the social importance of behavior, goals, and outcomes (Wolf, 1978) and social acceptability as the degree to which the intervention is perceived as fair, reasonable, and appropriate (Kazdin, 1977). The SIRF measured three components of social validity, suitability, perceived benefit, and convenience (Harrison, State, Evans, & Schamberg, 2016). If the intervention was perceived as suitable, then the raters: (a) liked the intervention, (b) found that

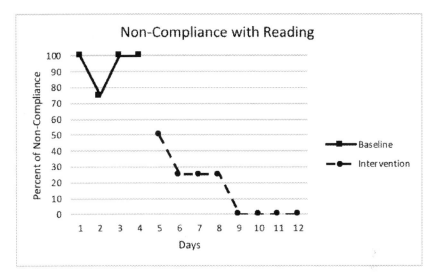

FIGURE 3.4 Noncompliance with reading during baseline and intervention phases

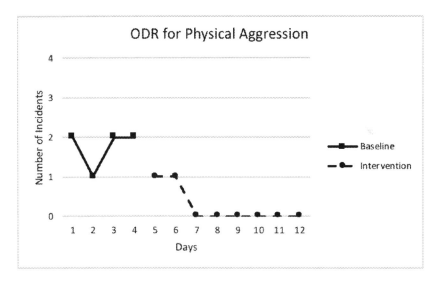

FIGURE 3.5 ODRs for physical aggression during baseline and intervention phases

it was a good fit for their classrooms, and (c) was not difficult to implement. If the raters indicated that the intervention was beneficial, then the raters believed that the student benefited from the intervention, and if they found the intervention to be convenient, then they indicated that they expended a reasonable amount of energy and resources to implement the intervention and the student experienced no negative side effects (Harrison et al.).

TE has been determined to be a socially valid/acceptable intervention (Soares et al., 2016). As such, it was not surprising that Ryan, Coach Bryce, and Mr. Kade rated the intervention as socially valid. Specifically, Ryan indicated that he liked that he could work for varying secondary reinforcers each week. Coach Bryce indicated that the combination of CICO and DBR was very suitable and convenient, as it allowed him to praise Ryan for his demonstration of replacement behavior in classes throughout the day, and Mr. Kade indicated that the DBR was very beneficial, as it allowed him to monitor Ryan's progress, which was very evident.

Intervention Considerations

For successful implementation of TE, school psychologists and other educators should consider several factors. First, it is important that students are successful in order to increase the likelihood that the appropriate behavior will continue. In order to ensure success at the beginning of the intervention, the behavior to be demonstrated by the student must be easily achieved and the number of primary tokens needed to earn a secondary token must be extremely achievable. For example, if we had required that Ryan read every time he was given the opportunity in order to earn any quality quarters, it is unlikely that he would have been able to earn his secondary reinforcer. This outcome would have decreased his motivation to read or use the red card. The reinforcement earned had to be sufficient for him to escape the undesired activity and want to stay in the classroom. He had previously mastered the ability to escape from the undesired activity; therefore, the replacement behavior had to be just as powerful.

Second, research indicates that TE is most effective with children older than five years old. This finding is fairly logical due to developmental differences. Children need to have the cognitive capacity to connect earning the token for demonstrating the expected behavior. Furthermore, students have to be able to identify secondary reinforcers for themselves. Each of these is more difficult for younger children. If an educator decides to use TE with younger children, then the steps would need to be simplified. For example, it is common for preschool teachers to use token boards with Velcro to attach pictures of tokens (when earned) and a picture of the reinforcer (as a motivator). The system is designed so that the secondary reinforcer can be earned fairly quickly, sometimes twice a day. Further, progress is monitored closely for effectiveness.

Third, research indicates that TE is most effective without verbal cueing or response cost (Soares et al., 2016). Teachers are often inclined to remind students of the expected behavior (frequently) while implementing a TE. In our work, we have often heard educators give reminders at the time of the misbehavior. For example, when Ryan began to verbally refuse to read, the teacher interrupted him with a prompt to use his red card. This type of prompting is not likely to increase the effectiveness of the intervention. This is also true of response cost. Response cost is the procedure of "taking away" tokens once earned. Again, in our work, we have seen teachers take away tokens until the student has none left. On one occasion, we saw a teacher take away tokens after the student had none left, leaving him owing the teacher tokens. These are not effective strategies and significantly decrease the effectiveness of the TE. Further, these unnecessary components increase the complexity of the intervention and in turn the likelihood that the TE will not be implemented as designed. As such, we strongly encourage educators to avoid these strategies.

Fourth, it is important that progress be monitored through data collection and interpretation and that the TE be adapted and modified as needed. It is highly likely that school psychologists will need to provide training to other educators who are collecting and interpreting data. Research indicates that these are skills are not frequently taught to teachers, and teachers report feeling less than confident in their ability to interpret data. As such, it is important that, prior to implementing an intervention, teachers are taught to read and interpret the data, including mean levels, immediacy of the effect, trend, and trajectory.

If the intervention is not sufficiently effective, consideration should be given to adaptations to address potential barriers. One barrier that we have experienced is differing expectations of co-teachers and/or teachers in regards to when/how the tokens should be delivered. To overcome this barrier, all adults passing out tokens should discuss scenarios for expectations and agree upon how/when to distribute tokens. Another barrier is selecting "reinforcers" that are not reinforcing to the student because they do not desire the reinforcer or because they have lost interest, which can happen when students earn the reinforcer frequently. When students show no desire to work for the secondary reinforcer, then it should be changed.

Fifth, we want to emphasize that TE fits well within a MTSS framework. A TE is flexible enough to be designed for whole group, small group, or an individual student. For example, a teacher could use the "marble in a jar" program within the class (Tier 1) to reinforce a specific expectation. The whole class would be earning marbles (i.e., tokens) and contributing to the class reinforcer (i.e., movie day, extra recess). As a Tier 2 intervention, TE could be implemented with a small group of students engaging in social skills instruction. The group of students could individually earn primary reinforcers for individual behavior that could then be exchanged for a group secondary reinforcer. For example, if the group is working on communicating feelings, then when a student appropriately communicated a feeling, he/she would earn a token. All of the individual tokens are then compiled to purchase a secondary reinforcer, such as a pizza party. In the case study used here with Ryan, the TE was set up for an individual student who demonstrated significant problem behaviors, likely a Tier 3 scenario.

Conclusion

It is undeniable that disruptive behavior is a hindrance to teaching and learning. Teachers can feel confident that the use of TE as a strategy employed in the teaching-learning process has a high probability of increasing teachers' opportunity to reinforce appropriate behavior while teaching without disruption. As demonstrated by our case study, with the implementation of TE, the student's use of the replacement behavior can be expected to increase, the problem behavior to decrease, and academic performance to become the focus of student and teacher time.

References

Alberto, P., & Troutman, A. C. (2009). *Applied behavior analysis for teachers*. Upper Saddle River, NJ: Merrill/Pearson.

Crone, D. A., Hawken, L. S., & Horner, R. H. (2010). *Responding to problem behavior in schools: The Behavior Education Program* (2nd ed.). New York: Guilford Press.

Fixsen, D., Blase, K., Metz, A., & Van Dyke, M. (2013). Statewide implementation of evidence-based programs. *Exceptional Children*, 79(2), 213–230. doi:10.1177/001440291307900206

Gersten, R., Fuchs, L. S., Compton, D., Coyne, M., Greenwood, C., & Innocenti, M. S. (2005). Quality indicators for group experimental and quasi-experimental research in special education. *Exceptional Children*, 71(2), 149–164. doi:10.1177/001440290507100202

Harrison, J. R., State, T. M., Evans, S. W., & Schamberg, T. (2016). Construct and predictive validity of social acceptability: Scores from high school teacher ratings on the School Intervention Rating Form. *Journal of Positive Behavior Interventions*, 18(2), 111–123. doi:10.1177/1098300715596135

Hartmann, D. P., Barrios, B. A., & Wood, D. D. (2004). Principles of behavioral observation. In S. N. Haynes & E. M. Heiby (Eds.), *Comprehensive handbook of psychological assessment, Vol. 3: Behavioral assessment* (pp. 108–127). Hoboken, NJ: John Wiley & Sons.

Ivy, J. W., Meindl, J. N., Overley, E., & Robson, K. M. (2017). Token economy: A systematic review of procedural descriptions. *Behavior Modification*, 41(5), 708–737. doi:10.1177/0145445517699559

Kazdin, A. E. (1977). Artifact, bias, and complexity of assessment: The ABCs of reliability. *Journal of Applied Behavior Analysis*, 10(1), 141–150. doi:10.1901/jaba.1977.10-141

Kazdin, A. E., & Bootzin, R. R. (1972). The token economy: An evaluative review. *Journal of Applied Behavior Analysis*, 5(3), 343–372. doi:10.1901/jaba.1972.5-343

Kern, L., & Gresham, F. (2002–2007). Research Exploring Alternatives for Children in Schools (REACH) (National Center Grant funded by the Department of Education, Office of Special Education Programs).

McDougal, J. L., Chafouleas, S. M., & Waterman, B. (2006). *Functional behavioral assessment and interventions in schools: A practitioner's guide (grades 1-8)*. Champaign, IL: Research Press.

Simonsen, B., Fairbanks, S., Briesch, A., Myers, D., & Sugai, G. (2008). Evidence-based practices in classroom management: Considerations for research to practice. *Education and Treatment of Children*, 31(1), 351–380. doi:10.1353/etc.0.0007

Soares, D. A., Harrison, J. R., Vannest, K. J., & McClelland, S. S. (2016). Effect size for token economy use in contemporary classroom settings: A meta-analysis and moderator analysis of single case research. *School Psychology Review*, 45(4), 379–399. doi:10.17105/SPR45-4.379-399

Wolf, M. M. (1978). Social validity: The case for subjective measurement or how applied behavior analysis is finding its heart. *Journal of Applied Behavior Analysis*, 11(2), 203–214. doi:10.1901/jaba.1978.11-203

Appendix A: A-B-C Observation Form

For a period of two weeks, document what happens before (Antecedent) and after (Consequence) each behavior of concern. Also, please describe the behavior in the "behavior" column.

Setting Information				
Date	Time	Antecedent (The thing or event that triggers the behavior)	Behavior (Problem behavior is behavior that is causing a problem)	Consequence (The outcome, what happens after the behavior)

Appendix B: Hypothesis A-B-C Summary Statement

Setting Event (Influenced by)	Antecedent (Triggered by)	Behavior (Student will)	Consequence (Resulting in)
			Therefore, the function is: • __ to get something • __ escape • __ social/attention • __ item/activity • __ sensory

Appendix C: Reinforcement Survey

Name: Date:

Student Questions	Student Response	Teacher Notations
Things I like to do after school are		
If I had ten dollars, I would		
My favorite TV programs are		
My favorite game at school is		
My best friends are		
My favorite toys/activities are		
My favorite music is		
My favorite subject in school is		
My favorite foods are		
My favorite inside activities are		
My favorite outside activities are		
My hobbies are		
Name three games you like to play or do		
It makes me mad when I cannot		
I wish my teacher would not		
When you do a good job, who would you like to know?		
A person at school I would do almost anything for is		
When I do something good at school, I wish my teacher would		
The friend or person I would most like to spend more time with at school is		

Beverages		Food		Recreation/Leisure	
Chocolate milk		Bagels		Computers	
Fruit juices		Chips, nuts, pretzels, popcorn		Dancing	
Lemonade		Cookies		Drawing	
Milk		Fruit		Listening to music	
Punch		Granola		Looking at books/magazines	
Sodas _____		Candy _____		Looking at YouTube videos	
Sparkling water		Hot dogs		Work jigsaw puzzles	
V-8 juice		Ice cream		Art project	

Token Economy 45

School/Classroom-Based Reinforcers		Individual Activities and Privileges
Computer time	Write a positive note to student	Answering questions
Allow student to be a peer tutor	Send the student/parent a letter through the mail	Assisting teacher to teach
Choice of assignment	Self-selected activity	Choosing activities
Special privilege	Magazine/book selection	Decorating room
Call student at home to congratulate	Listen to music	Leading student groups
Give student a "Free Homework Pass"	Library pass	Making school materials
Give student a free ticket to school activity (dance, sporting event)	Give student a job or responsibility	Special seating arrangement

Appendix D: Daily Behavior Report Card

Student: Ryan   *Date:* _____

Today, I met the following behavioral expectations:

1. I read when my teacher asked me to, or I used my red card to show I was passing on reading aloud.

Subject   2   1   0

Reading

Social Studies

Science

Total Points: _____   **Got afternoon incentive:**
                                               Yes   No

Adapted from *Functional Behavioral Assessment and Interventions in Schools: A Practitioner's Guide (Grades 1-8)*, by J. L. McDougal, S. M. Chafouleas, and B. Waterman, 2006, Champaign, IL: Research Press (800-519-2707; www.researchpress.com).

Appendix E: Treatment Fidelity Observation Form

Date: *Condition:*

Treatment Step:	Yes (Initials)	No (Initials)	Notes
Ryan attended CICO in the morning with Coach Bryce.			
Ryan and Coach Bryce reviewed the DBR.			
Ryan and Coach Bryce identified barriers to success (if any).			
Ryan and Coach Bryce identified strategies to overcome barriers.			
Ryan and Coach Bryce goal-set.			
Ryan attended CICO in the afternoon with Coach Bryce.			
Ryan and Coach Bryce reviewed the DBR.			
Ryan and Coach Bryce totaled the amount of tokens Bryce received.			
Ryan and Coach Bryce graphed the total tokens on his progress chart.			
Ryan and Coach Bryce discussed the day, problem-solved any issues, and made plans for the following day.			
Ryan picked up his DBR from Coach Bryce and gave it to his reading teacher.			
Ryan picked up his DBR from Coach Bryce and gave it to his social studies teacher.			
Ryan picked up his DBR from Coach Bryce and gave it to his science teacher.			
The reading teacher completed the DBR.			
The social studies teacher completed the DBR.			
The science teacher completed the DBR.			

Appendix F: School Intervention Rating Scale

Please complete the following questionnaire. For each item, please check the box that best indicates your feelings about the Token Economy Intervention.

	Not at all (5)	(4)	Somewhat (3)	(2)	Very (1)
How clear is your understanding of the TE after having used it with your student?					

How acceptable did you find TE to be regarding your concerns about your student/classroom?					
How willing were you to carry out this TE?					
Given your student's behavioral problems, how reasonable did you find the TE to be?					
How costly was it to carry out the TE?					
To what extent were there disadvantages in implementing the TE?					
How much time each day was needed for you to carry out this TE?					
How effective was this TE?					
Compared to other students, how serious are your student's problems?					
How disruptive was it to the class to carry out the TE?					
How effective was the TE for your student(s)?					
How affordable was the TE for your classroom?					
How much did you like the procedures used in the TE?					
How willing were other staff members to carry out the TE?					
To what extent did undesirable side effects occur as a result of the TE?					
How much discomfort did your student experience during the course of the TE?					
How severe are your student's behavioral difficulties now after using the TE?					
How willing were you to change your classroom routine to carry out the TE?					
How well did carrying out the TE fit into the classroom routine?					
To what degree are your student's behavioral problems of concern to you?					

Adapted from Kern, L., & Gresham, F. (2002–2007). Research Exploring Alternatives for Children in Schools (REACH) (National Center Grant funded by the Department of Education, Office of Special Education Programs).

4
TIME-OUT

Anna C.J. Long, Jessie A.G. Munson, and Catherine R. Lark

Introduction

Problem behavior within the classroom can be difficult for educators, as it interferes with their ability to deliver effective classroom instruction. Teachers have frequently reported feeling unprepared to deal with problematic behavior, which is concerning given that in the absence of effective intervention, challenging behaviors are likely to continue (Kern, Benson, & Clemens, 2010). Across the past decade, many schools have begun to adopt multi-tiered systems of support that are both positive and preventative, such as Positive Behavioral Interventions and Support (PBIS; Sugai & Horner, 2006). Nevertheless, despite the general focus on promoting positive behaviors, some students with more severe behavioral presentations require the use of punishment procedures to achieve sufficient behavior reductions. One such proven procedure for teachers to consider using is time-out, which can be applied to a variety of behaviors and school contexts. Importantly, the use of punishment procedures alone is less preferable given the potential detrimental impact on the student-teacher and parent-teacher relationships, as well as empirical data that suggest these procedures are most effective when paired with a reinforcement-based strategy.

Across several decades of research, time-out from positive reinforcement, or time-out for short, has been shown to be a common and highly effective behavioral management intervention used by both caretakers (Everett et al., 2010) and educators alike (O'Handley et al., 2019). Time-out involves the principle of negative punishment whereby contingent upon a target behavior there is the temporary loss of reinforcing stimuli, which results in decreased future frequency of the undesirable behavior (Cooper et al., 2007). Implicit in this definition of time-out is that the time-in environment must contain reinforcement in order for there to be a discrepancy between the time-in and time-out environments. Thus, time-out is typically used in conjunction with reinforcement strategies designed to increase positive behaviors in addition to decreasing maladaptive behaviors (O'Handley et al., 2019).

Eight parameters have been considered possible core components of time-out and, thus, garnered attention in the research: *location*, *schedule* (i.e., continuous use versus intermittent schedules), *warning* (i.e., short or no warning), *signal* (i.e., stimulus signaling time-out is an available consequence), *the form of administration* (i.e., instructional versus physical guidance to time-out), *verbalized reason* (i.e., explanation to the child of what behavior caused time-out), *contingent release* (i.e., release from time-out conditioned on something), and *duration*. A review of the eight parameters most often implemented with respect to time-out indicate that time-out is most effective when the time-out environment is non-reinforcing when compared to the time-in environment (O'Handley et al., 2019) and when duration is five minutes or less (Corralejo, Jensen, & Greathouse, 2018). Regarding location, best practice recommends attempting less intrusive methods (i.e., non-exclusionary time-out) before moving to more intrusive methods (i.e., exclusionary time-out). Concerning schedule, best practices indicate continuous use at first and then thinning to intermittent use when the target behavior is sufficiently suppressed. The review suggests that time-out is more acceptable to practitioners when a short, verbalized reason is given when implementing time-out, but the research regarding the use of a time-out signal is inconclusive. More research is also needed to evaluate the effectiveness of instructional versus physical administration. There is no evidence to suggest additional benefit or harm in the use of contingent release.

Case Study

Background Information

Ramona was a three-year-old preschooler with a speech-language delay in the three- to four-year-old classroom of the university laboratory preschool. She received speech-language pull-out services biweekly for 30 minutes. She was referred for problems related to aggression towards her peers, such as hitting and pulling things from her peers' hands. Ms. Podesta, the lead teacher, and Ms. Kelly, a teaching assistant for the classroom, instructed the other children to share with Ramona when this occurred and told Ramona, "no hitting." This was the most common outcome for the behavior, and no other interventions or strategies were typically employed.

There were 12 children enrolled in Ramona's classroom. Undergraduate students in the early childhood education program at the university were also present to assist and observe in the classroom a few days per week. The laboratory preschool follows the Reggio Emilia philosophy, a child-centered, experiential learning-based pedagogy. Modeling, coaching, redirection, and collaborative problem-solving are generally used with regard to behavior management, but no formal or systematic classroom management program or plan was utilized. To address Ramona's problem behaviors, a school psychologist was requested for behavior consultation services. The school psychologist provided a conjoint consultation with Ms. Podesta and Ramona's parents.

Description of the Problem Behavior

The school psychologist conducted problem-identification interviews with Ms. Podesta and Ramona's parents focusing on physically aggressive behaviors towards her peers. These behaviors were defined as Ramona pushing, hitting, or taking/grabbing in an attempt to secure an item or object that a peer was playing with or had in his/her possession. Ms. Podesta reported that Ramona would become visibly frustrated during center time, particularly around sharing. Ramona had deficits in verbal expression, so she did not make requests or communicate her wants/needs to her peers during those incidents. When she wanted an item that another child was using or playing with, she would first attempt to grab the item from the other child's hands. If she was unsuccessful, she would try to hit or push. The hitting and pushing were not particularly severe or dangerous and did not often result in injury but were highly disruptive and upsetting to her peers. Ms. Podesta reported that these aggressive behaviors would occur one to two times per day during center times with an average of eight incidents per five-day week. Ramona's parents reported that these behaviors occurred at home as well with aggression aimed towards Ramona's five-and-half-year-old sister. Consequences at home were similar to at school, with Ramona's parents typically asking her sister to share with Ramona or removing the toy or object from both children. Ramona's aggressive behaviors at home were slightly more severe and included biting, but occurred less frequently, four times per week on average.

The school psychologist used an A-B-C chart tool to facilitate direct observation in the classroom during center time and to compile qualitative descriptions of the behaviors. These data are presented in Table 4.1, and a blank example of an A-B-C chart is presented in Appendix A.

Problem Analysis

The school psychologist hypothesized that Ramona's aggressive behaviors were maintained by access to tangibles such as preferred toys or objects, and that her difficulty to express herself verbally served as a motivating operation. A typical scenario the school psychologist observed was characterized by the following: a child would be holding a toy that Ramona preferred, or another child would pick up a toy that Ramona had recently been playing with. This was followed by Ramona grabbing either the toy, the child's arms/hands, or pushing the other

TABLE 4.1 A-B-C Data for Direct Observation of Ramona's Problem Behaviors

A-B-C Data	Date: 9/1-9/5	Student: Ramona G.	
Setting Event	*Antecedent*	*Behavior*	*Consequence*
What was happening in the environment (e.g., outdoor play time)?	What happened right before the behavior (e.g., another child took a toy away from her/him)?	What was the behavior (e.g., biting)?	What happened immediately after the behavior (e.g., child that was bitten cried and teacher removed child from the classroom)?
9/1 Centers – Blocks	Another child picked up a block Ramona had just put down	Ramona pushed the other child	Ramona was told "no" by Ms. P, started crying until Ms. P handed block to Ramona
9/2 Centers – Art	Ramona attempted to grab crayon from another child	Ramona slapped the other child's arm	Ramona was walked by hand to Blocks center (preferred)
9/3 Centers – Art	Another child was playing with chalk that Ramona prefers	Ramona pushed the other child	Ramona was told "no" by Ms. P, instructed to apologize, and other child told to share chalk
9/4 Centers – Books	Another child was looking at a book Ramona enjoyed from morning circle	Ramona grabbed the other child's arms and did not let go	Ramona was walked by hand to Blocks center (preferred)
9/5 Centers – Art	Another child picked up the chalk Ramona had just put down	Ramona pushed the other child	Ramona was told "no" by Ms. K and walked to Blocks center (preferred)

child. After this occurred, Ms. Podesta, Ms. Kelly, or a student would ask the other child to share the toy with Ramona or would separate the children to different centers, often taking Ramona to another preferred center. During these incidents, Ramona's physical behavior would escalate to tantrum behaviors and she would appear visibly upset, often crying and pouting. She would return to baseline behavior when she had access to the toy or another preferred center.

Intervention Goals

The school psychologist collaborated with Ms. Podesta and Ramona's parents to identify goals related to her aggressive behaviors. With or without adult prompting, Ramona was expected to choose a different toy/activity and wait her turn in order to prevent her behavior from escalating to physically aggressive behaviors four out of five times (80%). Over the course of six weeks, Ramona's aggressive behaviors should be reduced from an average of eight incidents per week to zero.

Measurement of Target Behaviors, Data, Collection Strategies, and Progress Monitoring

The school psychologist recommended the use of frequency counts and school–home notes to monitor Ramona's progress. Ramona's behavior was rated twice each day, morning and afternoon, on a three-point scale (good, fair, poor) that was paired with smiley faces and corresponded to frequency counts of problem behavior. If Ramona engaged in zero incidents of aggressive behavior for that time period, an entire morning or afternoon, she was awarded a smiley face and two points. If she engaged in one incident, she received an unsure face, which was worth one point. For two or more incidents, she received a frowny face and zero points. Each week, Ramona had the opportunity to earn 20 points. Given her goals, Ramona was expected to earn 16 points at minimum (80%, or four out of five). These ratings were discussed with Ramona and she colored in the appropriate face that corresponded with her behavior rating. These notes were sent home, and she would receive rewards at home based on the number of points she earned. Ramona's parents provided praise and encouragement daily for all of her success. They decided to reward her for every 10 points she was able to "save up" and tracked her points with a chart visual. The school psychologist also participated in weekly check-ins with Ms. Podesta. Ms. Podesta, Ms. Kelly, and the early childhood education undergraduate students assigned to Ramona's classroom were trained in direct observation and how to use the data collection forms. An example of the school–home note used is presented in Table 4.2 with

TABLE 4.2 School–Home Note for Ramona's Problem Behaviors

School–Home Note for Ramona G.
Week: 10/8-10/12
Day: Monday

Goals	Morning			Afternoon		
I will wait my turn or choose another toy						

Note: A smile is worth 2 points and indicates 0 incidents of aggressive behaviors, an unsure face is worth 1 point and indicates 1 incident of aggressive behavior, and a frown is worth 0 points and indicates 2 or more incidents of aggressive behaviors.

TABLE 4.3 Frequency Chart for Direct Observation of Ramona's Problem Behaviors

Frequency Chart Target: Aggressive Behavior	Student: Ramona G.	Observer: Ms. P	Dates: 10/8 - 10/12
Date	Occurrences	Daily Total	Notes
Monday	|	1	
Tuesday	||	2	
Wednesday	|	1	
Thursday	||	2	
Friday	||	2	
Weekly Total:	8		

a blank note presented in Appendix B, and the frequency recording form and a blank form are presented in Table 4.3 and Appendix C, respectively.

Intervention Plan

Baseline data were collected for one week prior to intervention implementation, during which time the teachers continued class practices as usual (treatment as usual). Ms. Podesta and Ms. Kelly then used the following protocol for implementing time-out in conjunction with positive reinforcement. Ms. Podesta designated a spot within the classroom that was easy to block an escape from and out of the reach of tangibles, preferred centers or objects, or Ramona's peers. These location considerations helped ensure the time-out spot was non-reinforcing in comparison to the time-in environment. Each time Ramona engaged in the target behavior (a continuous-use parameter) such as hitting or pushing, Ms. Podesta or Ms. Kelly would stand within arm's reach of Ramona and deliver the following verbal reason as part of the instructional administration of time-out: "You may not hit/push. Go to time-out." If Ramona did not begin walking to the time-out spot within five seconds, she was gently and safely escorted to the time-out spot, and a timer for four minutes was set. While Ramona was in the time-out spot, she received no verbal attention from the teacher and any attempts by Ramona to elicit teacher attention were ignored. If Ramona attempted to escape the time-out spot, she was blocked by an adult without verbal attention or eye contact. If she remained in the time-out spot for the four-minute duration, adults would do nothing. At the conclusion of four minutes, Ramona was welcomed back into classroom activities by Ms. Podesta or Ms. Kelly. This time-out procedure was explained to Ramona's parents for use at home as well.

Best practices for time-out indicate this it is used most effectively in combination with positive reinforcement for desired behavior (Everett et al., 2010; O'Handley et al., 2019). Pre-correction for expected behaviors was employed to remind all students, including Ramona, of classroom expectations prior to engaging in the next activity. Simple, positively worded language was used, such as: "Class, we are going to play in centers next. Remember, if someone has a toy that we want, we need to wait our turn or ask our friends to share. We can play with other toys while we wait." Throughout the day, Ms. Podesta and Ms. Kelly provided Ramona with behavior-specific praise when they observed her engaging in appropriate behaviors, especially during center time. During center time, an adult would maintain close proximity to Ramona to monitor her behavior and provide positive reinforcement (behavior-specific praise or access to a preferred tangible) or engage in the time-out procedure in response to aggressive behavior.

Intervention Fidelity and Interobserver Agreement

The school psychologist collected intervention fidelity during approximately 33% of sessions using the Intervention Procedural Checklist (see Appendix D). Intervention fidelity was calculated by dividing the number of steps completed correctly by the total number of steps and multiplying by 100. Fidelity was 100% for the observed sessions.

The school psychologist also collected interobserver agreement (IOA) for aggression using the same data collection form as the primary observer during all of the sessions in which she was present. Percentage agreement was calculated by dividing the number of agreements by the sum of agreements and disagreements and multiplying by 100. Interobserver agreement for aggressive events was 100%.

Intervention Outcome Data

Ramona's progress as measured by daily frequency counts is illustrated in Figure 4.1. The average daily number of aggressive behaviors Ramona exhibited during baseline was 2.4. This was reduced to an average of 1.7 over the course of the intervention with incidents reduced to zero in the last five days, satisfying her goal. Her aggressive behaviors tended to briefly increase at the end of most weeks and in the afternoons but declined gradually overall. Her progress as measured by school–home notes and weekly points earned is presented in Figure 4.2. Ramona's weekly points earned increased gradually over the course of the intervention, from 10 points (50% appropriate behaviors) in the first week to 20 points (100% appropriate behaviors), satisfying her goal.

Summary of Intervention Effects

Ramona's aggressive behaviors were significantly reduced over the course of intervention implementation. Ms. Podesta reported that Ramona's relationships with her peers also greatly improved by week six of the intervention due to her decreased aggressive behaviors. By day 15 of the intervention, all instances of

Time-Out   55

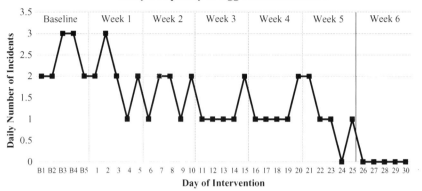

FIGURE 4.1 Daily frequency of aggressive behaviors
Note: Week 5 of the intervention phase was preceded by a week-long break from school for a holiday. The intervention resumed when school resumed.

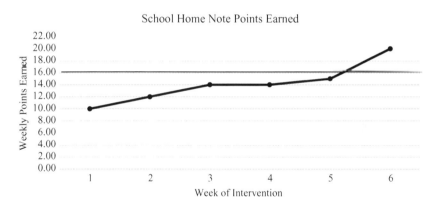

FIGURE 4.2 Weekly points earned
Note: The thin line represents Ramona's goal to exhibit appropriate behaviors 80% of the time, which corresponds to earning at least 16 points, as Ramona had the opportunity to earn 20 points per week total (two points each morning and afternoon for a total of four per day).

aggressive behaviors in the morning were eliminated. Ramona continued to display aggressive behaviors in the afternoon, as her fatigue was observed to increase closer to pick-up time each day. Ramona's team judged the intervention to be effective overall, as it greatly reduced her problematic aggressive behaviors over a short period of time, required only modest effort to implement (and could be implemented by undergraduate support students), and did not disrupt classroom activities.

Intervention Acceptability

Following the conclusion of data collection, Ms. Podesta and Ms. Kelly were asked whether they believed the time-out procedure was effective in reducing Ramona's aggressive behaviors and whether they would be likely to use this procedure in the future given similar problem behaviors. Ms. Podesta and Ms. Kelly indicated yes to both questions. They were also asked whether they believed the procedure to be easy to implement. Both indicated that the procedure was easy to implement given the number of adults typically present in the classroom but that the intervention would have been more difficult to implement if there had only been one adult present in the room. Each teacher was also asked about the ease of use regarding the data collection methods. Each indicated that the forms were easy to use and that they appreciated the collaborative nature of the school–home notes in that their use involved Ramona and her parents. The school psychologist concluded that this intervention was highly acceptable to both Ms. Podesta and Ms. Kelly.

Intervention Considerations

Dadds and Tully (2019) assessed historical and current conceptualizations of discipline in the context of child mental health across contemporary pillars of developmental theory including social learning, attachment, self and emotion regulation, and ecological systems to generate guidelines for the use of time-out. This analysis was conducted partially in response to recent popular media criticism of time-out as potentially harmful to children, particularly to children with attachment related problems and trauma histories. The authors categorize criticism of time-out along three general issues: attachment threat, as time-out necessarily separates the child from their caregiver; failure to teach new behaviors; and failure to address underlying causes of problem behavior. In reviewing the literature regarding the use of time-out in trauma-exposed populations and in the context of attachment, the authors found no evidence to support these criticisms.

Included in their guidelines for best practices with respect to time-out are recommendations related to the assessment of child behaviors that are appropriate targets for time-out intervention. Time-out should be used only for behaviors that the child has some control in producing. In the case example above, Ramona's aggressive behaviors were related to her speech delays, specifically her deficits in verbal expression. However, she had been receiving speech services or several months, which had developed her functional communication skills to be able to express her needs in the classroom. Time-out was an appropriate intervention for her aggressive behaviors, but it should not have been used if her functional communication skills had not first been developed or if it was being used to target distress reactions instead. Behaviors that represent a child's inability to perform a task or are in response to fear or overwhelming emotions are not appropriately targeted by time-out. Dadds and Tully (2019) also recommend time-out as part of a broader behavioral program that teaches positive replacement behaviors, as well as explicit communication that time-out is in response to a specific behavior that has been previously established to be inappropriate. In consideration of attachment processes of separation and reunion, time-out procedures must not carry messages related to abandonment or rejection (Dadds & Tully, 2019). Overall, the authors concluded that time-out is an effective positive discipline strategy.

In the case study above, a fixed-duration time-out procedure of four minutes was implemented. Another commonly recommended procedure for time-out involves the use of a release contingency. These are typically characterized by either resetting the time-out duration in response to problem behavior that occurs during time-out, or the requirement that no problem behaviors occur during a specified amount of time at the end of the time-out duration. Both of these contingencies are implemented to avoid reinforcing problem behavior with release from time-out. Donaldson and Vollmer (2011) compared the efficacy of fixed-duration time-out and release-contingency time-out and found that both procedures were effective in reducing problem behaviors, however a release-contingency did not eliminate problem behaviors while in time-out, and problem behaviors while in time-out did not predict problem behaviors in time-in. Thus, the authors recommend consideration of a fixed duration procedure first due to ease of implementation (Donaldson & Vollmer, 2011).

The level of prompting, either verbal or physical, required for the administration of time-out is an additional consideration in the ease of implementation, as full-physical guidance of the child to the time-out spot requires considerably more effort. In an evaluation of time-out procedures designed to increase compliance with verbally prompted time-out administration, evidence supported the use of a one-minute versus four-minute time-out duration contingent on the child complying with a verbal instruction to go to the time-out spot within 10 seconds of delivery of the verbal prompt. Children were made aware of the contingency beforehand and understood that if their teacher needed to help them walk to the time-out spot that the duration of their time-out would be longer (i.e., four minutes instead of one minute). The authors recommend this procedure for children who exhibit high levels of refusal for time-out and to maximize the amount of time-in.

A common recommendation regarding duration is matching duration to the child's age, with one to two minutes per year of age considered most appropriate (Frost, 2014). This recommendation has been disputed, as evidence suggests that fixed durations and age-dependent durations are equally effective (Kapalka & Bryk, 2007). A four-minute time-out duration, utilized in the case example above, is considered historically standard and has been shown to be as effective as longer durations in reducing problem behaviors while minimizing duration

(Benjamin, Mazzarins, & Kupfersmid, 1983; Donaldson & Vollmer, 2011, 2012; Hobbs, Forehand, & Murray, 1978; McGuffin, 1991). In a study that aimed to determine the shortest effective duration to reduce sibling aggression, the authors concluded that a one-minute time-out duration was equally effective (Corralejo, Jensen, & Greathouse, 2018). This study included children diagnosed with developmental delays and Attention Deficit Hyperactivity Disorder (ADHD), suggesting that time-out is also effective for children with diverse abilities. As duration may be the most impactful parameter regarding intervention effectiveness as well as an essential consideration for ease of use for caregivers and teachers and an important ethical consideration due to loss of instructional or social time for children, the shortest effective duration should be used (Corralejo, Jensen, Greathouse, & Ward, 2018).

Conclusion

Time-out, short for time-out from positive reinforcement, is a widely used and effective behavior reduction procedure. It can be used in a variety of school contexts to address a wide range of behaviors. Furthermore, it is a simple and socially acceptable strategy to implement. This chapter's case study demonstrates the swift and powerful effects of this intervention when used as recommended. Given that physical aggression is a safety concern for schools and can result in severely punitive and consequential outcomes for students, it is encouraging to know that educators have this easy yet impactful tool at their disposal.

References

Benjamin, R., Mazzarins, H., & Kupfersmid, J. (1983). The effect of time-out (TO) duration on assaultiveness in psychiatrically hospitalized children. *Aggressive Behavior*, 9(1), 21–27. doi:10.1002/1098-2337(1983)9:13.0.CO;2-H

Cooper, J. O., Heron, T. E., & Heward, W. L. (2007). *Applied behavior analysis* (2nd ed.). Upper Saddle River, NJ: Pearson.

Corralejo, S. M., Jensen, S. A., & Greathouse, A. D. (2018). Time-out for sibling aggression: An analysis of effective durations in a natural setting. *Child & Family Behavior Therapy*, 40(3), 187–203. doi:10.1080/07317107.2018.1487701

Corralejo, S. M., Jensen, S. A., Greathouse, A. D., & Ward, L. E. (2018). Parameters of time-out: Research update and comparison to parenting programs, books, and online recommendations. *Behavior Therapy*, 49, 99–112. doi:10.1016/j.beth.2017.09.005

Dadds, M. R., & Tully, L. A. (2019). What is it to discipline a child: What should it be? A reanalysis of time-out from the perspective of child mental health, attachment, and trauma. *American Psychologist*, 74(7), 794–808. doi:10.1037/amp0000449

Donaldson, J. M., & Vollmer, T. R. (2011). An evaluation and comparison of time-out procedures with and without release contingencies. *Journal of Applied Behavior Analysis*, 44(4), 693–705. doi:10.1901/jaba.2011.44-693

Donaldson, J. M., & Vollmer, T. R. (2012). A procedure for thinning the schedule of time-out. *Journal of Applied Behavior Analysis*, 45(3), 625–630. doi:10.1901/jaba.2012.45-625

Everett, G. E., Hupp, S. D., & Olmi, D. J. (2010). Time-out with parents: A descriptive analysis of 30 years of research. *Education and Treatment of Children*, 33(2), 235–259. Retrieved from www.jstor.org/stable/42900065. doi:10.1353/etc.0.0091

Frost, J. (2014). *Jo Frost's toddler rules: Your 5-step guide to shaping proper behavior*. New York: Ballantine Books.

Hobbs, S. A., Forehand, R., & Murray, R. G. (1978). Effects of various durations of timeout on the noncompliant behavior of children. *Behavior Therapy*, 9(4), 652–656. doi:10.1016/S0005-7894(78)80142-7

Kapalka, G. M., & Bryk, L. J. (2007). Two- to four- minute time-out is sufficient for young boys with ADHD. *Early Childhood Services*, 1, 181–188. Retrieved from https://www.pluralpublishing.com/journals_ECS.htm

Kern, L., Benson, J. L., & Clemens, N. H. (2010). Strategies for working with severe challenging and violent behavior. In G. G. Peacock, R. A. Ervin, E. J. Daly III, & K. W. Merrell (Eds.), *Practical handbook of school psychology: Effective practices for the 21st century* (pp. 459–474). New York: The Guildford Press.

McGuffin, P. W. (1991). The effect of timeout duration on frequency of aggression in hospitalized children with conduct disorders. *Behavioral Interventions*, 6(4), 279–288. doi:10.1002/bin.2360060405

O'Handley, R. D., Olmi, D. J., & Kennedy, A. (2019). Time-out procedures in school settings. In K. C. Radley & E. H. Dart (Eds.), *Handbook of behavioral interventions in schools* (pp. 482–500). New York: Oxford University Press. doi:10.1093/med-psych/9780190843229.003.0025

Sugai, G., & Horner, R. R. (2006). A promising approach for expanding and sustaining school-wide positive behavior support. *School Psychology Review*, 35, 245.

Appendix A: Blank Generic A-B-C Data Collection Form

A-B-C Data	Date:	Student:	
Setting Event	*Antecedent*	*Behavior*	*Consequence*
What was happening in the environment (e.g., outdoor play time)?	*What happened right before the behavior (e.g., another child took a toy away from her/him)?*	*What was the behavior (e.g., biting)?*	*What happened immediately after the behavior (e.g., child that was bitten cried and teacher removed child from the classroom)?*

Appendix B: Generic Blank Home Note

School–Home Note for:

Week:
Day:

Goals	Morning			Afternoon		
	🙂	😐	☹️	🙂	😐	☹️

Appendix C: Blank Generic Frequency Chart for Direct Observation

Frequency Chart
Target: *Student:*   *Observer:*   *Dates:*

Date	Occurrences	Daily Total	Notes
Monday			
Tuesday			
Wednesday			
Thursday			
Friday			
Weekly Total:			

Appendix D: Intervention Fidelity Checklist

Step	Procedure	Completion		
1	Pre-correction occurred before center time as a reminder of the classroom rules.	Yes	No	N/A
2	An adult remained within arm's length of Ramona during center time.	Yes	No	N/A
3	When the target behavior occurred, the reason for time-out was labeled.	Yes	No	N/A
4	Ramona was directed to go to time-out, and gentle guidance was used if she did not walk within five seconds.	Yes	No	N/A
5	The timer was set for four minutes.	Yes	No	N/A
6	No attention was provided during time-out, and any attempts to escape time-out were blocked without attention.	Yes	No	N/A
7	At the end of the four minutes, Ramona was welcomed back to the classroom activity.	Yes	No	N/A
8	Multiple incidents of behavior-specific praise were provided to Ramona during center time.	Yes	No	N/A

5
PREMACK'S PRINCIPLE AND VISUAL SCHEDULES

Susan Rattan and Mahri Wrightington

Introduction

Students are frequently faced with tasks they either experience as aversive or unpleasant. For many students, aversive or unpleasant tasks lead to mildly negative responses that require little teacher intervention. For other students, however, these aversive or unpleasant tasks are followed by more troubling responses such as noncompliance and disruptive behavior. For teachers managing such problems, identifying simple yet effective strategies for increasing student compliance is of paramount importance.

Premack's principle might be useful to consider when students are noncompliant and refuse to complete academic tasks. Premack's principle states that high-probability behaviors (e.g., behaviors that are more likely to occur independently) can be used to positively reinforce low-probability behaviors (Premack, 1959). In other words, the likelihood that a student engages in a low-probability behavior (e.g., math worksheets) can be increased when that behavior is regularly followed by a high-probability behavior (e.g., recess). Premack's principle has been colloquially referred to as "Grandma's rule." As the adage goes, Grandma says to her grandchild, "You can have a cookie after you finish your peas." Grandma is using the high-probability behavior (eating a cookie) to reinforce the low-probability behavior (finishing the peas). Premack's principle helps us arrange consequences so that contingent relationships might be established between high- and low-probability behaviors including preferred and non-preferred activities and tasks.

Premack's principle can be effectively used in educational settings to increase the occurrence of low-probability behaviors or non-preferred activities or tasks. Studies have found interventions derived from Premack's principle are effective in school settings to increase the occurrence of various non-preferred activities such as report writing (Hosie, Gentile, & Carroll, 1974) and academic work completion (Geiger, 1996), and to increase attending behavior (Van Hevel & Hawkins, 1974) and attentive calmness for students with attention deficit/hyperactivity disorders (Azrin, Vinas, & Ehle, 2007). These studies used preferred activities (i.e., high-probability behaviors) such as physical activity and playground time, free time, and time to engage in artistic activities to reinforce engagement in non-preferred tasks (i.e., low-probability behaviors).

There are a number of points to consider when implementing an intervention using Premack's principle. First, the intervention's success is largely dependent on correctly identifying preferred activities that might be used to reinforce low-probability behaviors. The intervention is not likely to be successful when, for example, computer time is used to reinforce finishing a math worksheet when computer time is not a preferred activity. Second, the student must have the skills necessary to successfully complete any non-preferred tasks. Put differently, the student's failure to complete the non-preferred task should be due to a performance deficit (i.e., "won't do") rather than a skill deficit (i.e., "can't do"). Third, expectations regarding completing the non-preferred task should be gradually increased to assist students in moving towards a higher level of independence. This is typically accomplished when the high-probability behavior is no longer needed to reinforce the low-probability behavior. Finally, visual schedules might be used to provide students with reminders of the preferred and non-preferred tasks (Johns, 2015). Perhaps more importantly, visual schedules offer a visual representation of the contingent relationship between the preferred and non-preferred tasks.

Visual schedules are visual representations of sequences of tasks to be completed. The visual representations most often involve pictures, symbols, or words. Students can refer to visual schedules to identify which tasks they should be working on and which tasks are coming. Visual schedules, which have strong empirical support, are commonly used for students with autism spectrum disorder (ASD) and intellectual disability (ID; Knight, Sartini, & Spriggs, 2015; Spriggs, Mims, van Dijk, & Knight, 2017). Following a comprehensive literature review, Knight et al. (2015) concluded that visual schedules were effective for increasing time on-task, decreasing work completion time, and decreasing the number of prompts needed during transitions for students with ASD. Similarly, Spriggs et al. (2017) found visual schedules improved daily living and academic skills, on-task behavior, and independence for students with ID (Spriggs et al., 2017). Unfortunately, there is less available research examining visual schedules used with students without disabilities, although one recent study found evidence supporting the effectiveness of visual schedules for decreasing challenging behaviors of young children without disabilities (Zimmerman, Ledford, & Barton, 2017).

The First-Then Board is a specific strategy that combines Premack's principle with a version of the visual schedule. This visual representation of Premack's principle displays the non-preferred task(s) on the left side of the board, typically under the word "first," and the preferred task(s) on the right side of the board, typically under the word "then." The tasks can be presented as pictures, symbols, or words depending on the student's ability to comprehend the schedule independently (Hume, 2009). In order for the use of the visual schedule to be a successful support, there should be a plan in place to teach students how to read and understand the schedule. Other considerations include deciding where the schedule will be kept, how often it will be used, and how its effectiveness will be determined. Additionally, those implementing the First-Then Board should always follow through on the promise that the preferred activity will be available contingent on completion of the non-preferred task (Hume, 2009). Successful implementation of an intervention based on the Premack principle relies on the establishment of a contingent relationship between the non-preferred task (First) and preferred activity it follows (Then).

Case Study

Background Information

Vincent was a 15-year-old ninth grade student at Ginsburg High School. He had a diagnosis of ASD and had been receiving special education services since first grade. His Individualized Education Plan (IEP) included goals in areas such as social skills (e.g., communicating appropriately and respectfully with others), executive functioning (e.g., initiating tasks, organizing assignments, time management), independent living skills (e.g., self-care, safety), and writing (e.g., initiating, expanding and elaborating). Vincent's reading and math scores generally fell within the average range on standardized tests, so he did not receive specialized instruction in these areas. Vincent attended classes that were co-taught by general and special education teachers, and received paraprofessional support throughout the majority of the school day.

Vincent's teachers requested a meeting with the school psychologist to discuss strategies to increase Vincent's writing output. At the meeting, they shared that Vincent appeared to be progressing in most skill areas when verbal responses, dictation, or hands-on materials were used, but that Vincent often refused to engage in tasks that required putting pencil to paper. While the team was willing to accommodate Vincent using verbal responses, technology, and other appropriate alternatives as often as possible, they unanimously agreed that Vincent should learn to tolerate some amount of writing in preparation for college and career options.

Description of the Problem Behavior

The team identified written work refusal as Vincent's primary concern. Written work refusal was defined as failing to complete assigned paper/pencil tasks within the allotted class time. Examples of written work refusal included completing only one of ten written math problems on a given worksheet in algebra class, writing only two words on an assigned ten-sentence journal prompt in history class, and putting his head down instead of completing a science note-taking activity. Examples of written work completion included completing written tasks with an appropriate level of neatness and accuracy based on Vincent's previous written work.

The school psychologist, Dr. Mae, planned her observations with the teachers to coincide with times when writing tasks would be assigned in class. Dr. Mae observed Vincent in five academic class periods over the course of one school week. During her observations, she used an A-B-C observation scheme to support the team's problem analysis process. The A-B-C data are presented in Table 5.1. In addition, Dr. Mae created a written work completion data collection form (see Figure 5.1) and asked each teacher to estimate the percent (e.g., 0%, 25%, 50%, 75%, or 100%) of the paper-pencil tasks that were completed by Vincent over the course of one week. This collection of data points in all academic subject areas across one school week served as baseline data. In an effort to ensure adequate estimation consistency among teachers, Dr. Mae conducted a brief training during which the team reviewed and practiced estimating completion rates of various types of assignments. Baseline data are presented in Table 5.2 and a visual representation of those data are presented in Figure 5.2. These data indicated that over the course of the baseline week, Vincent completed between 5–25% of the assigned written tasks across the different content areas. Work completion percentages averaged across subject areas indicated that Vincent was completing an average of 14% of the assigned written tasks over the course of the baseline week.

Problem Analysis

After interviewing Vincent's teachers and observing Vincent across settings, Dr. Mae hypothesized that the function of Vincent's written work refusal behavior was avoidance of non-preferred academic tasks. Specifically, Dr. Mae hypothesized that Vincent's work refusal behavior was initiated and maintained by successful avoidance of written tasks. Additionally, Vincent's teachers believed that he had the knowledge and skills to complete the assignments. They reported that he was successful when he was allowed to answer questions orally and that he had the physical skills to write those responses on paper. The team believed a reinforcement-based intervention might be effective at increasing Vincent's written work output, as it appeared the problem behavior was a result of a performance deficit and not a skill deficit.

Intervention Goals

Dr. Mae guided the team in analyzing and summarizing Vincent's baseline data collected during the problem analysis phase. These data revealed that Vincent

TABLE 5.1 A-B-C Data

Date/Time/Class	Written Task	Antecedent	Behavior	Consequence
Algebra	Complete worksheet with 24 problems	Paraprofessional placed worksheet on desk	V put arms and head down on desk for approx. 9 min	Teacher collected blank page from his desk
Physical Science	Take observation notes on organizer during video	Teacher passed out organizer and started video	V watched entire video, put name on organizer, did not write anything else	Teacher called on V to answer 2 questions about the video – he provided correct answers and received praise
U.S. History	Summarize important facts from chapter reading	Teacher put V with partner and para. Para suggested they share one sheet and take turns writing.	V agreed to go first and wrote one sentence. On his next turn, he stated, "Can I just tell you what to write?"	Peer said yes and completed 3 more sentences, while V participated verbally. Teacher praised them for getting it done.
Resource	Complete vocabulary organizer	Para asked student to complete organizer, then walked away to help another student	V folded paper into shape and tried to get it to stand on end. Then put head down.	Teacher asked students to put completed work in basket – V did not and was dismissed to next class with no discussion about it.
English 9	Complete journal entry on career aspirations	Teacher put writing prompt on board and asked students to retrieve journals from the shelf	V retrieved journal, picked up pencil and drew circles in journal. Para asked questions about career – V discussed interest in video game design but stated, "I just don't want to write."	Teacher asked to see what he got done – told him she needs to see more effort next time. V was dismissed to next class.

Premack's Principle and Visual Schedules 67

Directions: In each class period this week, please estimate the amount of written work (i.e, paper/pencil tasks) completed by Vincent during class.

Subject: _____   Week of: _____

Monday	Tuesday	Wednesday	Thursday	Friday
☐ 0%	☐ 0%	☐ 0%	☐ 0%	☐ 0%
☐ 25%	☐ 25%	☐ 25%	☐25%	☐ 25%
☐ 50%	☐ 50%	☐ 50%	☐ 50%	☐ 50%
☐ 75%	☐ 75%	☐ 75%	☐ 75%	☐ 75%
☐ 100%	☐ 100%	☐ 100%	☐ 100%	☐ 100%
☐ Absent	☐ Absent	☐ Absent	☐ Absent	☐ Absent
☐ No writing assigned today	☐ No writing assigned today	☐ No writing assigned today	☐ No writing assigned today	☐ No writing assigned today

Calculate average work completion rate across the week by adding percentages and dividing by 5. If student was absent OR no writing tasks were assigned, remove that day from the denominator.

Average work completion rate for this week: _____

FIGURE 5.1 Data collection form

TABLE 5.2 Baseline Data

Class	Teacher Estimate of Written Work Completion					Average Written Work Completion Percentage
	Mon	Tues	Wed	Thurs	Fri	
Algebra	0%	25%	0%	50%	0%	15%
Physical Science	0%	0%	25%	25%	0%	10%
U.S. History	25%	25%	50%	0%	25%	25%
Resource	0%	0%	25%	0%	0%	5%
English 9	0%	0%	25%	25%	25%	15%
Average of all classes across 1 week						14%

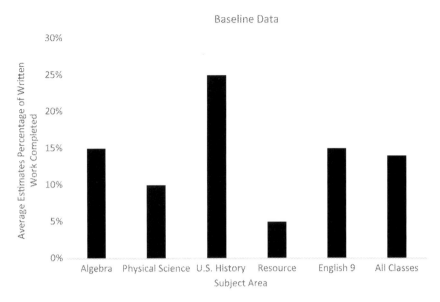

FIGURE 5.2 Average estimates of percentage of written work completed by subject area during baseline

was completing between 5% and 25% of assigned written tasks in each subject area, with an overall completion rate average of 14% of assigned written tasks in a week's time. The team discussed Vincent's long-standing difficulties with writing and that writing had always been a non-preferred academic task. They determined that a reasonable goal for Vincent would be to complete 50% of assigned written tasks independently using paper and pencil after approximately two months of intervention.

Measurement of Target Behaviors, Data Collection Strategies, and Progress Monitoring

The team defined the target behavior, written work completion, as putting pencil to paper to complete assigned writing tasks in class. They would continue to collect data using the same data collection format that Dr. Mae designed for the baseline phase. This method required Vincent's teachers to estimate the percentage of assigned written work that Vincent completed during each class period.

Prior to the start of the intervention, Vincent's teaching team attended another training session with Dr. Mae during which they practiced estimating written work completion percentages to ensure reliability of the collected data. The paraprofessional assigned to support Vincent would be responsible for conferring briefly with the teacher at the end of each class period to estimate the percentage of written work completed and record the necessary information on the form. The team agreed that the data collection chart would be submitted to Dr. Mae at the end of each week. Dr. Mae would be responsible for inputting, graphing, and analyzing the data for the team. This information would be summarized and sent in a weekly email to all of Vincent's teachers.

Intervention Plan

The team designed an intervention combining Premack's principle with visual schedules to increase Vincent's written output in school. Specifically, the intervention presented Vincent with a visual schedule using a First-Then Board to depict the non-preferred task (i.e., writing assignment) and the preferred activity (i.e., access to comic books). Dr. Mae interviewed Vincent's teachers and paraprofessional, Vincent's parents, and Vincent himself to help determine preferred activities that might positively reinforce Vincent's written work completion. Additionally, Dr. Mae conducted an interest inventory with Vincent to identify potential activities that might positively reinforce written work completion. Dr. Mae determined that preferred activities appropriate for school were reading comic books, using a tablet to play math games, and playing board games. Given time constraints within the classroom, the team decided to use access to comic books as the preferred activity.

For the intervention, the teacher first provided Vincent with explicit instructions about the written assignment individually after providing class-wide instructions. This helped ensure Vincent's understanding of assignment expectations, especially writing expectations (e.g., neatness). Second, the paraprofessional presented the First-Then Board depicting the non-preferred task (i.e., writing assignment) alongside the preferred activity (i.e., accessing comic books). Vincent was able to read his comic books only after completing the assigned writing task. The team determined that the paraprofessional would be responsible for transporting Vincent's visual schedule to each class throughout the day, as she traveled with him from class to class. The team expected Vincent to eventually be independent in carrying the visual schedule with his personal belongings after several weeks of intervention. A visual schedule template (see Appendix A) was created and laminated so the paraprofessional could write a brief description of the writing assignment in marker, wiping it off following each class.

Intervention Fidelity and Interobserver Agreement

To assess intervention fidelity, Dr. Mae completed one observation per week during class periods when teachers planned to assign written work. Dr. Mae rotated her observations so that over the course of eight weeks, she observed each subject at least twice. During observations, she used a Fidelity Checklist (see Figure 5.3) developed by the team that included the intervention's key components. Dr. Mae

Procedure	Completed (please circle)
Did the teacher provide explicit instructions to indicate exactly what needed to be completed in order for Vincent to earn access to his preferred activity?	Yes No
Was the visual schedule placed in Vincent's view while he worked on the written assignment?	Yes No
If Vincent completed his assignment, was he given immediate access to his preferred activity?	Yes No N/A
If Vincent did not complete his assignment, was his preferred activity withheld?	Yes No N/A

FIGURE 5.3 Intervention fidelity checklist

calculated fidelity at the end of both four-week intervention periods. Fidelity was 95% and 92% for the first and second four-week periods, respectively.

Dr. Mae also collected the Written Work Completion Data Collection Forms each week, so she was able to see that the teachers were consistently rating the percentage of written work completed each day. She randomly selected two days per week for each subject area to collect the completed written work and estimated the percentage of work completed that day in the selected subject. Then, she compared her estimate to the teacher's estimate. She calculated interobserver agreement (IOA) for each subject across the eight weeks of intervention. IOA ranged from 87.5% to 100% across teachers. Based on these data, the team determined that the intervention was being implemented with adequate fidelity.

Intervention Outcome Data

As stated previously, baseline data indicated that Vincent was completing about 14% of written work assigned across all of his classes during a one-week period. Dr. Mae collected data forms from each class period over eight weeks. She reviewed, analyzed, and summarized the intervention data at the end of each week. The team convened a meeting after week four to discuss the data and determine a need for changes. Intervention data are presented in Table 5.3. During the first three weeks of the intervention, Vincent's written work completion increased to 45%, 53%, and 61%, respectively. However, a decline was noted during week four, as Vincent's written work completion average was 29%. Several

TABLE 5.3 Baseline and Intervention Data: Average Estimates of Percentage of Written Work Completed

CLASS	Baseline	Week 1	Week 2	Week 3	Week 4	Week 5	Week 6	Week 7	Week 8
Algebra	15%	55%	50%	80%	25%	25%	55%	75%	65%
Physical Science	10%	25%	50%	50%	20%	35%	50%	60%	50%
U.S. History	25%	50%	55%	55%	10%	25%	65%	55%	75%
Resource	5%	20%	65%	45%	40%	10%	80%	50%	60%
English 9	15%	75%	45%	75%	50%	30%	45%	50%	55%
All classes	14%	45%	53%	61%	29%	25%	59%	58%	61%

team members hypothesized that reading comic books in school was no longer as reinforcing as it had been during the intervention's first three weeks. Teachers shared statements made by Vincent such as, "I already read those," and, "I can just look at my comic books at home later." Dr. Mae explained to the team that the decline in Vincent's interest was likely due to changes in the comic books' reinforcing value, given that he had access to them at school and home. A reinforcer will often lose some or all of its potency to affect behavior when accessed over and over. This phenomenon is known as reinforcement satiation.

Dr. Mae suggested combatting reinforcer satiation by offering Vincent choices of reinforcers each time the intervention was implemented. She also suggested that the team collaborate with the family to restrict Vincent's access to his most preferred comic books at home by sending them to school, thereby potentially increasing the reinforcing value of those comic books. Equipped with this knowledge, the team made two specific changes to the intervention. First, the team decided that Vincent would be allowed to choose from a menu of preferred activities (e.g., looking at comic books, using a tablet to play math games, playing a board game) when written work was completed. Second, the team collaborated with Vincent's family to have his most preferred comic books sent to school, restricting free access to only after his written work was completed. These intervention changes were implemented at the end of week five. Week five data continued to show a decline from previous weeks with an average written work completion rate of 25% across classes. Following week five, Vincent's written work output increased to 59% during week six, 58% during week seven, and 61% during week eight (see Figure 5.4).

Summary of Intervention Effects

The team convened again at the end of week eight to review and analyze the data. The team agreed that the changes to the intervention during week five had a positive effect on Vincent's written work completion. The team noted that Vincent

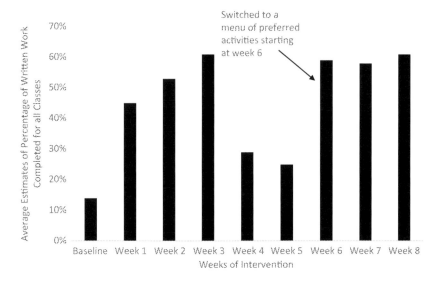

FIGURE 5.4 Average estimates of percentage of written work completed for all classes across baseline and intervention phases
Note: a change in intervention occurred between Week 5 and Week 6.

regularly selected different preferred activities and even identified additional preferred activities not on the activity menu. The team agreed that a necessary part of Vincent's continued success with this intervention would be to regularly add new preferred activities to the menu so that satiation does not occur.

The team also reviewed the fidelity and IOA data. Dr. Mae praised the teachers for their efforts to implement this intervention each day and for taking the time to carefully review Vincent's work to provide an accurate estimate of work completion. The team determined that it would be important to continue fidelity checks to guard against implementation drift.

Intervention Acceptability

Following the eight weeks of intervention, Dr. Mae met with each teacher and Vincent's paraprofessional to obtain feedback about their acceptability of this intervention. She asked them questions such as, "Was this intervention easy to implement?" and, "Do you think this intervention helped to increase Vincent's work completion?" All of the teachers agreed that Vincent's work completion greatly improved over the course of the intervention. Several teachers reported that on some occasions, estimating the correct percentage of work completion was challenging. Vincent's paraprofessional reported that she had an easy time displaying Vincent's visual schedule during written assignments and that he seemed to use the schedule to keep himself on track. She also stated that it was much easier for Vincent to start working on a written assignment when he knew he was working for his chosen preferred activity. Overall, there was agreement that, while there were some challenges to implementing the intervention, the benefits outweighed the costs in this situation.

Intervention Considerations

This case study described a high school student diagnosed with ASD experiencing difficulty completing written work during class time. The team developed and implemented an intervention using Premack's principle with a visual schedule. The intervention provided this student access to a preferred activity contingent on completing a non-preferred academic task using a First-Then Board. There were several considerations when conceptualizing the implementation of the First-Then Board. First, problem analysis involved assessing whether the target behavior was as a result of a skill or performance deficit. Based on their assessment, the team developed a hypothesis that Vincent had the skills to complete written assignments but did not like to write, which resulted in him frequently refusing to complete written assignments. The team selected an intervention employing Premack's principle because of its use of positive reinforcement to potentially increase the target behavior. An intervention based on positive reinforcement might have been much less successful if the target behavior was due to a skill deficit. In that case, a more appropriate intervention would have focused on improving Vincent's writing skills.

Second, identifying Vincent's preferred activities was crucial to the intervention's overall success. Interventions using Premack's principle must consider whether the activity or task following the target behavior is, in fact, reinforcing. In this case study, the team began with a preferred activity (i.e., viewing a comic book for five minutes) selected from several activities identified through an informal assessment involving an interest inventory and interviews with teachers, parents, and Vincent. Viewing a comic book for five minutes following completion of written work initially generated positive results. However, Vincent then had one week where his written work completion returned to baseline levels. This decrease in performance might have been influenced by changes in the reinforcing value of the comic book. Specifically, reinforcer satiation might have been responsible for the decrease in Vincent's written work completion percentage. At that point in the intervention, the team decided to make a change by developing a menu of preferred activities Vincent could select from following completion of written work. School psychologists using Premack's principle to design an intervention might consider a preferred activity menu over a single reinforcing activity.

Third, the team initially identified what was considered an achievable starting goal based on Vincent's written work completion assessed during baseline. Beginning the intervention with an achievable goal increases the possibility the student meets the goal and gains access to the preferred activity. Starting with a goal that is too difficult will likely result in the student rarely or never accessing the preferred activity. In addition, increasing the goal over time allows the team to shape the student's performance so that it comes to resemble desired performance levels. For example, the team might have eventually required Vincent to complete 75% and then 100% of written work to access the preferred activity.

Finally, the team in our case study determined that Vincent might benefit from the use of a visual schedule, as it appeared to act as a reminder of his written work and what he would be able to access after completing his written work. While the team was unable to determine whether the visual schedule was necessary in this case, Vincent's paraprofessional reported that he often used the visual schedule. Since there is research supporting visual schedules as an effective intervention for students with ASD and the visual schedule was not very intrusive within this intervention, the team might have continued to implement this component with Vincent or other students with similar behaviors.

The First-Then Board can be individualized based on students' age, language abilities, current level of functioning, and behavioral goals. In addition, the intervention's level of complexity can be adjusted based on contextual factors. For example, a simple visual schedule, similar to the one used in this case study, could be employed using the first-then format with pictures or symbols displayed to represent the activities or tasks. The intervention could also be made more complex for older students by using words rather than pictures to depict a series of sequentially ordered tasks (e.g., multiple assignments). Similarly, Premack's principle can be applied in simple or more complex ways depending on what needs to be done to earn access to the preferred activity. For example, a student might be required to complete only one non-preferred task in order to gain access to a preferred activity. Conversely, a student might be required to complete a series of tasks or maintain a specified level of task completion over time in order to earn the preferred activity. Additionally, the student's goal could change over time so that the intervention requires the student to meet increasingly higher expectations in order to access the reinforcer.

Conclusion

Applying the Premack principle with a visual schedule can create an effective intervention when challenging behaviors are thought to be related to a performance deficit (i.e., "won't do") rather than a skill deficit (i.e., "can't do"). The case study presented in this chapter illustrates how these strategies might be applied in a high school setting with a student struggling to complete academic tasks. Both intervention components can be adjusted based on students' unique situations. Moreover, Premack's principle and visual schedules could be used either alone or in combination to target a range of behaviors for students in the school setting.

References

Azrin, N. H., Vinas, V., & Ehle, C. T. (2007). Physical activity as reinforcement for classroom calmness of ADHD children: A preliminary study. *Child & Family Behavior Therapy*, 29(2), 1–8. doi:10.1300/J019v29n02_01

Geiger, B. (1996). A time to learn, a time to play: Premack's principle applied in the classroom. *American Secondary Education*, 25(2), 2–6.

Hosie, T. W., Gentile, J. R., & Carroll, J. D. (1974, Summer). Pupil preferences and the Premack principle. *American Educational Research Journal*, 11, 241–247.

Hume, K. (2009). *Steps for implementation: Visual schedules*. Chapel Hill, NC: The National Professional Development Center of Autism Spectrum Disorders, Frank Porter Graham Child Development Institute, The University of North Carolina.

Johns, B. H. (2015). *15 positive behavior strategies to increase academic success*. Thousand Oaks, CA: Corwin Press. doi:10.4135/9781483388489.n8

Knight, V., Sartini, E., & Spriggs, A. D. (2015). Evaluating visual activity schedules as evidence-based practice for individuals with autism spectrum disorders. *Journal of Autism and Developmental Disorders*, 45, 157–178.

Premack, D. (1959). Toward empirical behavior laws: I. Positive reinforcement. *Psychological Review*, 66, 219–233. doi:10.1037/h0040891

Spriggs, A. D., Mims, P. J., van Dijk, W., & Knight, V. F. (2017). Examination of the evidence base for using visual activity schedules with students with intellectual disability. *The Journal of Special Education*, 51, 14–26. doi:10.1177/0022466916658483

Van Hevel, J., & Hawkins, R. P. (1974). Modification of behavior in secondary school students using the Premack principle and response cost technique. *School Applications of Learning Theory*, 6(4), 31–41.

Zimmerman, K. N., Ledford, J. R., & Barton, E. E. (2017). Using visual activity schedules for young children with challenging behavior. *Journal of Early Intervention*, 39, 339–358. doi:10.1177/1053815117725693

Appendix A: Sample First-Then Visual Schedule

FIRST	THEN
Write 5 sentences in your journal. Each sentence must be neat, complete, and relevant.	Comic books for 5 minutes!

6
VIDEO MODELING

Scott Bellini and Olivia Heck

Introduction

Video modeling is an evidence-based practice (National Autism Center, 2019; Wong et al., 2015) that has been used across multiple disability categories to teach a wide variety of skills and behaviors, including motor behaviors, social skills, communication, compliance, self-monitoring, functional skills, vocational skills, athletic performance, and emotional regulation (Baker, Lang, & O'Reilly, 2009; Bellini & Akullian, 2007; Delano, 2007; Dowrick, 1999; Hitchcock, Dowrick, & Prater, 2003; Kehle & Bray, 2009; Losinski, Wiseman, White, & Balluch, 2016; Seok, DaCosta, McHenry-Powell, Heitzman-Powell, & Ostmeyer, 2018). A video modeling intervention involves an individual watching a video demonstration of a skill or behavior and then imitating the behavior or skill depicted in the video. Video modeling can be used to promote skill acquisition, enhance skill performance, and reduce problem behaviors. Video self-modeling (VSM) is a specific application of video modeling that allows the individual to imitate targeted behaviors by observing him or herself successfully performing a behavior. Results of meta-analytical research have supported the notion that skills learned via video modeling and VSM are acquired rapidly, are easily transferred across different settings and persons, and are maintained for months following the conclusion of the intervention (Baker, Lang, & O'Reilly, 2009; Bellini & Akullian, 2007; Losinski et al., 2016; Seok et al., 2018).

The success of video modeling and VSM has been conceptualized through a variety of theoretical lenses, including behavioral (Nikopoulos & Keenan, 2004), cognitive (Kehle, Bray, Margiano, Theodore, & Zhou, 2002), and social-cognitive perspectives (Dowrick, 1999). From a behavioral perspective, Nikopoulos and Keenan (2004) theorized that watching certain activities or play items on a video serves as a motivating operation, thereby increasing the reinforcing properties of the activities and items featured on the video. From a cognitive perspective, Kehle et al. (2002) speculated that watching edited self-modeling videos that depict positive and efficacious behavior may alter the viewer's memories of their past behaviors. That is, their memories of past maladaptive behaviors may be replaced by memories of exemplary behaviors. Finally, from a social-cognitive lens, Dowrick (1999) asserted that children not only acquire skills by observing themselves performing behaviors on video (i.e., modeling), but that they also increase self-efficacy through the viewing of their own efficacious behavior.

VSM interventions typically fall within two categories of implementation: *positive self-review* and *video feed-forward* (Dowrick, 1999). Positive self-review refers to individuals viewing themselves successfully engaging in a behavior or activity that is currently within their behavioral repertoire. It may be used with low-frequency behaviors or behaviors that were once mastered but are no longer performed. In this case, the individual is recorded while engaging in the low-frequency behavior and then shown a video of the behavior. An example of a positive self-review intervention can be applied to a child who rarely complies with adult directives. To implement the intervention, the child would be recorded while an adult provides a variety of task directives. The video would then be edited to remove all instances of non-compliance. Once the video is edited, the positive self-review intervention would involve the child repeatedly watching the instances of compliance with task directives. Positive self review is a relatively simple strategy to use from a technological standpoint. However, for very low-frequency behavior, it may require extensive amounts of raw video footage to capture even a small amount of the target behavior.

Video feed-forward is typically used when the individual already possesses most of the necessary skills in her behavioral repertoire but is unable to perform them in the proper sequence to complete an activity. For instance, the child may have the ability to get out of bed, brush her teeth, get dressed, and comb her hair, but she does not perform these skills together in the proper sequence during her morning routine. A video feed-forward intervention would involve video-recording her engaging in each of these tasks and then splicing the segments together to form the complete sequence of steps. The same may be done with typical social interaction behaviors. For instance, the child could be video-recorded demonstrating three different skills: initiating an interaction, maintaining a reciprocal interaction, and appropriately terminating the interaction. The three clips could then be blended together to portray one successful fluent and continuous social interaction. Feed-forward is also a good option for individuals who need additional assistance or support to complete tasks successfully through the use of *hidden supports*. For instance, the child may be video-recorded interacting with peers while an adult provides continual assistance through cueing and prompting. The adult prompt is then edited out (i.e., "hidden") so that when the child views the video segment, he sees himself as independent and successful.

Feed-forward requires additional technological capabilities as compared to positive self-review, but it typically requires a smaller amount of raw footage.

Case Study

Background Information

Mike was a sixth grade student identified as having an autism spectrum disorder (ASD) at Bloomington Middle School. He was referred for intervention by his parents and teacher because of concerns for his social, behavioral, and emotional functioning and to assist in the development of an intervention plan. In particular, his teacher reported that Mike frequently disrupts class with inappropriate statements or noises. A student, parent, and teacher interview, standardized behavioral checklists, and a functional behavior assessment (FBA) were administered to Mike, his mother, and his teacher to assess behavioral and affective functioning.

Mike's mother reported that he expresses interest in interacting with peers and talks frequently about making friends. Mike indicated that he has two friends at school, but his mother and teacher reported that he usually plays alone and that he has no friends. Mike stated that he enjoys playing video games and reading about ceiling fans. Mike's favorite subjects in school are math and reading. He was described by his teacher as an affectionate child who frequently attempts to hug and chase other children and adults. In addition, Mike has a history of making inappropriate noises and impulsive comments in class. His teacher reported that the vocalizations are disruptive to the instructional setting and distracting to other kids. His teacher also reported that Mike often engages in various "inappropriate" behaviors at lunch and has great difficulty in establishing positive peer interactions. Mike exhibits numerous expressive communication deficits (articulation, pragmatics, etc.) that negatively impact his social and behavioral functioning.

Description of the Problem Behavior

A modified problem-solving interview (Bellini, 2006a) was conducted with Mike's special education teacher that focused on elucidating the function of the problem behaviors and analyzing social skill deficits. The interview included four standard components: problem identification, problem definition, problem validation, and problem analysis. The primary purpose of the problem-identification phase was to identify, prioritize, and define specific social skill deficits and problem behaviors that were particularly problematic for Mike. The problem-identification phase also provided an opportunity to ask Mike's teacher what interventions have been tried in the past and how successful they have been. Mike's teacher reported that he often engages in "inappropriate social behaviors" during lunch with other children. She further described these behaviors as "touching other children, pushing them, chasing them, and calling them names." When asked to describe Mike's social skills, the teacher responded that they were "non-existent." Upon further prompting, she indicated that he particularly struggles with social initiation and responding skills. Mike's teacher reported that Mike does seem to have an interest in other children and often attempts to initiate interactions with them. However, she reported that his initiations are often ineffective and off-putting, and usually lead to peer rejection. During the interview, the teacher and school psychologist together labeled Mike's problem behaviors as "ineffective and problematic social interactions," and his teacher indicated that positive social initiations, social responding, and maintaining positive engagement with peers would be important skills to address during the intervention. The teacher reported that the school team previously attempted to teach social initiation skills using a social narrative strategy and a peer modeling strategy. However, neither intervention was effective according to his teacher.

In addition to the problem-solving interview, an assessment of social competence was conducted using the Autism Social Skills Profile-2 (ASSP-2; Bellini, 2016) to identify specific social skill deficits that could be contributing to problem behaviors, and to determine potential skills to target in his educational plan. The results of the assessment indicated significant deficits in joining in activities and responding to peer initiations.

Problem Analysis

The purpose of the problem analysis phase was to determine the function of the problem behaviors to identify motivating operations that may be contributing to the presence of the problem behaviors. In particular, the school psychologist was interested in determining how the presence of social skill deficits might be influencing the problem behaviors. The problem analysis phase provided an opportunity to gather information about the contexts or settings in which the problem behaviors and target social skills are most likely and least likely to occur. In addition, the problem analysis phase involved determining whether the targeted social skill deficits were the result of skill acquisition deficits or performance deficits. The problem analysis phase included both an interview with Mike's teacher and an A-B-C Observation during the lunch setting to elucidate the function of the problem behaviors.

Mike's teacher was asked to describe the rate, frequency, and the severity, or intensity, of the problem behavior and targeted social skills. She reported that the problem behaviors occur every day, and multiple times during the lunch period. She indicated that his behaviors are not severe in terms of aggressiveness (i.e., he has never hurt other children). However, she is concerned that these behaviors have significantly interfered with his ability to establish and maintain interactions with peers, and that peers have begun to reject and avoid him. His teacher was also asked to rate how well Mike initiates interactions relative to other children and maintains positive engagement with peers. She indicated that, compared to other children at the school, his initiation skills are in the bottom 1% of children in the sixth grade, and that he maintains positive engagement with peers less than 10% of the time he is around them. The A-B-C Observation conducted during the lunch period indicated that the likely function of the problem behaviors was to gain peer attention. When Mike pushes or grabs other children, the other children would sometimes laugh and engage in "chase behavior" with Mike, but most of the time they would tell him to leave them alone and "go away." These admonishments were often ignored by Mike, who, undeterred, would continue to engage in these undesired social behaviors.

Based on the results of the FBA, including the problem-solving interview and the A-B-C Observation data, it was determined that Mike was engaging in problematic social behaviors to gain peer attention. Further, based on the problem-solving interview and the results of the ASSP-2, it was determined that various social skill deficits (difficulty initiating, responding, and maintaining interactions with peers) were contributing to the presence of the problem behaviors. That is, Mike was engaging in problematic social behaviors to gain peer attention because he did not know how to effectively and appropriately gain their attention. As a result, the goal of the intervention was to reduce the problem behaviors by teaching Mike effective and appropriate social skills. Further, the assessment data indicated that these skill deficits could be conceptualized as skill acquisition deficits (i.e., skills not currently in Mike's repertoire). As such, it was determined that these skill deficits need to be taught using a skill acquisition strategy.

Intervention Goals

The school psychologist and Mike's teacher collaborated to identify goals related to the target problem behaviors and to select social skills to replace the problem behaviors. The goal of the intervention was to reduce ineffective and problematic social initiations by replacing them with positive and effective social behaviors. For the primary replacement behavior of positive engagement with peers, the goal was to increase these behaviors by 50% during the first nine weeks of the intervention compared to baseline. For the primary problem behavior of ineffective and problematic social interactions, Mike's teacher and the school psychologist indicated that the initial goal should be to reduce the number of behaviors by 50% in the first nine weeks of the intervention compared to baseline.

Measurement of Target Behaviors, Data Collection Strategies, and Progress Monitoring

Two outcome variables were assessed to facilitate progress monitoring: positive social engagement with peers and ineffective and problematic social interactions. Positive social engagement was defined as active participation in an activity, play sequence, or conversation with a peer. Instances of unprompted verbal and nonverbal social initiations and responses to peers were also coded as social engagement. Social initiations included requesting assistance, requesting information, requesting participation, joining-in play activities, greeting, providing compliments, giving/sharing/showing objects, and providing physical affection. Social responses involved providing assistance following a request, responding to questions, joining-in activities following an invitation, responding to a greeting or compliment, accepting a toy or object when offered, and accepting physical affection. Parallel play with separate or similar play items was not counted as engagement unless a reciprocal exchange of play items occurred during the interval. For instance, if the child was seated at a table with other children while completing a puzzle, the activity would not be counted as social engagement unless there was a reciprocal exchange of pieces (sharing) or the two children completed the same puzzle (e.g., making a shape together). Negative behaviors, such as taking an object from another student or pushing another student, were not counted as social engagement. Social interactions that were prompted by the school staff were not counted as social engagement. Ineffective and problematic social interactions were defined as an undesirable behavior used to initiate an interaction with a peer or respond to a peer's initiation that does not lead to positive engagement with the peer. Ineffective and problematic interactions include touching or grabbing other children, pushing them, chasing them, or calling them names.

Data were collected by the school psychologist three times per week during a 20-minute lunch period. The lunch period was structured to provide the students with 10 minutes to eat, and 10 minutes to socialize with peers. The sixth grade students were provided access to the playground that was shared with the adjacent elementary school, and an indoor "game room" that provided the students access to a variety of games and play items. The observations were conducted for two weeks prior to the intervention (baseline phase), during the four weeks of the VSM intervention (intervention phase), and for two weeks following the intervention (maintenance phase). Ineffective and problematic social interactions were recorded using a frequency count. Positive social engagement with peers was measured using a partial interval time sampling procedure with 10-second intervals.

Intervention Plan

A VSM intervention was implemented to teach Mike how to effectively initiate, respond, and maintain engagement with peers. VSM interventions can be used as both a skill acquisition strategy and performance enhancement strategy (Bellini, 2016). The VSM intervention followed the six-step approach for creating VSM interventions recommended by Bellini and Ehlers (2009), including: (1) determine target student and target behavior, (2) determine who else will be in video,

(3) plan the production, (4) film the behavior, (5) edit the raw footage, (6) show the video to the student. The target student was Mike, and the target behaviors were social engagements with peers, which included initiating, responding, and maintaining interactions with peers. The video recording also included two classroom peers who had a positive social history with Mike. Both students expressed a willingness to participate and provided assent to be video-recorded. Parental consent was also gained from the parents of all children appearing in the video.

After securing consent, the filming took place in the school's game room. Numerous games and reciprocal play items, such as board games, cornhole, and a Nerf basketball game, were provided. The feed-forward technique of "hidden support" (Dowrick, 1999) was used to facilitate social initiations and responses. During filming, the school psychologist provided numerous verbal prompts to instruct Mike to initiate, respond, and maintain engagement with his two peers using the prompting guidelines described by Bellini (2016). The level and type of prompt used was commensurate with Mike's developmental and skill level. Video footage was collected two weeks prior to collecting baseline data. The video recording took place across two days and approximately 30 minutes of raw footage was collected.

The video was edited by the school psychologist upon completion of the filming phase. Two one-minute video clips were produced that depicted Mike effectively initiating, responding, and maintaining engagement with peers. The videos were edited to remove the continual prompting delivered by the school psychologist (hidden supports) and to eliminate all interactions that were considered problematic or ineffective (e.g., solitary play, lack of response to peer initiations, inappropriate statements, violation of personal space) in order to portray Mike as independent and efficacious in his interactions with the peers.

The intervention phase (i.e., the showing of the video clips) lasted 17 school days and across four school weeks. Two days were missed because of the Thanksgiving holiday and Mike was absent for one school day during the intervention. During the intervention phase, Mike viewed one edited video clip per day. Teachers were instructed to alternate the showing of the video clips so that Mike did not view the same video on consecutive days. To promote consistency, Mike viewed the videotape prior to the lunch period. Mike watched the video in the presence of a designated member of the school staff (e.g., teacher or paraprofessional). The school staff member was instructed not to engage Mike in conversation during the viewing of the video other than to provide redirection in cases where he was not attending to the video screen. In such cases, the staff member was instructed to provide redirection in the form of verbal or nonverbal cues and prompts (e.g., "watch video," or by tapping the screen and saying "look"). Mike watched his videos in his teacher's office, which was connected to the classroom. Mike was told that he was going to watch a video "of you hanging out with your friends." After watching the video, Mike transitioned immediately to lunch. Teachers were instructed to refrain from prompting or reinforcing the social interactions of Mike during the 20-minute observational period.

Intervention Fidelity and Interobserver Agreement

The special education teacher of record (whom Mike had class with immediately prior to lunch) was given an intervention fidelity form to complete to confirm treatment compliance (see Figure 6.1). The fidelity form contained boxes representing the days of the week, and the teacher was asked to check the

Teacher(s): _____ Student: _____ Dates: _____

Please check the box below to indicate whether the student viewed the video on that day. If the child was absent, write "absent" in the box. If school was not in session that day, write "no school." If only a portion of the video was shown that day, write "PS" for partial showing. Finally, if you were not able to show the student the video because of equipment failure, please write "EF" in the box for that day.

Monday	Tuesday	Wednesday	Thursday	Friday

Please indicate how you think the intervention is going this week. Please circle the response that best describes this week of the intervention.

SD = Strongly Disagree D = Disagree A = Agree SA = Strongly Agree

The intervention has interfered with normal classroom activity

SD   D   A   SA

The intervention is distracting to the other students in the classroom

SD   D   A   SA

The student attended to the videos

SD   D   A   SA

The student enjoys watching the videos

SD   D   A   SA

The intervention is easy to implement

SD   D   A   SA

I believe the intervention is beneficial to the student

SD   D   A   SA

I enjoy being part of this intervention

SD   D   A   SA

Additional Comments:

FIGURE 6.1 Social validity and treatment fidelity form

box if Mike watched the video that particular day. The teacher was also asked to note whether the child was attentive to the video that day. The teacher was also instructed to check the DNS (Did Not Show) box if the video was not shown or check the PS (Partial Showing) if only a portion of the video was shown that day. The teacher was asked to note any equipment failure (or user error) that prevented the showing of the video on a particular day. According to his teacher, the video was shown as intended on 16 out of 17 days. The teacher noted a partial showing on day one due to inattention. The teacher noted that Mike required frequent prompting and redirection to look at the computer screen on this day.

The school psychologist provided a brief in-service training to Mike's education team (one special education teacher and two paraprofessionals) on the VSM intervention and the behavioral observation techniques that were used in the intervention. In addition, the school team had an opportunity to practice recording social interactions prior to beginning the study. In order to establish interobserver agreement (IOA) in training sessions, the school team engaged in practice sessions where they recorded behaviors while watching a video of Mike's social interactions with peers in the resource room. The school team recorded behaviors in 15-minute segments and then immediately compared their recordings to the school psychologist's recordings. Training continued in this fashion until the teachers achieved 90% agreement with the school psychologist. To confirm IOA, a member of the teaching staff recorded behavior alongside the school psychologist for 25% of all observation sessions. IOA was calculated by dividing agreements by agreements plus disagreements, then multiplying by 100. In this case, IOA was calculated by comparing the recordings of the school psychologist with the responses of each data collector. IOA for both outcome variables ranged from 80% to 100% with a mean of 98% across phases.

Intervention Outcome Data

The effectiveness of the intervention was determined through visual inspection of the graphical representation of the data, including the immediacy of change in the outcome variables following the introduction of the intervention, the degree of overlap in data points across phases, and an analysis of the slope and direction of the outcome variables across phases. A trend analysis was conducted via the construction of a split middle line of progress (see Alberto & Troutman, 2013). In addition to visual inspection, the magnitude of change in the outcome variables across phases was analyzed via descriptive analysis of mean rates of engagement across phases and via the calculation of the effect size metric, Improved Rate of Differences (IRD). IRD (Parker, Vannest, & Brown, 2009; Parker, Vannest, & Davis, 2011) is an effect size metric that represents the percentage of improvement between baseline and intervention phases. Parker et al. (2009) provides the following guidelines for interpreting the magnitude of IRD: scores less than or equal to .50 have questionable effects; scores between .50 and .70 have moderate effects, and scores greater than .70 have strong effects.

Mike's level of social engagement increased substantially following the introduction of the VSM intervention and the change in the outcome variable was rapid (see Figure 6.2). Mike's mean rate of social engagement during baseline was 17%. Mike's level of social engagement was stable and flat at baseline, ranging

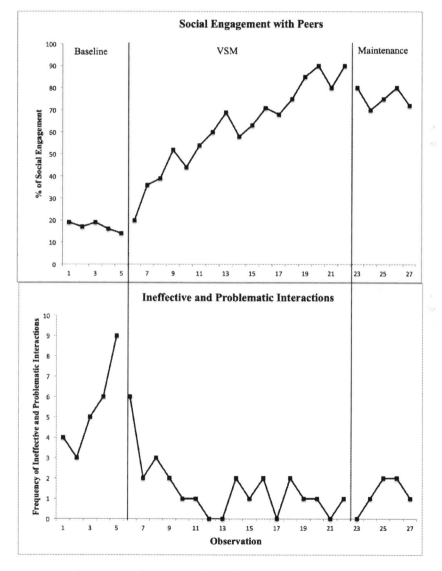

FIGURE 6.2 Percentage of unprompted social engagement and frequency of ineffective and problematic behaviors before, during, and after VSM intervention

from 14% to 19%. His engagement increased to 62% during the VSM intervention phase with an ascending trend line. All intervention data points were higher than the mean rate of engagement at baseline. IRD between baseline and VSM was 1.00, indicating a strong effect size for the VSM intervention. Mike's mean rate of social engagement was 75% during the maintenance phase. IRD between baseline and maintenance was also 1.00, indicating a strong rate of improvement between these two phases.

Mike's frequency of ineffective and problematic interactions decreased following the introduction of the VSM intervention and change in the outcome variable was rapid (see Figure 6.2). Mike's mean frequency of ineffective and problematic interactions during baseline was 5.4. Mike's frequency of ineffective and problematic initiations was highly variable during baseline, ranging from 3 to 9. His mean frequency of ineffective and problematic interactions decreased to 1.5 during the VSM intervention phase with a descending trend line. All but one of the intervention data points were lower than the mean of baseline. IRD between baseline and VSM was .89, indicating a strong effect size for the VSM intervention. Mike's mean number of ineffective and problematic interactions was 1.2 during the maintenance phase and IRD between baseline and maintenance was 1.00, indicating a strong rate of improvement between these two phases.

Summary of Intervention Effects

The primary goal of the intervention was to decrease ineffective and problematic interactions by replacing them with positive social engagement with peers. For positive engagement with peers, the goal was to increase these behaviors by 50% during the first nine weeks of the intervention. For ineffective and problematic social interactions, Mike's teacher and the school psychologist indicated that the initial goal should be to reduce the number of behaviors by 50% in the first nine weeks of the intervention. During the first nine weeks of the intervention, positive social engagement with peers increased over 300%, and ineffective and problematic interactions with peers decreased by over 70%. Moreover, the collection of maintenance data indicated that the positive results of the intervention were maintained after the VSM intervention was discontinued.

Intervention Acceptability

Each week, a social validity questionnaire (adapted from Bellini, 2016) was provided to Mike's special education teacher to measure her satisfaction with the intervention and her acceptance of the VSM procedure (see Figure 6.1). The questionnaire consisted of a series of questions using a four-point scale, which ranged from 1 (strongly disagree) to 4 (strongly agree). The questionnaire contained the following items: (a) the intervention interferes with normal classroom activity; (b) the intervention is distracting to other children in the classroom; (c) the student enjoys watching the video; (d) the intervention is easy to implement; (e) I believe the intervention is beneficial to the student, and; (f) I enjoy being a part of the intervention. Space was also provided on the questionnaire for the teacher to share additional comments or concerns.

The teacher's responses on the weekly social validity questionnaires indicated that the intervention did not interfere with normal classroom activities ($M = 1.88$) and that it was not distracting to other students ($M = 1.88$). She reported that the intervention was easy to implement ($M = 3.75$) and that she enjoyed being a part of the intervention ($M = 4$). Her responses indicated that she believed that the intervention was beneficial to Mike ($M = 4$). She also noted that Mike initially did not enjoy watching the videos ($M = 3.25$). Specifically, Mike told her that he did not like watching himself on video. During the first day, she noted that he required frequent prompting and redirection to maintain his attention to the computer screen. After the first day, she reported that Mike seemed to enjoy watching his video more as evidenced by his increased attention to the computer screen. She further noted that on several occasions, Mike verbally requested to watch his video before it was time to do so. On the open-ended item of the social validity questionnaire, the teacher reported that Mike was interacting with others more frequently in other settings and with multiple persons throughout the school day.

Results of the social validity questionnaire indicate that the VSM procedure was deemed acceptable and was well regarded by the school team. Mike's teacher reported that the VSM intervention was easy to implement and was beneficial to the student. She also reported that the procedure did not disrupt normal classroom activities, nor was it distracting to other children in the classroom.

Intervention Considerations

Based on the results of the assessment, including the problem-solving interview, FBA, and ASSP-2, it was determined that Mike was engaging in problematic social behaviors to gain peer attention and that his social skill deficits were contributing to the presence of the problem behaviors. As a result, the goal of the intervention was to reduce the problem behaviors by teaching Mike the skills necessary to effectively initiate, respond, and maintain interactions with peers. Further, the assessment data indicated that these skill deficits could be conceptualized as skill acquisition deficits. As such, the team selected an evidence-based skill acquisition strategy, VSM, to facilitate the acquisition of social skills.

The VSM led to rapid and substantial increases in unprompted social engagement and decreases in ineffective and problematic social interactions. In addition, levels of social engagement and problematic social behaviors were maintained after the VSM intervention was withdrawn. Most importantly, the VSM intervention promoted generalization to settings and peers not featured in the videos.

These results are important because the intervention led to increases in social engagement with peers in a natural setting (lunch time setting), rather than a controlled clinical setting. The case study's results are also important given the deleterious impact social withdrawal can have on the developmental outcomes of children with ASD. Poor social skills have been associated with a variety of adverse life outcomes, including social failure and peer rejection, bullying (for both the bully and victim), anxiety, depression, substance abuse, suicidal ideation, delinquency, and other forms of psychopathology (Bellini, 2006b; Cook, Williams, Guerra, Kim, & Sadek, 2010; Tantam, 2000).

It is also important to note that the current intervention involved the use of VSM alone, without the use of other intervention strategies, such as prompting and reinforcement for the successful completion of the target behaviors. Mike's social engagement was not reinforced during the 20-minute observational period, nor was he prompted by adults to interact with peers, the latter of which is highly important for educators working with students on the autism spectrum, as VSM can be a useful strategy for prompt fading and minimizing prompt dependency. In this intervention, children were only prompted to interact with peers during video recording. The adult prompts were removed during the editing process so that when Mike viewed video clips, he watched himself interacting independently and fluently with peers.

Though previous research on VSM interventions have documented its effectiveness with children with a variety of disabilities, including behavioral disorders (Baker, Lang, & O'Reilly, 2009; Losinski et al., 2016; Seok et al., 2018), VSM is a particularly powerful intervention modality for students on the autism spectrum, as it addresses many of the underlying deficits of ASD (Bellini & Akullian, 2007). The effectiveness of video-modeling interventions, in part, may be attributed to the fact that VSM integrates a powerful learning modality for children on the autism spectrum (visually cued instruction) with a well-studied intervention modality (modeling). Second, it may increase attention to the modeled task, which is essential to successful modeling. The use of video modeling allows the interventionist to remove irrelevant elements of the modeled skill or behavior through the video-editing process. This enables the individual on the autism spectrum to better focus on essential aspects of the targeted skill or behavior. Typically, when the video monitor turns on, the child will often immediately attend to the screen, and thus, the targeted skill. However, when inattention does occur, it may be necessary to deliver a combination of redirection and reinforcement for attending behaviors, as attention to the video clips is essential to a successful VSM intervention. In addition, the novelty of the intervention and the method of delivery (i.e., watching a video) may increase motivation to participate in the intervention. Anecdotal evidence and clinical experience suggest that watching videos is a highly desired activity for many children with and without an ASD. This could lead to increased motivation and attention to the learning task. In VSM, motivation to watch oneself on the video may be enhanced by the portrayal of predominantly positive behaviors, which may also increase self-efficacy. That is, children are shown their highlights, not their mistakes. Finally, VSM allows the individual to monitor and evaluate his own behavior. Watching oneself on video provides a visual representation of self, which may assist in the development of self-monitoring and self-awareness.

Finally, it is important to assess and monitor the social validity of the VSM intervention before and during the intervention. This is particularly important given the fact that VSM is still a relatively unknown intervention modality. In addition, video modeling requires some technological capabilities to implement. The teacher in the present intervention reported that the VSM intervention was easy to implement and was beneficial to the participant. She also reported that the procedure did not disrupt normal classroom activities, nor was it distracting to other children in the classroom. However, it is important to highlight the fact that the present intervention did not involve the school staff in the video-editing process, which requires additional technological skills, resources, and time. This added responsibility might increase resistance or rejection by some educators and families who may view their lack of technological proficiency as an obstacle to successful implementation. Given the emphasis placed on technological proficiency by the National Association of School Psychologists' Practice Model (Skalski et al., 2015), school psychologists should look for opportunities to provide a training and leadership role in the implementation of interventions involving the use of technology.

Though the results of the present intervention indicated improvements in the outcome variables of social engagement and problematic social behaviors during the intervention phase, it is important to note that progress monitoring alone does not ensure a functional relationship between the intervention and the outcome variable. That is, it does not account for confounding variables that could present threats to internal and external validity of the intervention. For instance, in this intervention, teachers were precluded from prompting social behaviors during the 20-minute observational period, but the school psychologist did not control for teacher behavior at other times of the day. It is possible that the introduction of the intervention may have impacted teacher behavior in a way that made them more attentive to social behavior, leading to an increase in prompting and reinforcement of social engagement throughout the day. Though this may provide a threat to internal validity from a researcher's perspective, it would certainly be considered a desired "side effect" from the point of view of a practicing school psychologist. In addition, the school psychologist did not directly measure intervention fidelity. Though there is no reason to doubt the truthfulness of classroom teachers, the reliance on self-report measures of intervention fidelity prevents us from concluding with absolute certainty that the intervention was implemented as intended. Further, the intervention only measured maintenance effects over a one-week period. The relatively short maintenance period limits our ability to draw conclusions on the long-term effects of the VSM procedure. As such, we recommend that the educational team continue to monitor the maintenance of social goals for multiple quarters following the withdrawal of the intervention. Another potential weakness of the intervention was the failure to collect data on social engagement across multiple settings. Collecting data across settings would ensure that the skills learned in the intervention were transferred across multiple settings and with multiple persons.

Finally, the use of a VSM intervention in a school setting requires special attention in regards to permission and consent. Most school districts will require the school team to secure additional consent from parents to record all children depicted in the video. Interestingly, Mike's school sends out letters to parents at the beginning of every school year to inform them that their child's classroom may be videotaped for various promotional and educational purposes, such as for media stories or to provide feedback to teachers regarding their instructional practices and to facilitate individual student interventions. If parents do not wish to have their children recorded, they are asked to contact the school directly to opt out of the recording policy. In spite of this, the school psychologist reached out to the parents of the children participating in the VSM intervention to gain written consent to film their children. We recommend that school psychologists also check with their building-level administrator prior to starting a VSM intervention to inform them of their specific procedures and to get their explicit approval to proceed. The administrator can also provide additional information on the district's policy regarding video-recording students within the school setting. It is important to inform all involved (parents and administrators) that the goal of the video recordings is to create a highlight reel of the child's best behavior and performances.

Conclusion

The intervention described in this chapter examined the effectiveness of a VSM intervention in increasing social engagement and decreasing problem social behaviors of a sixth grade student with ASD. The VSM procedure led to rapid and substantial increases in unprompted social engagement and decreases in problematic social behaviors with peers in a lunch setting. An ever-growing body of research has demonstrated the value of VSM in improving the social, communication, functional, and behavioral outcomes of children with a variety of disabilities and across a number of behaviors and skills. VSM is an evidence-based strategy and could be a valuable asset in the intervention tool chests of all school psychologists.

References

Alberto, P. A., & Troutman, A. C. (2013). *Applied behavior analysis for teachers* (9th ed.). Upper Saddle River, NJ: Prentice Hall.

Baker, S., Lang, R., & O'Reilly, M. (2009). Review of video modeling with students with emotional and behavioral disorders. *Education and Treatment of Children*, 32(3), 403–420. Retrieved April 29, 2020, from www.jstor.org/stable/42900030. doi:10.1353/etc.0.0065

Bellini, S. (2006a). *Building social relationships: A systematic approach to teaching social interaction skills to children and adolescents with autism spectrum disorders and other social difficulties.* Shawnee Mission, KS: Autism Asperger Publishing.

Bellini, S. (2006b). The development of social anxiety in high functioning adolescents with autism spectrum disorders. *Focus on Autism and Other Developmental Disabilities*, 2(3), 138–145. doi:10.1177/10883576060210030201

Bellini, S. (2016). *Building social relationships 2: A systematic approach to teaching social interaction skills to children and adolescents with autism spectrum disorders and other social difficulties.* Shawnee Mission, KS: Autism Asperger Publishing.

Bellini, S., & Akullian, J. (2007). A meta-analysis of video modeling and video self-modeling interventions for children and adolescents with autism spectrum disorders. *Exceptional Children*, 73, 261–284. doi:10.1177/001440290707300301

Bellini, S., & Ehlers, E. J. (2009). Video modeling interventions for youth with autism spectrum disorders: Practical suggestions for clinicians and educators. *Journal of Assistive Technology Outcomes and Benefits*, 6, 56–69.

Cook, C. R., Williams, K. R., Guerra, N. G., Kim, T. E., & Sadek, S. (2010). Predictors of bullying and victimization in childhood and adolescence: A meta-analytic investigation. *School Psychology Quarterly*, 25, 65–83. doi:10.1037/a0020149

Delano, M. E. (2007). Video modeling interventions for individuals with autism. *Remedial and Special Education*, 28, 33–42. doi:10.1177/07419325070280010401

Dowrick, P. W. (1999). A review of self-modeling and related interventions. *Applied and Preventive Psychology*, 8, 23–39. doi:10.1016/S0962-1849(99)80009-2

Hitchcock, C. H., Dowrick, P. W., & Prater, M. A. (2003). Video self-modeling interventions in school-based settings: A review. *Remedial and Special Education*, 24, 36–46. doi:10.1177/074193250302400104

Kehle, T. J., & Bray, M. A. (2009). Self-modeling. In A. Akin-Little, S. G. Little, M. A. Bray, & T. J. Kehle (Eds.), *Behavioral interventions in schools* (pp. 231–244). Washington, DC: American Psychological Association. doi:10.1037/11886-015

Kehle, T. J., Bray, M. A., Margiano, S. G., Theodore, L. A. & Zhou, Z. (2002), Self-modeling as an effective intervention for students with serious emotional disturbance: Are we modifying children's memories?, *Psychology in the Schools*, 39, 203–207. doi:10.1002/pits.10031

Losinski, M., Wiseman, N., White, S. A., & Balluch, F. (2016). A meta-analysis of video-modeling based interventions for reduction of challenging behaviors for students with EBD. *The Journal of Special Education*, 49(4), 243–252. doi:10.1177/0022466915602493

National Autism Center. (2019). National standards report, phase 2. Retrieved from: https://www.nationalautismcenter.org/national-standards-project/phase-2/

Nikopoulos, C. K., & Keenan, M. (2004). Effects of video modeling on social initiations by children with autism. *Journal of Applied Behavior Analysis*, 37(1), 93–96. doi:10.1901/jaba.2004.37-93

Parker, R., Vannest, K., & Brown, L. (2009). The improvement rate difference for single case research. *Exceptional Children*, 75, 135–150. doi:10.1177/001440290907500201

Parker, R., Vannest, K., & Davis, J. L., (2011). Effect size in single-case research: A review of nine nonoverlap techniques. *Behavior Modification*, 35, 303–322. doi:10.1177/0145445511399147

Seok, S., DaCosta, B., McHenry-Powell, M., Heitzman-Powell, L. S., & Ostmeyer, K. (2018). Systematic review of evidence-based video modeling for students with emotional and behavioral disorders. *Education Sciences*, 8(4), 170. doi:10.3390/educsci8040170

Skalski, A. K., Minke, K., Rossen, E., Cowan, K. C., Kelly, J., Armistead, R., & Smith, A. (2015). *NASP practice model implementation guide*. Bethesda, MD: National Association of School Psychologists.

Tantam, D. (2000). Psychological disorder in adolescents and adults with Asperger syndrome. *Autism*, 4, 47–62. doi:10.1177/1362361300004001004

Wong, C., Odom, S. L., Hume, K. A., Cox, A. W., Fettig, A., Kucharczyk, S., Brock, M. E., Plavnick, J. B., Fleury, V. P., & Schultz, T. R. (2015). Evidence-based practices for children, youth, and young adults with autism spectrum disorder: A comprehensive review. *Journal of Autism and Developmental Disorders*, 45, 1951–1966. doi:10.1007/s10803-014-2351-z

7
BEHAVIORAL SKILLS TRAINING AND POSITIVE PRACTICE

Clayton R. Cook and Shawn N. Girtler

Introduction

The acquisition and performance of social, emotional, and behavioral (SEB) skills are important to ensure healthy development and functioning over time (Alexander, Entwisle, Blyth, & McAdoo, 1988). Children who lack certain SEB skills are at risk for short- and long-term difficulties, including lower academic achievement (Durlak et al., 2011; Hinshaw, 1992), school truancy/absenteeism (Hootman & DeSocio, 2004), impaired relationships (Cook et al., 2010), substance abuse problems (Arthur et al., 2007), and school dropout (Greenberg et al., 2001). Given the prevalence and impact of children who lack SEB skills, there is a need to increase children's access to high-quality intervention as a way of promoting skills that enable improvements in their academic and life success.

The purpose of this chapter is to provide an overview of behavioral skills training and positive practice as essential methods to help children acquire and apply key social, emotional, and behavioral (SEB) skills, enabling them to better meet the demands and expectations of home and school life. This chapter discusses the importance of identifying the reasons a student is exhibiting a problem behavior in order to properly match the intervention to the student's needs. This will set up the discussion of behavioral skills training and positive practice as essential instructional techniques that support children's acquisition and use of important prerequisite skills that enable them to meet the demands of key host environments, such as home, school, and community settings. This chapter will conclude with a case example of Billie, a third grade student identified as in need of intervention, to highlight the process of designing and delivering behavioral skills training and positive practice as effective methods to address the identified problem and promote the skills of students with hypothesized acquisition deficits that undermine success in school.

Teaching Students with Acquisition Deficits

Students with acquisition deficits have a need for intervention that teaches them prerequisites SEB or academic skills that enable them to meet the demands of a given performance setting. Too often, adults make the mistake of telling students what to do without properly *teaching* them how to do the skill or what behavior is expected of them. When students do not possess a skill or behavior that is expected, there is an increased likelihood of a reactive approach that involves punitive, exclusionary discipline (Mitchell & Bradshaw, 2013). Punitive, exclusionary discipline may produce temporary relief from dealing with the behavior, but the use of these sanctions in response to behavior is associated with negative side effects, including harming the relationship with the student, decreasing a sense of belonging and connection to the setting, loss of opportunities to learn, and stigma (Skiba et al., 2014). For example, a student who lacks self-management skills to regulate behavior under certain academic situations (e.g., independent work involving learning something new) may exhibit off-task behaviors, which prompts the teacher to publicly reprimand the student for the behavior. In turn, the public reprimand can either cause the student to shut down or act out. Instead of a using a reactive approach, it is important for educators and caregivers to assess whether the student has the SEB skills to behave consistently with the expectations of the environment. If not, then there is a need to take a teaching approach that involves supporting the child in acquiring and applying the necessary SEB skills. The question then becomes: What is an effective way to teach students SEB skills?

Behavioral Skills Training

Behavioral skills training (BST) is a specialized form of instruction with demonstrated support to effectively help individuals acquire and apply knowledge and skills (Miles & Wilder, 2009; Reid et al., 2003; Rosales et al., 2009). BST is consistent with explicit instruction, which is an effective instructional model to teach students core academic skills (Marchand-Martella et al., 2013). BST is also as an effective approach to train professionals to deliver specific applied behavior analytic practices (Reid et al., 2011). There are slightly different approaches to BST, but most share five sequential steps that are designed to promote the acquisition of specific behaviors and skills: (1) tell, (2) show, (3) do, (4) feedback, and (5) review. Steps three and four of BST are often repeated until the person reaches skill mastery, which is being able to practice or rehearse the skill consistent with criteria of a behavioral definition. Each of these steps of the BST instructional process is described below.

1. **Tell or coach them what SEB skills they need to learn.** The *TELL* step involves the "what," "under what conditions," and "why" elements to effective instruction, with the goal of the student being able to comprehend the SEB skills to be performed, the situations in which the skills need to be used, and the reason why the skills are important. Students need to understand the contexts in which the SEB skills will be used, as well as understand how the skills fits in the big picture of helping them do and achieve things that are meaningful in the future. To adequately complete this step, trainers must behaviorally define the target skill using a tool such as a performance checklist (Lattimore, Stephens, Favell, & Risley, 1984).
2. **Show them so they can see what the SEB skills look like.** The *SHOW* step provides the student with the opportunity to see examples and non-examples of the SEB skills. Examples represent what the SEB skills looks like when applied well in a given situation, while non-examples demonstrate problematic or incorrect use of skills in a given situation. Together, modeling examples and non-examples of the SEB skills helps the student to discriminate and cultivates more accurate learning of the focal skills.
3. **Do the skills by providing opportunities for the student to practice.** The next step is to provide opportunities for the student to practice what was modeled. Also called behavioral rehearsal, in this step scenarios are presented that mimic application of the skill in real contexts. The goal is for the student to practice and then apply what they learned in a real-world context. Many times, adults do the first two steps, but are weak when it comes to *DO*. This results in the student displaying the skill inconsistently and/or inaccurately. When the *DO* step of BST is given the time and attention it needs, the student is able to more consistently and fluently display a given skill. Practicing the skill has been shown to be a critical feature for the success of BST (Nigro-Bruzzi & Sturmey, 2010; Rosales et al., 2009).
4. **Feedback to promote learning.** The *FEEDBACK* step is a critical aspect to provide information about the student's performance practicing the skill. Ward-Horner and Sturmey (2012) identified feedback as the essential component of BST that contributed to learner success. When feedback is delivered well, the student is able to make course corrections throughout the learning process and determine what to do next time to incrementally improve their ability to exhibit the skill.
5. **Review the skill and debrief.** The *REVIEW* step is important to provide a summary of the session, determine whether the learning objectives have been accomplished, and debrief about next steps. This step is also often paired with homework that outlines specific opportunities to practice the skill outside of the training session and report back on how it went.

The success of BST depends largely on the identification of keystone behaviors or skills the student acquires through the systematic instructional

Approach	Definition	Examples
Incompatible, desired behavior	Desired behavior that cannot occur at the same time as the problem behavior.	Teach the student specific behaviors to maintain on-task behaviors that are incompatible with engaging in off-task behaviors.
Functionally-equivalent replacement behavior	Socially acceptable behaviors that serve the same function (i.e., get/obtain wanted outcome or avoid/escape unwanted outcome) as the problem behavior.	Teach the student a more socially acceptable way to avoid doing unwanted academic work that is less disruptive to the learning environment.
General social skills	Socially acceptable learned behaviors enabling an individual to interact effectively with others.	Teach the student specific adult- and peer-related social skills, such as active listening, initiating positive conversations with others, respecting other's property, and solving conflicts productively.
Self-regulation skills	Skills designed to regulate thoughts, emotions, and behavior in response to specific situations that elicit problem behavior.	Teach the student specific emotion regulation (e.g., deep breathing, distraction tactic, self-soothing), attention regulation (e.g., self-monitoring), and behavior regulation skills that enable the student to stay in a regulated state when confronted with specific situations that previously elicited problem behavior.

FIGURE 7.1 Behavior and skills to teach through behavioral skills training

process. A keystone behavior or skill is one that has high contextual fit and is likely to make a significant difference in the student's functioning at school or in settings outside of school. There are three general approaches to conceptualize and identify the specific target behavior or skills to incorporate into BST: (1) incompatible, desired behavior, (2) functionally equivalent replacement behavior, (3) general social behaviors, and (4) self-regulation skills. One way to approach identifying the specific behaviors to train the student to do is to start with defining the problem behavior that is having a negative impact on self, others, and/or the learning environment. Once the problem behavior is defined, an appropriate replacement behavior is identified and taught using the BST steps described above (Figure 7.1).

Positive Practice

One shortcoming of training interventions is poor generalization of the skills beyond the training sessions (McIntosh & MacKay, 2008). Although BST emphasizes an approach that aims to promote skill mastery, there is a need for instructional techniques that go beyond the training session that aim to promote the generalization of newly learned skills. In particular, students need opportunities that increase the number of repetitions needed to build fluency (i.e., automaticity), as well as understand the specific situations in which the newly learned skills need to be applied. *Positive practice* is designed to support the student in learning when to apply the new skills. This procedure is also referred to as positive-practice overcorrection. The technical definition of positive practice is the required practice to demonstrate the appropriate skill contingent upon observed instances of the inappropriate behavior or missed opportunities to exhibit the skill (Weems & Costa, 2005). Positive practice involves the systematic, repeated practice of replacing an undesirable behavior with a desired behavior. For example, if a teacher was interested in having the student learn how to raise their hand and wait until called upon, instead of blurting out responses or asking questions without being called upon, the teacher would stop and have the student practice raising their hand and waiting up to three to five times. In the literature, the repeated practice component is called overcorrection, which can result in greater fluency and increases the likelihood of displaying the target behavior or skill the next time a situation calls for them. Essentially, the positive practice procedure stops the student immediately after a mistake is made, provides an example of the correct or more appropriate thing to do or say in that setting, and invites two or more repetitions before moving on. There is no anger or disapproval to the student, only full encouragement to take advantage of the practice opportunity. If the student practices, then praising the student for the energy and effort they put into practicing the skill is recommended to reinforce the effort and skill. The more a child does a certain desired behavior, the more likely that behavior is to happen. After the problem behavior, the student must repeatedly practice the correct response. Here are some examples of positive practice:

- *"You missed a chance to do the behavior we've been working on. Let's practice this behavior correctly four times so you'll be more likely to do it the next opportunity you have."*
- A student runs into the classroom, *"Wow, you seem excited, but let's try that again. I want you practice walking calmly into the classroom in the way that we've been discussing. That's one. Now back to the doorway again. Two. Two more times. Back to doorway one more time. Three. OK. Excellent, you got it. Thanks for being a good sport."*

Positive practice is beneficial because of one of two potential mechanisms of behavior change. First, it may be mildly aversive to the student and thus creates a punishment contingency that reduces the future likelihood of the problem behavior. Thus, for some students, repetitively performing a given behavior may itself be mildly punishing. For this reason, it is important to consider how positive practice is delivered. First, it should be done as privately as possible, using supportive and empathetic language (e.g., "*It seems like you're bored in class, which isn't that cool. Let's practice on how we can better handle when you get bored. I will also see what I can do to make that part of class less boring for you.*"). Second, positive practices create the opportunity for generalization of learned skills through creating opportunities to practice a newly learned skill within the context of where it should occur. Telling a child what to do in response to problem behavior is not the same as actually practicing the newly acquired behavior or skill. Imagine a coach just telling a basketball player what to do after they made a mistake without any real opportunity to go back and actually practice the specific thing the player should have done in the situation. Effective coaches calmly identify the mistake and have the player go back and do the skill over until they get it right. Although positive practice may be an effective way to promote skill acquisition and use on its own, when paired with systematic teaching approaches, like BST, it is likely to be more effective.

Behavioral Skills Training Plus Positive Practice

The combination of BST and positive practice potentially provide for a better approach to supporting students with acquisition deficits than either approach alone. In fact, they are complementary, as BST ensures that the student has the knowledge and ability to perform a given behavior or skill, while positive practice helps the student generalize the skill beyond the training sessions to build fluency and consistently use the newly learned skills in response to specific situations that call for them. Combining positive practice with BST adds another step to the instructional process that focuses explicitly on supporting the student to generalize the skill. Skill generalization and maintenance are the ultimate goals of instructional interventions. Response maintenance refers to the extent to which a student continues to perform a given skill or behavior after the intervention supports are systematically withdrawn. Setting/situation generalization is the extent to which the student exhibits the trained skill or behavior in settings or situations that are different from the setting in which the behavior was originally trained. The combination of BST and positive practice provides a more potent instructional intervention aimed at promoting the acquisition, generalization, and maintenance of important behaviors and skills that increase students' capability of meeting the social, emotional, and academic demands of school.

Case Study

To highlight the practical application of BST and positive practice to promote better outcomes for students with identified needs, a case study about Billie, a third grade student who was identified as having a need for intervention above and beyond Tier 1 classroom supports, is presented.

Background Information

Billie is a bright, energetic, playful student who enjoys socializing with other students and the teacher and attends third grade at Martin Luther King Elementary School, which is an elementary school in a culturally and socioeconomically diverse urban school district. Billie's elementary school conducts twice-yearly universal screening in order to proactively detect students who may be in need of supports above and beyond Tier 1. The school is actively implementing a restorative approach to school-wide positive behavior intervention and supports (SWPBIS). The Tier 1 implementation in the school involves (a) proactive restorative circles to cultivate a sense of community in the class and engage in planned teaching of the school-wide behavioral expectations (safe, respectful, and responsible), (b) a school currency in the form of good-behavior bucks to acknowledge and recognize students for exhibiting behavioral expectations, and (c) a progressive approach to responding to minor and major problem behavior, including restorative conferences for students who engage in major problem behaviors that negatively impact relationships with others. Billie was flagged as part of the fall universal screening effort due to the ratings indicating the presence of externalizing behaviors that were negatively impacting their learning and that of other students. Billie was brought to the attention of a problem-solving team who convenes as a group to considered whether they were in need of an intervention. Billie's teacher, Mr. Frank, has tried several strategies with them to address the externalizing behavior, but with uneven and limited success. The strategies tried included altering seating, proactively reminding Billie of the expectations, and creating a behavior-tracking chart linked to tangible rewards. The problem-solving team determined that Mr. Frank does reasonably well at implementing core components of PBIS and restorative practices with fidelity in the classroom, and that Billie has a need that warrants a Tier 2 intervention that is organized and supported by the problem-solving team.

Description of the Problem Behavior

The problem-solving team (PST) adheres to a structured problem-solving process that begins with problem identification, which entails providing a precise definition of the problem behavior. The team includes the principal, school psychologist, counselor, general education teacher leader, special education teacher leader, and a paraprofessional. The PST uses a problem-identification interview to gather information from Mr. Frank that informs the development of a precise behavioral definition of what Billie's externalizing behavior looks like, and the specific dimension of it (e.g., frequency, duration, intensity) that represents how Billie's externalizing behavior is having a negative impact on the classroom learning environment. Interview data indicated that Billie was exhibiting disruptive behaviors, which were defined as talking to peers about topics unrelated to the academic task at hand, making audible noises with objects (e.g., tapping pen or pencil loudly, thumping the desk with hand), and interrupting the teacher when talking to other students. The dimension of the behavior was frequency, and it was estimated that during a given 90-minute block of instruction, Billie exhibited 8-10 disruptive behaviors. According to Mr. Frank, although Billie exhibited disruptive behavior across different time points during the day, their disruptive behavior was more likely to occur during the literacy block than during other subjects. The interview revealed that Mr. Frank was most interested in the intervention promoting on-task behaviors that were incompatible with the disruptive behavior. On-task behavior was defined as orientation toward the task at hand, compliance with all directions, and working with appropriate materials.

Problem Analysis

As part of the Tier 2 process, the PST moves from problem identification to problem analysis. Specifically, the PST uses the acquisition–performance paradigm to identify the root cause that explains why the student's behavior problem is happening. An acquisition need hypothesizes that a problem occurs because the student does not possess the prerequisite skills/behaviors to meet the demands or expectations of an environment, while a performance need hypothesizes that the problem occurs because the student is insufficiently supported, encouraged, prompted, and/or motivated by the environment to exhibit the skills/behaviors they possess. Based on information gathered from the team Mr. Frank, Billie, and a classroom observation, the team hypothesized that Billie had an *acquisition* need, in that Billie did not possess specific skills to manage self in classroom. Billie possessed the prerequisite skills to participate and complete the academic work, but they appeared to lack self-management skills to regulate behaviors in the context of academic instruction. Data that supported this conclusion included reports indicating that even when provided with the opportunity to earn preferred tangible items, Billie exhibited disruptive behavior and struggled to manage self to exhibit desired, on-task behavior. Also, when Billie was asked about how to manage self to reduce disruptive behavior and improve on-task behavior, they had limited knowledge of skills that could be helpful. Thus, it was concluded that Billie had an acquisition need and would benefit from an acquisition-based intervention that focused on teaching self-management skills and provided Billie with opportunities to build fluency and generalize skills beyond the training sessions.

Intervention Goals

After gathering baseline data, measurable, monitorable, and change-sensitive goals were set to provide a reference point with the baseline data to evaluate Billie's response to the intervention. The goals for disruptive and on-task behavior, respectively, were set using social comparison data from typical peers. Typical

TABLE 7.1 Goal Statements for Billie's Disruptive and On-Task Behavior

Behavior	Who	Will Do What	At What Level	By When	How Will It Be Measured
Disruptive behavior	Billie	will reduce disruptive behavior	from an average of 8 occurrences per instructional block to an average of 1	by March 30th (four weeks from the start of the intervention)	as measured by daily direct behavior ratings completed by the teacher
On-task behavior	Billie	will increase on-task behavior	from an average of 55–60% of the time per instructional period to 80% of the time	by March 30th (four weeks from the start of the intervention)	as measured by daily direct behavior ratings completed by the teacher

peers (i.e., not students with problematic behavior nor students who exhibit exceptionally low problem behavior or exceptionally high on-task behavior). Using these data, the goal criterion for disruptive behavior was set at an average of 1 occurrence of disruptive behavior per instructional block (literacy and math), while the goal for on-task behavior was set at 80% of the class period. All of this information was then put into an effective goal statement that spells out the *who, will do what, by when, at what level,* and *how it will be measured* (Table 7.1).

Measurement of Target Behavior, Data Collection Strategies, and Progress Monitoring

To establish baseline data, the team constructed a direct behavior rating (DBR) tool (Christ et al., 2009) to capture the frequency of disruptive behavior and duration of on-task behavior. DBR is hybrid observation-rating tool used to gather data for well-defined target behaviors during a predetermined setting and length of time. The DBR data were gathered during the 90-minute literacy block in the morning and 45-minute math block in the afternoon. Across three different occasions, baseline data indicated that the median disruptive behavior in the literacy block and math blocks were 9 and 6 occurrences, respectively. With regard to on-task behavior, the median baseline estimates for the literacy and math blocks were 55% and 65% of the time, respectively (Table 7.2).

The baseline data provided a critical reference point to gauge Billie's response to intervention. In addition to the baseline data, the PST engaged in a process to establish intervention goals that represent what they want to achieve for Billie as a result of implementing the intervention.

TABLE 7.2 Baseline Data for Disruptive Behavior (Frequency) and On-Task Behavior (Duration)

Target Behaviors	Setting and Time	Monday	Wednesday	Friday	Median
Disruptive behavior frequency (# of occurrences)	Literacy Block	11 occurrences	9 occurrences	8 occurrences	9 occurrences
	Math Block	6 occurrences	6 occurrences	4 occurrences	6 occurrences
On-task behavior duration (% of time)	Literacy Block	55% of the time	70% of the time	40% of the time	55% of the time
	Math Block	60% of the time	80% of the time	65% of the time	65% of the time

Monitoring Data

During the intervention implementation process, the PST prepared to gather two critical pieces of data to inform decisions when it came time to meet as a team and make a data-driven decision as to the next action step to take with Billie. The two sources of data included (a) progress-monitoring data using the same DBR form as the one used to gather baseline data and (b) intervention fidelity data to monitor the degree to which the interventions were delivered as planned. The intervention fidelity data were gathered once a week to capture whether the core components of BST and positive practice were being delivered as planned. The PST were preparing to support the delivery of the BST plus positive practice intervention for Billie over the course of four weeks and scheduled a meeting to reconvene together to review data and make a decision as to the next step to take to support Billie.

Intervention Plan

The team decided that *BST plus positive practice* was an appropriately matched acquisition-based intervention to support Billie's acquisition and generalization of self-management skills to maintain on-task behavior during academic instruction. Specifically, the intervention focused on teaching Billie specific behavioral expectations for on-task behavior, including examples of what it looks like and non-examples of what it does not look like, and two self-management skills to maintain on-task behavior (stop & think, and self-monitoring). Below are the behavioral definitions of the on-task behavior and self-management skills. The PST believed it was important for Billie to understand the expectations of on-task behavior and what it does and does not look like, as well as to be supported to use specific self-management skills that enable them to regulate on-task behavior in response to situations that may provoke off-task behavior (Table 7.3).

Action and Coping Plans

At a recent professional conference, members of the team learned about implementation planning as a way to increase the likelihood of delivering interventions with fidelity (Collier-Meek et al., 2016). Implementation planning includes two plans that together facilitate the effective delivery of the intervention, so the student actually receives the intervention in a way that research has shown it to be effective. The PST began the implementation planning process by developing the first plan, which is an action plan. The action plan included components that add specificity and detail to facilitating successful delivery of the intervention (i.e., *what, who, when and for how long, descriptive details,* and *reminders*).

Next, the team created the second plan, which is a coping plan (Sanetti et al., 2014). A coping plan involves anticipating barriers that will obstruct the delivery

TABLE 7.3 Intervention Target Behavior and Skills

Target Behavior/Skills	Behavioral Definitions
On-Task Behavior	Defined as times when the student is working on the academic tasks or activities and paying attention to the teacher or other students who are discussing information relevant to the academic task. Examples of on-task behavior include writing, reading aloud, raising a hand and waiting patiently, talking to the teacher or other student about assigned material, listening to a lecture and looking up information that is relevant to the assignment.
Self-Management Skills	<u>Stop & Think</u>: This skill was defined as noticing an urge to say or do something off-task and placing a stamp next to a visual stop/think cue on the table or class binder as a reminder to engage in on-task behavior. <u>Self-Monitoring Sheet</u>: This skill was defined as reflecting on on-task behavior when prompted by the MotivAider® device and recording behavior on a chart. Billie was prompted every 15-minutes by the device to reflect on and record whether they were on-task or off-task.

of the action plan and identifying specific solutions to overcome those barriers. The PST identified three barriers that would prevent the delivery of different components of the intervention: (1) disruptions to pulling Billie out of class to participate in BST, (2) forgetting to react to disruptive behavior and implement positive practice, and (3) lack of time to complete DBRs to monitor progress. The PST linked specific solutions to each barrier: (1) identify a time for BST sessions that does not conflict with mandated educational activities (e.g., testing) and secure an agreement among all parties that Billie's participation in BST is a priority and should not be disrupted, (2) create daily prompts and reminders to prevent Mr. Frank from forgetting to use the positive practice procedure with Billie, and (3) protect time at the end of the instructional block by having an independent activity that students engage in to free up Mr. Frank to complete the DBR.

Intervention Fidelity and Interobserver Agreement

The intervention fidelity data were gathered through creating a brief observation tool that broke down BST and positive practice into their core components and provided operational definitions of each of these components so they were observable and measurable. One of the team members was assigned the responsibility of conducting observations to gather fidelity data once per week. On one of the occasions, another team member joined the observation session to gather interobserver agreement (IOA) data to verify that the observational data were reliable. In this way, data were gathered at the same time and occurrence as the

TABLE 7.4 Intervention Fidelity Data for BST and Positive Practice

Components	Week of 3/2	Week of 3/9	Week of 3/16	Week of 3/23	Component Integrity
BST					
Tell	X	X	X	X	100%
Show	X	X	X	–	75%
Do	X	X	X	X	100%
Feedback	X	X	X	X	100%
Review	–	X	X	–	50%
Positive Practice					
Respond to problem behavior	X	X	X	X	100%
Communicate calmly and privately	–	X	X	X	75%
Repeated practice of desired skill/behavior	X	X	X	X	100%
Weekly Integrity	75%	100%	100%	75%	**Total Integrity = 87.5%**

BST and positive practice interventions were being delivered. Fidelity data across both interventions indicated that the core components were delivered with 87.5% fidelity over the course of the four weeks. Moreover, IOA data indicated that the two observers' agreement was 100%, suggesting that data were reliable. The intervention component with the lowest fidelity was the *review* component of BST, with 50% adherence. Five of the components were delivered with 100% adherence. Overall, data suggested that Billie largely received the two interventions as planned (Table 7.4).

Intervention Outcome Data

The results of the progress-monitoring data were graphed to display the information in such a way that team members could conduct a visual analysis to make a data-driven decision. While the average duration of on-task behavior was 55% at baseline, it increased to an average of 81% over the last four measurement occasions. This was an increase of 26 percentage points. When visually examining the progress-monitoring data for disruptive behavior, the PST noticed a similar an observable decrease in disruptive behavior during the intervention phase when compared to baseline, indicating a positive response to the intervention. In this case, the average frequency of disruptive behavior at baseline was nine occurrences, and once the intervention plan was implemented this reduced to an average of 3.25 occurrences over the last four measurement occasions. Overall, visual analysis comparing the level of performance during the baseline phase relative to the intervention phase indicated that Billie's behavior changed significantly in level. Moreover, the goal lines suggested that for both on-task and disruptive behavior, Billie's performance was meeting the predetermined goals (Figure 7.2).

Summary of Intervention Effects

The PST was committed to evaluating the effectiveness of Billie's intervention using the two sources of data discussed above: (a) intervention fidelity data and (b) progress-monitoring data. The question they sought to answer was, "Did the intervention plan work?" They used the below grid to guide their decisions using the two sources of data. As one can see, when the student demonstrates sufficient response and fidelity is good, the PST's discussions center on maintaining or gradually withdrawing aspects of the intervention. When the response is insufficient, the PST decides that it is necessary to determine the strength of fidelity. If fidelity is insufficient, then the PST's decision is likely to involve revisiting the implementation plan and identifying how to improve fidelity. If fidelity is sufficient, then the decision is to focus on changing aspects of the intervention or staying course because the student has not received sufficient exposure for the intervention to exhibit it effects (Figure 7.3).

The PST had a structured way of meeting to evaluate Billie's intervention plan. The structure allowed each team member time (three minutes) to review the data independently, select a defensible decision that was supported by the data, and discuss with the team why they selected a particular decision based on the data as the best next step to take to support Billie. The goal of this structured process was for the PST to reach consensus on the decision the majority of the group believed was the most defensible according to the data.

Each team member reviewed both the progress-monitoring data and the intervention fidelity data. After each person took their turn sharing their decisions, it was concluded that there was uniform agreement that Billie demonstrated a positive response to the intervention via observable changes in the level of behavior when comparing baseline data to progress-monitoring data. This was confirmed with the intervention fidelity data that indicated Billie generally received the interventions as planned over the course of the four weeks. They then discussed what next action step they would take with Billie. They believed it was premature to stop the intervention, yet they wanted to relax on the frequency of the BST sessions, so they reduced it to one session per week. The plan was to continue to implement the intervention as planned for the next four weeks, at which point they will reconvene to make a decision. The PST interviewed Mr. Frank and Billie about the intervention to examine their acceptability of it. Mr. Frank indicated that it was challenging to be consistent, but overall the intervention was worth it because Billie's behavior was improving and he had more time to devote to instruction and other students in class. Billie indicated a

Behavioral Skills Training and Positive Practice **107**

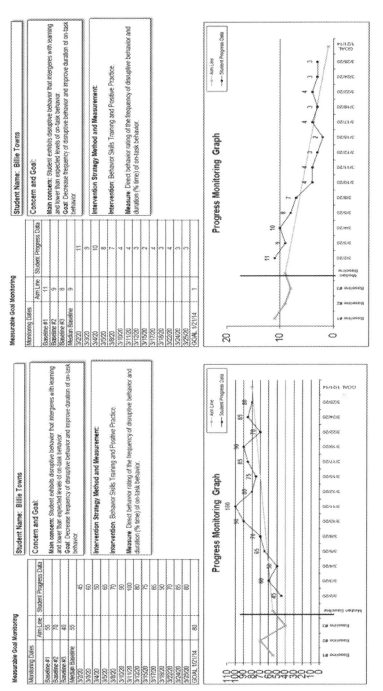

FIGURE 7.2 Progress monitoring graphs for on-task and disruptive behavior

FIDELITY DATA

	Sufficient Fidelity	Insufficient Fidelity
Sufficient Response	Maintain or Exit (1) Maintain/continue intervention, (2) Change the goal, (3) Begin fading intervention	Improve Fidelity or Exit Improve fidelity, Exit student from process
Insufficient Response	Change Intervention (1) Change intervention, (2) Consider bumping up to a more intensive tier	Improve Fidelity Improve fidelity by addressing barriers to delivery of specific intervention components

(PROGRESS MONITORING)

FIGURE 7.3 Data-based decision-making grid

preference for the BST sessions over having to practice the skills and behaviors in class. Altogether, the PST viewed this intervention as a success.

Intervention Acceptability

The PST adopted a standard method of assessing both student and staff perceptions of the intervention, as well as gathering feedback on how the interventions could be adapted to be more suitable and acceptable for use in the future. Specifically, they used the Usage Rating Profile-Intervention (URP) and the Children's Usage Rating Profile (CURP) to gather data on the acceptability of the interventions. To make for a more efficient assessment, the PST only administered items from the URP *acceptability* and CURP *personal desirability* subscale. They learned that the staff implementing the interventions found both interventions to be generally acceptable, with BST endorsed as more acceptable than positive practice. The teacher delivering the positive practice intervention recommended to generate more discrete ways for the student to engage in repeated practice after the incident of a problem behavior so it does not distract other students as a way to improve its acceptability. The student reported that the BST was acceptable but that the positive practice intervention was less personally desirable. This was expected, as one potential aspect of positive practice that enables it to work is a punishment contingency that introduces an unwanted experience contingent on problem behavior, which likely produces an unfavorable experience for the child.

Intervention Considerations

Billie's case study demonstrates the importance of conducting root cause analyses that determine *why* a particular problem is happening. As illustrated in this chapter, many students struggle socially, emotionally, and behaviorally because they lack the prerequisite skills and behaviors that enable them to meet the social and academic demands of school. For this reason, it is imperative that schools have acquisition-based interventions such as BST and positive practice available as part of the continuum of supports they provide to students with hypothesized acquisition deficits that explain why SEB problems are happening. Effective acquisition interventions support students to acquire, build fluency, and ultimately use new behaviors and skills during the times and situations in which they are expected and needed. Too often interventions fall short of accomplishing this. The combination of BST plus positive practice, however, provides an effective instructional intervention for students with acquisition needs.

Conclusion

BST and positive practice represent effective interventions to support students to acquire and apply new behaviors and skills that enable them to be more successful in school. In the case of Billie, the hypothesized root cause explaining why disruptive behavior was happening was an acquisition deficit. Acquisition deficits reflect students who are experiencing SEB problems because they have not yet acquired prerequisite skills necessary to meet the demands of a given performance setting (e.g., classroom). For students with acquisition deficits, the intervention must be instructional in nature and involve effective teaching methods that support the student to acquire and generalize behaviors and skills to enable them to be more successful in school.

References

Alexander, K., Entwisle, D., Blyth, D., & McAdoo, H. (1988). Achievement in the first 2 years of school: Patterns and processes. *Monographs of the Society for Research in Child Development*, 53(2), 1–157. doi:10.2307/1166081

Arthur, M., Briney, J., Hawkins, J., Abbott, R., Brooke-Weiss, B., & Catalano, R. (2007). Measuring risk and protection in communities using the Communities That Care Youth Survey. *Evaluation and Program Planning*, 30(2), 197–211.

Christ, T. J., Riley-Tillman, T. C., & Chafouleas, S. M. (2009). Foundation for the development and use of Direct Behavior Rating (DBR) to assess and evaluate student behavior. *Assessment for Effective Intervention*, 34(4), 201–213. doi:10.1177/1534508409340390

Collier-Meek, M. A., Sanetti, L. M. H., & Boyle, A. M. (2016). Providing feasible implementation support: Direct training and implementation planning in consultation. *School Psychology Forum*, 10(1), 106–119.

Cook, C. R., Williams, K. R., Guerra, N. G., Kim, T. E., & Sadek, S. (2010). Predictors of bullying and victimization in childhood and adolescence: A meta-analytic investigation. *School Psychology Quarterly*, 25(2), 65–83. doi:10.1037/a0020149

Durlak, J. A., Weissberg, R. P., Dymnicki, A. B., Taylor, R. D., & Schellinger, K. B. (2011). The impact of enhancing students' social and emotional learning: A meta-analysis of school based universal interventions. *Child Development*, 82(1), 405–432. doi:10.1111/j.1467-8624.2010.01564.x

Greenberg, M. T., Domitrovich, C., & Bumbarger, B. (2001). The prevention of mental disorders in school-aged children: Current state of the field. *Prevention & Treatment*, 4(1), Article 1a. doi:10.1037/1522-3736.4.1.41a

Hinshaw, S. P. (1992). Academic underachievement, attention deficits, and aggression: Comorbidity and implications for intervention. *Journal of Consulting and Clinical Psychology*, 60(6), 893.

Hootman, J., & DeSocio, J. (2004). School nurses' important mental health role. *Behavioral Health Management*, 24(4), 25–29.

Lattimore, J., Stephens, T.E., Favell, J.E., & Risley, T.R. (1984). Increasing direct care staff compliance to individualsed physical therapy body positioning prescriptions: Prescriptive checklists. *Mental Retardation*, 22, 79–84.

Marchand-Martella, N. E., Martella, R. C., Modderman, S. L., Petersen, H. M., & Pan, S. (2013). Key areas of effective adolescent literacy programs. *Education and Treatment of Children*, 36(1), 161–184.

McIntosh, K., & MacKay, L. D. (2008). Enhancing generalization of social skills: Making social skills curricula effective after the lesson. *Beyond Behavior*, 18(1), 18–25.

Miles, N. I., & Wilder, D. A. (2009). The effects of behavioral skills training on caregiver implementation of guided compliance. *Journal of Applied Behavior Analysis*, 42(2), 405-410. doi:10.1901/jaba.2009.42-405

Mitchell, M., & Bradshaw, C. (2013). Examining classroom influences on student perceptions of school climate: The role of classroom management and exclusionary discipline strategies. *Journal of School Psychology*, 51(5), 599–610. doi:10.1016/j.jsp.2013.05.005

Nigro-Bruzzi, D., & Sturmey, P. (2010). The effects of behavioral skills training on mand training by staff and unprompted vocal mands by children. *Journal of Applied Behavior Analysis*, 43(4), 757–761.

Reid, D. H., O'Kane, N. P., & Macurik, K. M. (2011). Staff training and management. In W. W. Fisher, C. C. Piazza, & H. S. Roane (Eds.), *Handbook of applied behavior analysis* (pp. 281–294). New York: The Guilford Press.

Reid, D. H., Rotholz, D. A., Parsons, M. B. M. L., Braswell, B. A., Green, C. W., & Schell, R. M. (2003). Training human service supervisors in aspects of positive behavior support: Evaluation of a state-wide, performance-based program. *Journal of Positive Behavior Interventions*, 5(1), 35. doi:10.1177/10983007030050010601

Rosales, R., Stone, K., & Rehfeldt, R. A. (2009). The effects of behavioral skills training on implementation of the Picture Exchange Communication system. *Journal of Applied Behavior Analysis*, 42(3), 541–549. doi:10.1901/jaba.2009.42-541

Sanetti, L., Collier-Meek, M., Long, A., Kim, J., & Kratochwill, T. (2014). Using implementation planning to increase teachers' adherence and quality to behavior support plans. *Psychology in the Schools*, 51(8), 879–895. doi:10.1002/pits.21787

Skiba, R., Arredondo, M., & Williams, N. (2014). More than a metaphor: The contribution of exclusionary discipline to a school-to-prison pipeline. *Equity & Excellence in Education*, 47(4), 546–564. doi:10.1080/10665684.2014.958965

Ward-Horner, J., & Sturmey, P. (2012). Component analysis of behavior skills training in functional analysis. *Behavioral Interventions*, 27(2), 75–92. doi:10.1002/bin.1339

Weems, C., & Costa, N. (2005). Encyclopedia of behavior modification and cognitive behavior therapy. In M. Hersen, J. Rosqvist, A. M. Gross, R. S. Drabman, G. Sugai, & R. Horner (Eds.), *Encyclopedia of behavior modification and cognitive behavior therapy* (pp. 961–962). Thousand Oaks, CA: SAGE Publications. doi:10.4135/9781412950534.n2092

8
BEHAVIORAL MOMENTUM

Michael I. Axelrod, Melissa Coolong-Chaffin, and Renee O. Hawkins

Introduction

Following teacher instructions is a foundational skill essential for students' classroom success. Compliance, generally considered a keystone behavior or behavior that leads to positive outcomes across other behaviors and situations, is necessary for learning more complex skills (see Banda, Neisworth, & Lee, 2003). Failure to follow teacher instructions is one of the more common behavior problems exhibited by children and adolescents (Lipschultz & Wilder, 2017). Noncompliance may inhibit learning, limit opportunities to participate in classroom activities, negatively impact peer relations, and escalate to more serious forms of disruptive behavior (e.g., aggression). Moreover, noncompliance of even one student in a classroom takes teacher time and resources, potentially resulting in a loss of both academic and social instructional opportunities.

School psychologists looking for a proactive (versus reactive), easy-to-implement strategy to improve students' compliance might consider behavioral momentum. Behavioral momentum (BM) takes advantage of a high-probability command sequence (HPCS) to increase the likelihood of a student complying with a low-probability command. More specifically, BM involves the delivery of a set of simple instructions in which the student is likely to comply immediately prior to the delivery of an instruction that has a lower probability of compliance. For example, a teacher might request a student slide her chair closer to the desk, give the teacher a high-five, and pick up her pencil (all high-probability instructions) before asking the student to write her name at the top of the worksheet (low-probability instruction). In addition, brief praise statements are often used following compliance with each command.

The development of HPCSs to increase compliance is largely based on the principle that a quick series of high-probability request-response-reinforcement (RRR) trials administered just prior to delivering a low-probability request increases the probability of compliance with the low-probability request (Oliver & Skinner, 2002). The high rate of responding and reinforcement (i.e., complying with the high-probability instructions followed by reinforcement contingent on compliance) is thought to create a momentum of compliance, which may increase compliance with the low-probability request (Lipschultz & Wilder, 2017). In theory, BM also increases the rate of reinforcement for compliance as a response class (i.e., responses or behaviors that are alike and serve a similar function) and establishes a learning history whereby students' previous experiences with HPCSs increases the probability of compliance with future HPCSs (Axelrod & Zank, 2012).

Reviews of the research suggest that interventions utilizing HPCSs and BM are effective at improving the behavior of individuals ranging from preschoolers to adults (Lee, 2005). Research also indicates these interventions improve the behavior of individuals with various diagnoses and in various settings (Lipschultz & Wilder, 2017). Specific to school settings, HPCSs and BM have been shown to improve student behavior (Knowles, Meng, & Machalicek, 2015). For example, Axelrod and Zank (2012) demonstrated that an intervention based on sequencing high- and low-probability requests could have a profound impact on the compliance of two students identified with a behavioral disorder within a general education classroom. The researchers noted that "interventions based on behavioral momentum allow teachers to be proactive in their management of noncompliant behavior and perhaps prevent problem behavior from escalating" (p. 130).

Case Study

Background Information

Casey was a fifth grade student at Rock Creek Elementary School. He was referred to the student assistance team because of problems associated with compliance with adult instructions. Casey was not receiving special education services at the time of the intervention. Tier 1 programming included a standard social/emotional learning curriculum delivered to Casey and his class in the general education setting by the school counselor and a School-Wide Positive Behavior Interventions and Supports (SWPBSIS) model emphasizing small rewards contingent on individual and group behaviors (e.g., assisting peers, lining up appropriately, homework completion). Previous attempts at intervention at the Tier 2 level included Check In/Check Out implemented daily by his classroom teacher and a contingency contract developed collaboratively between Casey and the school psychologist. Both Tier 2 interventions targeted compliance with adult instructions and escalations in problem behavior resulting from noncompliance (e.g., ongoing failure to following instructions, physical and verbal aggression towards teacher and peers, leaving the classroom). The Tier 2 interventions were implemented separately for six weeks each and together for four weeks. According to Mr. Brenner, Casey's teacher, Casey's compliance with adult instructions slightly improved with the implementation of the Tier 2 interventions. However, Mr. Brenner noted that the frequency of noncompliance remained well below expectations. Furthermore, Casey continued to engage in noteworthy behavior problems following noncompliance. Per Mr. Brenner's report and corroborated with assessment data, Casey's academic skills were comparable to same grade peers.

Mr. Brenner was in his sixth year as a fifth grade teacher. He admitted to having little training in applied behavior analysis or the implementation of behavioral interventions either at the individual or group level. The class consisted of 24 students. A paraprofessional, Mrs. Martin, trained in instructional delivery methods and classroom management techniques, was available to work with students during reading and math instruction each day.

Description of the Problem Behavior

The school psychologist conducted a problem-identification interview with the classroom teacher focusing on Casey's noncompliant behavior. Compliance with instructions was defined as initiating an adult request within 10 seconds of the request being verbally given and completing the request within an appropriate amount of time as determined by the staff member making the request. Noncompliance was defined as engaging in a behavior other than the behavior that was requested (e.g., arguing with the teacher, verbal refusal to complete the task, walking away). Mr. Brenner also noted that Casey often escalated his behavior when the demand was not removed. Specifically, he often engaged in aggressive or argumentative behavior, or left the classroom when Mr. Brenner verbally restated the instruction. Finally, Mr. Brenner indicated that Casey was most likely to engage in noncompliant behavior when given an adult request during reading and math instructional time and independent seatwork. Reading instructional time and independent seatwork occurred for 45 minutes in the morning. Math instructional time and independent seatwork occurred for 45 minutes in the afternoon. Mr. Brenner stated that Casey rarely received positive feedback or peer attention during these times of the day. Consequential events immediately following the noncompliant behavior generally included not completing the task, accessing a preferred activity, and teacher or peer attention.

The school psychologist used an A-B-C narrative observation scheme to conduct several classroom observations during reading and math instruction and independent seatwork. Table 8.1 summarizes qualitative data collected from the observation. The school psychologist also collected data on the frequency of Casey's and a male peer's compliance with low- and high-probability instructions.

TABLE 8.1 Summary of A-B-C Data Collected during Classroom Observations

Classroom Activity	Antecedent	Behavior	Consequence
Independent seatwork (reading)	Teacher (T) issued instruction to sit down in chair	Student (S) said, "no"	T reissued instruction
Independent seatwork (reading)	T issued instruction to put toy in desk, get back to assignment	S continued playing with toy	T reissued instruction, took away toy
Math instruction	T issued instruction to walk back to desk	S continued to use pencil sharpener and talk with peer	T reissued instruction, S continued talking with peer
Reading instruction	T issued instruction to stop talking to peer and sit forward	S followed instruction	T complimented S for complying with request
Reading instruction	T issued instruction to read paragraph	S said, "no"	T reissued instruction

The school psychologist noted that Mr. Brenner issued about one instruction to Casey every 15 minutes, which was slightly more often than the peer, and that Casey complied with requests approximately 50% of the time, which was significantly less than the peer. The school psychologist also reported that Casey escalated his behavior approximately once every other day, which was also more often than peers.

Problem Analysis

The school psychologist hypothesized that both positive (e.g., teacher attention, access to tangible items) and negative (e.g., avoidance of academic task) reinforcement maintained Casey's noncompliant behavior. In addition, the team hypothesized that limited teacher and peer attention prior to periods when the problem behavior was most frequent served as a motivating operation. Finally, the team concluded that Casey's academic skill level was not likely contributing to the problem behavior. Academic tasks were at Casey's instructional level and supports were deemed appropriate.

The school psychologist decided to collect data to identify high-probability instructions. According to Lee, Belfiore, and Budin (2008), the purpose "is to identify tasks that are quick to complete and generally result in compliance" (p. 67). Mr. Brenner developed a list of 40 common classroom instructions he knew Casey could complete independently. He issued Casey each instruction during both the reading and math instructional and independent seatwork periods, randomly, 10 times, over a two-week period. All instructions constituted an

TABLE 8.2 Casey's Percentage Compliance with Instructions Identified as High-Probability

Instruction	Percentage of compliance (%)
Give me a high-five	100
Pick up writing utensil (e.g., pencil, pen, color pencil)	100
Smile	100
Slide chair closer to desk	100
Stand up	90
Put down writing utensil	90
Move eraser from one side of desk to other side of desk	90
Put hands on lap	90
Put hands on desk	90
Read sentence from passage	80
Put name on paper	80
Sit or stand still	80
Look at my eyes/give me eye contact	80
Put calculator on desk	80

initiation command (i.e., do or start something). Following the two-week period, the school psychologist calculated percentage compliance for each instruction. The team decided, using criteria from previous research (e.g., Axelrod & Zank, 2012), to categorize high-probability instructions as instructions complied with 80% of the time or greater. Table 8.2 provides the instructions identified as high-probability and their percentage of compliance during the two-week period.

Intervention Goals

The school psychologist and Mr. Brenner collaborated to identify goals related to the target behaviors. For the primary target behavior of compliance, Casey was expected to follow low-probability instructions issued by the teacher 60% of the time by the end of intervention's third week and 80% after six weeks of intervention (minus three days of return to baseline). For escalations in problem behavior, the frequency of Casey's aggressive behavior, arguing, and elopement from the classroom following noncompliance was expected to be two per week by the intervention's fourth week, one per week by the intervention's sixth week, and zero per week by the intervention's eighth week.

Measurement of Target Behaviors, Data Collection Strategies, and Progress Monitoring

The school psychologist and Mr. Brenner elected to measure Casey's percentage compliance with low-probability instructions. Percentage compliance was calculated by dividing the number of instances of compliance by the number of instances of compliance plus the number of instances of noncompliance and multiplying by 100. Mr. Brenner asked the team to also track the frequency of escalations resulting from Casey's noncompliance. Escalations were defined as physical or verbal aggression, arguing immediately following an instruction, and leaving the classroom without permission.

Appendix A provides an example of a frequency-recording data collection form. Mr. Brenner and Mrs. Martin were responsible for collecting progress-monitoring data each day. The school psychologist trained each in behavioral observation data collection methods including how to use each of the data collection forms. The training involved a 20 minute presentation followed by opportunities to practice collecting data using the two data collection forms.

Observations corresponded to when the BM intervention was scheduled to be implemented in the classroom (i.e., reading and math instructional and independent seatwork periods). In consultation with the school psychologist, Mr. Brenner and Mrs. Martin determined an observational schedule that made sense given each professionals' responsibilities during the observation period.

A Goal Attainment Scale (GAS) was also used as a measure of progress (see Coffee & Ray-Subramanian, 2009). The school psychologist and Mr. Brenner identified goals and corresponding benchmarks along a five-point scale (−2 to +2) for the target behavior of compliance with low-probability instructions (see Table 8.3). Mr. Brenner completed the GAS every afternoon during all phases (baseline, intervention, follow-up). He was told to consider Casey's compliance with low-probability instructions across the entire day, not only during reading and math instructional and independent seatwork periods.

TABLE 8.3 Goal Attainment Scale

Level of Attainment	Percentage Compliance w/Low-Probability Instructions
(-2) Much less than expected	Casey is compliant with low-probability instructions less than 20% of the time
(-1) Somewhat less than expected	Casey is compliant with low-probability instructions between 20% and 40% of the time
(0) Expected level of outcome	Casey is compliant with low-probability instructions between 40% and 60% of the time
(+1) Somewhat more than expected	Casey is compliant with low-probability instructions between 60% and 90% of the time
(+2) Much more than expected	Casey is compliant with low-probability instructions more than 90%
Comments:	

Intervention Plan

Several "phases" or conditions were implemented across the intervention. An initial three-day baseline condition was followed by a BM condition using a 3:1 high- to low-probability command ratio lasting 15 days. A second three-day baseline condition was followed by a BM using a 1:1 high- to low-probability instruction ratio. The team decided to initially reduce the high- to low-probability ratio from 3:1 to 1:1 so that the intervention would eventually more closely resemble what typically happens in the classroom environment. However, the team decided to move from 1:1 to 2:1 after Casey's compliance with low-probability instructions steadily decreased following Day 26. The team had Mr. Brenner return to a 1:1 ratio at Day 39 when Casey's percentage compliance met the 80% goal three out of four days.

The intervention was delivered during reading and math instruction and independent seatwork periods. During the 3:1 high- to low-probability instruction ratio condition, Mr. Brenner issued three high-probability instructions followed by a low-probability instruction. During the 1:1 and 2:1 high- to low-probability instruction ratio condition, he issued one and two high-probability instruction, respectively, followed by a low-probability instruction. Mr. Brenner selected instructions that fit the context of the classroom activity. Casey was provided behavior-specific praise (e.g., "thank you for scooting your chair closer to your desk," "great job picking up your pencil") following compliance with both low- and high-probability commands. Mr. Brenner issued instructions no longer than five seconds after providing praise for compliance with the previous instruction. He continued managing Casey's noncompliance through reprimands, restatements, redirections, and planned ignoring, and his escalations in behavior by contacting the school's principal immediately following an incident.

Intervention Fidelity and Interobserver Agreement

Mrs. Martin assessed intervention fidelity twice per week using the Behavioral Momentum Procedural Checklist (see Table 8.4). The school psychologist independently assessed intervention fidelity during one intervention session per week using the same checklist. Percentage agreement (i.e., fidelity) was calculated by dividing agreements by agreements plus disagreements and multiplying by 100. Fidelity was 97% during the observed sessions. In addition, Mr. Brenner and Mrs. Martin both indicated the intervention was implemented every day school was in session. Taken together, the team concluded the intervention was implemented with fidelity.

Interobserver agreement (IOA) for compliance with low-probability instructions was evaluated by the school psychologist independently observing one intervention period per week during baseline and intervention phases using the same data collection form as the primary observer. Percentage of agreement (i.e.,

TABLE 8.4 Behavioral Momentum Procedural Checklist for 3:1 Condition

Step	Procedure	Completed (circle one)
1.	Obtain eye contact with student	Yes No
2.	Issue first high-probability instruction	Yes No
3.	Behavior-specific praise statement for compliance within 10-s	Yes No N/A
4.	Issue second high-probability instruction (within 5-s of praise statement)	Yes No
5.	Behavior-specific praise statement for compliance within 10-s	Yes No N/A
6.	Issue third high-probability instruction (within 5-s of praise statement)	Yes No
7.	Behavior-specific praise statement for compliance within 10-s	Yes No N/A
8.	Issue low-probability instruction (within 5-s of praise statement)	Yes No
9.	Behavior-specific praise statement for initiating compliance within 10-s and completing task in appropriate amount of time	Yes No N/A
10.	For noncompliance (circle all that apply): • Restatement of instruction • Redirection of student • Planned ignoring	Yes No N/A
11.	For escalation following noncompliance	Yes No N/A

IOA) was calculated by dividing agreements by agreements plus disagreements and multiplying by 100. Interobserver agreement was 96% during the observed sessions suggesting the data were reliable.

Intervention Outcome Data

Percentage Compliance with Low-Probability Instructions

Figure 8.1 provides a visual of Casey's progress with percentage compliance with low-probability instructions during the intervention. His mean percentage compliance with low-probability instructions during three days of baseline was approximately 37% (range: 33.33%–40%). Data were generally stable, resulting in the implementation of the BM intervention using the 3:1 ratio. Casey's mean percentage compliance during the 3:1 ratio phase was just under 64% (range: 45.45%–77.78%). The lowest data point observed in the 3:1 ratio condition was higher than the highest data point during baseline. The team decided to return to baseline after 15 days in the 3:1 condition, which coincided with the timing of the first goal (i.e., 60% compliance with low-probability instructions after three weeks of intervention). Casey's mean percentage of compliance with

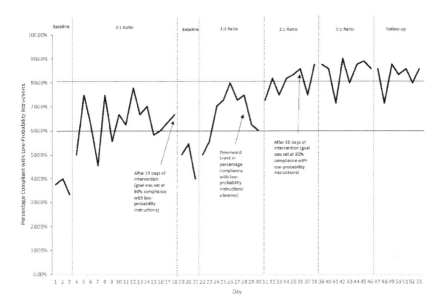

FIGURE 8.1 Casey's percentage compliance with low-probability instructions

low-probability instructions during the second three days of baseline was slightly under 50% (range: 40%–54.55%), which was higher than Casey's percentage of compliance during the initial baseline phase but lower than his percentage of compliance during the 3:1 condition.

Casey's mean percentage of compliance with low-probability instructions was 66.5% (range: 50%–80%) during the first 1:1 condition. His percentage compliance peaked at 80% on Day 26, then steadily declined to 60% on Day 30. The team decided to move to a 2:1 high-probability to low-probability instruction ratio after Day 30. Casey's percentage compliance with low-probability instructions was 80% (range: 72.73%–87.5%) during the 2:1 condition. Following an intervention high of 87.5% compliance with low-probability instructions observed on Day 38, Mr. Brenner returned to the 1:1 condition. Casey's mean percentage compliance with low-probability instructions during the second 1:1 condition was 84.59% (range: 71.43%–90%). Beginning with Day 36 when the second intervention goal was set, Casey achieved 80% compliance with low-probability instructions on nine of 11 days.

During the follow-up phase (i.e., a final return to baseline), Casey's mean percentage of compliance with low-probability instructions was 82.77% (range: 71.43–87.50). Only once during the follow-up phase (i.e., seven days) did his percentage compliance drop below the goal line of 80%. Mr. Brenner and the team decided to discontinue data collection after Casey achieved five days of 80% or more compliance with low-probability instructions.

TABLE 8.5 Frequency of Escalations of Behavior by Condition

Condition (# of days)	Number of Escalations	Number of Escalations per day
Baseline (3 days)	2	.67
3:1 Ratio (15 days)	4	.27
Return to Baseline (3 days)	1	.33
1:1 Ratio (9 days)	2	.22
2:1 Ratio (8 days)	1	.13
1:1 Ratio (8 days)	0	0
Follow-up (7 days)	0	0

Frequency of Escalations Resulting from Noncompliance

Table 8.5 provides data on the frequency of escalations of Casey's behavior (i.e., aggressive behavior, arguing, elopement) following noncompliance during the intervention. The number of Casey's escalations per day during the initial three days of baseline was .67. During the 3:1 ratio phase, the number of escalations decreased to .27 per day. Casey escalated his behavior once during the three days when baseline was reintroduced. The number of his escalations per day during the 1:1, 2:1, and second 1:1 ratio phases were .22, .13, and 0, respectively. Casey did not escalate his behavior following noncompliance during the follow-up phase. Based on these data, Casey met the intervention goal of zero instances of behavioral escalations following noncompliance by the intervention's eighth week.

Goal Attainment Scale

Figure 8.2 provides a visual of Casey's progress with percentage compliance with low-probability instructions as measured by the GAS completed daily by Mr. Brenner. The data are consistent with other measures (e.g., direct observation of percentage compliance with low-probability instructions), indicating Casey made progress during the intervention. Most notable was Mr. Brenner's ratings of Casey's behavior during the 2:1 ratio, second 1:1 ratio, and follow-up conditions. Specifically, Mr. Brenner rated Casey as exceeding expectations on all days during those conditions.

Summary of Intervention Effects

Based on the data presented above, Casey's compliance with low-probability instructions increased significantly during the intervention and maintained an appropriate level when the intervention was finally withdrawn. Perhaps more importantly, data from the GAS indicated Casey's overall compliance with

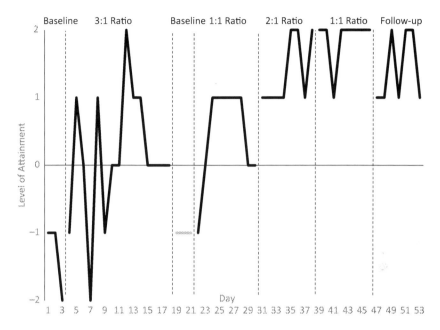

FIGURE 8.2 Goal attainment scale for percentage compliance with low-probability instructions

low-probability instructions, not just times when the intervention was implemented (i.e., reading and math instruction and independent seatwork periods), improved significantly, suggesting some degree of generalization. In addition, the frequency of Casey's escalations resulting from noncompliance decreased to zero when the intervention was faded and, ultimately, withdrawn. Taken altogether, Mr. Brenner and the team decided Casey met all intervention goals. Finally, a single-case experimental design (i.e., ABACDCA) was used to demonstrate the effects of the BM intervention on the target behaviors and establish a causal relationship between the intervention and observed changes to the target behaviors. Given this variation of the ABAB design and the exceptionally high intervention fidelity and IOA values, the team concluded that the BM intervention was likely responsible for Casey's improved compliance with low-probability instructions. Stated differently, Mr. Brenner and the team believed Casey responded remarkably well to the BM intervention.

Intervention Acceptability

Mr. Brenner and Mrs. Martin each completed an intervention feedback questionnaire (see Appendix B). They both strongly agreed that the BM intervention was effective at improving Casey's compliance with instructions and decreasing his behavior resulting from noncompliance (i.e., aggression, arguing, elopement).

They also both indicated being highly likely to use the intervention again for students exhibiting similar behavior problems and recommend it to colleagues as a strategy to improve students' compliance with instructions. Mr. Brenner agreed and Mrs. Martin strongly agreed that the intervention was easy to implement. Both were neutral about the data-collection process being easy to implement. Finally, Mr. Brenner and Mrs. Martin reported being satisfied with the outcome of the BM intervention. Taken altogether, the team agreed that the intervention was highly acceptable to both Mr. Brenner and Mrs. Martin. However, everyone was in agreement that the data-collection process might have been cumbersome given the job responsibilities of both staff members.

Intervention Considerations

This case study demonstrates how BM might be used with one elementary-age student in a general education classroom setting. However, BM could have the same effect on the noncompliance of preschool and middle/high school students. In his synthesis of the behavioral momentum literature, Lee (2005) found comparable levels of compliance among these different age groups following exposure to interventions derived from HPCSs. BM might also be used in settings other than general education classrooms. Research has found BM to be an effective intervention in separate schools for students with significant behavior disorders, self-contained classrooms, and special education resource rooms (Knowles et al., 2015), although the intervention might also be successfully employed in any setting in which a student receives adult instructions (e.g., cafeteria, playground, hallway). Finally, BM can also address problems involving latency to begin a task or comply with a request, transitions during the school day (e.g., moving from one activity to another), and academic work completion. When targeting academic work completion, teachers might design assignments with a sequence of high-probability tasks (e.g., skills that are in the maintenance stage) immediately preceding the low-probability task (e.g., skills being targeted for instruction). For example, several easier multiplication problems (i.e., high-probability tasks) can be placed immediately before more difficult double-digit multiplication problem (i.e., low-probability task; see Appendix C).

BM is applicable at all levels of a multi-tier approach to support students with behavior problems (e.g., Response to Intervention [RTI]). This case study conceptualized the intervention at the Tier 3 level after the student failed to respond to school-wide and general education programming or more individualized interventions at the Tier 2 level. However, BM can easily be implemented school-wide at the Tier 1 level (e.g., part of a teacher's classroom management system) or used with several students in general and special education. Moreover, BM can be combined with other evidence-based interventions, especially when BM by itself fails to improve compliance. For example, pairing behavior-specific praise with a reward system following the student's compliance with a high-probability instruction could be easily incorporated into the BM intervention protocol, or BM could be placed immediately after explicit skill instruction.

There are two other aspects of this case study considered important for practice. First, a cause and effect relationship was established through the use of single-case experimental design methodology. Specifically, an ABACDCA design was used to determine the intervention's effects. While formally documenting a causal relationship is not often a priority for most practitioners, it does enhance accountability and is preferred over anecdotal report when making high-stakes decisions about individual students. It should be noted, however, that, in practice, employing an ABAB design does not always go as planned. The current case study illustrates the need to sometimes makes decisions about changing phases or conditions after considering the data. For example, the initial plan called for a baseline phase followed by a 3:1 high- to low-probability instruction ratio, a second baseline, a 1:1 ratio, and a follow-up or final return to baseline phase. However, the student failed to adequately respond when the 1:1 ratio was implemented, leading the team to implement a 2:1 ratio phase. This process of data-based decision making via ongoing data analysis is a hallmark of school psychology practice. Second, intervention acceptability data suggested the data-collection process might have been unmanageable for the teacher and paraprofessional. Given most educators' responsibilities, conducting behavioral observations 90 minutes a day for 10 consecutive weeks might be unrealistic. In such cases, the team might consider dividing the responsibility of conducting observations among more people or using video to capture the student's behavior and teacher's implementation of the intervention.

School psychologists and other educators might consider the following when using BM as an intervention. First, high-probability instructions should be identified before implementing the intervention. Poor compliance with high-probability instructions likely leads to poor compliance with the low-probability instruction, as compliance with the quick series of RRR trials serves as an antecedent that increases the likelihood of compliance with the low-probability instruction (see Axelrod & Zank, 2012). In this case study, the teacher issued 40 common classroom instructions systematically to determine high-probability instructions (see *Problem Analysis* section above). Practitioners might select different high-probability instructions or reassess instructions to determine their probability of compliance. Other factors in selecting high-probability instructions include the time it takes the student to complete the instruction and the effort of the response (Oliver & Skinner, 2002). Naturally, quick responses that involve low effort are initially preferred.

Second, the time interval between high-probability RRR trials should initially be between one and five seconds. Moreover, low-probability instructions should initially be issued immediately after the series of high-probability RRR trials to ensure "momentum" is established and maintained. Attending to these details when initially designing the intervention should encourage positive effects. Furthermore, time intervals should be included in intervention fidelity checklists, and feedback should be provided when those implementing the BM intervention fail to follow these guidelines. Third, behavior-specific praise should be delivered contingent on and immediately after compliance with both high- and low-probability instructions. When the intervention fails to produce improvements, practitioners should consider other forms of reinforcement for compliance (e.g., tangibles, edibles, activities, nonverbal gestures), especially compliance with low-probability instructions. For example, BM might be implemented within a token economy (TE) system where the student earns tokens for compliance with high- and low-probability instructions. Practitioners employing a TE might even assign more value to compliance with low-probability instructions by having the student earn more tokens for those specific behaviors.

Finally, practitioners should carefully consider the ratio of high-probability instructions to low-probability instructions used in the BM intervention. While most studies employ a 3:1 ratio (see Knowles et al., 2015), the literature provides little guidance on which ratio is most effective for students exhibiting problems with noncompliance. Practitioners are encouraged to take a data-based decision-making approach by beginning with a reasonable ratio (e.g., 3:1) and considering changes after the collection of several outcome data points. In this case study, the team started with a 3:1 ratio, moved to a 1:1 ratio following some success, and then decided to increase the ratio from 1:1 to 2:1. The move to a 2:1 ratio followed a downward trend in Casey's percentage compliance with low probability instructions. Also, practitioners should consider systematically fading the number of high-probability instructions before removing the intervention altogether (e.g., moving from a 3:1 to 1:1 ratio). This procedure is likely to help with the maintenance of effects by providing students with continued access to reinforcement (i.e., teacher praise) for compliance with high-probability instructions before the teacher issues the low-probability instruction (Axelrod & Zank, 2012). Other recommended approaches to facilitating maintenance include slowing the rates of reinforcement (e.g., delivering high-probability instructions that take more time to complete or require more effort, increasing the time between delivering each high-probability instruction, increasing the time between completion of the final high-probability instruction and the low-probability instruction), fading high-probability reinforcement quantity (e.g., reinforce compliance following the final high-probability instruction), and gradually decreasing the time between compliance with high-probability instruction and reinforcement (see Oliver & Skinner, 2002 for more detail). Practitioners should remember the intervention's goal is for the student to comply with teacher requests without being supported by the sequence of high-probability instructions.

Conclusion

BM has been found to be an effective way to address students struggling with complying with teacher requests (see Knowles et al., 2015; Lipschultz & Wilder, 2017). This chapter's case study parallels the literature indicating HPCSs can improve a student's compliance with low-probability instructions. Taking advantage of the "momentum" derived from the quick series of high-probability RRR trials, teachers and other educators can proactively target students' noncompliance without needing noncompliance to occur. This is particularly important, as noncompliance can quickly escalate to other, more serious problems, and commonly employed reactive behavior management strategies (e.g., loss of privileges) have the capacity to be antecedents to other behavioral excesses (e.g., aggression, arguing). In addition to improving compliance, this case study illustrates how BM might impact noteworthy problem behavior resulting from a student's initial noncompliance. BM has the potential to decrease noncompliance, which, in turn, can decrease the frequency of escalations of in problem behavior.

References

Axelrod, M.I., & Zank, A.J. (2012). Increasing classroom compliance: Using a high-probability command sequence with noncompliant students. *Journal of Behavioral Education, 21,* 119–133. doi:10.1007/s10864-011-9145-6

Banda, D.R., Neisworth, J.T., & Lee, D.L. (2003). High-probability request sequences and young children: Enhancing compliance. *Child and Family Behavior Therapy, 25,* 17–29. doi:10.1300/J019v25n02_02

Coffee, G., & Ray-Subramanian, C.E. (2009). Goal attainment scaling: A progress-monitoring tool for behavioral interventions. *School Psychology Forum: Research in Practice, 3,* 1–12.

Knowles, C., Meng, P., & Machalicek, W. (2015). Task sequencing for students with emotional and behavioral disorders: A systematic review. *Behavior Modification, 39,* 136–166. doi:10.1177/0145445514559927

Lee, D.L. (2005). Increasing compliance: A quantitative synthesis of applied research on high-probability request sequences. *Exceptionality, 13,* 141–154. doi:10.1207/s15327035ex1303_1

Lee, D.L., Belfiore, P.J., & Budin, S.G. (2008). Riding the wave: Creating a momentum of school success. *TEACHING Exceptional Children, 40,* 65–70. doi:10.1177/004005990804000307

Lipschultz, J.L., & Wilder, D.A. (2017). Behavioral assessment and treatment of noncompliance: A review of the literature. *Education and Treatment of Children, 40,* 263–298. doi:10.1353/etc.2017.0012

Oliver, R., & Skinner, C.H. (2002). Applying behavioral momentum theory to increase compliance: Why Mrs. H. RRRevved up the elementary students with the hokey-pokey. *Journal of Applied School Psychology, 19,* 75–94. doi:10.1300/J370v19n01_06

Appendix A: Frequency Recording Form

Student Observed: Casey

Teacher: Mr. Brenner   **Grade:** Fifth

Date: March 5th   **Observer:** Mrs. Martin

Time Begin: 10:15   **Time End:** 11:00

Target Behavior(s) & Definition(s): Compliance - initiating adult request with 10-s, completing the request in appropriate amount of time. Noncompliance - engaging in a behavior other than the behavior that was requested. Escalation - aggression, arguing, leaving classroom.

Behavior	Occurrences	Total Number
Compliance with low-p instruction	⁄⁄⁄⁄	5
Noncompliance with low-p instruction	⁄⁄⁄	3
Escalation following noncompliance	⁄	1

Percentage compliance with low-p instructions = $(5 \div 8) \times 100 = 62.5\%$

Appendix B: Intervention Feedback Questionnaire

In order to obtain feedback about the intervention, we ask that you complete this brief survey. This information will help the student assistance team consider, develop, and implement similar interventions in the future.

The behavioral momentum intervention was easy to implement.	Strongly Agree	Agree	Neutral	Disagree	Strongly Disagree
The data-collection process was easy to implement.	Strongly Agree	Agree	Neutral	Disagree	Strongly Disagree
I was satisfied with the overall outcome of the behavioral momentum intervention.	Strongly Agree	Agree	Neutral	Disagree	Strongly Disagree
The behavioral momentum intervention improved Casey's compliance with instructions.	Strongly Agree	Agree	Neutral	Disagree	Strongly Disagree
The behavioral momentum intervention improved Casey's behavior resulting from noncompliance (e.g., aggression, arguing, elopement).	Strongly Agree	Agree	Neutral	Disagree	Strongly Disagree
I would consider using the behavioral momentum intervention with students exhibiting similar behavior problems.	Strongly Agree	Agree	Neutral	Disagree	Strongly Disagree
I would recommend the behavioral momentum intervention to colleagues as a strategy to improve students' compliance with instructions.	Strongly Agree	Agree	Neutral	Disagree	Strongly Disagree

Appendix C: Multiplication Worksheet

Student Name: _____   Date: _____

High-probability task	High-probability task	Low-probability task	High-probability task	High-probability task	Low-probability task
4 × 4	3 × 6	12 × 6	2 × 5	8 × 3	19 × 4
5 × 8	7 × 4	23 × 5	6 × 4	8 × 4	43 × 3
9 × 2	3 × 5	38 × 5	7 × 7	9 × 7	33 × 4
2 × 2	6 × 5	52 × 7	7 × 3	4 × 3	21 × 2
8 × 2	9 × 3	15 × 4	6 × 6	4 × 5	45 × 6

9
RESPONSE EFFORT AND OVERCORRECTION

Todd Haydon, Cara Dillon, Alana M. Kennedy, and Tina Stanton-Chapman

Introduction

Children who display behavioral struggles in early childhood often continue to exhibit behavior problems in subsequent years of schooling if they do not receive early intervention (Hart et al., 2016). Specifically, young children who exhibit challenging behaviors are at an increased risk of experiencing negative relationships with peers and teachers, and are more likely to experience later academic failure (Coleman et al., 2013). Therefore, early identification and treatment of behavior problems is essential for students' long-term success in school.

Interventions targeting behavior problems in young learners range from universal prevention efforts to highly-individualized behavior support plans. Many early childhood education programs organize this continuum of services within a Positive Behavior Interventions and Supports (PBIS) framework. Within this framework, universal prevention efforts should meet the behavioral needs of the majority of children. Targeted and intensive interventions are developed for those students who continue to struggle in the classroom environment despite these class-wide supports. For the children who exhibit the most challenging or severe behavior problems, Functional Behavior Assessments (FBAs) are conducted to plan individualized intervention. FBAs are an evidence-based strategy used to identify components of the educational environment that can be altered so as to help prevent problem behaviors, reinforce appropriate behavior, and address problem behaviors consistently when they do occur (Dunlap & Fox, 2011).

The effort required to engage in a behavior is an important factor that influences individual's choices among the response options. Altering response effort has been shown to effectively reduce problem behavior in multiple settings. In a review of the literature surrounding response effort, Friman and Poling (1995) discussed the use of increasing response effort as an alternative to punishment-based interventions, as well as reducing response effort to promote desirable behaviors. However, punishment procedures are often utilized when reinforcement-based plans are not effective enough to decrease rates of a child's problem behavior. One such punishment procedure employed at this stage of intervention development is overcorrection.

Overcorrection

Overcorrection is defined as a behavioral strategy incorporating elements of positive punishment, which requires a student to "engage in effortful behavior that is directly or logically related to fixing the damage" caused by an individual's problem behavior (Cooper, Heron, & Heward, 2019, p. 796). There are two different types of overcorrection – restitution overcorrection and positive practice overcorrection. Restitution overcorrection is utilized when a student's problem behavior has caused damage to the educational environment and requires him or her to fix the effects of the behavior (Carey & Bucher, 1981). This approach may be used when a student vandalizes school property and is directed to clean the affected spaces *and then* do something additional to bring the environment to a better state than it was before. Positive practice overcorrection requires the learner to practice a pertinent behavior that is incompatible with the problem behavior (Carey & Bucher, 1981). For example, contingent upon an instance of running in the hallway, a student would practice appropriate walking behavior several times. Overcorrection has been contrasted with other punishment procedures because it includes an "educative" component for appropriate behaviors (Axelrod, Brantner, & Meddock, 1978). However, research to date has not demonstrated a consistent link between overcorrection and an increase in appropriate behaviors (Peters & Thompson, 2013).

Researchers have demonstrated that overcorrection, used alone and as part of a packaged intervention, can be implemented to effectively address inappropriate behaviors for preschool children (Doke & Epstein, 1975), school-aged students (Azrin & Powers, 1975), and adults who may exhibit adaptive and intellectual skill deficits (Singh & Bakker, 1984). Children whose behaviors have been targeted via overcorrection include typically functioning students served in a general education classroom as well as those with medical/educational disabilities (i.e., autism) served in an alternative education or hospital setting. General guidelines when using overcorrection procedures include providing straightforward descriptions of the overcorrection procedure to the student, close monitoring of the student throughout the entirety of the process, limiting praise for correct responding during the procedure, and implementing overcorrection as soon as possible after an occurrence of problem behavior (Cooper et al., 2019). Overcorrection is often used when other reinforcement-based interventions have been ineffective and when it is necessary to quickly terminate instances of problem behavior (McAdam & Knapp, 2013).

Overcorrection has been used to address a variety of behaviors, including self-injurious behavior (SIB) such as eye-gouging (Conley & Wolery, 1980), head-banging (Harris & Romanczyk, 1976), nail-picking (Freeman, Graham & Ritvo, 1975), and decreasing rates of disruption (Azrin & Powers, 1975). In addition, overcorrection has been used to address hand-flapping, toilet-training (e.g., Brown, & Middleton, 1998; Butler, 1976; Doan & Toussaint, 2016; Foxx & Azrin, 1973), pica (e.g., Singh & Bakker, 1984), stereotypy (Peters & Thompson, 2013), inappropriate hand-mouthing (e.g., thumb-sucking; Doke & Epstein, 1975), and inappropriate sexual behaviors (Clay, Bloom, & Lambert, 2018). Procedures used for SIB and stereotypy typically include the use of positive practice overcorrection with physical guidance. For example, contingent upon the occurrence of a SIB such as nail-picking, the participant's hands are physically guided by the interventionist down to the participant's sides and held there for a short interval of time. Alternatively, the individual may be guided to toys or other preferred items and physical guidance may be utilized to initiate appropriate interaction with the items in place of the inappropriate behavior (Peters & Thompson, 2013). Treatment of pica and hand-mouthing similarly incorporate positive practice overcorrection, often in conjunction with graduated guidance (Foxx & Martin, 1975). Procedures often include directing an individual to stop or expel the object, and then instructing him to engage in tooth brushing or mouth rinsing with an antiseptic for a specified period of time, contingent upon the target behavior (Doke & Epstein, 1975). The least amount of physical guidance needed to assist a child with engagement in the specified sequence is provided. Instances of inappropriate behavior (talking out of turn or leaving one's seat without permission) were followed by immediate or delayed overcorrection, which included practicing appropriate hand-raising and seated behavior during the students' recess. Another strategy that is helpful in reducing rates of responding is increasing the effort or force required to perform the behavior (Cooper et al., 2019)

Response Effort

Response effort is defined as the amount of exertion a person must utilize to effectively complete a specific task and has been hypothesized to be an important factor that influences individuals' choices among response options (Friman & Poling, 1995). Response effort increases the efficiency of appropriate behaviors and decreases the efficiency of inappropriate behaviors. This method serves as one alternative to punishment of inappropriate behavior that can reduce behavior without introducing an aversive stimulus or taking away an enjoyed stimulus (Friman & Poling, 1995). In a review of the literature surrounding response effort, Friman and Poling (1995) suggested the use of increasing response effort as an alternative to punishment-based interventions because it produces enduring and rapid decreases in behavior.

Altering response effort has been shown to effectively reduce problem behavior in multiple settings. For example, Zhou, Goff, and Iwata (2000) demonstrated that increasing the effort required to engage in hand-mouthing via the application of sleeves resulted in reduced self-injurious behavior and increased appropriate object manipulation in four adults. Piazza, Roane, Keeney, Boney, and Abt (2002) increased the response effort required to engage in pica items. In this study, engagement in pica items decreased when it was associated with more difficulty in accessing the pica item. In another study, researchers used wrist weights to make face-slapping more effortful and effectively reduce its occurrence (Van Houten, 1993). Increasing effort of response has been used successfully to decrease inappropriate behaviors including aggression, SIBs, thumb-sucking, and frequent task-switching (Friman & Poling, 1995). Researchers have demonstrated that lowering required effort for desired behaviors can result in increases in appropriate behavior in areas such as food intake (Patel, Piazza, Layer, Coleman, & Swartzwelder, 2005), recycling (O'Connor, Lerman, Fritz, & Hodde, 2010), and therapists' safety behaviors (Casella, Wilder, Neidert, Rey, Compton, & Chong et al., 2010).

While varying the level of effort can be a great tool for a practitioner to use, training appropriate behaviors and offering additional reinforcement in conjunction to changing response effort may be necessary. Fischetti et al. (2012) describes this in a study of compliance with children with autism. While the researchers decreased the distance to a toy bin when asking the children to put a toy away, that alone was not enough to increase compliance with the demand. Compliance increased when response effort was paired with a preferred edible; however, the edible enough was not sufficient to maintain the desired rate of compliance without response effort (Fischetti et al., 2012). This shows that response effort was essential to the intervention, but more components were vital to the overall success.

Researchers have utilized response effort paired with functional communication training to address aggressive behaviors (Richman, Wacker, & Winborn, 2001). Richman and colleagues targeted aggression with a three-year-old child with a developmental disability. The researchers used the intervention package to teach the child to use a request card or verbalize "please" rather than striking an adult. Results demonstrated that the mand card was more efficient than the aggression, but the verbalization was more efficient than the mand card as appropriate behaviors were at the highest level during the verbalization phase (Richman et al., 2001). Functional communication skills that require less response effort are more likely to be utilized by the target individual. This is important to consider when creating an intervention package because there may be behaviors with lower response cost that can be used. For example, researchers have used functional communication training for accessing "help" (i.e., pointing to a "help" sign) to obtain edibles to determine which communication required the least response effort (Lira, Browder, & Sigafoos, 1998). The authors suggest developing interventions that would help children acquire the most appropriate responses and require the least response effort.

Case Study

Background Information

Tammy was a three-year-old African-American female with Down syndrome attending preschool for the first time at a learning center operated by a local university. Tammy had limited language ability and often pinched or grabbed others to access play or gain attention from peers.

The inclusive preschool accepted students of a large demographic. The school uses a combination of child-directed and teacher-based learning and follows the High Scope Curriculum (i.e., plan-do-review unstructured time, small-group activities, large-group activities). Each classroom serves approximately 15 children with a lead teacher, two assistant teachers, and one student teacher. Related service providers (i.e., speech-language pathologists, occupational therapists, physical therapists) provide push-in services for those students who are scheduled for such services on their Individualized Education Plan (IEP). Tammy is enrolled in a half-day classroom with 11 peers, a lead teacher, and an assistant teacher. Peers without disabilities were four years old while peers with disabilities ranged from three to five years old. There are three students with disabilities including Tammy. The classrooms are equipped with multiple exploratory areas (e.g., block center, manipulative center, dramatic play center) for students to interact with, and the students also had teacher-led access to the playground and motor room.

Description of the Problem Behavior

The school psychologist conducted a problem-identification interview with the classroom teachers and determined that Tammy would pinch (use fingers to apply pressure on another person's body), grab (using one or two hands or arms to encircle a body part of another person and apply pressure), or push (use one or two flat hands on another's body, which causes movement on that person's body) peers in the classroom or on the playground. Collectively, these behaviors were referred to as aggression. The teachers were unsure of the function of the behavior but noted that Tammy often receives attention from peers and teachers as a consequence. The school psychologist then observed Tammy in her classroom environment to collect more information about the behavior with an A-B-C recording and frequency recording of the behavior (Cooper et al., 2019). The school psychologist noted that both attention and

TABLE 9.1 A-B-C Recording Data from Classroom Observations

Activity	Antecedent	Behavior	Consequence
Independent Play	Peer (P) takes toy car from Tammy (T)	T follows P and pinches P's arm	P drops toy and T takes toy
Motor Room	Staff (S) turns from T to talk to a P	T pushes P to the ground	S tells T that pushing is not nice and discusses saying sorry
Independent Play	Class is told to find an area to play in	T sits beside P playing with blocks and grabs P's arm and reaches for blocks	P gives T three blocks
Outdoor Play	Ps are sitting at a picnic table playing with a dollhouse	T pinches one P on the back three times	P moves from picnic bench and T sits down
Outdoor Play	S is talking to a P about leaves	T grabs P's wrist and takes leaf from P	S asks T to return the leaf and helps T find her own leaf

access to play were consequences of Tammy's behaviors, and this is demonstrated in the A-B-C recordings in Table 9.1.

Problem Analysis

The school psychologist hypothesized that both attention from peers and teachers as well as access to play were the functions of Tammy's behavior. Tammy pinched, grabbed, or pushed during unstructured times (i.e., plan-do-review) when she did not have attention from others and when she was not given a task. These unstructured times showed the most instances of the target behaviors. Tammy's teachers agreed on the hypothesized functions of the behavior. The school psychologist further hypothesized that Tammy uses these behaviors to access attention and play because of her limited language ability.

Intervention Goals

In collaboration with the lead teacher, the short-term goal of the intervention is to reduce the target behavior of aggression from an average of six instances per hour to four instances per hour over the course of two weeks and be able to use the picture cards appropriately for 30% of attempts. The long-term goal is that aggression will be reduced to zero, consistent with peer behavior, and Tammy will use the picture cards appropriately for 90% of attempts to access play or attention.

Measurement of Target Behaviors, Data Collection Strategies, and Progress Monitoring

Aggression

The school psychologist and the lead teacher collected frequency of the target behaviors for one hour during unstructured play times. Aggression includes pinching (using fingers to apply pressure to another person), grabbing (using hands to apply pressure to another person), and pushing (using two hands against another person that results in their body moving). These behaviors were frequent but short in duration, which makes frequency counting an appropriate measure (Cooper et al., 2019). Because these behaviors could be dangerous, data on the target variables were collected twice a week to closely monitor progress. The problem-solving team agreed that the intervention would be altered if Tammy did not reach the short-term goals described above.

Appropriate Use of Cards

Appropriate use of the card system was also recorded. Appropriate card use included finding the correct card on the lanyard and showing another individual the card without exhibiting aggression. The lead teacher calculated a rate using the formula: (appropriate uses of a card/ (appropriate uses of the card + target behavior)) × 100.

Intervention Plan

The school psychologist and the lead teacher determined that a functional intervention would be most appropriate for Tammy. The school psychologist chose a picture exchange system that would allow Tammy to exchange cards for access to attention or play. This intervention would still serve the function but in an appropriate manner. Tammy already used picture cards to access food, water, and the bathroom. Further, picture exchange systems have been used successfully with children with Down syndrome that have limited language (Davis, Camarata, & Camarata, 2016; Foreman & Crews, 1998). Overcorrection will be implemented when a target behavior occurs to overcorrect for the use of the picture card.

To promote appropriate communication skills, Tammy was trained in the use of picture cards prior to the intervention. She is able to successfully use cards to access food, water, the bathroom, and general help. The lead teacher was familiar with the system since Tammy had used cards to communicate those needs. The school psychologist then trained Tammy on two additional cards: play and hug. These cards would allow Tammy to access play and attention from peers or staff. Cards were on a ring attached to a lanyard that Tammy carried with her at all times, and these cards were added during baseline. Tammy was trained to use the cards in similar ways described in Davis, Camarata, and Camarata (2016) and

Foreman and Crews (1998). The school psychologist would entice Tammy with play or turn away from her to entice her to seek attention. When Tammy would reach out to engage with the school psychologist, the lead teacher would direct Tammy's hand to take the correct card and hand it to the school psychologist. The school psychologist would then reward Tammy's correct responses with play or a hug and name the card Tammy gave her.

Once Tammy was able to use the cards without prompting in this contrived setting, the lead teacher would teach the other students what the cards meant when Tammy gave them a card. This occurred during circle time. The lead teacher showed the class the cards and explained what each meant. The lead teacher then practiced with the class by handing them a card and asking them what it meant. The class was 85% accurate after two 10-minute sessions. An accurate peer was then used to generalize the card use to students in the classroom. The lead teacher would watch Tammy interact with peers. Praise was offered when she used the cards correctly. If Tammy did not use the card correctly or exhibited a target behavior instead, the lead teacher would use overcorrection to promote practice of the cards. The lead teacher would prompt the use of the card, provide praise when the card was used, and allow 30 seconds of play or a hug. This overcorrection process was repeated two additional times.

Response effort was also implemented to reduce pinching and grabbing behaviors. These behaviors could be dangerous to peers, so increasing the effort to perform those behaviors was key to ensuring the safety of Tammy's peers. Mittens with padding were placed on Tammy's hands so that pinching and grabbing with enough force to harm peers was more difficult to perform. Tammy would have to take off the mittens to perform the target behaviors, but Tammy could still effectively use the cards as they were on a ring and could still be flipped through. In this way, the target behaviors were no longer as efficient as using the cards.

Intervention Fidelity and Interobserver Agreement

The school psychologist collected adherence data through a checklist completed while observing the intervention. Adherence was monitored one day a week (20% of interventions) to ensure fidelity of the intervention. While training Tammy to use the picture cards, adherence averaged 90%. During the intervention, adherence averaged was 95% with a goal of at least 90%.

Interobserver agreement (IOA) was taken with the school psychologist and the lead teacher in the classroom setting described above for 30% of intervals during the baseline and intervention phases, which is greater than the recommended 20% (Kennedy, 2005). Total count IOA was used wherein the smaller count was divided by the larger count and then multiplied by 100 to achieve the percentage IOA. Observer agreement was an average of 94.3% for aggression and 95.8% for card use, which is over the 80% standard (Kennedy, 2005).

Intervention Outcome Data

The average baseline rate of Tammy's behavior was six instances of the target behavior per hour as seen in Figure 9.1. After two weeks, Tammy demonstrated the target behavior of aggression three instances per hour. Figure 9.2 shows the percentage of attempts where Tammy effectively used the picture exchange cards. During baseline, Tammy was not using the cards. However, following training, Tammy used the cards appropriately for approximately 50% of attempts. Tammy did meet the short-term goal set by the school psychologist and the lead teacher. After four weeks of intervention, Tammy demonstrated aggression at zero instances per hour. Tammy used the cards appropriately for 100% of attempts. Tammy did meet the long-term goal set by the school psychologist and the lead teacher.

Summary of Intervention Effects

Based on the data presented above, the intervention was effective in reducing Tammy's aggression towards peers and increasing an acceptable replacement behavior. Levels were significantly different between the baseline and intervention period. Initially during the intervention phase, levels of aggression remained similar to baseline levels for the first week of the intervention. The lead teacher and the assistant teacher discussed this matter, and this was most likely due to

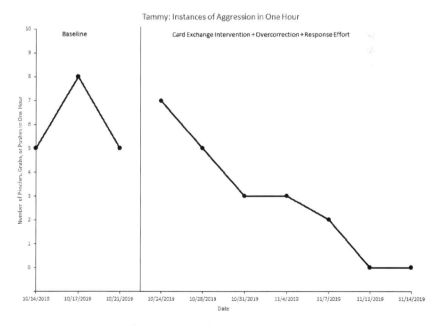

FIGURE 9.1 Instances of aggression per hour

138 Haydon et al.

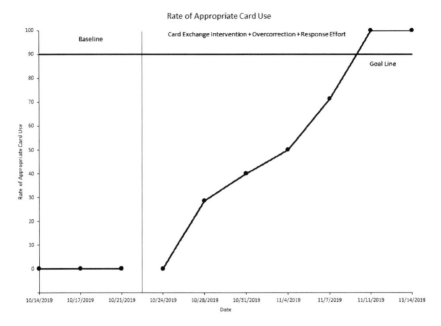

FIGURE 9.2 Rate of appropriate card use in one hour

Tammy still acquiring the card use skill and generalizing it to the classroom. However, Tammy still met the short-term goal, and the intervention remained the same. Tammy continued to use the card skill appropriately and met the long-term goal as well.

Intervention Acceptability

Social validity was measured through the Adapted Version of the Intervention Rating Profile (Adapted from Witt & Elliot, 1985), which was completed by the lead teacher to assess for intervention acceptability. The teachers scored the intervention acceptability as a 78 on the scale from 15 to 90 points as seen in Table 9.2. This number suggests that the intervention was high in acceptability. The intervention was created in a collaborative effort by the school psychologist and the lead teacher, which may have increased the level of acceptability of the intervention.

Intervention Considerations

This case study demonstrates the use of response effort and overcorrection as an intervention package to improve appropriate communication for a preschooler with Down syndrome. While a component analysis was not used to determine

TABLE 9.2 Social Validity Scale: Intervention Rating Scale Profile-15

Item	Rating
1. This was an acceptable intervention for the child's need.	Strongly Agree
2. Most teachers would find this intervention appropriate for children with similar needs.	Agree
3. This intervention proved effective in supporting the child's needs	Strongly Agree
4. I would suggest the use of this intervention to other teachers.	Agree
5. The child's needs were severe enough to warrant the use of this intervention.	Agree
6. Most teachers would find this intervention suitable for the needs of this child.	Strongly Agree
7. I would be willing to use this intervention in the classroom setting.	Agree
8. This intervention would be appropriate for a variety of children.	Slightly Agree
9. This intervention was consistent with those I have used in the classroom setting.	Agree
10. The intervention was a fair way to handle the child's needs.	Agree
11. This intervention was reasonable for the needs of the child.	Agree
12. I liked the procedures used in this intervention.	Agree
13. This intervention was an appropriate way to handle this child's needs.	Agree
14. Overall, this intervention was beneficial for the child.	Strongly Agree

which aspects of the intervention were most effective, these intervention components have been found to be useful as parts of other interventions relating to communication training. The student was pretrained in the use of communication cards, and therefore required less training than another student who has not been exposed to the system prior. Moreover, this student attended a preschool with a low staff to student ratio where all intervention components could be implemented with fidelity without removing staff from other students. This intervention package used evidence-based practices to target the student's needs.

Conclusion

Tammy, a preschool student with Down syndrome, exhibited pinching, grabbing, and pushing behaviors to peers in order to gain attention and access play. The school psychologist and Tammy's teacher collaborated to create an intervention package with components of communication training, overcorrection, and response effort. While Tammy initially demonstrated similar levels of aggression during the intervention, Tammy met the short-term goal of reduced aggression and increased use of the communication cards. Tammy was then able to meet the long-term goal of zero aggression and above 90% card use. The lead teacher rated the intervention as highly acceptable.

References

Axelrod, S., Brantner, J. P., & Meddock, T. D. (1978). Overcorrection: A review and critical analysis. *The Journal of Special Education*, 12(4), 367–391. doi:10.1177/002246697801200404

Azrin, N. H., & Powers, M. A. (1975). Eliminating classroom disturbances of emotionally disturbed children by positive practice procedures. *Behavior Therapy*, 6(4), 525–534. doi:10.1016/S0005-7894(75)80009-8

Brown, G., & Middleton, H. (1998). Use of Self-as-a-model to Promote Generalization and Maintenance of the Reduction of Self-stimulation in a Child with Mental Retardation. *Education and Training in Mental Retardation and Developmental Disabilities*, 33(1), 76–80.

Butler, J. F. (1976). Toilet training a child with spina bifida. *Journal of Behavior Therapy and Experimental Psychiatry*, 7(1), 63–65. doi:10.1016/0005-7916(76)90045-8

Carey, R. G., & Bucher, B. (1981). identifying the educative and suppressive effects of positive practice and restitutional overcorrection. *Journal of Applied Behavior Analysis*, 14(1), 71–80. doi:10.1901/jaba.1981.14-71

Casella, S. E., Wilder, D. A., Neidert, P., Rey, C., Compton, M., & Chong, I. (2010). The effects of response effort on safe performance by therapists at an autism treatment facility. *Journal of Applied Behavior Analysis*, 43, 729–734. doi:10.1901/jaba.2010.43-729

Clay, C. J., Bloom, S. E., & Lambert, J. M. (2018). Behavioral interventions for inappropriate sexual behavior in individuals with developmental disabilities and acquired brain injury: A review. *American Journal on Intellectual and Developmental Disabilities*, 123(3), 254–282. doi:10.1352/1944-7558-123.3.254

Coleman, J. C., Crosby, M. G., Irwin, H. K., Dennis, L. R., Simpson, C. G., & Rose, C. A. (2013). Preventing challenging behaviors in preschool: Effective strategies for classroom teachers. *Young Exceptional Children*, 16(3), 3–10. doi:10.1177/1096250612464641

Conley, O. S., & Wolery, M. R. (1980). Treatment by overcorrection of self-injurious eye gouging in preschool blind children. *Journal of Behavior Therapy and Experimental Psychiatry*, 11(2), 121–125. doi:10.1016/0005-7916(80)90009-9

Cooper, J., Heron, T., & Heward, W. (2019). *Applied behavior analysis* (3rd edition). Columbus: Prentice Hall/Merrill.

Davis, T. N., Camarata, S., & Camarata, M. (2016). Cross modal generalization of receptive and expressive vocabulary in children with Down syndrome. *Journal of Down Syndrome & Chromosome Abnormalities*, 2(1), 1–9.

Doan, D., & Toussaint, K. A. (2016). A parent-oriented approach to rapid toilet training. *International Electronic Journal of Elementary Education*, 9(2), 473–486.

Doke, L. A., & Epstein, L. H. (1975). Oral overcorrection: Side effects and extended applications. *Journal of Experimental Child Psychology*, 20(3), 496–511. doi:10.1016/0022-0965(75)90122-8

Dunlap, G., & Fox, L. (2011). Function-based interventions for children with challenging behavior. *Journal of Early Intervention*, 33(4), 333–343. doi:10.1177/1053815111429971

Fischetti, A. T., Wilder, D. A., Myers, K., Leon-Enriquez, Y., Sinn, S., & Rodriguez, R. (2012). An evaluation of evidence-based interventions to increase compliance among children with Autism. *Journal of Applied Behavior Analysis*, 45(4), 859–863. doi:10.1901/jaba.2012.45-859

Foreman, P., & Crews, G. (1998). Using augmentative communication with infants and young children with Down syndrome. *Down Syndrome Research and Practice*, 5(1), 16–25. doi:10.3104/reports.71

Foxx, R. M., & Azrin, N. H. (1973). Dry pants: A rapid method of toilet training children. *Behaviour Research and Therapy*, 11(4), 435–442. doi:10.1016/0005-7967(73)90102-2

Foxx, R. M., & Martin, E. D. (1975). Treatment of scavenging behavior (coprophagy and pica) by overcorrection. *Behaviour Research and Therapy, 13*, 153–162. 10.1016/0005-7967(75)90009-1

Freeman, B. J., Graham, V., & Ritvo, E. R. (1975). Reduction of self-destructive behavior by overcorrection. *Psychological Reports, 37*(2), 446–446. doi:10.2466/pr0.1975.37.2.446

Friman, P. C., & Poling, A. (1995). Making life easier with effort: Basic findings and applied research on response effort. *Journal of Applied Behavior Analysis, 28*, 583–590. doi:10.1901/jaba.1995.28-583

Harris, S. L., & Romanczyk, R. G. (1976). Treating self-injurious behavior of a retarded child by overcorrection. *Behavior Therapy, 7*(2), 235–239. doi:10.1016/S0005-7894(76)80281-X

Hart, K. C., Graziano, P. A., Kent, K. M., Kuriyan, A., Garcia, A., Rodriguez, M., & Pelham, W. E. (2016). Early intervention for children with behavior problems in summer settings: Results from a pilot evaluation in head start preschools. *Journal of Early Intervention, 38*(2), 92–117. doi:10.1177/1053815116645923

Kennedy, C. H. (2005). *Single-case designs for educational research*. Boston: Pearson/A & B.

Lira, L., Browder, D.M., & Sigafoos, J. (1998). The role of response effort and motion study in functionally equivalent task designs and alternatives. *Journal of Behavioral Education, 8*, 81–102. doi:10.1023/A:1022816824572

McAdam D., & Knapp V. M. (2013). Overcorrection. In Volkmar F.R. (Ed), *Encyclopedia of autism spectrum disorders*. Springer, New York, NY

O'Connor, R. T., Lerman, D. C., Fritz, J. N., & Hodde, H. B. (2010). Effects of number and location of bins on plastic recycling at a university. *Journal of Applied Behavior Analysis, 43*, 711–715. doi:10.1901/jaba.2010.43-711

Patel, M.R., Piazza, C.C., Layer, S.A., Coleman, R., & Swartzwelder, D.M. (2005). A systematic evaluation of food textures to decrease packing and increase oral intake in children with pediatric feeding disorders. *Journal of Applied Behavior Analysis, 38*, 89–100.

Peters, L. C., & Thompson, R. H. (2013). Some indirect effects of positive practice overcorrection. *Journal of Applied Behavior Analysis, 46*(3), 613–625. doi:10.1002/jaba.63

Piazza, C.C., Roane, H.s., Keeney, K.M., Boney, B.R., & Abt, K.A. (2002). Varying response effort in the treatment of pica maintained by automatic reinforcement. *Journal of Applied Behavior Analysis, 35*, 233–246

Richman, D. M., Wacker, D. P., & Winborn, L. (2001). Response efficiency during functional communication training: Effects of effort on response allocation. *Journal of Applied Behavior Analysis, 34*(1), 73–76.

Singh, N. N., & Bakker, L. W. (1984). Suppression of pica by overcorrection and physical restraint: A comparative analysis. *Journal of Autism and Developmental Disorders, 14*(3), 331–341. doi:10.1007/BF02409583

Van Houten, R. (1993). The use of wrist weights to reduce self-injury maintained by sensory reinforcement. *Journal of Applied Behavior Analysis, 26*(2), 197–203. doi:10.1901/jaba.1993.26-197

Witt, J. C., & Elliott, S. N. (1985). Acceptability of classroom intervention strategies. In TR Kratochwill (Ed.), *Advances in school psychology* (Vol. 4, pp. 251–288). Hillsdale, NJ: Lawrence Erlbaum Associates

Zhou, L., Goff, G.A., & Iwata, B.A. (2000). Effects of increased response effort on self-injury and object manipulation as competing responses. *Journal of Applied Behavior Analysis, 33*, 29–40.

10
RESPONSE COST RAFFLE AND MYSTERY MOTIVATOR

Gina Coffee and Sally Whitelock

Introduction

Masterful teachers have skills and knowledge that make teaching and learning look easy and straightforward; however, teaching in today's public schools is a complex process. High-quality education requires teachers to support 25 or more students from various cultural backgrounds and experiences, create a positive and engaging classroom culture, have expertise in the academic content and grade-level standards, understand best instructional practices, respond to the many learning and social–emotional needs of each student, and regularly assess and differentiate instruction to ensure that each student grows academically. Teachers consistently report that students' disruptive behaviors are one of their biggest frustrations, which negatively impact the learning of not only students who are having behavioral challenges, but also the learning of others and the teacher's ability to provide quality instruction. Therefore, implementation of effective, evidence-based, social/emotional/behavioral interventions is necessary to support teachers in meeting the educational needs of all students. Additionally, because evidence-based interventions are often not implemented with fidelity and are not sustained over time, the collaboration of the school administrator, school psychologist, and teacher is, therefore, necessary in order to advise and coach teachers to administer evidence-based interventions, especially class-wide interventions, with fidelity in a quality and sustainable manner.

One way for teachers to proactively address behavioral challenges that might either occur frequently or with multiple students in a classroom is through the implementation of a class-wide behavioral intervention. Two class-wide interventions that have been shown to be effective in addressing behavioral challenges are Response Cost Raffle and Mystery Motivator (Burns, Riley-Tillman, & Rathvon, 2017). Because both interventions can be designed as group contingencies, they are especially fitting for use with whole classrooms or with small groups of students.

When a teacher uses Response Cost Raffle with whole classrooms, the intervention begins with each student receiving a specified number of tickets at the beginning of the intervention period. Then, throughout the intervention period, tickets are removed when students engage in challenging behaviors, and remaining tickets are entered into the raffle ticket box. At the end of the week (or each intervention period), a ticket is removed from the raffle ticket box, and the student whose name is on the ticket has the opportunity to choose a prize from the raffle prize list. If a ticket with the word "group" is drawn, then the whole class may receive a class prize such as a classroom party, free time, or a homework pass. Response Cost Raffle can easily be adapted for use with individuals, small groups, or teams. At an individual level, Response Cost Raffle has been shown to be effective in addressing junior high students' (n = 4) engagement in disruptive behaviors (Proctor & Morgan, 1991). Similarly, use of a response cost intervention with a preschool classroom also resulted in a reduction of disruptive behaviors (Conyers et al., 2004).

Incorporating similar principles of positive reinforcement, Mystery Motivator gives whole classrooms the opportunity to earn meaningful rewards. However, unlike Response Cost Raffle, the opportunity to earn a reward is intermittent, not fixed (i.e., students do not have an opportunity to earn a reward at the end of each intervention period). To begin, the teacher creates a calendar for the class and randomly inserts a mystery M on certain days to designate a Mystery Motivator day (the M is not visible to the class, as it is either covered with a note card or written with invisible ink). The class then defines a class goal (e.g., 75% assignment completion). At the end of each intervention period, the class determines if it has met the goal, and if it has, a student reveals whether or not that particular day has an M. If it does, the class chooses a reward from a reinforcement chart. If it does not, the teacher praises the class for effort and reminds them that they will have another opportunity to earn a reward during the next intervention period. Studies have demonstrated the effectiveness of Mystery Motivator in addressing disruptive behaviors within preschool (e.g., Murphy, Theodore, Aloiso, Alric-Edwards, & Hughes, 2007), elementary (e.g., Kowalewicz & Coffee, 2014), and secondary (e.g., Schanding & Sterling-Turner, 2010) classrooms.

The case study that follows illustrates collaboration between a mental health team (school psychologist, school psychology intern, and school psychology practicum student), two elementary classroom co-teachers, and a school principal to implement, monitor, and evaluate class-wide outcomes of Response Cost Raffle and Mystery Motivator through an alternating-treatments design (Kazdin, 2011).

Case Study

Background Information

Sunflower Elementary School is a neighborhood elementary school with 590 students from early childhood education through fifth grade. Each grade level has 3–4 classrooms, with a teacher-student ratio of 1:27, and all students at Sunflower Elementary School receive academic, behavioral, and social–emotional support within a multi-tiered system. Across grade levels, Tier 1 academic instruction is primarily delivered by classroom teachers. Additionally, students receive Tier 2 and Tier 3 academic support from instructional interventionists and from special education teachers who rotate between classrooms and push in to classrooms to co-teach with classroom teachers and to deliver differentiated instruction in small group settings within classrooms.

Behavioral and social–emotional supports are also primarily delivered by classroom teachers and further supported by the school's Positive Behavioral Interventions and Supports (PBIS) coordinator, school psychologist, school psychology intern, school psychology practicum student, and school administration (principal and assistant principal). At Tier 1, Sunflower Elementary School aligns with a School-Wide Positive Behavior Support model, and all classrooms use Class Dojo (Class Dojo, 2020) as a framework for supporting positive behaviors and for facilitating communication with teachers and families. In addition, classroom teachers hold daily morning meetings focused on building community, and the PBIS coordinator and school psychologist deliver class-wide lessons to each classroom focused on social–emotional coping, mindfulness, problem-solving/conflict resolution, and bullying prevention. Finally, the PBIS coordinator and school staff designed and oversee structured Playworks recess periods to increase opportunities for prosocial play (Playworks, 2020).

At Tiers 2 and 3, the school psychologist, school psychology intern, and school psychology practicum student (Sunflower Elementary School's mental health team) facilitate social–emotional learning (SEL) small groups focused on supporting the development of coping skills and prosocial behaviors. Groups are composed of students in grades 3–5 whose internalizing and/or total score on the universal administration of the BASC-3 Behavioral and Emotional Screening System (BESS; Kamphaus & Reynolds, 2015) in the fall fell in the very elevated range and of students in grades 1–2 who have been referred by grade-level teams. The mental health team also provides individualized direct intervention to students who are in need of additional supports and consistently consults with classroom teachers to either facilitate transfer of skills students learn in sessions with the mental health team to the classroom or indirectly support students' acquisition and maintenance of behavioral skills within the classroom. Finally, the mental health team and school administration partner to support student crises and use of restorative practices related to discipline.

Recently, Ms. Munro and Ms. Montoya, co-teachers on the second grade team at Sunflower Elementary School, contacted their instructional coach (Ms. Dunne, the school principal) and the school psychologist (Dr. Coffield) seeking guidance about behaviors that are occurring during math. They had noticed that several students in the classroom were engaging in similar behaviors, and they were worried that these behaviors were interfering with all students' learning. Ms. Munro and Ms. Montoya co-teach math each afternoon, alternating who teaches the whole-group lesson and who teaches small groups of students. The physical arrangement of the classroom includes flexible seating with options for students to sit/work on the carpet at the front of the classroom, lowered desks with seating on the floor, standard desks with seating on standard chairs or ergonomic stools, and small tables with seating on standard chairs, and the math period consists of 30 students. Behaviors Ms. Munro and Ms. Montoya were consistently noticing during math, especially during independent work time, included making audible sounds and talking with peers about off-task topics, drawing, playing with items in their desks, swiveling around in chairs, and looking around. Independent work time occurs daily for approximately 20–30 minutes following whole-group math instruction.

Description of the Problem Behavior

The mental health team and Ms. Dunne collaboratively conducted a problem-identification interview with Ms. Munro and Ms. Montoya to identify and define the keystone target behavior. Ms. Munro and Ms. Montoya described the behaviors they have been observing during independent work time and estimated that approximately 75% of the students engaged in off-task behaviors for the majority of the period. Together, the team hypothesized that by first addressing the making audible sounds and talking with peers behaviors, then perhaps the additional identified behaviors would also decrease and engagement in academic tasks would increase. Making audible sounds and talking with peers during independent work time was identified as *off-task verbal behavior* and defined as "any audible verbalizations that are not permitted and/or are not related to an assigned academic task" (Shapiro, 2011, p. 44). Examples included making any audible sounds such as humming, singing, or calling out and talking with peers about any topic without teacher permission. Ms. Munro and Ms. Montoya shared that students typically begin talking with one another immediately following the whole-group lesson when the teachers give students instructions to independently work on math assignments. Conversely, *on-task verbal behavior* was identified as quietly working on the math task assigned by a teacher.

The school psychologist and school psychology practicum student conducted systematic observations of off-task verbal and on-task verbal behaviors by adapting the Behavioral Observation of Students in Schools (BOSS) model for use with whole classrooms (Shapiro, 2011). Baseline observations were conducted for

30 minutes during independent work time in math each day for one week. Off-task verbal behaviors were measured and recorded every 15 seconds using partial-interval recording, and on-task verbal behaviors were measured and recorded every 15 seconds using momentary time sampling. Interobserver agreement (IOA) was 100%, and daily baseline data are displayed in Figure 10.1. Across the week of baseline data collection, students were engaged in off-task verbal behaviors during independent work time for an average of 80% of observed intervals and engaged in on-task verbal behaviors for an average of 20% of observed intervals.

To supplement data collected via the BOSS, the school psychologist and the school psychology intern completed A-B-C narrative observations during independent work time in math to identify the environmental factors around students' engagement in off-task verbal behaviors (Table 10.1). The primary antecedent immediately preceding students' engagement in off-task verbal behaviors was Ms. Munro and/or Ms. Montoya finishing a whole-group lesson and giving students instructions to independently work on math assignments. Following engagement in the keystone target behavior, students immediately accessed conversations with peers while teachers were either working with small groups of students or walking around the classroom to help students. When teachers verbally redirected students by instructing them to "reset," students worked quietly for 1–3 minutes and gradually began talking again. Students also worked quietly when they sat with a small group and one of their teachers at the kidney table, when one of their teachers stood near them, or when their teachers specifically praised them for working quietly.

Finally, teachers also calculated the percentage of completed math assignments during independent work time each day (one assignment per student per day)

TABLE 10.1 Example Data from A-B-C Narrative Observations

Antecedent	Behavior	Consequence
Ms. Munro finished whole-group lesson and instructed students to work on math assignments	Students talked with peers while transitioning to desks and continued talking	Ms. Munro verbally instructed students to "reset" and begin working on the assignment
Ms. Munro walked around the classroom assisting students	Students talked with peers	Ms. Munro verbally praised students who were working quietly
Ms. Montoya worked with a small group of students at the kidney table	Students working at the kidney table worked quietly	Ms. Montoya verbally praised students who were working quietly

Subject: Math (Independent Work Time)

during the baseline data collection period. On average, 30% of students completed the math assignment each day.

Problem Analysis

At the end of the week, the mental health team, Ms. Dunne, and the classroom teachers met again to review and analyze the baseline data. Together, they hypothesized that students' engagement in off-task verbal behaviors were maintained by accessing peer attention and avoiding completion of math assignments. Conversely, students' engagement in on-task verbal behaviors were maintained by teacher proximity and teacher attention (e.g., instructions to "reset" and specific praise). Given that math instruction and assignments were differentiated and aligned with each student's instructional level, the team decided that task difficulty did not influence students' behaviors during independent work time.

Given that the data collected and analyzed during baseline data collection suggested class-wide behavioral challenges, the mental health team described two class-wide intervention options with Ms. Munro and Ms. Montoya: Response Cost Raffle and Mystery Motivator (Burns et al., 2017). After reviewing and discussing the options, Ms. Munro and Ms. Montoya expressed an interest in both interventions and asked the mental health team and Ms. Dunne if it would be possible to try both to determine which is most acceptable to their students, is most feasible to implement during independent work time, and is most effective at addressing the target behaviors. The team agreed to collaboratively design a plan for the classroom teachers to implement both interventions.

Intervention Goals

Using the baseline data to inform next steps, the mental health team, Ms. Dunne, and the classroom teachers identified three goals: one goal focused on decreasing engagement in off-task verbal behaviors, a second goal focused on increasing engagement in on-task verbal behaviors, and a final goal focused on increasing work completion. The class would engage in off-task verbal behaviors during no more than 60% of observed intervals after three weeks of intervention, no more than 40% of observed intervals after six weeks of intervention, and no more than 20% of observed intervals after eight weeks of intervention. In addition, the class would engage in on-task verbal behaviors during at least 40% of observed intervals after three weeks of intervention, at least 60% of observed intervals after six weeks of intervention, and at least 80% of observed intervals after eight weeks of intervention. Finally, at least 60% of students would complete the daily assignment after three weeks of intervention and at least 80% of students would complete the daily assignment after six weeks of intervention.

Measurement of Target Behaviors, Data Collection Strategies, and Progress Monitoring

The team agreed that the mental health team would complete systematic observations of off-task verbal and on-task verbal behaviors daily for 30 minutes during independent work time. Consistent with baseline data collection, the mental health team completed observations of off-task verbal and on-task verbal behaviors using the Behavioral Observation of Students in School (BOSS; Shapiro, 2011) and calculated the percentage of observed intervals students engaged in the behaviors during each observation period. The school psychologist, school psychology intern, and school psychology practicum students rotated observations so that each team member completed an equal number of observations distributed across different intervention phases. To measure completion of assignments, Ms. Munro and Ms. Montoya independently tallied the number of completed assignments each day and calculated a percentage of completion.

Intervention Plan

Given Ms. Munro and Ms. Montoya's interest in implementing both the Response Cost Raffle and the Mystery Motivator interventions class-wide, the intervention plan consisted of two phases and three subphases within an alternating-treatments design (Kazdin, 2011). Phase I was the baseline data collection that occurred prior to intervention implementation (Week 1). Phase II was the intervention phase that included three subphases (Weeks 2-9): Response Cost Raffle, Baseline, and Mystery Motivator. During Phase II, the two interventions were counterbalanced within each week to minimize carryover effects, to maximize exposure to each intervention, and to allow for the inclusion of a brief baseline subphase throughout implementation. Ms. Munro and Ms. Montoya implemented Response Cost Raffle on Monday and Tuesday and Mystery Motivator on Thursday and Friday of Weeks 2, 4, 6, and 8. Conversely, they implemented Mystery Motivator on Monday and Tuesday and Response Cost Raffle on Thursday and Friday of Weeks 3, 5, 7, and 9. To balance intervention implementation, Ms. Munro and Ms. Montoya each led implementation for each intervention only one day per week. For example, during Week 2, Ms. Munro implemented Response Cost Raffle on Monday, while Ms. Montoya implemented Response Cost Raffle on Tuesday. Similarly, Ms. Munro implemented Mystery Motivator on Thursday, while Ms. Montoya implemented Mystery Motivator on Friday. The classroom teachers alternated days in subsequent weeks. Neither intervention was implemented on Wednesday, so one day each week served as a baseline subphase. To prepare for and carry out implementation, the instructional coach/school principal offered Ms. Munro and Ms. Montoya additional planning time in their schedules as well as supplies and resources for implementation.

Before beginning Phase II, the mental health team taught, modeled, and coached preparation and implementation of each intervention, and the classroom teachers described the interventions to their math class. Specifically, at the beginning of the intervention periods for the separate Response Cost Raffle and Mystery Motivator subphases, the classroom teachers announced to the class which intervention would be implemented that day, displayed the corresponding visuals (e.g., Raffle Prize List, Mystery Motivator calendar), and distributed relevant materials (e.g., raffle tickets).

Intervention Fidelity and Interobserver Agreement

Ms. Munro and Ms. Montoya measured and recorded intervention fidelity on two separate intervention fidelity checklists: the Response Cost Raffle Daily Fidelity Checklist (Appendix A) and the Mystery Motivator Daily Fidelity Checklist (Appendix B). A member of the mental health team also measured and recorded intervention fidelity by simultaneously using the same checklists one time per week for each intervention. For example, during Week 2, the mental health team measured (along with, yet independent from, a classroom teacher) intervention fidelity of Response Cost Raffle on Tuesday and intervention fidelity of Mystery Motivator on Thursday. Observations of intervention fidelity were balanced across the two teachers' implementation of the two interventions. Point-by-point agreement (Kazdin, 2011) was calculated by dividing the number of agreements on the checklist between a mental health team member and a classroom teacher by the sum of agreements and disagreements and multiplying by 100. Intervention fidelity was 98% during the observed sessions for Response Cost Raffle and 97% for Mystery Motivator, indicating strong fidelity during implementation of both interventions.

IOA using point-by-point agreement (Kazdin, 2011) was also calculated for observations of off-task verbal and on-task verbal behaviors, as well as work completion. Thirty percent of observations within each intervention phase and subphase were completed by two mental health team members to establish an estimate of IOA. IOA of off-task verbal behaviors across 30% of observations was 99% and of on-task verbal behaviors was 100%, indicating reliable observation data. Similarly, interrater agreement between Ms. Munro and Ms. Montoya's daily measurement of completed assignments was 100%, indicating reliable work completion data.

Intervention Outcome Data

Off-Task Verbal Behaviors

Student outcome data for off-task and on-task verbal behaviors are displayed in Figures 10.1 and 10.2, respectively. Baseline data collected during Phase I (Week 1) showed that students engaged in off-task verbal behaviors during an

150 Coffee and Whitelock

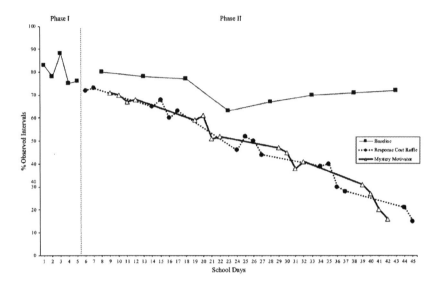

FIGURE 10.1 Off-task verbal behaviors. Each data point represents the percentage of observed intervals students in the classroom engaged in off-task verbal behaviors during math independent work time each school day of Phase I (Week 1) and Phase II (Weeks 2-9). Every five school days represent one school week

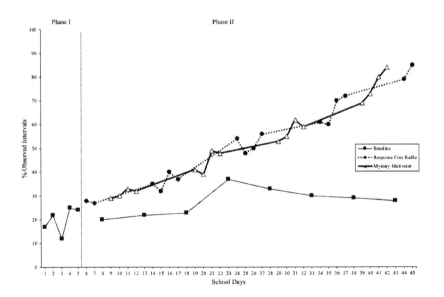

FIGURE 10.2 On-task verbal behaviors. Each data point represents the percentage of observed intervals students in the classroom engaged in on-task verbal behaviors during math independent work time each school day of Phase I (Week 1) and Phase II (Weeks 2-9). Every five school days represent one school week

average of 80% of the observed intervals (range: 76%-88%). Baseline data collected each Wednesday of Phase II (Weeks 2–9) showed that students engaged in off-task verbal behaviors during an average of 72% of the observed intervals (range: 63%-80%), indicating a return to near-baseline levels when both interventions were removed. Aligned with the identified intervention goals, students engaged in off-task verbal behaviors during 59%-63% of observed intervals in Week 4 of Phase II, 38%-41% of observed intervals in Week 7 of Phase II, and 15%-21% of observed intervals in Week 9 of Phase II. Furthermore, engagement in off-task verbal behaviors did not differ significantly between the two interventions. That is, students engaged in off-task verbal behaviors during an average of 47% of observed intervals across all weeks of Phase II during the implementation of Response Cost Raffle and during the implementation of Mystery Motivator.

On-Task Verbal Behaviors

Baseline data collected during Phase I (Week 1) showed that students engaged in on-task verbal behaviors during an average of 20% of the observed intervals (range: 15%-27%). Baseline data collected each Wednesday of Phase II (Weeks 2-9) showed that students engaged in on-task verbal behaviors during an average of 29% of the observed intervals (range: 22%-36%), indicating a return to near-baseline levels when both interventions were removed. Aligned with the identified intervention goals, students engaged in on-task verbal behaviors during 37%-41% of observed intervals in Week 4 of Phase II, 59%-62% of observed intervals in Week 7 of Phase II, and 79%-85% of observed intervals in Week 9 of Phase II. Similar to the occurrence of off-task verbal behaviors, engagement in on-task verbal behaviors did not differ significantly between the two interventions. That is, students engaged in on-task verbal behaviors an average of 52% of observed intervals across all weeks of Phase II during the implementation of Response Cost Raffle and during the implementation of Mystery Motivator.

Assignment Completion

Student outcome data from assignment completion are displayed in Figure 10.3. Baseline data collected during Phase I (Week 1) showed that 30% of students were completing the daily assignment (range: 23%-37%). Baseline data collected each Wednesday of Phase II (Weeks 2-9) showed that 36% of students completed the daily assignment (range: 29%-40%), indicating a return to near-baseline levels when both interventions were removed. Aligned with the identified intervention goals, 58%-63% of students completed the daily assignment in Week 4 of Phase 2, and 80%-90% of students completed the daily assignment in Week 7 of Phase II. Students maintained assignment completion through the remainder of Phase II. Assignment completion did not differ significantly between the two interventions and maintained or increased during the duration of Phase II. That

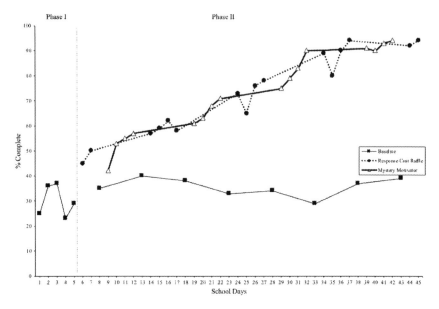

FIGURE 10.3 Assignment completion. Each data point represents the percentage of students who completed the daily math assignment during independent work time each school day of Phase I (Week 1) and Phase II (Weeks 2-9). Every five school days represent one school week

is, an average of 72% of students completed the daily assignment across all weeks of Phase II during the implementation of Response Cost Raffle and during the implementation of Mystery Motivator.

Summary of Intervention Effects

For this class-wide case study, implementation and evaluation of Response Cost Raffle and Mystery Motivator occurred within an alternating-treatments design, a single-case experimental design that directly facilitates the evaluation of two or more interventions (Kazdin, 2011). An alternating-treatments design was particularly fitting for this case study because neither intervention was likely to have carryover effects on days that it was not being implemented, and changes in target behaviors (i.e., verbal behaviors and assignment completion) were also unlikely to have lasting effects in the absence of intervention implementation. Counterbalancing implementation of the two different interventions as well intervention change agents (i.e., Ms. Munro and Ms. Montoya), maintaining strong intervention fidelity, and establishing high interobserver/rater agreement also minimized threats to validity and contributed to the establishment of a causal relationship between each intervention and changes in the target behaviors.

As such, data collected via systematic observations and assignment completion during Phase I and Phase II indicated that class-wide engagement in off-task verbal behaviors decreased and on-task verbal behaviors and assignment completion increased during the implementation of Response Cost Raffle as well as the independent implementation of Mystery Motivator. Visual inspection of changes in level and trend were consistent with intervention goals, and variability of data was minimal. All intervention goals were met, and differential effects of the two interventions were not observed.

Intervention Acceptability

At the completion of Phase II, the mental health team and Ms. Dunne collaboratively conducted a plan evaluation interview with Ms. Munro and Ms. Montoya to learn about their experiences with, and perceptions of, implementing Response Cost Raffle and Mystery Motivator during independent work time in math. Ms. Munro and Ms. Montoya also independently completed an adaptation of the Behavior Intervention Rating Scale (BIRS) for each intervention (Elliott & Von Brock Treuting, 1991; Appendix C). Ms. Munro and Ms. Montoya each reported strong satisfaction regarding acceptability, effectiveness, and time to effect for both interventions. Qualitatively, the classroom teachers noted some initial discomfort removing tickets when implementing Response Cost Raffle but become more comfortable when they noticed that removal did not appear to negatively impacts students. When implementing Mystery Motivator, teachers and students enjoyed identifying a class goal and working together to achieve it. Ms. Munro and Ms. Montoya also shared that students appeared to enjoy the interventions, and teachers found value in limiting implementation daily to only short periods in the day when classroom behaviors were more disruptive because the interventions then would not lose their novelty and student would remain excited about the interventions. Importantly, the teachers expressed that the planning time and resources they received from the school principal were invaluable.

Intervention Considerations

In order to increase the opportunity for an intervention to be effective and sustainable over time, change agents like school psychologists should consider the key components that increase the likelihood of successful implementation. Principal support and support from other administrators; teacher support; financial resources; high-quality training and technical assistance; alignment of the intervention with school philosophy, goals, policies, and other programs; visibility of the impact of the intervention to key stakeholders; and development of methods to deal with turnover in school staff and administrators were viewed as key in supporting successful implementation EBIs (evidence-based interventions;

Forman et al., 2013). Principals and school psychologists are in prime leadership roles to encourage, facilitate, and reinforce staff for altering their previous, traditional responsibilities (Eagle et al., 2015). School psychologists provide expertise related to content knowledge of evidence-based interventions, mental health issues, and systematic problem-solving procedures. School principals provide expertise in organizational systems, school culture, professional development, and instructional best practices. Together, school psychologists and school principals can provide leadership to achieve successful implementation of interventions.

Administrator support for interventions establishes an environment for success and sustainability. Administrator support assures school staff that implementation will be supported by allocating resources (e.g., time, incentives, training), communicating expectations, and addressing competing practices that may decrease resources (Blase & Fixsen as cited in Mathews et al., 2014). School leaders consistently make decisions regarding financial resources, professional development, discipline policies, and coaching opportunities. School leaders model the expectations regarding how adults interact with and build relationships with students. The central motivation for the current work is the question of how to allocate school and community mental health resources in ways that will have a greater effect on children – specifically, support to teachers to enhance classrooms (Cappella et al., 2011). With this in mind, a strong team of school principal and school psychologist can model and communicate school values related to relationships with students and implementation of interventions. School leaders and school psychologists can ensure that all teachers receive professional development and develop strong skills in classroom management and social–emotional interventions. They can ensure that coaching provides teachers with opportunities to get support and grow in their ability to provide interventions with fidelity. This partnership between the school psychologist and the principal can create an environment in which teachers have buy-in and skills to effectively implement interventions with fidelity.

Once teachers have received professional development, have the skills to implement an intervention, and even have buy-in, for implementation to be successful and sustained over time, ongoing coaching is necessary. Due to their training and expertise, school psychologists are well positioned to serve in the role of coach and support progress monitoring of interventions. School-based consultation can apply implementation drivers to support change at multiple levels, including the individual student (client-centered), classroom (consultee-centered), building, or district (systems-level; Eagle et al., 2015). Access to this support allows the continued refinement of implementation, as school personnel can successfully contextualize the practice when responding to the demands of a changing host environment (Baker, Gersten, Dimino, & Griffiths as cited in Mathews et al., 2014). After a principal, school psychologist, and teacher decide to implement an intervention, and the teacher is trained in the intervention, a collaborative principal will create a culture of support and problem solving. Then, in a consultative role, the school psychologist (as social–emotional expert) and teacher (as educational expert) work together to implement the intervention, gather data, progress-monitor, and make adjustments to support success of the students. Coaches need to be able to deliver key content while remaining flexible enough to differentiate between teachers who needs more support (Reinke et al., 2013). Though each staff member has a role to play – administrator setting the values, creating the systems, and ensuring the resources; school psychologist providing training, coaching, and progress monitoring; and teacher implementing the intervention in the classroom – it is the collaborative relationship that increases the likeliness that interventions are implemented with fidelity and sustained over time.

Schools are complex environments and even with administrator support, strong systems, professional development, and coaching, teachers often continue to struggle to implement interventions with fidelity and students often fail to respond as expected to interventions. Several studies have found that the level of implementation of EBIs in schools is low (Atkins, Frazier, Adil, & Talbott, 2003; Gottfredson & Gottfredson, 2002), and this provides a compelling rationale for the importance of implementation and of advancing implementation science in school psychology (Forman et al., 2013). The goals of implementation science have been to understand barriers to and facilitators of implementation, to develop new approaches to improving implementation, and to examine relationships between an intervention and its impact (Forman et al., 2013). Implementation science focuses on understanding the processes and factors related to successful integration of EBIs in a specific type of setting, such as a school (Forman et al., 2013). Within an implementation science paradigm, principals and school psychologists provide distinct expertise in competency (school psychologists) and organizational (principals) drivers and complementary and collaborative skills within leadership drivers (Eagle et al., 2015). Through the role of change agent, school psychologist practitioners have the potential to increase and improve the implementation of EBIs in schools, given knowledge and skill related to effective means of communicating about EBIs within the school organizational and social system context (Forman et al., 2013). School psychologists, in collaboration with school principals, are in unique positions to use implementation science to support effectiveness of classroom interventions. As school psychologists collaborate with principals and teachers to implement interventions, using the steps of implementation science could be beneficial: 1) In the *exploration* stage, a school team defines the problem, researches possible solutions, and considers adopting or implementing a new intervention; 2) The second phase is the *installation* stage in which school teams participate in training and agree on a protocol or process for intervention implementation; 3) In the *initial implementation* stage, the school team begins using the intervention, gathers data regarding implementation fidelity and outcomes, and makes modifications to the protocol/process as needed, 4) Lastly is *full implementation* in which the school team fully implements the intervention across multiple classrooms and throughout the school. Through this process, school psychologist and principals can support implementation while also making adjustments to improve outcomes and sustainability.

Conclusion

As school psychologists collaborate with teachers to implement Response Cost Raffle and Mystery Motivator interventions, it behooves them to collaborate closely with the school principal while also supporting the classroom teacher. Consideration of school values and systems, in addition to professional development and resources, will be necessary to improve outcomes. Additionally, school psychologists should strategically plan how they will provide ongoing advice and coaching to teachers implementing the intervention and how the principal can support this in occurring. Lastly, implementation science is a useful tool to support fidelity of implementation of interventions and sustainability.

References

Atkins, M.S., Frazier, S.L., Adil, J.A., & Talbott, E. (2003). School-based mental health services in urban communities. In M.D. Weist, S.W. Evans, & N.A. Lever (Eds.), *Handbook of school mental health: Advancing practice and research* (p. 165–178). New York: Kluwer Academic.

Burns, M.K., Riley-Tillman, T.C., & Rathvon, N. (2017). *Effective school interventions: Evidence-based strategies for improving student outcomes* (3rd ed.). New York: Guilford Press. ISBN: 978-1-4625-2614-7.

Cappella, E., Jackson, D.R., Bilal, C., Hamre, B.K., & Soule, C. (2011). Bridging mental health and education in urban elementary schools: Participatory research to inform intervention development. *School Psychology Review, 40*(4), 486–508.

Class Dojo. (2020). *Class Dojo*. Retrieved March 1, 2020, from https://www.classdojo.com

Conyers, C., Miltenberger, R., Maki, A., Barenz, R., Jurgens, M., Sailer A., Haugen, M., & Kopp, B. (2004). A comparison of response cost and differential reinforcement of other behavior to reduce disruptive behavior in a preschool classroom. *Journal of Applied Behavior Analysis, 37*(3), 411–415. doi:10.1901/jaba.2004.37-411

Eagle, J.W., Dowd-Eagle, S.E., Snyder, A., & Holtzman, E.G. (2015). Implementing a Multi-Tiered System of Support (MTSS): Collaboration between school psychologists and administrators to promote systems-level change. *Journal of Educational and Psychological Consultation, 25*, 160–177. doi:10.1080/10474412.2014.929960

Elliott, S.N., & Von Brock Treuting, M.B. (1991). The behavior intervention rating scales: Development and validation of a pretreatment acceptability and effectiveness measure. *Journal of School Psychology, 29*, 45–51. doi:10.1037/t07574-000

Forman, S.G., Shapiro, E.S., Codding, R.S., Gonzales, J.E. Reddy, L.A., Rosenfield, S.A., Sanetti, L.M.H., & Stoiber, K.C. (2013). Implementation science and school psychology. *School Psychology Quarterly, 28*(2), 77–100. doi:10.1037/spq0000019

Gottfredson, D.C., & Gottfredson, G.D. (2002). Quality of school-based prevention programs: Results from a national survey. *Journal of Research in Crime and Delinquency, 39*(1), 3–35.

Kamphaus, R.W., & Reynolds, C.R. (2015). *BASC-3 behavioral and emotional screening system (BESS)*. Bloomington, IN: NCS Pearson, Inc.

Kazdin, A.E. (2011). *Single-case research design: Methods for clinical and applied settings* (2nd ed.). New York, NY: Oxford University Press. ISBN: 978-0-19-534188-1.

Kowalewicz, E., & Coffee, G. (2014). Mystery Motivator: A Tier 1 classroom behavioral intervention. *School Psychology Quarterly, 29*(2), 138–156. doi:10.1037/spq0000030

Mathews, S., McIntosh, K., Frank, J.L., & May, S.L. (2014). Critical features predicting sustained implementation of school-wide positive behavioral interventions and supports. *Journal of Positive Behavior Interventions, 16*(3), 168–178. doi:10.1177/1098300713484065

Murphy, K.A., Theodore, L.A., Aloiso, D., Alric-Edwards, J.M., & Hughes, T.L. (2007). Interdependent group contingency and mystery motivators to reduce preschool disruptive behavior. *Psychology in the Schools, 44*(1), 53–63. doi:10.1002/pits.20205

Playworks. (2020). Playworks. Retrieved March 1, 2020, from https://www.playworks.org

Proctor, M.A., & Morgan, D. (1991). Effectiveness of a response cost raffle procedure on the disruptive classroom behavior of adolescents with behavior problems. *School Psychology Review, 20*, 97–109.

Reinke, W.M., Herman, K.C., Stormont, M., Newcomer, L., & David, K. (2013). Illustrating the multiple facets and levels of fidelity of implementation to a teacher classroom management intervention. *Administration and Policy in Mental Health, 40*, 494–506.

Schanding, G.T., & Sterling-Turner, H. (2010). Use of the Mystery Motivator for a high school class. *Journal of Applied School Psychology, 26*(1), 38–53. doi:10.1080/15377900903379448

Shapiro, E.S. (2011). *Academic skills problems* (4th ed.). New York: Guilford Press.

Appendix A: Response Cost Raffle Daily Fidelity Checklist

Response Cost Raffle Steps	*Completed* (circle 1 for each step)			*Teacher Notes*
1. Announced that the class will be playing Response Cost Raffle today.	Yes	No	–	
2. Displayed the Raffle Prize List.	Yes	No	–	
3. Distributed raffle tickets to students.	Yes	No	–	
4. Removed raffle tickets from individual students for each instance of engaging in off-task verbal behaviors.	Yes	No	–	
5. At the end of the intervention period, placed remaining tickets into the raffle ticket box.	Yes	No	–	
6. At the end of the intervention period, removed a ticket from the raffle ticket box.	Yes	No	–	
7. Allowed the student whose name was on the ticket chose a prize from the raffle prize list.	Yes	No	–	
8. If the ticket drawn had the word "group" on it, the whole class received a class prize.	Yes	No	N/A	
9. Praised the class for effort.	Yes	No	–	
10. Reminded the class that they will have another opportunity to earn a reward during the next intervention period.	Yes	No	–	

Appendix B: Mystery Motivator Daily Fidelity Checklist

Mystery Motivator Steps	Completed (circle 1 for each step)			Teacher Notes
1. Announced that the class will be playing Mystery Motivator today.	Yes	No	–	
2. Displayed the Mystery Motivator Calendar.	Yes	No	–	
3. Displayed the reinforcement chart.	Yes	No	–	
4. Collaboratively determined with the class a daily goal focused on less engagement in off-task verbal behaviors.	Yes	No	–	
5. At the end of the intervention period, collaboratively determined with the class if the daily goal was met or not.	Yes	No	–	
6. If the goal was met, asked a student to reveal whether or not today has an M.	Yes	No	N/A	
7. If an M was revealed, allowed the class to choose a reward from the reinforcement chart.	Yes	No	N/A	
8. If the goal was not met or an M was not revealed, praised the class for effort.	Yes	No	N/A	
9. If the goal was not met or an M was not revealed, reminded the class that they will have another opportunity to earn a reward during the next intervention period.	Yes	No	N/A	

Appendix C: Behavior Intervention Rating Scale (BIRS)

Please complete the items listed below by circling the number next to each item that best indicates how you feel about the intervention.

	Strongly Disagree	Disagree	Slightly Disagree	Slightly Agree	Agree	Strongly Agree
1. This was an accep table intervention to address off-task verbal behaviors.	1	2	3	4	5	6
2. Most teachers would find this intervention appropriate for behaviors other than off-task verbal behaviors.	1	2	3	4	5	6
3. The intervention proved effective in changing off-task verbal behaviors.	1	2	3	4	5	6

4. I would suggest the use of this intervention to other teachers.	1	2	3	4	5	6
5. Off-task verbal behaviors were disruptive enough to warrant use of this intervention.	1	2	3	4	5	6
6. Most teachers would find this intervention suitable for addressing off-task verbal behaviors.	1	2	3	4	5	6
7. I would be willing to use this again in the classroom setting.	1	2	3	4	5	6
8. The intervention did not result in negative side effects for students in my classroom.	1	2	3	4	5	6
9. The intervention was an appropriate intervention for a variety of students.	1	2	3	4	5	6
10. The intervention was consistent with those I have used in classroom settings.	1	2	3	4	5	6
11. The intervention was a fair way to handle off-task verbal behaviors.	1	2	3	4	5	6
12. The intervention was reasonable for addressing off-task verbal behaviors.	1	2	3	4	5	6
13. I liked the procedures used in the intervention.	1	2	3	4	5	6
14. This intervention was an appropriate way to handle off-task verbal behaviors.	1	2	3	4	5	6
15. Overall, the intervention was beneficial for students in my classroom.	1	2	3	4	5	6
16. The intervention quickly improved off-task verbal behaviors.	1	2	3	4	5	6
17. The intervention produced a lasting improvement in off-task verbal behaviors.	1	2	3	4	5	6

18. The intervention improved off-task verbal behaviors to the point that these behaviors would not noticeably deviate from other behaviors.	1	2	3	4	5	6
19. Soon after using the intervention, I noticed a positive change in off-task verbal behaviors.	1	2	3	4	5	6
20. I believe that off-task verbal behaviors will remain at an improved level even after the intervention is discontinued.	1	2	3	4	5	6
21. Using the intervention will likely not only improve off-task verbal behaviors during independent work time in math, but also in other settings/subjects.	1	2	3	4	5	6
22. When comparing off-task verbal behaviors during independent work time in math before and after use of the intervention, off-task verbal behaviors during different times of the day/subjects will likely be more alike after using the intervention.	1	2	3	4	5	6
23. The intervention is likely to produce enough improvement in off-task verbal behaviors so that off-task verbal behaviors are no longer a problem during independent work time in math.	1	2	3	4	5	6
24. Other behaviors related to off-task verbal behaviors are also likely to be improved by the intervention.	1	2	3	4	5	6

Adapted from Elliott and Von Brock Treuting (1991).

11
SELF-MONITORING

Faith G. Miller and Alexandria C. Muldrew

Introduction

Teachers are often responsible for delivering behavioral interventions in addition to a myriad of other responsibilities, including managing and instructing a classroom of students. The burden placed on teachers' time has grown exponentially in recent years, undoubtedly contributing to issues of burnout and retention. Yet, they do not always need to serve as sole interventionists to support student behavior. For many students, a self-monitoring (SM) intervention may be appropriate in improving their problem behavior. SM interventions include several key features: use of a cue (e.g., timer) that prompts the student to measure, through self-reflection, and record, through self-rating, their behaviors. These interventions can be administered flexibly either through technological (e.g., tablet or handheld device) or analog methods. Regardless of the mode of administration, students systematically observe and evaluate their own behavior, and then record the extent to which those behaviors align with operationally defined targets. This procedure occurs during specified intervals, and students receive a prompt to record their behavior at the end of each interval. The features of SM interventions can be customized; for example, the prompts can either come from a technological source or the teacher can cue the student, and the recording methods can include a technological source or paper and pencil. The versatility of SM interventions is perhaps one of their greatest strengths.

The basic theory underlying SM interventions is that self-regulation, or the ability for one to manage their own personal state of functioning, is reliant, in part, on one's ability to monitor this state. SM then is a developmental process that evolves over time as part of cognitive development through executive functioning processes. However, it can also be developed and supported through the use and implementation of SM interventions. In one of the earliest studies involving SM, Snyder (1974) defined SM as a combination of self-reflection and self-control that is driven by both situational prompts and social expectations. Multiple theories of change have been offered to explain why SM interventions positively impact student behavior (Webber, Scheuermann, McCall, & Coleman, 1993). One explanation stems from Snyder's (1974) view that the process of monitoring helps develop self-awareness, increasing the likelihood that behaviors will change to meet expectations. Another plausible explanation is that the very act of SM is inherently self-reinforcing or punishing, which leads to shifts in behaviors (Kanfer, 1970). Regardless of the exact theory of change, decades of robust empirical evidence support both technology-based and analog administration of SM interventions as effective in improving the behaviors of students (for comprehensive reviews, see Bruhn et al., 2015; Sheffield & Waller, 2010; Webber et al., 1993). Indeed, SM has been found to be beneficial across differing age groups (e.g., Gulchak, 2008; Wills & Mason, 2014), subject areas (e.g., Prater, Hogan, & Miller, 1992), and ability levels (e.g., Rock, 2005).

SM interventions fall under the umbrella of self-management interventions – or interventions that are student-managed as opposed to teacher-managed. Given the teachers' many responsibilities, such interventions offer clear advantages in terms of feasibility of implementation. In addition to being student-managed, the use of technology can further facilitate and enhance implementation of SM interventions (Schardt, Miller, & Bedesem, 2019). Electronic devices such as digital timers, tablets, cell phones, or other electronic devices can be used to prompt and/or record behavior. Some technology-based SM interventions utilize applications on tablets or portable devices and are able to electronically store and digitally display data that can help with decision-making related to verifying the effectiveness of an intervention. While technology-based SM interventions can streamline implementation, they are but one option. Universal accessibility of analog methods, including visual or verbal prompts from teachers or peers and paper–pencil administration of SM interventions, can make implementation of this intervention more feasible when access to specific technological devices is not available.

Like most behavioral interventions, the effectiveness of SM interventions can be maximized when the function of the student's behavior is identified and utilized to create the intervention plan (Briere & Simonsen, 2011). However, SM interventions are flexible enough that they do not have to directly relate to the function of a student's behavior in order to improve student behavior. So, while it is best practice to match the function of a student's behavior to the SM intervention, this is not absolutely necessary to demonstrate improvements in student behavior (Bruhn et al., 2015).

The versatility of SM interventions makes them appropriate to meet the behavioral needs of students who are exhibiting challenges with staying on-task and overall difficulty with meeting the expectations of a classroom. This includes students with general behavioral difficulties as well as students with disabilities.

For example, research supports SM interventions with students diagnosed with Emotional Behavioral Disorders (EBD; Blood et al., 2011), Autism Spectrum Disorder (ASD; Legge, DeBar, & Alber-Morgan 2010), and Attention-Deficit/Hyperactivity Disorder (ADHD; Reid et al., 2005; Wills & Mason, 2014). Here, we provide a case study to support academic engagement of a middle school student with ADHD. It is important to note that the effectiveness of SM interventions is not limited to improving engagement for students with ADHD. Indeed, students with noticeable, but not diagnosable, attentional difficulties, overall disengagement, and disruptive behavior could potentially benefit from SM interventions (Davis et al., 2016; Mooney et al., 2005; Rafferty, 2012). Furthermore, SM interventions need not be restricted to purely social, emotional, or behavioral concerns; they can also be effective for academic concerns as well.

Case Study

Background Information

Kai was a sixth-grade student who recently transitioned to Washington Middle School (WMS) from a smaller elementary school in the district. His homeroom and math teacher, Ms. Lopez, referred him to the student assistance team due to concerns about his engagement throughout the school day. Specifically, several of Kai's teachers noted that he seemed to have difficulty staying focused and completing work. They noted he often seemed to be daydreaming in class, staring off and not following along with the rest of his peers. He was falling behind in his coursework and assignments. Review of Kai's file indicated that he had been diagnosed with ADHD by his pediatrician in second grade, but that no additional supports or services had been provided by his previous school. Tier 1 supports at WMS were embedded within a Positive Behavioral Interventions and Supports (PBIS) framework, and included clear school-wide behavioral expectations depicted by the acronym SOAR (Safe, On-Task, Always Do Your Best, and Responsibility). In addition to direct instruction and modeling of SOAR expectations, WMS also utilized a system for recognizing appropriate behavior (SOAR Tickets) and responding to inappropriate behavior (redirections and office disciplinary referrals). Despite implementation of these Tier 1 supports with high fidelity, the grade-level team determined that Kai was nonresponsive, and he was falling below expectations for on-task behavior. Tier 2 supports were needed, but Ms. Lopez expressed that she did not know what to do.

Ms. Lopez shared with the student assistance team that she had limited experience dealing with this kind of issue and that most of her behavior-management experience related to students with disruptive behavior. She reported that she and the other grade-level team members were at a loss for what to do, and that maybe she should suggest to Kai's parents that they needed to consider medication to address the problem. The student assistance team assured Ms. Lopez that they could support her and the rest of the grade-level team in developing an intervention for Kai that could help him be more successful in school.

Description of the Problem Behavior

Members of the student assistance team first worked to better understand the nature of the problem by meeting with members of Kai's grade-level team, interviewing them, and collecting preliminary data. In working to define the problem, the primary target for intervention emerged as academic engagement, or actively or passively participating in classroom activities. Each of Kai's grade-level teachers estimated that Kai was typically academically engaged for less than 50% of classroom instruction, and that this was consistent across days, activities, and subjects. To more formally assess Kai's current levels of performance, each grade-level teacher was asked to complete a Direct Behavior Rating (DBR; Briesch et al., 2016) to estimate the proportion of time that Kai was academically engaged during class instruction. During class, teachers were instructed to mentally monitor Kai's behavior throughout the duration of class. Then, at the end of class, they provided a rating on a 0%-100% scale to estimate the proportion of time that Kai was academically engaged. They completed DBR ratings daily for one week.

Problem Analysis

After the initial week of data collection, the DBR ratings from Kai's classroom teachers were evaluated. Results from the DBR ratings indicated that Kai was rated as academically engaged for 45% of the time across teachers. The student assistance team reviewed the information collected through interviews, behavior ratings, and a file review, and worked to develop and evaluate several working hypotheses regarding Kai's inattention in class. First, the team hypothesized that Kai's attention difficulties were due to the class content being either too difficult or too easy for him. An evaluation of Kai's achievement testing data, grades, and classwork all suggested that this was not the case, and that classwork was appropriately matched to his instructional level. Second, the team hypothesized that Kai's attention difficulties were due to either a skill deficit, wherein Kai lacked the necessary skills to properly pay attention in class, or a performance deficit, wherein Kai mastered the skills necessary to pay attention but did not perform them consistently. The school psychologist advised that an SM intervention in this case could benefit Kai; clearly, he had some ability to engage but was not utilizing it consistently, which is more consistent with a performance deficit. In this case, the SM intervention could help him become more self-aware and better maintain attention while also encouraging more consistent use of those skills. The team decided that they would initially implement the SM intervention in Ms. Lopez's class as a starting point, evaluate Kai's response, and then work to implement and generalize the intervention to additional classes and settings.

Intervention Goals

Based on results from DBRs in baseline, the intervention goals for Kai focused on increasing his time on-task and work completion. Specifically, it was expected that within six weeks, teacher DBR ratings would reflect that on average, Kai would be academically engaged for 70% of the time (a 25% point increase from baseline). Additionally, it was expected that in six weeks, Kai would complete on average 70% of the items on worksheets assigned in class. The team hoped that Kai's progress would exceed these benchmarks in less than six weeks, but wanted to ensure a reasonable starting point.

Measurement of Target Behaviors, Data Collection Strategies, and Progress Monitoring

Given limited resources available at the school, the team prioritized ensuring feasible data collection procedures in order to monitor Kai's response to the SM intervention. Therefore, DBR and permanent products would serve as progress monitoring methods. On the DBR form, academically engaged behavior (AEB) was defined as: actively or passively participating in classroom activities (e.g., writing, raising hand, looking at instructional materials). At the end of the instructional period, Ms. Lopez simply reflected back on the approximate proportion of time that she observed Kai to be academically engaged and provided a rating on a zero (never) to 10 (always) scale. The paper DBR forms were then delivered to the school psychologist, who graphed the data each week in a spreadsheet. This served as the primary outcome measure; however, Kai also recorded his behavior using a paper–pencil SM sheet (see Figure 11.1). These data were also collected and reviewed as part of the intervention. Lastly, because the ultimate goal of the SM intervention was not just to ensure that Kai was academically engaged during instruction, but also completed his work appropriately, permanent products in the form of worksheets completed during class were also collected and reviewed. The proportion of items complete on each worksheet was calculated and graphed as a secondary outcome measure.

Intervention Plan

After defining the problem, analyzing information to develop intervention goals, and then finalizing the approach to data collection, the team set out to work on developing the intervention plan. The target behavior of academic engagement was previously identified and defined, and it was determined that the intervention would take place during math instruction (a 50-minute class period) as a starting point. Next, the team developed the SM form and decided to use a MotivAider®, a small device that vibrates at a predetermined interval, in order to cue Kai to measure and record his behavior. This device, they determined,

Self-Monitoring Form

Name:	Date:	Activity:

Directions: Each time the MotivAider buzzes, mark a [+] if you were academically engaged. If you were not academically engaged, mark a [-]. Do your best to answer honestly and truthfully.

Academically engaged (AE) means to be actively or passively participating in classroom activities. <u>Some examples include</u>: writing, raising hand, answering a question, talking about a lesson, listening to the teacher, reading silently, or looking at instructional materials. <u>Some non-examples</u> include: looking out the window, playing with objects, drawing, staring off, or talking with others unless directed to.

Interval	1	2	3	4	5	6	7	8	9	10
AE										

Interval	11	12	13	14	15	16	17	18	19	20
AE										

Interval	21	22	23	24	25	26	27	28	29	30
AE										

Interval	31	32	33	34	35	36	37	38	39	40
AE										

Interval	41	42	43	44	45	46	47	48	49	50
AE										

A. Total number of + _____
B. Total number of intervals _____
C. A/B = _____

C x 100 = _____ % Academically Engaged during class today!

FIGURE 11.1 Self-monitoring form

would be best because it is unobtrusive. Given the relatively low occurrence of AEB, they decided to set the cue to one-minute intervals. At the end of each interval, the MotivAider® would buzz and Kai would record whether he was academically engaged (+) or not (−). At the end of the 50-minute period, Kai would calculate the proportion of time he was academically engaged and submit the form to Ms. Lopez.

Next, the team considered whether to implement the SM intervention alone, or to include SM with reinforcement or punishment. Although SM interventions alone can be reinforcing for students, adding external reinforcement is also an option. SM interventions with external reinforcement are utilized after the student either accurately records their behavior or achieves a goal. Thus, the student is provided with a reward (e.g., edible or tangible items, unique privileges) that encourages them to produce correct ratings and/or stay on-task. SM interventions with punishment are utilized when a student receives a consequence for not achieving a goal that encourages them to stay on-task in the future (e.g., missing recess, extra homework, loss of privilege). While it is important to know that SM interventions with punishment are an option, within the context of the present case, an SM intervention with and without external reinforcement was ultimately implemented to encourage a more positive approach towards implementation of this intervention. The team decided to start with SM alone, but was open to adding external reinforcement if that in and of itself was not sufficient in producing the desired change.

With the intervention logistics determined, the team provided instruction to Ms. Lopez for how to introduce the SM intervention to Kai and teach him the process. The training for Kai included several steps. First, an informational discussion was held to (a) describe the purpose and importance of the intervention, (b) provide examples and non-examples of academically engaged behaviors, (c) introduce the MotivAider® and how to operate it, (d) introduce the SM sheet and how to complete it, and (e) discuss specific goals. Next, Ms. Lopez modeled how to use the materials and then provided a practice session where Kai had the opportunity to practice the intervention. During this time, she provided feedback to him and stressed the importance of accurately and honestly recording his behavior. She explained she would compare his daily self-ratings to her daily DBR ratings, and they would discuss any major discrepancies (i.e., greater than 10%).

To assess the effectiveness of the SM intervention, an ABABB' withdrawal design was implemented. Such designs add significant strengths to data interpretation efforts, as a causal inference can be made in such cases. In the initial baseline (A) phase, Ms. Lopez used DBR to estimate the percentage of time Kai was academically engaged during the math class period. For the next phase (B), Kai was trained in the SM procedures and implemented the SM intervention along with assistance from Ms. Lopez, who also continued to estimate Kai's academic engagement. In the third phase (A), Kai did not implement the SM intervention, but Ms. Lopez still measured his academic engagement. For the fourth phase (B), Kai independently implemented the SM intervention and Ms. Lopez monitored his academic engagement. Based on Kai's data in this final phase, the team decided to add an additional (B*) phase, which continued the SM intervention and added external reinforcement to encourage Kai to meet his daily goal of staying academically engaged for at least 70% of the time. Ms. Lopez asked Kai to complete a brief survey in order to identify rewards that he would be motivated to earn. If Kai remained on-task for at least 70% of the class period, then he immediately received the reinforcer from Ms. Lopez.

Intervention Fidelity and Interobserver Agreement

Intervention fidelity was evaluated through permanent products and an SM fidelity checklist. Permanent products included the SM forms completed by Kai and the DBR forms completed by Ms. Lopez. The fidelity checklist included each step of the intervention and was completed by Ms. Lopez each day during math instruction (see Appendix A). Given Ms. Lopez's buy-in to the intervention, she was very eager to implement it. Fidelity was found to be very high for the intervention, with 98% adherence overall by Ms. Lopez.

Interobserver agreement (IOA) was calculated twice per week by Ms. Lopez's student teacher, who also observed Kai during math instruction and completed DBR ratings. A criterion for agreement was set to include a margin of one DBR rating point. That is, adequate agreement was determined when the DBR ratings were within one point of each other (e.g., a rating of eight by Ms. Lopez and a rating of nine by her student teacher would still count as agreement). Percentage agreement was then calculated by dividing the number of agreements by the total number of IOA ratings and multiplying by 100. Percent agreement was found to be very high, with Ms. Lopez and her student teacher in agreement 98% of the time.

Intervention Outcome Data

Direct Behavior Ratings (DBR)

Figure 11.2 provides a visual depiction of Kai's academic engagement (AE) during math class throughout the intervention. During baseline, Kai did not receive outside interventions or support and Ms. Lopez went about her classroom routine with Kai in a business-as-usual fashion. In this phase, Kai's AE was at least 30% points lower than the goal and the lowest data point was the last one in this phase, with Kai demonstrating AE behaviors 20% of the time. On average, Kai was only academically engaged for 38% of the time during baseline. At the start of the intervention, Kai's AE experienced an immediate level change from 20% to 60%, suggesting that Ms. Lopez perceived a noticeable improvement in Kai's AE during math. This positive trend continued throughout the phase and Kai was able to successfully meet his goal in the last three sessions during this phase. On average, Kai was academically engaged 66% of the time during the first SM intervention phase. To confirm that the SM intervention was causing these positive effects, the team decided to temporarily discontinue the SM intervention for several days

Self-Monitoring 169

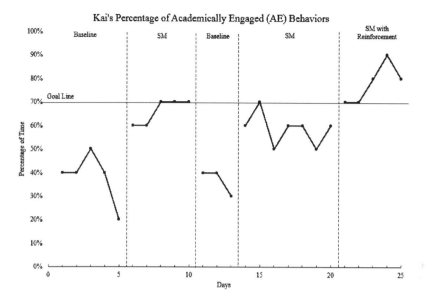

FIGURE 11.2 Percentage of time of AEBs across baseline, self-monitoring, and self-monitoring with reinforcement conditions

and continue to monitor Kai's performance. At this time, Kai's AE immediately dropped from 70% to 40% and never increased to the levels observed during the SM intervention phase. On average, he was only academically engaged for 37% of the time when the SM intervention was withdrawn. Therefore, the team quickly decided to reinstate the SM intervention and once again, there was an immediate level change with Kai's AE increasing from 30% to 60%. Although Kai was making progress during this phase, he was still not attaining his goal. On average, Kai was only academically engaged 59% of the time during the time the SM intervention was reinstated. The team first evaluated the fidelity data and determined that the intervention was being implemented with 100% fidelity. Therefore, the team decided to make a slight modification and add a reinforcement component to the SM intervention. With Kai receiving a daily reinforcer contingent on meeting his goal, his AE in this phase remained above the goal line. In this condition, Kai was academically engaged on average 80% of the time, indicating that this intervention condition was effective, and the addition of reinforcement provided the boost in performance that the team was hoping for.

Permanent Products

Figure 11.3 illustrates Kai's average rate of completion for items on worksheets during math class. To evaluate Kai's academic performance, permanent products (i.e., class worksheets) were collected and monitored for completeness. Prior to

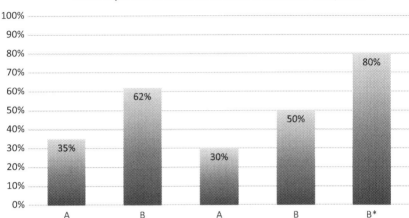

FIGURE 11.3 Proportion of items completed on in-class worksheets. A (baseline); B (SM intervention); A (baseline); B (SM intervention); B★ (SM intervention + reinforcement)

implementation of the intervention, Kai struggled to complete math worksheets assigned in class, and he averaged 35% completion in the first week during baseline. At the start of the SM intervention, Kai's average completion nearly doubled to 62%. During the second baseline, Kai's average completion rate dropped from 62% to 30%, which was lower than the average obtained in the original baseline. Upon reintroduction of the SM intervention, Kai once again completed worksheets on average 50% of the time. The highest percentage of work completion observed for Kai occurred in the final condition with both the SM intervention and reinforcement of goal attainment in place. During this condition, Kai completed on average 80% of items on his worksheets in class. Overall, similar to the effects observed in Ms. Lopez's ratings of Kai's AE, there was a notable improvement in Kai's in-class work completion during intervention phases.

Summary of Intervention Effects

Based on the data obtained, Kai demonstrated substantial improvement in his behavior. Although some positive effects were obtained when the SM intervention alone was implemented, Kai clearly benefited from the addition of external reinforcement. Due to these improvements, the team decided to revise Kai's goal to include at least 80% work completion in addition to 80% engagement. With this performance sustained in math class, the team would then work to implement the SM intervention in Kai's other classes. Eventually, to encourage Kai to internalize the process and apply the skills independently, the SM intervention would be gradually faded.

Intervention Acceptability

Assessing the social validity of an intervention is absolutely critical – an implementer can develop the best and most effective intervention in the world, yet if it is not feasible to implement and acceptable to users, it will fail. To this end, Ms. Lopez and Kai were asked to complete a brief six-item questionnaire regarding their experience engaging in the SM intervention using a five-point Likert scale with the following response options: strongly disagree, slightly disagree, neutral, slightly agree, strongly agree. The questions included the following: (1) I found this approach to be helpful, (2) This approach was easy for me to do, (3) This approach provided meaningful information, (4) I think this approach is a good way to help students, (5) I would use this approach again in the future, and (6) I liked the procedures used in this approach. Responses from both Kai and Ms. Lopez indicated that they found the SM intervention to be both acceptable and feasible. Responses on all items ranged from neutral to strongly agree, with neither respondent indicating either slight or strong disagreement to any of the items. Therefore, the SM intervention was deemed to have strong social validity according to both users of the intervention.

Intervention Considerations

This case study provides an overview of an SM intervention for a middle school student with ADHD, and it is just a single example of how SM procedures can be used. As previously reviewed, these methods can be implemented in a variety of ways, using a variety of methods to target diverse behaviors in different settings with students across a range of ages and disabilities. Within a multi-tiered system of support (MTSS) framework, SM interventions can be used at Tier 1 class-wide, for targeted students at Tier 2, or as part of a comprehensive behavior support plan (BSP) at Tier 3. This versatility makes SM interventions well-suited for any number of referral concerns. There are, however, additional considerations that should be made when selecting and implementing an SM intervention. In particular, Rafferty (2010) outlined several important considerations, which we summarize here. First, SM interventions are most appropriate for performance, as opposed to skill, deficits. That is, SM alone cannot be used to teach a student a new skill that they do not already have in their repertoire. In these cases, skills training is absolutely essential. Second, SM intervention should not be used with dangerous behaviors – those that pose a potential harm to self or others. Third, implementers should consider developmental and cognitive levels of the student and whether they can (a) understand the target behaviors and (b) recognize when they are engaging in them. Fourth, implementers should consider a student's background and whether the target behaviors are congruent with a student's cultural norms. For example, in some cultures, increasing eye contact may not be a culturally appropriate target behavior.

Finally, implementers should consider the best mode of administration of SM interventions to include appropriate cues and recording methods.

Conclusion

A significant body of research conducted over several decades supports the effectiveness of SM interventions. These interventions offer an efficient, flexible, and feasible option for supporting student behavior, and help to reduce the stress and burden placed on teachers. SM interventions help students gain the essential skill of self-awareness, which is a critical component of self-regulation and self-control. SM interventions are highly adaptive and can be used for a multitude of challenges related to behavioral or academic performance deficits in the classroom. Novel applications involving the use of technology for SM are also constantly evolving and offer a promising and streamlined approach to prompting and recording behavior. When incorporated as a behavior management strategy within MTSS, SM interventions offer many unique advantages to support positive student behavior.

References

Blood, E., Johnson, J. W., Ridenour, L., Simmons, K., & Crouch, S. (2011). Using an iPod touch to teach social and self-management skills to an elementary student with emotional/behavioral disorders. *Education and Treatment of Children, 34*, 299–321. doi:10.1353/etc.2011.0019

Briere III, D. E., & Simonsen, B. (2011). Self-monitoring interventions for at-risk middle school students: The importance of considering function. *Behavioral Disorders, 36*(2), 129–140. doi:10.1177/019874291103600204

Briesch, A. M., Riley-Tillman, T. C., & Chafouleas, S. M. (2016). *Direct behavior rating: Linking assessment, communication, and intervention.* New York: Guilford Press.

Bruhn, A., McDaniel, S., & Kreigh, C. (2015). Self-monitoring interventions for students with behavior problems: A systematic review of current research. *Behavioral Disorders, 40*(2), 102–121. doi:10.17988/bd-13-45.1

Davis, J. L., Mason, B. A., Davis, H. S., Mason, R. A., & Crutchfield, S. A. (2016). Self-monitoring interventions for students with ASD: A Meta-analysis of school-based research. *Review Journal of Autism and Developmental Disorders, 3*(3), 196–208. doi:10.1007/s40489-016-0076-y

Gulchak, D. J. (2008). Using a mobile handheld computer to teach a student with an emotional and behavioral disorder to self-monitor attention. *Education and Treatment of Children, 31*, 567–581. doi:10.1353/etc.0.0028

Kanfer, F. H. (1970). Self-monitoring: Methodological limitations and clinical applications. *Journal of Consulting and Clinical Psychology, 35*, 148–152. doi:10.1037/h0029874

Legge, D. B., DeBar, R. M., & Alber-Morgan, S. R. (2010). The effects of self-monitoring with a MotivAider® on the on-task behavior of fifth and sixth graders with autism and other disabilities. *Journal of Behavior Assessment and intervention in Children, 1*(1), 43. doi:10.1037/h0100359

Mooney, P., Ryan, J. B., Uhing, B. M., Reid, R., & Epstein, M. H. (2005). A review of self-management interventions targeting academic outcomes for students with emotional and behavioral disorders. *Journal of Behavioral Education, 14*(3), 203–221. doi:10.1007/s10864-005-6298-1

Prater, M. A., Hogan, S., & Miller, S. R. (1992). Using self-monitoring to improve on-task behavior and academic skills of an adolescent with mild handicaps across special and regular education settings. *Education and Treatment of Children, 15,* 43–55.

Rafferty, L. A. (2010). Step-by-step: Teaching students to self-monitor. *Teaching Exceptional Children, 43,* 50–58. 10.1177/004005991004300205

Rafferty, L. A. (2012). Self-monitoring during whole group reading instruction: Effects among students with emotional and behavioral disabilities during summer school intervention sessions. *Emotional and Behavioural Difficulties, 17*(2), 157–173. doi:10.1080/13632752.2012.672866

Reid, R., Trout, A. L., & Schartz, M. (2005). Self-regulation interventions for children with attention deficit/hyperactivity disorder. *Exceptional Children, 71,* 361–377.

Rock, M. L. (2005). Use of strategic self-monitoring to enhance academic engagement, productivity, and accuracy of students with and without exceptionalities. *Journal of Positive Behavior Interventions, 7,* 3–17. doi:10.1177/10983007050070010201

Schardt, A. A., Miller, F. G., & Bedesem, P. (2019). The effects of CellF-Monitoring on students' academic engagement. *Journal of Positive Behavior Interventions, 21,* 42–29. doi:10.1177/1098300718773462

Sheffield, K., & Waller, R. J. (2010). A review of single-case studies utilizing self-monitoring interventions to reduce problem classroom behaviors. *Beyond Behavior, 19,* 7–13.

Snyder, M. (1974). Self-monitoring of expressive behavior. *Journal of Personality and Social Psychology, 30,* 526. doi:10.1037/h0037039

Webber, J., Scheuermann, B., McCall, C., & Coleman, M (1993). Research on self-monitoring as a behavior management technique in special education classes: A descriptive review. *Remedial and Special Education, 14,* 38–56. doi:10.1177/074193259301400206

Wills, H. P., & Mason, B. A. (2014). Implementation of a self-monitoring application to improve on-task behavior: A high-school pilot study. *Journal of Behavioral Education, 23*(4), 421–434. doi:10.1007/s10864-014-9204-x

Appendix A: Fidelity Checklist: Self-Monitoring Intervention

Teacher :—————————   Student :—————————

Week of :—————————

Intervention Step	M	Tu	W	Th	F
Provided student with self-monitoring form.	Y N	Y N	Y N	Y N	Y N
Provided student with MotivAider.	Y N	Y N	Y N	Y N	Y N
Directed student to begin self-monitoring.	Y N	Y N	Y N	Y N	Y N
Reviewed self-monitoring sheet with student at end of class.	Y N	Y N	Y N	Y N	Y N
Compared student ratings to teacher DBR ratings.	Y N	Y N	Y N	Y N	Y N
If ratings agreed within 10%, student was praised. If ratings deviated by more than 10%, this was discussed and resolved.	Y N	Y N	Y N	Y N	Y N
If student met goal of _____, reward was given if applicable.	Y N	Y N	Y N	Y N	Y N
Total # of "Y"s					
Total # of intervention steps observed or applicable					
A/B					

12
COGNITIVE BEHAVIORAL THERAPY

Michael Handwerk and Jessamine Manack

Introduction

By most accounts, no other psychological intervention has as much empirical support for its effectiveness as does Cognitive Behavioral Therapy (CBT; David et al., 2018; O'Donohue & Fisher, 2012). CBT has been demonstrated to be effective for a vast array of psychological problems and disorders across an incredible developmental age span (Hofmann et al., 2012). It has been demonstrated to be effective in treating mood disorders, anxiety and trauma disorders, substance use, personality disorders, sleep problems, psychotic disorders, anger and aggression, adult ADHD, somatic and pain disorders, eating disorders, and general and occupational stress. While there are many hundreds of well-designed studies demonstrating the effectiveness of CBT with adults, the evidence-base for CBT for children and adolescents is more limited, though still impressive (Stallard, 2009).

CBT can be traced to the early works of Aaron Beck (1964) and Albert Ellis (1958), both of which placed primacy on cognitive appraisal as central to understanding human functioning and, more specifically, maladaptive psychological conditions. Beck (1964) posited that it is not the situation in and of itself that determines how people feel, but rather the way in which they perceive it. Ellis' Rational Emotive Therapy (RET) emphasized the causative role that evaluative and, specifically, irrational beliefs of perceptions of events played in leading to an individual's negative affective and behavioral responses (Walen, DiGiuseppe, & Dryden, 1992). While both of these therapy systems placed primary emphasis on the 'cognitive' element of CBT, both also utilized behavioral techniques to help induce a change in client behaviors. As cognitive therapy became more popular and demonstrated accumulating empirical evidence of its effectiveness in treating psychological problems, subsequent theorists and clinicians, many of whom were trained in a traditional behavioral approach (e.g., Kazdin, 1982), added to the conceptual framework of early cognitive therapies, emphasizing more 'behavioral' elements, particularly as CBT was applied to children and adolescents (Kendall & Braswell, 1997).

Despite the overwhelming amount of evidence for its effectiveness, precise operational definitions of CBT are elusive. At its core, the CBT model is a mediational model (Dobson, 2003) meaning that thoughts, emotions, and behaviors are inherently interwoven in a bidirectional loop of cause and effect: how individuals feel is influenced by how they perceive and think about events, how they act is influenced by their mood, how they behave influences how they perceive and think about things. The practice of CBT varies widely and includes a multitude of strategies, practices, and tactics (including many of the interventions and techniques described in this book). Although CBT involves both cognitive and behavioral components, some forms of CBT stress the primacy of altering cognitions; other forms emphasize the importance of altering behaviors (Lorenzo-Luaces, Keefe, & DeRubeis, 2016). Techniques such as Socratic questioning, examining alternative explanations for beliefs, and cognitive restructuring fall on the 'cognitive' end of the spectrum, while techniques like exposure, activity scheduling, and role-playing fall more on the 'behavioral' end of the spectrum. While there is raging empirical debate among CBT scholars regarding the necessity of altering cognitions to effect symptom improvement (Lorenzo-Luaces et al., 2016), in practice, almost all major models of CBT incorporate a mix of strategies that incorporate both cognitive and behavioral techniques. In sum, CBT acknowledges and emphasizes the importance of cognitions (e.g., beliefs, expectancies), yet maintains a concern for behaviors, both in treatment and as an outcome measure (Kendall & Braswell, 1997).

CBT can be described as a collaborative empiricism model whereby the therapist and client establish a collaborative relationship in which the patient works together with the therapist as a team to define problems and gain skills in managing these problems (Wright, 2006). CBT is problem-focused (i.e., on the identified target), structured (i.e., therapy sessions have a specific purpose and identified tasks/activities), and time-limited (i.e., not indefinite, often 6-12 sessions). Perhaps more so than other therapies, CBT tends to have a distinctive pedagogical overtone where the therapist is teaching skills and self-evaluative methods to a presumably motivated client.

Case Study

Background Information

Karla was a 14-year-old, ninth grade student enrolled at Creole Falls High School, a small, rural high school of 330 students in southern Illinois. She was an only child who lived with both of her biological parents. Her father was frequently away from home for work several weeks at a time; her mother was a stay-at-home parent. Karla began demonstrating notable problems with depression and anxiety during the middle of 8th grade. Her mother reported Karla was withdrawn and tearful, slept more, and appeared sadder and more pessimistic. She was also experiencing peer relationship problems (e.g., intense arguments with friends) and mild school avoidance. Karla maintained excellent grades in all of her classes, many of which were advanced or accelerated, although occasionally she would receive a poor grade on an assignment because she did not complete make-up work on days she was absent. Karla's mother noted that Karla would often become overwhelmed at home if she had make-up schoolwork to do. Karla's mother had taken her to the pediatrician on numerous occasions, but there were no notable medical problems.

At the start of ninth grade, Karla transitioned to the high school. Although there was communication between the middle school and high school regarding Karla's struggles, the interventions implemented during eighth grade did not remain in place when she started high school. Karla was attending school regularly for the two months, though her mother noted an increase in verbal and somatic complaints with a concomitant slow increase in missed school days. At that time, Karla became ill and tested positive for influenza, causing her to miss five consecutive days of school on her physician's orders. After this period, although her overt symptoms were resolved, Karla requested to stay home stating she still didn't feel well, but with coaxing, drove to school with her mother; once there, she became very emotional and pleaded with her mother to allow her to stay at home for another day, which her mother reluctantly allowed. Karla's school attendance plummeted, as she averaged attending school less than 2 days a week for another two weeks. During that period, Karla's mother met with the school principal and a teacher that served as the high school's special education coordinator. After this meeting, several interventions were implemented, including allowing Karla to complete school assignments at home, having Karla to meet with a teacher once a week after school at the local library (which Karla requested), allowing Karla to attend partial days with no penalties, and identifying several adults at school (i.e., the school librarian, school counselor, her art teacher, assistant principal) that Karla could talk to if she were feeling anxious and overwhelmed. These interventions were in place for two weeks, but Karla's attendance did not improve.

Description of the Problem Behavior

The school counselor met with Karla and her mother to conduct a clinical intake interview and collaborate on problem-identification. The interview consisted of collecting historical and contextual information regarding Karla's school avoidance, conducting a functional assessment of Karla's school avoidance, and creating an initial anxiety hierarchy through collaboratively identifying a variety of common and unique situations associated with school avoidance and having Karla rate her level of anxiety in each situation. Additionally, the school counselor met with the school team (i.e., principal, a favorite teacher, a least favorite teacher).

During the intake interview, Karla reported "liking school," but that she started to become very anxious when she was at school starting around the middle of the eighth grade when she and her best friend had an intense argument when other friends were present. She indicated that until that time, she had a "large group of friends" (i.e., about six to seven individuals) that she interacted with on a daily basis at school. After this incident, Karla reported feeling "awkward" around her ex-best friend and larger friend group. She felt that they were "looking, judging, and talking about her." An attempt at reconciliation with her ex-best friend was not successful. Karla stated that "things have gone downhill, and now they have spiraled out of control." Karla identified "feeling depressed," not having any friends, and being "overwhelmed and anxious" when thinking about being at school and around people at school. She reported currently having few people to talk with on a regular basis. At school, she incessantly frets about the quality of her work, her performance on tests and assignments, and being judged negatively by others. Karla felt very uncomfortable in classes where students were loud or didn't listen to the teacher, and "hated" walking the crowded hallways between classes. Further, she indicated feeling overwhelmed with schoolwork that accumulated as a result of her extended absences. Karla identified several reasons to return to school including her love for learning, being around teachers she likes, making/having friends, and meeting requirements that she needs to attend a good university. Karla's mother identified depression, school attendance, and anxiety about school as her primary concerns.

The school counselor also interviewed members of the school team. Themes included Karla being an excellent student but taking a long time to complete assignments and having difficulty accepting feedback in class. One teacher noted Karla was very eager to help others, but sometimes too much so, which resulted in other students viewing her "as a know-it-all" and rejecting her attempts at social interaction. Because Karla was not attending school, no observational data could be collected. The team identified school attendance as the primary problem behavior.

Problem Analysis

Although Karla had previously experienced mild to moderate school refusal, her current episode escalated quickly and was relatively severe. During the intake interview, the school counselor gave Karla and Karla's mother the School Refusal Assessment Scale-Revised (Kearney & Albano, 2018), a measure that asks children and parents to rate a series of questions about possible functions of school avoidance. The instrument identifies four functions: (1) avoidance of negative stimuli/situations (e.g., tests); (2) escape negative peer situations or performance evaluation; (3) attention from caretakers; and (4) reinforcement from activities outside of school (e.g., access to videogames). Indeed, Karla's and her mother's ratings demonstrated high elevations for both the negative reinforcement functions. Although attention from caretakers was a distant third in terms of averaged ratings, Karla's mother rated three questions as occurring frequently. Reinforcement from outside activities did not appear to have significant contributions to Karla's school avoidance as a whole.

Based on all available data, the treatment team hypothesized that Karla's school avoidance was predominantly attributable to negative reinforcement, though positive reinforcement also contributed to maintaining the behavior. Specifically, Karla experienced intense anxiety when at school, and avoiding (i.e., staying home from, leaving) school reduced this feeling. She was able to avoid what she perceived as negative teacher and peer evaluation. She also avoided situations that were very uncomfortable for her (e.g., walking in crowded hallways, being in loud classrooms, performance on tests). Additionally, when she was at home, she was able to watch TV, have interactions with her mother, play with her pets, and engage in other preferred activities (e.g., work on art projects). Finally, Karla reported that when she missed school, she became overwhelmed by the amount of make-up homework she had to complete and felt paralyzed to even start, further exacerbating her anxiety and avoidance.

Intervention Goals

Due to problems associated with non-attendance, the primary goal of CBT was to increase school attendance as quickly as possible. Karla's attendance goal was to fully return to school, being present all day, every day. Reduction in anxiety was also a primary goal of CBT, as the treatment team hypothesized that reducing anxiety would directly impact school avoidance. The decision was made to limit intervention goals as the team conceptualized the primacy of avoidance of anxious feelings leading to school avoidance, which in turn contributed to other reported problems such as depression and social relationship difficulties. It is much more difficult to engage in social relationships without a forum for that to occur, and for most children, school provides that venue. Similarly, Karla's depression was likely a related consequence of experiencing failure to attend school and lack of social reinforcement. Thus, both her peer relationships and her depression would likely improve if Karla regularly attended school. This is not to imply that peer relationship difficulties and depressed affect did not contribute to her anxiety and school avoidance, only that they were not prioritized as primary goals, though were included in the CBT intervention.

A primary goal for CBT was a reduction in anxiety. We hypothesized a bidirectional relationship between school attendance and anxiety reduction. That is, the team hypothesized that reductions in anxiety through CBT interventions would increase the probability of school attendance, and conversely, attending school would lead to reductions in reports of anxiety by means of exposure. The goal for anxiety reduction was for Karla to report a 50% reduction on her level of anxiety for her most anxiety-provoking situations at school.

Measurement of Target Behaviors, Data Collection Strategies, and Progress Monitoring

As the ultimate goal was for Karla to be present at school the whole day, every day, the primary measure of school attendance was the number of full days Karla attended school (and was in class) each week. However, as Karla was rarely attending school at all at the start of the intervention, partial attendance, defined as at least two hours at school for a day, was deemed to be a potential indicator of success and was also recorded. Further, given her affinity for one or two classes, but high aversion for others (and other situations), it was hypothesized that Karla might demonstrate initial success at returning to school for brief periods of time (e.g., attend classes she particularly likes), but it might be more difficult for her to increase attendance at other less-preferred class times (English) or situations (i.e., in the morning). As such, we also measured the number of hours Karla was at school each week (35 total hours/per week). School attendance was measured by looking at school attendance records at the end of each week (which were provided by the principal with Karla's and Karla's mother's permission) as well as from a log that Karla's mother kept. Hours at school were collected from Karla's mother's log, as she was asked to record time in and time out of school each day.

Anxiety was measured by having Karla rate her level of anxiety in the 12 situations identified in the initial assessment (see Table 12.1) using a zero to 10 scale

TABLE 12.1 Karla's Anxiety Hierarchy with SUDS Ratings from the First CBT Session

Situation	(0–10)
Being at school the whole day★	10
Walking into the school building in the morning★	10
Being at school for a partial day (at least 2 hours)★	9
Being in the hallways during class transition★	9
Being at school for English★	9
Being at school for lunch★	8
Talking about school in therapy session/to counselor during school	6
Being at present at school for art class	6
Being at school in the library	6
Meeting with a teacher after school	3
Talking about school in therapy session/to counselor after school	2
Being in the school building when school is not in session	2

Note: Items marked with an asterisk denote Karla's most highly related SUDS items that were the primary outcome measure for assessing reductions in anxiety and presented in Figure 12.3.

(i.e., subjective units of distress [SUDS]; zero = no anxiety, 10 = extreme anxiety). Karla rated her level of anxiety for each of these situations at the beginning of every CBT session, and these ratings served as the primary measure of anxiety.

An AB design with a post-intervention/generalization phase was utilized to assess intervention effects. For attendance, the three-week period prior to starting CBT served as baseline data for school attendance, with the intervention phase lasting for six weeks, and a post-intervention phase for seven weeks (with the fifth post-intervention week including a "CBT booster therapy" session). Anxiety (SUDS) ratings were collected at the beginning of every therapy session (12 sessions plus a booster session).

Intervention Plan

In the week prior to intervention implementation, the school psychologist and school counselor collaboratively identified and reviewed evidenced-based CBT strategies for school avoidance and anxiety. This process culminated in the creation of an individualized CBT treatment manual for the school counselor to utilize with Karla's specific presentation that included standard CBT elements tailored to school avoidance, including 1) psychoeducation, 2) relaxation and emotional regulation, 3) cognitive restructuring, 4) exposure, 5) skill building, 6) problem-solving, and 7) parental involvement. CBT consisted of Karla meeting with the school counselor twice a week for 45-60 minutes over a six-week period (i.e., 12 CBT therapy sessions). The CBT treatment manual defined the topics to cover for each session, identified the specific content for sessions, including therapist scripts, and contained the written materials for each session (e.g., handouts, homework assignments). The school psychologist and school counselor reviewed and practiced the implementation of sessions by identifying critical/crucial tactics or strategies, role-playing implementation of CBT, and problem-solving anticipated implementation issues prior to each session.

Twice per week sessions were deemed necessary given the length of time Karla had been out of school and the importance of getting her back to school as soon as possible. Karla's mother was also asked to attend CBT sessions, sometimes alone with the counselor or concurrently with Karla, to discuss the CBT model, review Karla's progress, discuss interventions that she might implement, review strategies that Karla was working on and how her mother could support them, and problem-solve issues that arose between sessions, making necessary adjustments to the treatment plan as needed. As Karla was typically not at school, these sessions initially occurred away from school at an affiliated office site. Moving therapy sessions to the school was one of the goals of CBT, and this occurred starting the second week. We had also planned for the possibility of a post-intervention "booster session" depending on the success of the initial CBT intervention as well as Karla's ability to maintain any treatment gains after CBT was terminated.

Although providing an in-depth description of each of the 12 CBT sessions is beyond the scope of this chapter, the content and material for much of the treatment in this case was adapted from a few primary sources, and the interested reader is encouraged to consult these treatment manuals for more thorough descriptions of session-by-session content (Heyne & Rollings, 2002; Kearney & Albano, 2018). In the remainder of this section, we elucidate some important overarching themes in conducting CBT and provide a few examples of dialogue from a couple of sessions to illustrate some of the concepts of CBT in more depth.

Psychoeducation

Psychoeducation is a critical first phase in CBT, as it sets the stage for everything that comes after. It is more than simply educating the client about how thoughts, feelings, and behaviors interact (although that is important); psychoeducation, particularly in this case, involves providing rationales for why the interventions that follow are important as well as attempts to build engagement and motivation for doing difficult work. Most human beings avoid things that are unpleasant; thus, normalizing escape and avoidance is critical, and framing the student's behavioral responses in the context of typical human behavior can go a long way in building rapport, eliminating guilt and shame, and providing an expectation that improvement is possible. Explaining to students that escape/avoidance "works" to eliminate anxious feelings as a short-term coping strategy often validates what they already know. It is also essential, however, that the student understand that avoidance perpetuates the anxiety cycle, reinforces irrational beliefs, and, as a long-term strategy, is one that limits opportunities for reinforcement, growth, and the extraordinary possibilities of life. The following dialogue illustrates a portion of the conversation between Karla and the school counselor involving psychoeducation about anxiety:

KARLA (K): I feel overwhelmed when I think about walking through those doors. I shake uncontrollably. And when I stay home, I feel so much better.

SCHOOL COUNSELOR (SC): No doubt! I totally get how being anxious about going to school is overwhelming. And when you don't go, what happens to that feeling? It goes away!!!

K: Yeah, exactly!

SC: So, what's wrong with that, right? Why are we even here talking about this today?

K: Yeah, why are we?!?! [K & SC laugh]

SC: Well, if that were the end of the story, we wouldn't be. But it's not the end of the story, is it? I mean, yeah, in the short-run, you don't feel anxious or overwhelmed, and you feel better. But in the long-run, is it a good strategy?

I mean, you are missing out on being with friends, making friends, laughing with friends, experiencing the excitement and challenges of life with other people, being with teachers you like, learning about topics that excite you, preparing yourself for college and being a pediatrician. In short, you are missing out on a big chunk of your life, don't you think?

K: Yeah, I know... I want to go, I do... it's just... [long pause]

THERAPIST: I *do* know!!! It's hard, like REAL hard, seemingly almost impossible to make yourself walk through those doors. That overwhelming sense of dread, all the negative thoughts that invade your head, the shaking, and feeling ill. AND... you know that you have this escape hatch... that if you leave, or don't walk in, that feeling goes away. Like the crushing weight of a giant boulder is lifted from your chest. But you also know why it's important to be there. And every time you walk away, every time you stay at home, your mind learns: it's easier just to not go. Right???

K: Yeah, that pretty much sums it up!

SC: But I can almost guarantee you that at some point in your life, you had another fear, maybe not something quite so big as this is now, but still big... maybe the first time you tried to ride your bike, maybe getting on a roller coaster, maybe getting shots at the doctor's office... I'm not sure what it may have been for you, but I'm guessing that there was something you really feared but did anyway for whatever reason... maybe your parents made you... but you did it... and afterward, you learned it wasn't as bad as you thought it was going to be.

K: [laughing] I used to be terrified of riding roller coasters! I don't know why. But now I love them... I asked to go to Six Flags for my birthday every year so I can ride all the roller coasters.

SC: See!!! And how would you have known that what your mind was telling you about roller coasters was not accurate unless you actually got on one? Can you imagine your life if you avoided everything that made you anxious, nervous, fearful, or uncomfortable??? We'd never do ANYTHING! The good news is that you have mastered your anxiety before, probably a lot more than you even know, and I think that with help and support, you can master it again.

As the dialogue above illustrates, psychoeducation is not simply presenting the notion of anxiety and avoidance to a client; it involves making it relevant, personal, and meaningful. The conversation between Karla and the school counselor includes elements of normalization; the connection between thoughts, feelings, and behaviors; rationales for therapy; and evoking motivation to engage in difficult work (e.g., therapeutic homework and exposure). Although CBT is pedagogical in nature, this does not imply that it should not be collaborative, interactive, engaging, and personally interesting. Research has consistently shown that youth engagement in CBT and therapeutic alliance with the therapist positively influences outcomes; conversely, manualized CBT consistently outperforms therapy as usual (i.e., non-directive, supportive therapy). Thus, when working with children and adolescents, it is imperative that the therapist balance engagement and CBT fidelity.

Relaxation

Relaxation techniques are critical in CBT for anxiety to reduce the physiological effects of arousal. Deep breathing, progressive muscle relaxation, and visual imagery are considered core techniques, and all were utilized with Karla. We have found that it is imperative to utilize a variety of relaxation strategies when conducting CBT with youth, as some youth do not resonate with certain techniques, contextual factors can influence the use of certain techniques (e.g., it's difficult to listen to a meditation script in the middle of class), and varying levels of anxiety may require utilization of different techniques (or a combination; e.g., deep breathing might be more effective for a youth at the onset of anxiety rather than once highly escalated).

Cognitive Restructuring

Cognitive restructuring goes by many names, and there are numerous techniques for having students examine their thinking processes and adopt new ways for perceiving and evaluating problematic situations. In the CBT intervention for Karla, we used several cognitive restructuring principles including cognitive defusion and cognitive reappraisal through implementation of various techniques (e.g., examination of common thought distortions, examining the evidence for thoughts/beliefs, positive coping statements, visualization exercises for "thoughts are just thoughts"). Although each has different assumptions and methods for cognitive restructuring, the goal of each is to have Karla change the way she perceives, experiences, and evaluates her anxiety. The following dialogue illustrates some of the nuances in one such technique:

SC: We've been reviewing how you've been doing the last few days, and went over some of your entries in your log. Let me ask you a question, Karla... How do you know you if your thoughts are accurate?

K: [long pause] I don't know, I mean, they are *my* thoughts.

SC: No doubt, and I didn't mean to imply they aren't real for you... not at all. My question is more about the content of your thoughts. Let me give you an example of what I mean. Do you believe in Santa?

K: [smiles] No, I'm 14 years old! I know there's no Santa Clause.

SC: Right, I figured... Do you remember when you did believe in Santa?

K: Well, yeah, every kid believes in Santa when they are younger.

SC: Exactly. And when you believed in Santa, you KNEW there was a Santa, and he came every Christmas Eve and left you presents. YOU KNEW IT!!! You ABSOLUTELY believed it, right?

K: Yeah, I suppose I did...

SC: But... turns out... you were wrong about Santa... what if you are wrong about your thoughts and beliefs about school??? What if that is like Santa? What if you absolutely believe it's true, but it's not?

K: [inquisitive look]

SC: So... how do you know that your thoughts about school, those thoughts about how people evaluate you when you're walking in the hallway, how devastating it would be to not do well on a test... those thoughts that lead to fears, worries, and anxieties about school... how do you know if they are accurate? It's not an easy question to answer, really. We all just assume that our thoughts are accurate. But in order to really know, we have to be a "thought detective."

K: What do you mean "thought detective"?

SC: Well, you told me you're afraid people are judging you, and your wrote in your log that you believe that they think you're "a loser." What's your evidence for that? Has anyone ever told you that?

K: Well, no, not exactly, but my best friend betrayed me, left me.

SC: OK, I get that must have been heartbreaking, but does that mean you are a loser?

K: Maybe...

SC: OK, well, "maybe" is different than "I definitely am a loser." Has anyone else called you a loser or betrayed you?

K: Well, not exactly, but some of my other old friends now don't talk to me... they hang out with [ex-best friend].

SC: So does that mean you are a loser? Are there any possible other explanations you can think of for why that happened?

K: They like her better.

SC: OK, and even if that's true, it still doesn't mean you are a loser. Maybe they hang out with her because they are upset with you, or thought you didn't handle the situation very well, or you didn't apologize sincerely, or a whole host of other possibilities... would you at least agree that really, you don't know with 100% certainty that they think you are a loser?

K: Well, when you put it like that, yeah, I guess I agree.

SC: Kinda sounds a little bit like Santa Clause. Can you think of any other reasons why people don't talk to you a lot at school, other than you are a loser?

K: I don't know... maybe because I don't talk a lot to them. Maybe because I'm kinda shy?

SC: Honestly, that seems a lot more plausible than you're a loser. Just because you have thoughts that come into your mind doesn't mean they are always right. You have to be a thought detective. What's the evidence for your thoughts and beliefs? As part of your homework, I'd like you to start including "thought detective" for some of your entries in your log, OK?

Exposure

Exposure is the backbone of CBT when used with internalizing disorders and, with moderate to severe school avoidance (i.e., not attending school for lengthy periods of time), it is recommended that exposure occur early in the intervention process. It is critical that children get back to school as soon as possible, so graduated exposure needs to happen early in the process, with increasingly challenging exposures as success builds and mastery develops. Of course, this is always balanced by the need to adequately prepare the student to handle their anxiety (through teaching coping strategies and other CBT strategies) before (and during) exposure. In the current CBT intervention, imaginal exposure started at the end of the first week of the intervention, and in-vivo exposure occurred at the start of the second week of the intervention (i.e., Karla attended the therapy session at school with her mother). As an example of imaginal exposure, Karla was instructed to close her eyes and visualize herself walking into art class, with the counselor verbalizing the exposure (e.g., "Visualize yourself walking down the hallway toward the art room… you approach the door… you pull the door open and see the teacher and other students getting seated…"). Karla was encouraged to use coping strategies discussed in the current or previous sessions, and these were scripted by the therapist for some of the exposure scenarios (e.g., "I want you to try deep breathing now"). In-vivo exposure exercises started at the beginning of week two (CBT session three) when therapy moved from off-campus to school. This was extraordinarily difficult for Karla and to help facilitate mastery, the first session at school was held 30 minutes before school, and Karla's mother came with Karla to the session, escorting and encouraging her prior to the session. This was done to ensure there would be few, if any, students around when Karla had to enter the building, but also make sure that she would be present in the building when the first bell rang (even though she was in the school counselor's office). Subsequent therapy sessions were scheduled at various times throughout the day based on Karla's progress and level of anxiety for particular situations (e.g., her art class was in the afternoon, so several sessions were scheduled in the afternoon, starting when most high schoolers were in class).

Homework

From a behavioral perspective, generalization of the skills and concepts being discussed in therapy sessions is more likely to occur if the student practices, implements, or otherwise is active using the skills and techniques between sessions when the problem is actually happening. In the current CBT intervention, almost every session had a between-session homework component. It is also important to recognize that adolescents, particularly those that have an aversion to school, often do not want to complete homework (rates of CBT therapy homework completion for adolescents is about 50%; Gaynor et al., 2006). Thus, it is important that the therapist try to provide useful, understandable, personally meaningful rationales for the homework. It is also important that the therapist adopts a strategy for addressing homework non-completion that is reasonable, empathetic, and based on a functional assessment (i.e., what variables are primarily responsible) of the non-completion. There are no consensus rules about the best approaches for dealing with homework non-completion, but trying to elicit reasons for nonadherence and problem-solving potential barriers has resulted in improved completion rates (Jungbluth & Shirk, 2013). Appendix A provides an example of a homework assignment frequently used with Karla between sessions.

Intervention Fidelity and Interobserver Agreement

As the "gold-standard" method of assessing fidelity for CBT typically involves a review of video/audio recordings of sessions by an expert, assessment of fidelity in the current case was not a straightforward task. Recording of video sessions was not feasible in this case due to the lack of time and resources to train a staff member to become facile with coding CBT recordings, then devote time to review and code a percentage of audio/video recordings of CBT sessions. Additionally, Karla did not assent to having sessions recorded.

In lieu of assessing fidelity via coding of sessions, three strategies were implemented to assess and enhance fidelity. The first was the use of several questions on the Therapeutic Alliance and Outcome Questionnaire (TAOQ; student and parent forms), a measure created and designed by the treatment team to assess therapist-client alliance, CBT implementation, and treatment satisfaction (see Appendices B & C), that asked Karla and her mother to rate the counselor's CBT skill utilization during the sessions. The second method was the use of supervised behavioral rehearsal. In this method, a therapist implements a CBT skill during an analog therapy session with a trained model/actor, and a supervisor observes (directly or through video recordings). The method is more flexible than direct observation methods and may serve as an intermediary step between direct methods (i.e., coding via observations of sessions) and indirect methods (i.e., self-reports; Beidas, Cross, & Dorsey, 2014). As it was not feasible to train a model/actor to represent a mock patient, the method was modified in this case, and the school psychologist role-played being a teenager presenting with school avoidance with anxiety, and the school counselor practiced implementation of core elements of CBT, followed by evaluation and feedback. The third approach was for the school psychologist to conduct a weekly clinical case review with the school counselor for one or both weekly CBT sessions, which included the

TABLE 12.2 Therapeutic Alliance & Outcome Questionnaire (TAOQ) Ratings

Youth	Session 2	Session 12	All sessions
Get along	4	5	4.7
Collaborated on goals	4	5	4.6
Explained topic/skills★	5	5	4.9
Demonstrated/practiced skills/strategies★	5	5	4.9
Understand thoughts/feelings/behaviors★	4	5	4.7
Helping accomplish goals	3	5	4.4
Recommend to another student	4	5	4.8

Parent	Session 2	Session 12	All Sessions
Get along	5	5	5.0
Feel included	4	5	4.9
Informed about progress	4	5	4.8
Helps me understand my child's problems	5	5	4.9
Helps/demonstrates tactics/strategies to help★	5	5	4.9
Feel like therapy is helping child	3	5	4.7
Recommend to another parent	3	5	4.8

Note: Questions with an asterisk denote items related to CBT fidelity. TAOQ ratings were not collected at the first session. "All sessions" is the average TAOQ item rating across all sessions.

therapist answering questions regarding CBT fidelity (i.e., how a skill, strategies, theme, or technique was implemented by the school counselor) and responses of the student (or her mother) from sessions.

Only one of these strategies produced objective data, and results from the three questions on the Therapeutic Alliance & Outcome Questionnaire (TAOQ)-Student form and one question on the TAOQ-Parent form related to CBT fidelity are presented in Table 12.2. As illustrated, both Karla and her mother indicated a high level of agreeability that the school counselor utilized CBT techniques in the therapy sessions with both Karla and her mother. Interrater reliability calculated for the one duplicate question on the youth and parent form was 91% across the 11 sessions for which it was collected and completed.

Intervention Outcome Data

School Attendance

The number of school days with full and partial attendance and average hours at school are presented in Figures 12.1 and 12.2, respectively. Karla's school attendance increased over the course of the intervention across all measures. As predicted, partial attendance increased rapidly relative to full-day attendance. During the first week of CBT, Karla was able to attend three partial days of school (compared to one partial day during the entire three-week baseline period), and by the third week of implementation of CBT, she was going to school every day

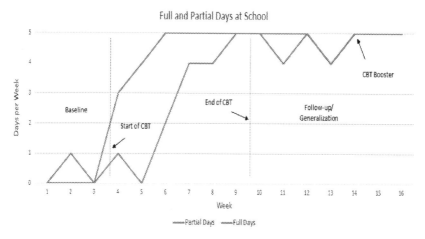

FIGURE 12.1 School days with full and partial attendance

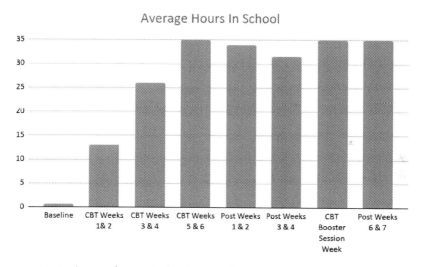

FIGURE 12.2 Average hours at school per week

for at least part of the day and maintained this throughout the CBT intervention. However, full-day attendance increased more slowly, and Karla did not attend a full, entire week of school until the sixth and last week of the CBT intervention. Interestingly, during weeks four and five of the intervention, Karla was at school the whole day every day, but she did not always attend the class she was scheduled for, instead preferring to go to another area (e.g., library). Karla's time at school also demonstrated a similar pattern and is reflective of her initial successes returning to school to attend several of her favorite classes. During the second and fourth week of CBT, she was able to be present at school for other more neutral classes and situations, but she was still struggling with being present for certain highly anxiety provoking situations (e.g., English class, walking through the school doors at or before morning bell; see SUDS ratings below). Generally speaking, Karla's attendance gains were maintained during follow-up, though minor fluctuations in full and partial day attendance during the four weeks following the end of CBT necessitated a "booster CBT" session during the 5th week following termination of the original CBT intervention.

SUDS Ratings

Karla's SUDS ratings are presented in Figure 12.3. Of the 12 situations that Karla rated at each CBT session, only six are presented in the graph, as these represent situations rated as most anxiety-provoking. As can be seen in the figure, Karla's SUDS ratings for all situations were lower at the end of CBT relative to her initial ratings. However, some SUDS ratings demonstrated rapid decline, whereas others remained somewhat elevated even at the end of CBT. Her SUDS ratings for going to the school library and going to art class (not presented in the graph) both dropped from a six to a three between the third and fourth CBT sessions which corresponded to in-vivo exposure exercises conducted during CBT sessions for these two classes. Similarly, her SUDS ratings for attending English class remained elevated until the eighth session, when there was a noticeable drop. In the seventh CBT session, the therapist and Karla were engaged in an in-vivo exposure exercise (e.g., walking down the hallway past her English classroom

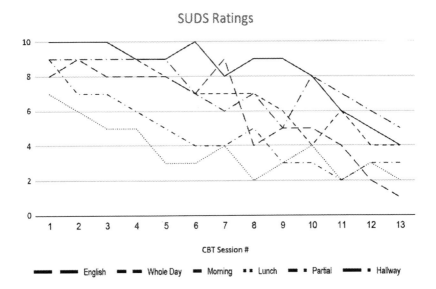

FIGURE 12.3 SUDS ratings for CBT sessions

while it was in session) when her English teacher walked out of the room. She had not been to his class more than once in over a month. Surprised to see her, the teacher smiled and said "Karla!!! I've missed you! Where have you been? I hope to have you back in the classroom soon... you are one of my brightest students and I miss hearing your opinions." Karla, though barely able to make eye contact, smiled broadly, and managed to say, "Thanks Mr. Forrest, I didn't know that's how you felt." Later, in the school counselor's office, Karla and the counselor discussed how her perceptions of this teacher didn't map onto the interaction that had just occurred and further engaged in "thought detective" dialogue. Karla agreed to go to English class the next day (a plan was devised so that she would walk into the class with another student). If she was able to do that, she could pick from pre-identified rewards (e.g., $10 gift card to local art supply store, spending an hour with art teacher after school). This resulted in Karla going to English class the next day and her reporting at the next session that "Mr. Forrest's not so bad... he's just really opinionated, and I don't always agree with him, but he doesn't agree with a lot of students, so it's not just me." All of her SUDS ratings dropped by 50% or more over the course of the intervention, and remained low at the booster session, with the exception of her anxiety when in the hallway during transition time, which declined from a nine at the first CBT session to six at the final session (and five at the booster session). Partially because of this, as long as she was at school, she was allowed to leave class five minutes early to transition to her next class in order to avoid the crowded hallways.

Summary of Intervention Effects

The CBT intervention dramatically improved Karla's school attendance over the course of CBT and was maintained over follow-up. The number of full school days attended, partial days attending, and time at school all improved over the course of the intervention. As hypothesized, partial attendance increased more rapidly, with slower gains in time at school and full-day attendance. Concurrently, Karla's report of anxiety related to various school situations decreased as well, with all but one situation (i.e., being in the hallways) showing decreases of 50% or more from initial ratings. Intervention effects were relatively immediate for some variables (e.g. partial days, SUDS ratings for moderately high anxiety situations), though were more gradual for the most difficult of situations (e.g., full days, walking into school in the morning, attending a non-preferred class, being in the hallways at school).

Intervention Acceptability

Throughout the intervention, both Karla and her mother completed the TAOQ that included questions about rapport, goals, CBT implementation, and perceptions of effectiveness and satisfaction (see Table 12.2). The treatment team decided to create their own measure of these constructs as existing alliance, outcome, fidelity, and satisfaction measures either were too costly or did not capture all the elements of interest in one measure. These ratings were completed weekly. Both Karla and her mother indicated a high degree of satisfaction with CBT and with her therapist. Although alliance, rapport, and CBT implementation ratings showed ceiling effects (i.e., ratings were highly elevated from the beginning and showed little variability), both Karla's and her mother's ratings of the effectiveness showed marked improvement over the course of the intervention, as would have been expected given that Karla was not going to school much during the first couple sessions (see Table 12.2 for pre, post, and averaged TAOQ ratings).

Intervention Considerations

Perhaps unlike some of the other interventions in this volume, CBT is not an intervention that can be easily implemented by most paraprofessionals, teachers, or even all school counselors or school psychologists (if they are not adequately trained in CBT). To be executed well, CBT requires knowledge, training, and practice, as numerous studies have reported significant reductions in treatment effects when CBT is implemented by therapists with inadequate training and/or supervision. Fortunately, many school psychologists and school counselors have training in CBT. Almost all evidenced-based CBT protocols for youth problems are manualized and many are freely available (or available at low cost), affording practitioners ample opportunity to become more knowledgeable about CBT interventions for students. We also note that although adherence to CBT manuals is important, even critical, when delivering CBT, it is also imperative to implement the content of the manual in a manner that resonates with and engages the student. Particularly when therapists have a thorough understanding of core CBT principles, rich clinical experiences in utilizing CBT, and/or enhanced clinical supervision, they can and should supplement, expand, tailor, modify, enrich, and generally bring to life the specific CBT methods delineated in any particular manualized CBT. In our opinion, the ultimate goal for any CBT practitioner is not to master the content of various treatment manuals, but rather to gain a rich, thorough understanding of the common elements inherent in almost all CBT treatment manuals. This is particularly relevant to schools as they consider adopting CBT therapies or interventions, as it would not be feasible for any one person to become an expert in all of the multitude of manualized CBT treatments for the range of problems likely to be encountered. However, mastery of core elements of CBT allows for an easier understanding and adoption of various CBT manuals, as well as the ability to implement manualized CBT interventions with flexibility, individualization, and enhanced client engagement (Kendall & Beidas, 2007).

For schools and school districts who have therapists trained in CBT, can afford to train professional staff in CBT, and/or have someone with expertise in CBT who can train and provide clinical supervision to school counselors/therapists, CBT can provide an extraordinarily valuable tool to the intervention arsenal. Given the expertise and effort required to implement CBT, it most likely should be reserved for students with significant behavioral, emotional, and/or social problems that have not responded to other interventions. It is also worth noting that CBT can be delivered effectively in a group format, which would afford practitioners some ability to reach more students, though attention to other issues would be needed (participant selection, group size, open/closed group, number of staff needed to run the group, pulling numerous students from class simultaneously, homogeneity of group members, etc.).

Conclusion

CBT is one of the most well-studied, effective interventions for a variety of child and adolescent problems. This case study demonstrates how CBT can be applied to the problem of school avoidance with a 14-year-old, female ninth-grader. CBT can be a highly effective tool for school personnel to address a variety of presenting problems across a wide age range. One of the strengths of CBT is that it is comprehensive, flexible, adaptable, and problem-focused. As illustrated by this case example, CBT incorporates a variety of different interventions targeted at the problem behaviors in a very short period of time. For this case study, within a span of four weeks, elements of behavioral parent training, school–home communication, psychoeducation, relaxation strategies, cognitive restructuring, and exposure strategies were introduced. Further, the presumption of CBT is that, when successful, it alters the way the individual perceives and processes information from their environment. Thus, inherent in the philosophical underpinnings of CBT is the notion of generalizability. After termination of CBT, the individual often continues treatment gains, as was true of Karla's case.

References

Beck, A. T. (1964). Thinking and depression: Theory and therapy. *Archives of General Psychiatry*, *10*, 561–571. doi:10.1001/archpsyc.1964.01720240015003

Beidas, R., Cross, W., & Dorsey, S. (2014). Show me, don't tell me: Behavioral rehearsal as a training and analogue fidelity tool. *Cognitive and Behavioral Practice*, *21*(1), 1–11. doi:10.1016/j.cbpra.2013.04.002

David, D., Cristea, I., & Hofmann, S. (2018). Why cognitive behavioral therapy is the current gold standard of psychotherapy. *Frontiers in Psychiatry*, *9*, 1-3. doi:10.3389/fpsyt.2018.00004

Dobson, K. (2003). *Handbook of cognitive-behavioral therapies* (2nd ed.). New York, NY: Guilford Press.

Ellis, A. (1958). Rational psychotherapy. *Journal of General Psychology*, *59*, 35–49.

Gaynor S., Lawrence P., & Nelson-Gray, R. (2006). Measuring homework compliance in cognitive-behavioral therapy for adolescent depression: review, preliminary findings, and implications for theory and practice. *Behavior Modification*, *30*(5), 647–672

Heyne, D., & Rollings, S. (2002). *School refusal*. Leicester: British Psychological Society.

Hofmann, S., Asnaani, A., Vonk, I., Sawyer, A., & Fang, A. (2012). The efficacy of cognitive behavioral therapy: A review of meta-analyses. *Cognitive Therapy and Research, 36*(5), 427–440. doi:10.1007/s10608-012-9476-1

Jungbluth, N., & Shirk, S. (2013). Promoting homework adherence in cognitive-behavioral therapy for adolescent depression. *Journal of Clinical Child & Adolescent Psychology, 42*(4), 545–553. doi:10.1080/15374416.2012.743105

Kazdin, A. (1982). *Single-case research designs* (1st ed.). New York: Oxford University Press.

Kearney, C.A., & Albano, A.M. (2018). *When children refuse school: A cognitive-behavioral therapy approach / Therapist's guide* (3rd ed.). New York: Oxford University Press. doi:10.1093/med-psych/9780190604059.001.0001

Kendall, P. C., & Beidas, R. S. (2007). Smoothing the trail for dissemination of evidence-based practices for youth: Flexibility within fidelity. *Professional Psychology: Research and Practice, 38*(1), 13–20. doi:10.1037/0735-7028.38.1.13

Kendall, P., & Braswell, L. (1997). *Cognitive-behavioral therapy for impulsive children* (2nd ed.). New York, NY: Guilford Press.

Lorenzo-Luaces, L., Keefe, J., & DeRubeis, R. (2016). Cognitive-behavioral therapy: Nature and relation to non-cognitive behavioral therapy. *Behavior Therapy, 47*(6), 785–803. doi:10.1016/j.beth.2016.02.012

O'Donohue, W., & Fisher, J. (2012). The Core Principles of Cognitive Behavior Therapy. In W O'Donohue & J Fisher (eds), *Cognitive behavior therapy: Core principles for practice*, 1–12. Hoboken, NJ: Wiley. doi:10.1002/9781118470886.ch1

Stallard, P. (2009). *Anxiety: Cognitive behaviour therapy with children and young people*. London: Routledge.

Walen, S. R., DiGiuseppe, R., & Dryden, W. (1992). *A practitioner's guide to rational-emotive therapy* (2nd ed.). New York: Oxford University Press.

Wright, J. (2006). Cognitive behavior therapy: Basic principles and recent advances. *Focus, 4*(2), 173–178. doi:10.1176/foc.4.2.173

Appendix A: Example of Between-Session Homework

MY TEB LOG
(Thoughts/Emotions/Behavior)

Over the next week, please keep notes on events that happen between sessions. Most of these events should be related to going/not going to school.

Event: _____

_____

My thoughts: How I felt: How I acted/behaved:

_____   _____   _____

_____   _____   _____

_____   _____   _____

_____   _____   _____

SUDS Rating (0–10):

Outcome: _____

_____

Appendix B: Therapeutic Alliance and Outcome Questionnaire (TAOQ)-Youth

In order to help us understand if what we are doing is working, we are asking that you answer the following questions as honestly as you can. They will be shared with your therapist, but only so that they can better understand what's working and not working, and how to help you better in therapy in order to reach your goals.

	(5)	*(4)*	*(3)*	*(2)*	*(1)*
My therapist and I get along well	Strongly Agree	Agree	Neutral	Disagree	Strongly Disagree
My therapist and I discuss my progress towards my treatment goals	Strongly Agree	Agree	Neutral	Disagree	Strongly Disagree
I felt like my therapist explained to me the importance of the topic or skill of the session in way I could understand	Strongly Agree	Agree	Neutral	Disagree	Strongly Disagree
Skills and/or strategies presented in sessions were demonstrated, practiced, and/or role-played	Strongly Agree	Agree	Neutral	Disagree	Strongly Disagree
My therapist helped me understand how my thoughts, feelings, and behaviors contribute to my difficulties	Strongly Agree	Agree	Neutral	Disagree	Strongly Disagree
I feel like therapy is helping me accomplish my goals	Strongly Agree	Agree	Neutral	Disagree	Strongly Disagree
I would recommend CBT to other students with similar problems	Strongly Agree	Agree	Neutral	Disagree	Strongly Disagree

Appendix C: Therapeutic Alliance and Outcome Questionnaire (TAOQ)-Parent

In order to help us understand if what we are doing is working, we are asking that you answer the following questions as honestly as you can. They will be shared with your therapist, but only so that they can better understand what's working and not working, and how to help you better in therapy in order to reach your goals.

	(5)	(4)	(3)	(2)	(1)
My child's therapist and I get along well	Strongly Agree	Agree	Neutral	Disagree	Strongly Disagree
I feel included in my child's therapy	Strongly Agree	Agree	Neutral	Disagree	Strongly Disagree
My child's therapist keeps informed about her progress	Strongly Agree	Agree	Neutral	Disagree	Strongly Disagree
My child's therapist helps me to better understand my child's problems	Strongly Agree	Agree	Neutral	Disagree	Strongly Disagree
My child's therapist has helped me to implement tactics and strategies to improve my child's functioning	Strongly Agree	Agree	Neutral	Disagree	Strongly Disagree
I feel like therapy is helping my child accomplish her goals	Strongly Agree	Agree	Neutral	Disagree	Strongly Disagree
I would recommend CBT to other parents that have students with similar problems	Strongly Agree	Agree	Neutral	Disagree	Strongly Disagree

13

EXPOSURE THERAPY

Rachel E. Mathews, Michael L. Sulkowski, and Cary Jordan

Introduction

A central component in the treatment of anxiety disorders is exposure-based intervention. Exposure, also known as Exposure and Response Prevention (ERP) or exposure therapy, is an evidence-based treatment approach to address fear-provoking stimuli (Craske, Treanor, Conway, Zbozinek, & Vervliet, 2014). While a cognitive perspective conceptualizes anxiety as involving automatic, negative, and often fearful thoughts, a behavior analytic approach posits that an individual's anxious or fearful behavior is negatively reinforced when the behavior results in the removal of fear-provoking stimuli. Repeated removal (or avoidance) of fear-provoking stimuli eventually shapes escape/avoidant responses to those fear-provoking stimuli. Failure to habituate to fear-provoking stimuli or decrease anxiety levels in the absence of fear-refusing behavior further exacerbates anxiety-related problems. Thus, engaging in exposure involves having individuals stay with or proximal to aversive stimuli until their escape/avoidant behaviors are no longer negatively reinforced, and eventually extinguished. Exposure therapy may be implemented using graduated or intense models and through imagery or in-vivo experiences (Merrell, Ervin, & Gimple, 2006).

Exposure therapy falls under the broad umbrella of Cognitive Behavioral Therapy (CBT), but typically does not involve cognitive restructuring, which is a central tenet of CBT. Rather, exposure therapy consists of identifying the individual's most acute and intrusive worries and developing a fear hierarchy. The anxiety associated with one's fears are measured using the Subjective Units of Distress scale (SUDS), often ranging from one to 10 or one to 100, with one indicating little to no anxiety and 10 or 100 denoting profound anxiety (Marazziti & Consoli, 2010). Using SUDS ratings, the individual's fears are ranked from least distressing to most distressing, and the therapist and client develop an exposure schedule to determine which fear-provoking stimuli will be introduced in subsequent sessions.

Once the fear hierarchy and exposure schedule are established, the client is asked to repeatedly confront the anxiety-provoking situations until extinction of escape/avoidant behavior occurs and response prevention is maintained. That is, an individual must be exposed to the fear-provoking stimuli until his or her anxiety decreases naturally through the process of habituation. Following standard practice, the client and therapist begin with lower numbers on the fear hierarchy and gradually work up toward more fear-provoking stimuli (Pence, Sulkowski, Jordan, & Storch, 2010).

There are two important concepts to consider when executing exposure tasks. These include anxiety sensitivity and habituation. Anxiety sensitivity is defined as the belief that anxiety and anxiety-related bodily sensations may result in harmful social, psychological, or physiological consequences (Epkins, Gardner, & Scanlon, 2013). Anxiety sensitivity varies from person to person based on a variety of factors including genetic makeup and lived experiences. Additionally, habituation must be considered. Habituation, in the context of exposure therapy, is defined as the reduction of a physiological and/or emotional response to a repeated stimulus (Foa et al., 2002), and generally takes between 10 and 45 minutes to occur, as clients demonstrate individual differences in how quickly or slowly they habituate. In exposure therapy, it is essential to communicate to clients that exposures will evoke some discomfort, which is an important part of the habituation process.

Systematic desensitization (SD) is one particular treatment modality that has been shown to be effective in treating anxiety and related disorders. Originally developed by Wolpe (1961), SD is a gradual approach in which an individual reduces his or her maladaptive anxious response to an aversive stimulus by being slowly and methodically exposed to the stimulus (Lang, 2017). SD is based on the theory of classical conditioning and typically contains three components: relaxation training, fear hierarchy construction, and desensitization to the stimulus (Wolpe, 1961). The case presented in this chapter highlights the use of systematic desensitization in the treatment of anxiety and escape/avoidance behaviors of an adolescent girl.

Case Study

Background Information

Anna was an 11th-grade student at Great Plains High School. She was initially referred to the student assistance team because of school refusal and social anxiety related to peer relationship problems occurring in and out of school. Anna was not receiving special education services through an Individualized Education Program (IEP), nor was she receiving accommodations through a Section 504 Plan. However, she had recently started therapy with a doctoral-level school psychologist named Dr. Daniels at an integrated behavioral healthcare clinic. At the time of intervention implementation, Anna had attended only the intake and one session at the outpatient clinic. Anna and Dr. Daniels had created her fear hierarchy at their first skill-building session but had not started the exposure-based part of treatment.

To address the academic and social–emotional/behavioral concerns of its students, Anna's school utilized Multi-Tiered Systems of Support (MTSS). The MTSS process is divided into three broad tiers based on the intensity of support delivered therein: Tier 1 (universal screening), Tier 2 (targeted support), and Tier 3 (intensive support; Sulkowski, Joyce, & Storch, 2012). Tier 1 social–emotional programming implemented at Anna's school was comprised of a Positive Behavior Interventions and Supports (PBIS) model. Through PBIS, students could earn rewards individually or as a group for demonstrating pro-social behaviors that aligned with the program. The Tier 2 social–emotional-behavioral interventions that were offered consisted of small-group sessions with the school psychologist in which students with similar needs (e.g., divorce, grief, etc.) were clustered together for weekly sessions using a CBT framework. The school psychologist had previously recruited Anna to join a coping skills group several times; however, Anna refused to attend and did not obtain consent from her mother to participate.

Anna's homeroom science teacher, Mrs. Bailey, reported that Anna missed school or skipped her class more frequently when interactive tasks were assigned. For example, she noted that Anna was often absent or left her class when students were asked to work with partners on lab assignments. Anna's language arts teacher, Mr. Lee, noted similar observations and indicated that Anna often missed class when students were given time to work collaboratively on group projects, discuss current or upcoming assignments, or grade one another's homework. Interestingly, Anna's math teacher, Mrs. Melody, reported virtually no difficulties with Anna coming to her class when she attended school. However, she indicated that the majority of work assigned in her class was completed individually and she rarely required students to pair up for activities. All of Anna's teachers agreed that her academic performance was above average, although her grades were beginning to suffer as a result of missing multiple days of school per week.

Description of the Problem Behavior

The school psychologist conducted a problem-identification interview with Anna and Anna's teachers. During their individual meeting, Anna disclosed that she began feeling nervous about coming to school following an incident with her peers several months prior to the emergence of school-refusal behaviors. Anna reported she had attended a party with friends in October and tried drinking alcohol for the first time. After having several drinks, Anna began to feel nauseated and panicky. She asked her friends with whom she had ridden if they could go home, but they would not leave the party. Her friends also indicated they would get in trouble if she admitted they had been drinking and prevented her from calling her parents. Anna described symptoms similar to those of a panic attack (e.g., chest tightness, shallow breathing, dizziness and, as Anna described, "this feeling that I was going to die"). Anna stated she felt powerless, scared, and disrespected by her peers, which led her to avoid her friends during free time. Anna reported that she eventually told her mother about her experience at the party because she felt guilty and her mother became very angry. Anna noted she then began feeling nervous anytime she saw her friends, not just when spending time together on the weekends. Anna stated she felt worried that her mother would assume she was doing "bad things" with her friends, even when she was attending school during the day.

After obtaining this information, the school psychologist and teachers consulted about Anna's school refusal and avoidance. School refusal has been previously defined as absences from school that are child-motivated and not due to medical illness or injury (Kearney, 2008). In this case, school refusal was operationalized to include missing a sum total of two or more days of school per week because of active noncompliance (e.g., fighting with her mother, crying, driving partway to school and then turning around to go home) or passive noncompliance (e.g., not getting out of bed, waiting for her mother to leave for work before going back to bed). Similarly, school avoidance has been previously defined as difficulty remaining at school for the duration of a full school day (Kearney, 2008. In Anna's case, school avoidance was any incident in which Anna attended school for some part of the day, but then left to go home.

When attendance data were accessed from the office, the school psychologist found that Anna was attending 2.04 full school days per week on average. In other words, Anna was attending school 40.8% of the time. Of the 35 hours in a typical school week, Anna was receiving approximately 14.28 hours of instruction. Thus, Anna was missing approximately 60% of instruction per week, which amounted to about 20.72 hours. Given this trajectory, Anna was missing over 80 hours of instruction per month.

In addition to fully refusing to attend school (e.g., avoiding school by staying home), Anna also frequently attempted to abscond when her mother required her to attend. Similar to the aforementioned procedures for calculating the number of days/hours Anna was attending per week, the school psychologist accessed attendance data from the high school office. Across a period of eight weeks, Anna left school approximately 2.25 times per week on average. As such, Anna was attending but then leaving school 45% of the time during a typical five-day school week. Anna was therefore leaving school approximately nine times per month.

Problem Analysis

The school psychologist hypothesized that the function of Anna's behavior was escape/avoidance of peers and therefore avoidance of attending school, which was maintained through negative reinforcement. Specifically, Anna's escape-maintained behaviors consisted of absenteeism, leaving school early, avoidance of social interactions with peers, and calling her mother for permission to go home when she felt anxious. Anna's avoidance-maintained behaviors consisted of school refusal, which occurred approximately three times per week and school avoidance, which occurred about twice per week.

The team considered Anna's cognitive and academic functioning in reference to her escape/avoidance behaviors. Anna was a native English speaker who had attended the same school district since preschool. She consistently earned above-average grades and teachers did not report concerns related to a potential learning disability. The team determined that Anna's school/peer avoidance was not likely due to her academic functioning. However, Anna's grades had begun slipping to Cs and Ds since she began frequently missing school.

Fear Hierarchy Development

The school psychologist elected to work with Dr. Daniels to collect data regarding aversive school-related stimuli and anxiety-provoking situations. Dr. Daniels shared the fear hierarchy he and Anna had begun to create during their first therapy session (see Appendix A). Dr. Daniels assisted the school psychologist with identifying stimuli that Anna categorized as less aversive (e.g., seeing a picture of her school) to more aversive (e.g., attending full days of school for five consecutive days). Dr. Daniels assisted the school psychologist with identifying exposure exercises that were related to school and could be implemented before or during the formal school day. The school psychologist and Dr. Daniels also consulted about adjusting some potential exposure exercises so they could be more readily implemented in a school setting. Such adjustments included considerations for Anna's schedule (e.g., using part of a study hall to practice an exposure), identifying a location to practice exposure exercises, and engaging Anna's teachers in practices to avoid accommodating her anxiety (e.g., not allowing excessive trips to the restroom).

Intervention Goals

Anna's school psychologist and teachers participated in ongoing consultation with Dr. Daniels. At the end of the eight-week intervention, Anna was expected to attend school 95% of the time or 4.75 days per week. However, given her baseline data of attending just 2.04 out of five school days, the team determined that an intermediate attendance goal of 80% (four out of five days) would be appropriate for the fourth week of intervention. Thus, tiered success criteria were designed with 80% attendance at week four and 95% at week eight.

The team also developed a goal targeting Anna's school avoidance. The team established that Anna would not leave school early more than once per month because of her anxiety (5% of the time). This goal extended to remaining in class (e.g., not leaving to "use the restroom" for extended periods of time), with Anna attending 95% of school hours per week.

Measurement of Target Behavior, Data Collection, and Progress Monitoring

The team selected three outcome variables to measure Anna's school attendance: (1) number of days attended per week; (2) number of hours spent in school per day; and (3) number of attempts of self-removal from school per week. The school psychologist was responsible for accessing Anna's overall attendance data each day, monitoring the number of hours Anna spent in school, and tracking the number of times she left school each week. See Appendix B for the school psychologist's data collection form.

Intervention Plan

Anna had been previously recruited by the school psychologist to participate in a Tier 2 small group for students with internalizing disorders (e.g., anxiety, depression). However, Anna refused to attend the group and did not obtain her mother's consent for participation. Given Anna's ongoing difficulties in participating in the Tier 2 small group intervention, a Tier 3 intervention was developed. This intervention utilized systematic desensitization (SD) to address Anna's escape/avoidant behavior and absenteeism.

Anna's eight-week intervention plan consisted of four primary phases using an ABAB single-subject design to evaluate its effects on the outcome variables. The first phase of Anna's intervention plan was comprised of a two-week baseline condition, which data related to her school refusal and avoidance were collected. Following the baseline condition, the intervention phase was implemented. This phase consisted of graduated exposure exercises, in which SD was used to address Anna's attendance and her remaining at school during the day. The school psychologist and Dr. Daniels worked closely to identify school-related fears on Anna's hierarchy that could be systematically introduced to increase attendance.

Based on Dr. Daniels' recommendations and the treatment protocol for exposure therapy, the team determined they would implement the exposure exercises in hierarchical order, from less anxiety-provoking to more aversive, with the final goal of Anna attending full days of school for five consecutive days. The team chose to have a return to baseline condition approximately halfway through the treatment protocol (after week 4) and at the conclusion of the intervention (week 8) to evaluate Anna's behavior without the inclusion of exposure exercises.

The exposure exercises were delivered before and during school hours, five days per week. They consisted of Anna physically coming to school, remaining in class, and limiting self-removal from school. Each morning, Anna met with the school psychologist to discuss the exposure exercises she would complete that day. In each session, the school psychologist provided psychoeducation to Anna about anxiety and the rationale for the exposure exercise. The school psychologist and Anna would then choose one exposure exercise with which she felt relatively comfortable. The school psychologist communicated Anna's daily exposure exercises to her teachers to ensure they understood the behavioral expectations for the day and limit their accommodation of Anna's avoidance and escape behaviors.

In addition to classroom-based exposure exercises, the school psychologist met daily with Anna during part of her study hall to practice being exposed to fear-provoking stimuli. For example, one session included Anna and the school psychologist creating an exposure script of negative thoughts that Anna frequently experienced. The school psychologist asked Anna to read and reread the script until her anxiety reduced to at least two or three out of 10 SUDS. The purpose of this particular session was for Anna to acknowledge her automatic, negative thoughts and habituate to them until they no longer provoked an anxious response (e.g., feeling nervous, increase in respiration, chest tightness, dizziness).

Finally, Dr. Daniels discussed the assignment of homework when Anna attended therapy sessions at the outpatient care clinic. Homework, defined as any maintenance activities that clients are asked to complete outside of therapy, is a core component of exposure therapy. To facilitate generalization, exposure-related homework can be implemented in a number of settings (e.g., home, school, community; Wheaton et al., 2016). In addition to addressing school refusal during sessions with Dr. Daniels, Anna's homework focused on increasing interactions with peers because of her fears about interacting with them after the party.

Intervention Fidelity and Interobserver Agreement

Intervention fidelity was evaluated once per week using a modified version of the Prolonged Exposure Therapy (PE) Fidelity Checklist (Foa, Hembree, & Rothbaum, 2007). Dr. Daniels evaluated the school psychologist's intervention fidelity using this modified checklist once per week by observing the intervention session via telehealth (see Appendix C). During the sessions observed by Dr. Daniels, fidelity was calculated to be 94%. In light of the percentage of agreement among raters, it was determined the intervention was being implemented with fidelity for the duration of the intervention period.

In addition to fidelity, interobserver agreement (IOA) was utilized to assess Anna's attendance. More specifically, IOA was calculated to examine raters' agreement about Anna's absenteeism (e.g., was she absent from school, was the absence due to anxiety). This was conducted once per week during the baseline and intervention periods. Interobserver agreement was calculated to be 98%, suggesting high reliability among raters.

Intervention Outcome Data

School Days Attended per Week/Month

The team implemented an initial, two-week baseline period. During the first week of baseline, Anna spent 2.04 full days at school. Her mean percentage attendance at baseline was 40.8%. During the second week of baseline, Anna's mean percentage attendance was 68%, with an average attendance of 3.4 days per week. At week 3, the team implemented the first intervention phase (i.e., SD), which was evaluated after two weeks. During week 3, Anna attended 3.84 days of school, which was 76.8% of the typical school week. At week 4, she attended 4.17 days of school (83.4%). Anna's team elected to return to baseline after the fourth week, at which time Anna was expected to attend approximately four days of school per week. At week 5, Anna attended school 4.48 days of school. Her mean percentage attendance was approximately 89.6% during this baseline period. Anna's progress was measured again at week six; at this point, her mean percentage attendance was 92.6% or 4.63 days per week. At week 7, the team resumed the exposure therapy intervention and Anna attended 4.72 (94.4%) days of school. At the conclusion of the intervention (week 8), Anna was attending school 4.89 days per week. Her mean percentage of attendance when the intervention ended was 97.8%, which exceeded the team's goal of 95% attendance per week. Thus, Anna's team elected to discontinue data collection and intervention implementation at that time. Figure 13.1 displays the number of days per week Anna attended school during baseline and intervention phases.

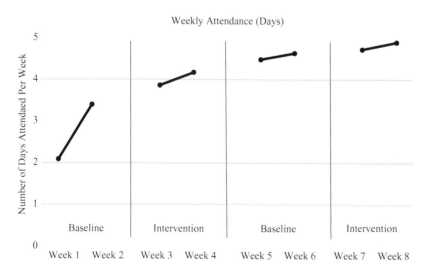

FIGURE 13.1 Number of days attending school per week during baseline and intervention phases

Time Spent in School

During the first week of the two-week baseline period, Anna was spending 14.28 hours per week in school receiving instruction. Her mean percentage of instruction time at baseline was 40.8%, indicating she was missing approximately 60% of instruction per week. During week two of baseline, Anna attended school for 17 hours (48.57% of the school week). The team implemented the exposure therapy intervention (i.e., systematic desensitization) for approximately two weeks. During week three, Anna attended 24.57 (70.2%) hours of school. At the conclusion of the first intervention phase (week four), Anna spent 20.85 hours per week in school, with a mean percentage instruction time of 59.57%. At the return to baseline (week five), Anna spent 27.32 hours in school per week. Her mean percentage instruction time during this period was 78%, which was an increase of more than 20% from the initial baseline phase. At the six-week mark, Anna spent 23.15 hours in school per week, with a mean percentage of 66.1%. Thereafter, the team returned to the intervention period for approximately two more weeks. In week seven, Anna attended 29.94 hours of school, which was nearly 86% of the school week. At the eight-week mark, Anna spent 34.23 hours per week in school receiving instruction. In one month, Anna received 136.92 hours of instruction out of 140 possible hours. Therefore, Anna's mean percentage of receiving instruction time was 97.8%, which exceeded the team's goal of spending at least 95% of school time in class per week. Figure 13.2 displays the number of hours per week Anna spent in school during baseline and intervention phases.

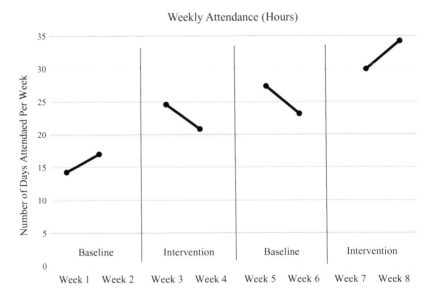

FIGURE 13.2 Number of hours per week Anna spent in school during baseline and intervention phases

Frequency of Self-Removal

An additional issue that Anna struggled with was leaving school early because of elevated anxiety. At baseline, Anna was leaving school between 2 and 2.25 times per week ($M = 2.13$). Each time Anna left school, she did not return for the rest of the day. Thus, Anna's mean percentage ranged from 40% to 45%. The team established a goal for Anna to self-remove no more than one time per month (95% no self-removal). At weeks three and four, Anna self-removed herself one time per week. After the first intervention phase, the team returned to baseline for two weeks. During this time, Anna left school one time during week five. Her mean percentage during the return to baseline was 80%, indicating improvement in remaining at school, despite feelings of anxiety. Anna did not self-remove herself from school at all during week six (100%). The team returned to the intervention phase for approximately two more weeks. During weeks seven and eight, Anna did not self-remove herself from school at all. Her mean percentage was again 100%, which was greater than the goal set forth by her educational team. Figure 13.3 depicts the number of times Anna attempted to leave school per week during baseline and intervention phases.

Summary of Intervention Effects

Given the results of the data presented in this case study, Anna's school refusal, avoidance, and self-removal significantly decreased during the intervention phases. Furthermore, the effects of the interventions maintained when returning to baseline, suggesting that Anna was becoming less reactive to fear-provoking stimuli

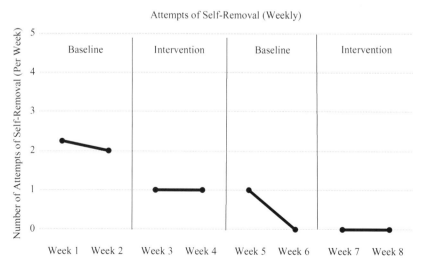

FIGURE 13.3 Number of times Anna attempted to leave school per week during baseline and intervention phases

associated with peers and school. Given Anna's significant progress with school attendance, the team concluded she had met her intervention goals. Furthermore, high levels of intervention implementation fidelity and high IOA support the conclusion that the exposure-based intervention had a positive effect on Anna's school attendance. In sum, the team concluded that Anna responded positively to the exposure exercises and demonstrated significant improvement in attendance.

Intervention Acceptability

At the conclusion of the intervention phase, Dr. Daniels and Anna's teachers completed an intervention acceptability questionnaire to provide feedback about the implementation, quality, and social validity of the exposure therapy intervention (see Appendix D). Results indicated that the team strongly agreed that the exposure therapy was effective at increasing attendance and decreasing the frequency of leaving school. The team also strongly agreed that they would utilize exposure therapies within a school context in the future and would recommend this intervention to other educational personnel.

Both the school psychologist and Dr. Daniels strongly agreed that ongoing consultation among providers was key to Anna's success, highlighting the importance of interdisciplinary consultation between school mental health and clinical professionals. Anna's teachers agreed that consultation was important but did not emphasize the need for clinical guidance to the same degree as the school psychologist and Dr. Daniels. Anna's math and language arts teachers strongly agreed that the intervention was easy to implement, while her science teacher somewhat agreed that it was easy to implement. All teachers strongly agreed that the data collection process was easy to implement and reported being highly satisfied with the intervention's outcomes related to attendance. Thus, Anna's team indicated that the intervention was acceptable for ongoing implementation to address anxiety-based school refusal and avoidance.

Intervention Considerations

The case example presented in this chapter illustrates the use of exposure therapy with a female high school student within a general education setting. Additionally, this case examines the implementation of a more clinically oriented behavioral intervention and how it can be modified for use in a school-based setting. While this case outlined the utility of an exposure-based therapy with a high school student demonstrating school refusal and avoidance, such a treatment modality could be used with a broad range of children demonstrating a variety of anxiety and related disorders. Research by Compton et al. (2004) posits that anxiety is a collection of classically conditioned responses that develop as a result of previous aversive life experiences. Through continued negative reinforcement (i.e., removal of the aversive stimulus), anxious behavior is reinforced and maintained. Fortunately, the behavior therapy literature indicates that anxious responses can be unlearned or counter-conditioned through repeated exposure to fear-provoking stimuli and responses that are incompatible with anxiety (e.g., Compton et al., 2004; Kazdin, 2003). Therefore, exposure-based interventions systematically introduce fear-provoking stimuli to individuals with a range of anxiety disorders to promote habituation and extinction of the anxiety response (Kazdin, 2003).

There are several ways that families and schools can provide valuable assistance to children with anxiety disorders. Parents and educators can provide insight into the frequency, duration, and intensity of the child's anxiety, especially when the child is developmentally unable to verbalize his or her fears and responses. Additionally, adults can aid in providing accountability for the child, both in conceptualizing their anxiety and reinforcing active participation in treatment when exposure exercises become uncomfortable (Vreeland & Peris, 2018). Finally, information gleaned from therapy sessions should be communicated to school personnel to ensure consistency in treatment across settings.

Another way that parents and schools can be involved in a child's exposure therapy is by participating in homework (Storch et al., 2007). Homework typically involves asking clients to put themselves in a situation that evokes anxiety, while resisting avoidance of compensatory behaviors. Clients are typically not asked to complete an exposure for homework that they have not already successfully completed in the therapist's office. Adults often play a critical role in exposure homework. First, parents can ensure that the child is adhering to the therapeutic plan. The homework assignment also helps the parent become aware of the assigned therapy exercises for the week. Additionally, exposure homework can assist parents with resisting accommodating the child's avoidant or escape behaviors (Lewin et al., 2005). For example, if a parent or teacher is made aware that he or she have been accommodating the child's anxiety symptoms, the exposure homework exercise can help replace accommodating behaviors with constructive options (e.g., teaching the child to manage his or her feelings of anxiety independently, without reassurance from the parent).

Finally, it is important to recognize that school psychologists receive a substantial amount of training in a broad range of areas, including mental health service delivery (National Association of School Psychologists, 2019). Therefore, school psychologists are in a unique position to provide school-based supports to children with a number of mental health concerns including anxiety as well as collaborate with other mental health professionals and facilitate awareness of services available in the community. The case provided in this chapter illustrates the importance of addressing student needs, recognizing one's own scope of practice, and consulting with other professionals when necessary. To this end, school psychologists can serve as liaisons among families, mental health providers, and other community agencies to provide comprehensive care for students.

Conclusion

The extant literature supports exposure therapies as an effective treatment for anxiety and related disorders (e.g., Craske, Treanor, Conway, Zbozinek, & Vervliet, 2014). The case study presented in this chapter reflects the importance of ongoing, graduated contact with a fear-provoking stimulus when an anxiety disorder is present, as well as preventing the anxiety-reducing response (e.g., escape) when exposed to that stimulus. In this particular case, systematic desensitization effectively addressed problem behavior (i.e., school refusal) that could have pervasive long-term consequences including but not limited to school dropout and poor psychiatric outcomes (Kearney, 2004). Additionally, this chapter delineated how in-vivo exposure exercises can be implemented in non-clinical settings, when appropriate training and consultation are included. In sum, exposure-based therapies are an effective treatment for anxiety disorders that can be translated to school settings through collaboration among school and clinical professionals.

References

Compton, S. N., March, J. S., Brent, D., Albano, A. M., Weersing, V. R., & Curry, J. (2004). Cognitive-behavioral psychotherapy for anxiety and depressive disorders in children and adolescents: An evidence-based medicine review. *Journal of the American Academy of Child & Adolescent Psychiatry, 43*, 930–959. doi: 10.1097/01.chi.0000127589.57468.bf

Craske, M. G., Treanor, M., Conway, C. C., Zbozinek, T., & Vervliet, B. (2014). Maximizing exposure therapy: An inhibitory learning approach. *Behaviour Research and Therapy, 58*, 10–23. doi: 10.1016/j.brat.2014.04.006

Epkins, C. C., Gardner, C., & Scanlon, N. (2013). Rumination and anxiety sensitivity in preadolescent girls: Independent, combined, and specific associations with depressive and anxiety symptoms. *Journal of Psychopathology and Behavioral Assessment, 35*, 540–551.

Foa, E., Hembree, E., & Rothbaum, B. (2007). *Prolonged exposure therapy for PTSD: Emotional processing of traumatic experiences therapist guide* (2nd ed.). New York, NY: Oxford University Press. doi:10.1093/med:psych/9780195308501.001.0001

Foa, E. B., Huppert, J. D., Leiberg, S., Langner, R., Kichic, R., Hajcak, G., & Salkovskis, P. M. (2002). The Obsessive-Compulsive Inventory: Development and validation of a short version. *Psychological Assessment, 14*, 485–496. doi: 10.1037/1040-3590.14.4.485

Kazdin, A. E. (2003). Psychotherapy for children and adolescents. *Annual Review of Psychology, 54*, 253–276. doi:10.1146/annurev.psych.54.101601.145105

Kearney, C. A. (2008). School absenteeism and school refusal behavior in youth: A contemporary review. *Clinical Psychology Review, 28*, 451–471. doi: 10.1016/j.cpr.2007.07.012

Lang, P. J. (2017). Stimulus control, response control, and the desensitization of fear. In D. Levis's (Ed.), *Foundations of behavioral therapy* (pp. 148–173). New York, NY: Routledge.

Lewin, A. B., Storch, E. A., Merlo, L. J., Adkins, J. W., Murphy, T., & Geffken, G. A. (2005). Intensive cognitive behavioral therapy for pediatric obsessive-compulsive disorder: A treatment protocol for mental health providers. *Psychological Services, 2*, 91–104. doi: 10.1037/1541-1559.2.2.91

Marazziti, D., & Consoli, G. (2010). Treatment strategies for obsessive-compulsive disorder. *Expert Opinion on Pharmacotherapy, 11,* 331–343. doi: 10.1517/14656560903446948

Merrell, K. W., Ervin, R. A., & Gimpel, G. A. (2006). *School psychology for the 21st century: Foundations and practices.* New York, NY: Guilford Press.

National Association of School Psychologists. (2019). *Who are school psychologists?* Retrieved from http://www.nasponline.org/about-school-psychology/who-are-school-psychologists

Pence Jr., S. L., Sulkowski, M. L., Jordan, C., & Storch, E. A. (2010). When exposures go wrong: Trouble-shooting guidelines for managing difficult scenarios that arise in exposure-based treatment for obsessive-compulsive disorder. *American Journal of Psychotherapy, 64,* 39–53. doi:10.1176/appi.psychotherapy.2010.64.1.39

Storch, E. A., Geffken, G. R., Merlo, L. J., Mann, G., Duke, D., Munson, M., ... & Goodman, W. K. (2007). Family-based cognitive-behavioral therapy for pediatric obsessive-compulsive disorder: Comparison of intensive and weekly approaches. *Journal of the American Academy of Child & Adolescent Psychiatry, 46,* 469–478. doi: 10.1097/chi.0b013e31803062e7

Sulkowski, M. L., Joyce, D. K., & Storch, E. A. (2012). Treating childhood anxiety in schools: Service delivery in a response to intervention paradigm. *Journal of Child and Family Studies, 21,* 938–947. doi: 10.1007/s10826-011-9553-1

Vreeland, A., & Peris, T. S. (2018). Involving family members of children with OCD in CBT. In E. A. Storch, J. F. McGuire, and D. McKay (Eds.), *The clinician's guide to cognitive-behavioral therapy for childhood obsessive-compulsive disorder* (pp. 135–154). Waltham, MA: Academic Press. doi:10.1016/B978-0-12-811427-8.00008-3

Wheaton, M. G., Galfalvy, H., Steinman, S. A., Wall, M. M., Foa, E. B., & Simpson, H. B. (2016). Patient adherence and treatment outcome with exposure and response prevention for OCD: Which components of adherence matter and who becomes well? *Behaviour Research and Therapy, 85,* 6–12. doi: 10.1016/j.brat.2016.07.010

Wolpe, J. (1961). The systematic desensitization treatment of neuroses. *Journal of Nervous and Mental Disease, 132,* 189-203. doi:10.1097/00005053-196103000-00001

Appendix A: Fear Hierarchy – Anna

10 = Attending a full day of school (7:30a-2:30p) for five consecutive days for one month
9 = Attending a full day of school (7:30a-2:30p) for five consecutive days
8 = Sitting through a full class period when doing peer/group activities
8 = Attending a full day of school (7:30a-2:30p)
7 = Attending school for five consecutive days
6 = Thinking about getting in trouble with her mother
5 = Seeing friend group at school
5 = Driving to school in the car
4 = Driving past the school
3 = Sitting through a full class period when doing individual work
2 = Seeing a picture of the school
2 = Hearing the word "school"

Appendix B: Data Collection Form

Week #1	Monday, 1/1	Tuesday, 1/2	Wednesday, 1/3	Thursday, 1/4	Friday, 1/5	Total Weekly
Absent (Y/N)						
Self-Removal (Y/N)						
Number of Hours Before Self-Removal (#)						

Appendix C: Exposure Therapy Fidelity Checklist

Instructions: Please indicate the exposure elements you delivered for this case by placing an 'X' on the line next to each exposure therapy element.

Case identifying number: _____   Number of Exposure therapy sessions: _____

Exposure therapy elements provided in this case:

____ 1. Presented the overall rationale for exposures.

____ 2. Explained the rationale for exposure.

____ 3. Developed an exposure hierarchy using patient's Subjective Units of DistressScale (SUDs) with range of items not restricted to high or low items.

____ 4. Administered self-reports at least every other session.

____ 5. Assigned homework for exposure.

If you excluded any exposure therapy elements, please give a brief explanation of your reasons for modifying the exposure therapy protocol in this case (explain below or use back of form if you need more space).

_____   _____   _____
Clinician Printed Name   Clinician Signature   Date

Appendix D: Intervention Acceptability Survey

Anna's exposure therapy intervention was easy to understand (e.g., rationale, choice of exposures, etc.)	Strongly Disagree	Disagree	Neutral	Agree	Strongly Agree
The exposure therapy intervention was easy to implement in the classroom.	Strongly Disagree	Disagree	Neutral	Agree	Strongly Agree
Collecting attendance/self-removal data for the exposure therapy intervention was easy.	Strongly Disagree	Disagree	Neutral	Agree	Strongly Agree
The exposure therapy intervention improved Anna's overall attendance, time spent in class, and number of self-removals from school.	Strongly Disagree	Disagree	Neutral	Agree	Strongly Agree
I would consider using an exposure-based therapy intervention with other students demonstrating similar school refusal and avoidance behaviors.	Strongly Disagree	Disagree	Neutral	Agree	Strongly Agree
I would recommend an exposure-based intervention to other educators as a method of addressing school refusal and avoidance behaviors.	Strongly Disagree	Disagree	Neutral	Agree	Strongly Agree
Overall, I was satisfied with the outcomes associated with the exposure therapy intervention.	Strongly Disagree	Disagree	Neutral	Agree	Strongly Agree

14
BEHAVIORAL ACTIVATION

Laura Nabors, Christina Klein, and Myia Graves

Introduction

Cognitive-behavioral interventions encompass a collection of techniques and are effective for a wide array of issues facing children and adolescents including conduct and attention/impulse control problems, trauma, developmental disabilities, and mood disorders (see Kendall, 2012, for detailed information). Cognitive Behavioral Therapy (CBT) is one such technique that can be especially helpful for children and adolescents experiencing anxiety and depression (Huberty, 2012). Garber and Weersing (2010) recommended using CBT techniques to reduce negative thinking and alter negative emotional reactions thereby increasing positive responses to stress. CBT strategies may also help youth understand behavioral responses to mood states and cognitions (Huberty, 2012). For example, mood monitoring may assist in linking adolescents' behavior, emotions, and thoughts. Cognitive restructuring, another cognitive strategy common to CBT, addresses negative or distorted thought patters (Huberty, 2012; Weisz, McCarty, & Valeri, 2006). Behaviorally oriented components of CBT typically focus on changing behavioral patterns (e.g., increasing engagement in pleasurable activities) and increasing the frequency of pro-social behavior (e.g., McCauley et al., 2016). Finally, relaxation training, another important component of CBT, may potentially alleviating physical symptoms associated with mood disorders (Curry & Meyer, 2018).

School psychologists searching for CBT strategies that are easy to implement with children and adolescents in a school-based context might consider Behavioral Activation (BA; McCauley et al., 2016). BA is based conceptually on understanding consequences "contributing to and maintaining depressive behaviors and [gaining knowledge of] what behaviors/events are necessary to curtail it"

(McCauley et al., 2016, p. 292). This approach is built on research indicating changes in the environment result in depressive behaviors that lead to fewer positive experiences, which, in turn decrease opportunities for positive reinforcement of healthy, nondepressed behavior (Axelrod, 2017). In addition, depressive behaviors are either positively or negatively reinforced, which increases the probability of those behaviors occurring in the future (Axelrod, 2017). For example, social isolation might elicit sympathy from parents and teachers (positive reinforcement) and, at the same time, allow the individual to avoid uncomfortable social interactions with peers (negative reinforcement). This pattern of positive and negative reinforcement for a depressed behavior likely increases the frequency of that depressed behavior. BA may be employed by school psychologists looking to address common characteristics of depression including anhedonia and social withdrawal. Table 14.1 highlights common elements of most BA interventions used with adolescents.

The specific use of BA involves increasing adolescents' engagement in healthy, pro-social behaviors that allow for opportunities to access positive reinforcement, increase access to individuals who provide positive reinforcement, and decrease engagement in behaviors that maintain depression (e.g., isolation, exposure to aversive events; Dimidjian, Barrera, Martell, Muñoz, & Lewinsohn, 2011; Hopko, Lejuez, Ruggiero, & Eifert, 2003). This is accomplished by identifying sources of reinforcement of depressed behavior and altering contingencies to facilitate nondepressed behavior. Features of BA include antecedent and functional assessment, goal-setting, teaching skills, and activity scheduling (Axelrod, 2017). The concept of shaping is also critical in BA, as positive reinforcement of small approximations of healthy, nondepressed behavior might be especially important when the depression is significant or the individual is resistant to treatment. Mood monitoring and journaling may also assist in identifying behaviors, and antecedent and consequential events that can later become targets for treatment (Dimidjian et al., 2011). Finally, Chu et al. (2016) emphasized addressing pathological avoidance, especially when depression is accompanied by anxiety. In such cases, systematic exposure to fear-provoking and depression-maintaining stimuli serve to change an individual's avoidant responses.

School psychologists using BA work collaboratively with the referred student, as well as parents, teachers, and peers, to identify depression-maintaining stimuli, identify possible functions of the depressed behavior, set appropriate goals, develop competencies for becoming more successful, and schedule activities that are likely to serve as reinforcement for healthy behavior (Axelrod, 2017). Again, the primary objective is to use goal-setting and activity scheduling to increase involvement, modify the environment to increase opportunities for positive reinforcement, and devise strategies to reduce avoidance of activities that lead to depressed behavior. School psychologists and other educational professionals are in a great position to employ BA, as they can work with the adolescent directly and also gain valuable support from the adolescent's parents, teachers, and peers.

TABLE 14.1 Common Behavioral Activation Elements Used With Adolescents

Area	Suggestions for Adolescents
Avoidance cycle	If you avoid activities and others, you do not get as many positives. If you avoid because it feels stressful to be involved in activities, you can actually increase the stress you feel the next time an opportunity for activities you might like occurs.
Feelings, thoughts, and behaviors are linked	The adolescent can develop a table of feelings related to sad mood and behaviors that occur when he or she is sad. Then, the clinician can help link feelings and behaviors (use a diagram when needed). There is a reciprocal relationship among these factors.
Goals, values, and preferred activities	What activities to you like? What has been fun for you in the past? Which friends are fun and what do you like to do together? Develop a table with a list of activities you enjoy, why you like them, and ideas to get involved in them. Values are what the adolescent finds important (e.g., relationships, hobbies, social life).
Activity schedule	Identify rewarding activities. Develop a schedule of activities, add steps about how the adolescent can become involved in activities. Schedule activities during times and in environments where the adolescent is most likely to succeed.
Problem-solving	Identify barriers to engaging in fun activities. Develop an action plan with goals to achieve. Break down goals into small steps and make sure that goals are attainable and realistic.
Identify and change negative self-talk	What do you say to yourself? Is this really true – or are you being too hard on yourself? What are some positive statements you can use if negative messages or tapes start playing in your head?
	If positive statements are not as easy to implement, what positive thoughts or images could you use to interrupt the negative messages or tapes, so that you could take a positive action?
Mood monitoring	Often a five- or seven-point Likert scale can be used from very sad to very happy. The adolescent should monitor mood when engaging in activities and at different points during the day.
Reminder: change often occurs in small steps	Start small, perhaps using a timer, and engage in activities for just five minutes. Find a friend or accountability partner to help you keep active. Use visual reminders to remember to be active. Set small and specific goals and praise yourself at each small step. Do one thing at a time (try not to multitask).
Increasing rewards and positive feedback	Teach the adolescent to provide positive statements for activity completion. Encourage rewarding effort and mastery steps. Parents can be involved in praising increased involvement.

Case Study

Background Information

Asia was 13 years of age, in the eighth grade, and African American. She was an only child residing with her mother. Her father lived several states away and she saw him for monthly visits and holidays. She reported having a good relationship with both parents. Asia lived in an inner-city housing project with limited opportunities for neighborhood activities. At the time of the referral, she was eating a lot of unhealthy snacks and drinking beverages high in sugar. Asia was a basketball star, but a serious knee injury sidelined her for the school year. However, her physician cleared her for walking, stretching, riding an exercise bicycle, and engaging in light exercise. After being injured and not being able to practice with her team, Asia reported she began feeling "blue." As time progressed, she withdrew from friends and stopped doing homework.

Asia came to the attention of the school psychologist after not turning in homework assignments, which was unusual given her previous academic performance. Asia's mother consented to treatment and the school psychologist elected to use BA as an intervention. Asia and the school psychologist agreed to involve and update Asia's mother about treatment as necessary. The team (i.e., school psychologist, mother, Asia) decided to meet regularly to develop and review interventions aimed at improving Asia's mood and social involvement.

Description of the Problem Behavior

During the initial session, Asia reported often feeling, "as if I'm no good, everything I do is wrong, and I'm not worth anything." She reported feeling "blue" for the past six months and "sad" about not getting along with her friends. They were going to parties often, which was an activity that no longer interested Asia. She was staying in her room most of the time and reported being "glued" to her iPad reviewing social media. Social withdrawal, eating unhealthy food, not engaging in physical activity, and not completing homework were identified as problem behaviors. Not unusual for a parent, Asia's mother frequently discussed Asia's withdrawn behavior with Asia, which was likely inadvertently reinforcing some of Asia's depressed behavior. During the initial session, Asia denied experiencing suicidal or homicidal ideation. Although there was no history of self-harm behavior, the school psychologist reviewed safety procedures for the home (e.g., removing sharp objects and medications that might be dangerous if taken in large quantities) with Asia's mother. Asia also denied substance use, which was confirmed by her mother.

The school psychologist referred Asia to her pediatrician to help assess Asia's current functioning and recommend additional treatment components. The pediatrician suggested that an exercise routine, perhaps involving yoga or riding an exercise bicycle, to potentially improve Asia's mood and help her maintain flexibility and muscle tone for when she returned to playing basketball. The pediatrician and school psychologist believed a diagnosis of Persistent Depressive Disorder (PDD) was most appropriate. The school psychologist discussed with Asia and her mother that PDD occurs when individuals experience feelings of sadness during most days for a year or more (see American Psychiatric Association, 2013). They also discussed other depressive symptoms including feeling tired, changes in sleep and eating, poor self-concept, loss of interest in daily activities, hopelessness, and difficulty making decisions and concentrating (see Merianos, 2016).

Problem Analysis

The school psychologist conducted informal antecedent and functional assessments of Asia's depressed behaviors. The school psychologists identified social isolation, eating unhealthy food, and spending time on social media as likely antecedents to Asia's depressed behavior. In addition, Asia's self-reports of sadness and worthlessness (e.g., "feeling worthless because I'm not doing anything") and negative statements (e.g., "I'm a failure," "there's a lot wrong with me") were also identified as likely antecedents. These events were more frequent as Asia reported more problems with depression, contributing to further withdrawal from friends and activities.

To begin assessing the possible function of Asia's depressed behaviors, the school psychologist asked Asia to consider the consequences of her withdrawn behavior. Asia indicated being afraid her friends would no longer be interested in spending time with her because she was no longer a "star" on the basketball team. The school psychologist observed that Asia was receiving a lot of attention for depressed behaviors, especially from her mother. Taken together, the school psychologists concluded that Asia's depressed behavior was likely maintained by positive reinforcement (e.g., attention from parents and peers) and negative reinforcement (e.g., avoidance of social situations).

The school psychologist analyzed difficulties with school performance, healthy eating, and exercise. In terms of school performance, problems typically involved not turning in work and not studying for quizzes. Unhealthy eating involved eating foods high in fat for snacks and not eating at mealtime. The lack of exercise was related to not having opportunities to engage in alternative exercise that would help Asia maintain some muscle strength and tone while she was recuperating from her injury.

Intervention Goals

The school psychologist, Asia, and her mother identified several intervention goals. First, Asia would decrease social isolation and increase her engagement in activities with friends. Second, Asia would increase the frequency of physical activity and exercise. Third, Asia would eat healthy by increasing consumption of fruits, vegetables, and lean protein, increase water intake, and decrease consumption of unhealth foods. Finally, Asia would use more positive statements. These goals were identified to increase Asia's opportunities to access positive reinforcement for healthy, nondepressed behavior. The primary objective of treatment was improved mood. In terms of completing schoolwork, Asia was expected to regularly check her school's e-learning system for assigned homework and quizzes. She also was to build in time to her schedule for studying and homework. She would work with her friends during specific homework sessions and make a commitment to complete her most difficulty homework by 8:00 pm. Her mother agreed to review Asia's progress twice a week by accessing the e-learning system to understand assignments and ensure Asia was making progress academically.

Measurement of Target Behaviors, Data Collection Strategies, and Progress Monitoring

Measurement of the target behaviors initially included collecting survey data from two instruments. First, the Children's Depression Rating Scale-Revised (CDRS-R), a 17-item survey with questions assessing affective, cognitive, psychomotor, and somatic symptoms related to depression (rating scale from one to seven, with seven indicating severe difficulties; Poznanski & Mokros, 1999), was used to evaluate depressive symptoms. This measure has adequate psychometric properties for use with adolescents (Mayes, Bernstein, Haley, Kennard, & Emslie, 2010). The CDRS-R was administered prior to treatment, after months one and two, and at the end of treatment.

Second, the depression scale from the PROMIS data bank was used to assess negative mood, anhedonia, negative view of self (e.g., worthlessness and negative social cognitions (e.g., loneliness, interpersonal alienation) (e.g., Cella et al., 2010; Pilkonis et al., 2011). The PROMIS measures focus on assessment of patient-centered outcomes and were designed to enhance communication among providers and clients. Items on the depression measure assess feelings of unhappiness, sadness, loneliness, stress, being sad made it hard to do things with my friends, feeling like "everything in my life went wrong" or "I can't do anything right" (five-point rating scale from "never" to "almost always"). T-scores are used for scoring with scores of less than 55 indicating none or slight levels for depression. The school psychologist determined that the PROMIS would be administered to Asia prior to treatment, at biweekly intervals for progress monitoring, and at the end of treatment.

After a joint meeting with the school psychologist, Asia's mother agreed to assist Asia in completing a daily journal and keep her own daily record of Asia's involvement in daily activities. Asia was asked to record information at the end of each day in her journal (see Table 14.2). Later in the intervention process, Asia recorded her physical activity and eating behaviors in the daily journal. Asia turned in her daily journals to the school psychologist each Friday. The

TABLE 14.2 Daily Journal

Day of the week/time of day	Activity	Minutes spent in activity	What I think and say to myself	Mood (circle the number for your mood, 1 – low or very sad, 3 – in the middle, 7 – very positive or very happy)
				1 2 3 4 5 6 7
				1 2 3 4 5 6 7
				1 2 3 4 5 6 7
				1 2 3 4 5 6 7

Soda and water consumed today

Breakfast – food & portions

Lunch – food & portions

Snacks – food and portions

Dinner – food & portions

Increase my physical activity to 30-60 min per day. Record exercise and time engaged in exercise

Note: The health educator worked with Asia to learn to estimate portion size.

school psychologist and Asia reviewed information in the journal and tabulated averages for the number of daily activities, positive statements, and mood ratings. The school psychologist contacted Asia's mother by telephone each week to review progress and record her mother's report of number of daily activities.

Intervention Plan

Education about Depression and BA

The school psychologist provided education on depression and BA to Asia and her mother. Specifically, the school psychologist discussed the course of depression and its symptoms. In addition, the school psychologists discussed BA, including the importance of changing the environment so that the Asia would engage in more healthy behavior. The school psychologist emphasized to Asia's mother the importance of praising Asia's efforts to engage with friends, eat healthy, and exercise more often. Finally, the school psychologist described how goal-setting and activity scheduling would be used to improve Asia's mood.

Asia agreed to use the journal, meet with a health educator to learn about and implement a healthier dietary plan, and begin to exercise. Her mother agreed to review her weekly homework and encourage Asia to study for quizzes. Also, Asia's mother planned to shop for healthier foods (e.g., fruits, vegetables, lean proteins) and buy reduced amounts of salty, high-fat snacks and soda. Asia also completed the PROMIS scale biweekly, and she and the school psychologist discussed her ratings on this scale and how involvement with friends and exercising were related to improvements in sadness.

Goal-Setting

In consultation with the school psychologist, Asia and her mother developed a set of goals based on the target behaviors. Goal-setting attempted to oriented Asia to becoming more goal-directed rather than mood-directed. First, Asia selected at least one activity with friends or her mother to engage in each day. These activities could include working on homework with friends, meal planning and cooking with her mother, watching her teammates practice and talking with them before or after practice, or doing something fun with friends (e.g., going to a coffee shop). The school psychologist and Asia's mother added calling or texting a friend, as Asia has stopped communicating with friends when at home. Second, Asia met with a health educator at the school to learn about and develop goals targeting healthy eating. The school psychologist, health educator, and Asia discussed healthy eating goals, including eating more fruit and swapping potato chips for vegetable chips or carrots and celery. Asia was also encouraged to reduce intake of ice cream and substitute low-fat yogurt with strawberries and blueberries as a dessert. Asia's mother agreed to cook more lean meats and vegetables for dinner, buy vegetable chips instead of potato chips, and purchase more yogurt, fruits, and vegetables. Asia developed daily goals for eating more fruits, vegetables, and lean proteins, drinking more water, and reducing intake of unhealthy foods. Third, Asia and her mother set goals around exercising three to four times per week. Involving family members in positive change can create a support system, which can be important for encouraging adolescents who reside in environments which have not been supportive of physical activity and healthy eating (Heidelberger & Smith, 2016). Asia and her mother set time to meet twice a week to review her progress for completing homework and studying. Finally, Asia set the goal of completing her daily journal. This served as a method to assess progress, self-monitor target behaviors, and maintain accountability.

Activity Scheduling

The purpose of activity scheduling was to identify and plan for activities that would increase Asia's contact with reinforcement for health behavior. Based on the set goals, the school psychologist and Asia developed a list of activities to be scheduled across the week. Daily activities were scheduled that were consistent with Asia's goals. For example, Asia identified times during the week in which she would exercise, spend time with friends, shop with her mother, and watch her teammates play basketball. With her mother, Asia also planned to go on weekly shopping trips, learn more about purchasing healthy foods, and exercising. Asia developed a plan to also exercise with her friends. She considered attending basketball practices and games with her friends to further encourage an exercise routine.

Asia and her mother agreed to meet on Mondays and Wednesdays to review academic progress. Most of the quizzes were on Thursdays or Fridays, and these "check-in times" allowed Asia and her mother to discuss how to best allocate time for homework and studying. Asia and her mother also planned to discuss Asia's overall academic performance (e.g., exam grades, class participation). Asia developed a schedule to complete her most difficult homework assignments first or with friends in her homework group.

Therapy Plan

The school psychologist discussed a therapy plan for sessions with Asia and her mother. The plan included weekly sessions for three months with decreasing session length. For the first six weeks, sessions with Asia were scheduled for approximately 45 minutes. For the remaining six weeks, sessions were expected to be approximately 15-30 minutes. The school psychologist received permission from Asia's mother and Asia to work with Asia's teachers to track academic progress.

Intervention Fidelity and Interobserver Agreement

Treatment integrity was assessed using two methods. First, the school psychologist collected Asia's Daily Journal every Friday. This allowed the school psychologist to determine the degree to which Asia was meeting her goals. Specifically, the Daily Journal tracked Asia's engagement in scheduled activities, healthy eating, and physical activity. Second, the school psychologist developed a six-item survey, which was completed weekly by Asia and her mother. Survey items assessed whether the journal was used on a daily basis and whether Asia provided accurate recordings of scheduled activities, healthy eating, and physical activity. They provided ratings for the six items on five-point scales ("1" strongly disagree, "2" disagree, "3" agree, "4" agree, and "5" strongly agree). Asia and her mother agreed that the Daily Journal was used most days, which matched the school psychologist's assessment of treatment integrity.

To assess interobserver agreement (IOA), Asia's mother kept a daily record of Asia's scheduled activities, healthy eating, and physical activity. IOA was calculated by comparing the Asia and her mother's daily records (agreements/[agreements + disagreements] *100%). The average IOA was 96% (range 94%-100%),

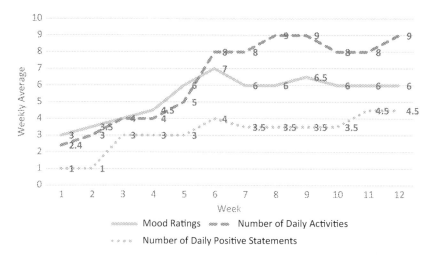

FIGURE 14.1 Asia's average weekly average for daily mood ratings, number of daily activities, and number of daily positive statements during baseline and intervention phases

which is considered acceptable. The school psychologist concluded that the intervention was implemented as designed and the outcome data were reliable.

Intervention Outcome Data

Figure 14.1 displays Asia's average weekly ratings for mood and the average number of activities and positive statements per day during baseline (weeks one and two) and treatment (weeks three through twelve). Asia reported more positive or happier moods from the beginning to end of treatment. Specifically, she self-reported her mood to be, on average, a three out of seven during the first week. At week six, her self-reported average mood rating peaked at a seven and maintained above a six until week 12 when treatment stopped. Asia reported using more positive statements, being happier, and engaging more with friends and family during treatment. This was consistent with Asia's ratings on the PROMIS scale (see Table 14.3).

Table 14.3 presents Asia's PROMIS scale results and items for discussion during therapy. Asia's ratings reflect improvements from baseline to week 12. Asia's ratings on the CDRS-R also showed positive changes from baseline to the end of the intervention. Specifically, her score was 65 during baseline, 55 after weeks one and two, and 48 at post-intervention follow-up. Asia's ratings on the CDRS-R indicated specific improvements in appetite, depression, schoolwork, social withdrawal, fatigue, and difficulty having fun. Also, Asia's reports of engaging in more activities per day during the course of treatment coincided with improved mood

TABLE 14.3 Asia's Ratings on the PROMIS Scale and Discussion Items With for Therapy

Time	PROMIS Scale Ratings	Discussion Items
Pre-intervention	64	**Low mood/sadness:** what activities (e.g., text or call a friend, do some yoga) can you engage in to improve your mood? **Feeling hopeless or helpless:** what were you doing when you felt this way? What activities (e.g., homework club, go to basketball practice) can you do to feel hope and feel like you are doing something positive? **Feeling I can't do anything right (worthless):** what are you doing when you feel valuable (e.g., being a part of basketball team, doing fun things with friends)?
Week 2	60	**Low mood/sadness:** what factors might be contributing to your low mood ("I'm not going to homework sessions with my friends") and how might you address this? **Feeling worthless:** can you engage in activities where you might experience a sense of accomplishment (e.g., cooking with mom, starting and completing homework)? **Loneliness:** Consider joining homework sessions with friends, attending basketball practice, or exercising with mom.
Week 4	60	**Alone:** consider texting peers, attending basketball practice, or engaging in yoga with mom. **Sadness:** discuss link between being alone and withdrawn, and feeling sad.
Week 6	54	**Improvements in feelings alone, sad/ unhappy, or worthless:** noted linkage among being active with others and mood; praise continued efforts for engaging friends socially.
Week 8	54	**Continued improvements:** emphasize improved school performance, attending basketball practices, and continuing to exercise and eat healthier
Week 10	50	No reports of feeling helpless; ratings of mood continue to improve; Asia is exercising with friends and eating healthier; Asia reports "feeling like I am taking care of myself"
Week 12	50	Improvements continue; Asia reports interacting with friends and basketball team; exercise and healthy eating continue

and decreased sadness. During the first week of baseline, she indicated engaging in slightly more than two activities per day. The average number of activities Asia engaged in per day steadily increased and by the end of treatment, she was averaging between eight and nine activities per day.

Asia's consumption of healthy foods and beverages also improved during treatment. She and her mother indicated in the Daily Journal increased consumption of fruits, vegetables, and lean proteins, increased water intake, and decreased consumption of unhealthy foods and beverages. In addition, Asia reported increased physical activity and exercise. She indicated exercising for 10 minutes two days per week during the first four weeks of treatment. During the last eight weeks of treatment, she reported exercising 30 minutes five days per week. She also started taking yoga classes with friends and steadily increased her riding time on the exercise bike.

Asia and her mother were meeting twice a week to discuss homework and set aside times to study for quizzes. The school psychologist interviewed Asia's teachers at weeks five, eight, and 12 to assess Asia's homework completion and overall academic performance. All teachers reported noteworthy improvements in homework completion, class participation, and performance on graded assignments and tests. Asia's overall academic performance improved so substantially that she was earning As in all classes by the end of the intervention.

Summary of Intervention Effects

Intervention goals were met by the end of treatment. Specifically, improvements were noted in the following areas: (1) decreased social isolation and increased engagement in social activities; (2) increased frequency of physical activity; (3) increased healthy eating; and (4) increase use of positive statements. Results from the CDRS-R and PROMIS revealed noteworthy improvements in mood and activity level. While Asia continued to meet the diagnostic criteria for PDD based on the length of time of depressed symptoms, intervention outcome measures indicated significant improvements in functioning.

Intervention Acceptability

Assessing the social impact of treatment provides information about stakeholders' views of how the intervention works and contributes to an understanding of the intervention's clinical significance (Kazdin, 2003). Asia responded to seven questions on a six-point Likert scale ranging from (one = "very much or very helpful" to six – "not at all or not at all helpful"; see Klingman & Hochdorf, 1993). Questions included items such as: (1) to what extent the program (e.g., interventions) had changed attitudes; (2) attractiveness of the interventions (how much the client likes interventions); (3) how much interventions had changed behavior; and (4) whether one would recommend the interventions to peers. Asia's ratings for the were ones and twos, indicating high social validity. Her mother answered similar questions and her responses indicated she felt the program was successful and could help other adolescents.

Intervention Considerations

One potential advantage of BA is that school psychologists, teachers, other school professionals, parents, and teenagers can collaborate to develop practical interventions, which impact teenagers' daily lives by involving them with others and seeking solutions to their social problems. In this case study, the health educator was heavily involved in the intervention process. However, it may be the case that teachers can assist in developing plans for youth involving peers study groups or after-school tutoring. Moreover, teachers can suggest ideas for after-school clubs to facilitate social activities and encourage the student to engage socially with peers and others.

Noncompliance with BA can also be an issue for students. Having parents record activities with their child may improve record-keeping. If this is not successful, the school psychologist could schedule short sessions with the student, either daily or weekly, to assist in recording behaviors, activities, positive statements, and mood. Should the adolescent fail to quickly begin engaging in social activities, the school psychologist might consider working with parents to develop a reward system. The school psychologist might also have to facilitate the process of developing ways to increase social interaction by collaborating with parents. If appropriate permissions are obtained, the school psychologist might consider including the student's friends to assist in developing a plan for involvement in social activities. Finally, peers might encourage the student to engage in social activities.

Fading the intervention may be critical to its success. In this case study, session times were reduced and involvement with the health educator decreased over time. Fading could involve meeting every other week with a goal of moving to monthly sessions. Fading of parent support could have occurred in this case study as well. It would have been interesting to see if Asia would have continued with recording information in her journal without her mother's support. When developing a fading plan, the school psychologist should consider circumstances where the intervention might need to be strengthened in terms of increasing or reinstating its intensity should depressed behaviors resume. This should be discussed with the client and his or her parents. For example, the school psychologist could mention that if depression and isolation recurred and if unhealthy eating habits returned, then meetings would resume to develop a new plan to increase involvement in activities and reinstate healthy eating habits. Journaling could resume to record and monitor intervention progress.

Conclusion

The case study in this chapter described BA applied to an adolescent girl with depression. While BA is typically included as part of a larger CBT intervention, this particular case study emphasized taking a functional approach to addressing the student's depression. The aim of BA is to decrease depressive behaviors by removing reinforcement of those behaviors (i.e., extinction) and, at the same time, increasing the frequency of reinforcement for healthy, nondepressed behaviors. In this case study, the school psychologist worked with the student and her mother to increase opportunities for reinforcement via social interactions, physical activity and exercise, healthy eating, and homework completion. As a result of the intervention, the student's healthy behavior increased, depressed behavior decreased, and mood improved.

References

American Psychiatric Association. (2013). *Diagnostic and statistical manual of mental disorders: DSM-V* (Fifth ed.). Washington, DC: American Psychiatric Publishing. doi:10.1176/appi.books.9780890425596

Axelrod, M.I. (2017). *Behavior analysis for school psychologists*. New York: Routledge. doi:10.4324/9781315650913

Cella, D., Riley, W., Stone, A., Rothrock, N., Reeve, B., Yount, S., … PROMIS Cooperative Group. (2010). The Patient-Reported Outcomes Measurement Information System (PROMIS) developed and tested its first wave of adult self-reported health outcome item banks: 2005-2008. *Journal of Clinical Epidemiology*, *63*(11), 1179–1194. doi:10.1016/j.jclinepi.2010.04.011

Chu, B. C., Crocco, S. T., Esseling, P., Areizaga, M. J., Lindner, A. M., & Skriner, L. C. (2016). Transdiagnostic group behavioral activation and exposure therapy for youth with anxiety and depression: Initial randomized controlled trial. *Behavior Research and Therapy*, *76*, 65–75. doi:10.1016/j.brat.2015.11.005

Curry, J. F., & Meyer, A. E. (2018). Treatment of depression. In P. C. Kendall (Ed.), *Cognitive therapy with children and adolescents: A casebook for clinical practice* (3rd ed., pp. 94–121). New York, NY: Guilford Press.

Dimidjian, S., Barrera, M. Jr., Martell, C., Muñoz, R. F., & Lewinsohn, P. M. (2011). The origins and current status of Behavioral Activation Treatments for Depression. *Annual Review of Clinical Psychology*, *7*, 1–38. doi:10.1146/annurev-clinpsy-032210-104535

Garber, J., & Weersing, V. R. (2010). Comorbidity of anxiety and depression in youth: Implications for treatment and depression. *Clinical Psychology*, *17*(4), 293–306. doi:10.1111/j.1468-2850.2010.01221.x

Heidelberger, L., & Smith, C. (2016). Low-income, urban children's perspectives on physical activity: A photovoice project. *Maternal and Child Health Journal*, *20*(6), 1124–1132. doi:10.1007/s10995-015-1898-4

Hopko, D. R., LeJuez, C. W., Ruggiero, K. J., & Eifert, G. H. (2003). Contemporary behavioral activation treatments for depression: Procedures, principles, and progress. *Clinical Psychology Review*, *23*, 699–717. doi:10.1016/S0272-7358(03)00070-9

Huberty, T. J. (2012). *Anxiety and depression in children and adolescents: Assessment, Intervention, and Prevention*. New York, NY: Springer-Verlag. doi:10.1007/978-1-4614-3110-7

Kazdin, A. E. (2003). Clinical significance: Measuring whether interventions make a difference. In A. E. Kazdin (Ed.), *Methodological issues & strategies in clinical research* (pp. 691–710). Washington, DC, USA: American Psychological Association.

Kendall, P. C. (Ed.) (2012). *Child and adolescent therapy: Cognitive-behavioral procedures* (4th ed.). New York, NY: Guilford Press.

Klingman, A., & Hochdorf, Z. (1993). Coping with distress and self-harm: The impact of a primary prevention program among adolescents. *Journal of Adolescence, 16*, 121–140. doi:10.1006/jado.1993.1012

Mayes, T. L., Bernstein, I. H., Haley, C. L., Kennard, B. D., & Emslie, G. J. (2010). Psychometric properties of the *Children's Depression Rating Scale-Revised* in adolescents. *Journal of Child and Adolescent Psychopharmacology, 20*(6), 513–516. doi:10.1089/cap.2010.0063

McCauley, E., Gudmundsen, G., Schloredt, K., Martell, C., Rhew, I., Hubley, S., & Dimidjian, S. (2016). The adolescent Behavioral Activation program: Adapting Behavioral Activation as a treatment for depression in adolescence. *Journal of Clinical Child and Adolescent Psychology, 45*(3), 291–304. doi:10.1080/15374416.2014.979933

Merianos, A. (2016). Depression, Chapter 8. In *Medical and mental health during childhood*, N. Singh (Ed.) (pp. 133–150). Springer Series on Child and Family Studies. Switzerland: Springer Nature. doi:10.1007/978-3-319-31117-3_8

Pilkonis, P. A., Choi, S. W., Reise, S. P., Stover, A. M., Riley, W. T., Cella, D., & PROMIS Cooperative Group. (2011). Item banks for measuring emotional distress from the Patient-Reported Outcomes Measurement Information System (PROMIS®): Depression, anxiety, and anger. *Assessment, 18*(3), 263–283. doi:10.1177/1073191111411667

Poznanski, E. O., & Mokros, H. B. (1999). *Children depression rating scale--revised (CDRS-R)*. Los Angeles, CA: Western Psychological Services.

Weisz, J. R., McCarty, C. A., & Valeri, S. M. (2006). Effects of psychotherapy for depression in children and adolescents: A meta-analysis. *Psychological Bulletin, 132*(1), 132–149. doi:10.1037/0033-2909.132.1.132

15
GOOD BEHAVIOR GAME

Evan H. Dart, Keith C. Radley, Christley McGirt, Jordyn Martin, Talia Shuman, and Rachael Hite

Introduction

Effective classroom management involves the application of evidence-based behavior intervention strategies to establish a productive academic environment and facilitate learning. Common strategies included under the scope of classroom management include frequent behavior specific praise (BSP; e.g., Haydon & Musti-Rao, 2011), antecedent interventions such as setting clear expectations and providing precorrection (Kern & Clemens, 2007), using elements of effective instruction delivery (EID; Dufrene et al., 2012), and providing students with many opportunities to respond (e.g., Sutherland, Alder, & Gunter, 2003). Generally, these interventions are effective and are thought to represent first line classroom management strategies that all teachers should implement; however, it is possible that these strategies are not sufficient in managing student behavior due to a particularly difficult time of day, academic subject, or activity. Additionally, some teachers may require additional behavioral support depending on the classroom composition (e.g., self-contained classroom for students with behavioral disorders). In all of these cases, group contingencies (GCs) have been identified as effective intervention strategies that can be implemented alongside regular classroom management practices.

In schools, GCs are best summarized as a reinforcement contingency with a single criterion that is applied to a group of students. They can be structured in three ways: (1) independent GCs, (2) dependent GCs, or (3) interdependent GCs. Independent GCs allow any student to meet the criterion for reinforcement based solely on their own behavior (e.g., "Whoever gets 90% or higher on their spelling test will get a sticker). Under independent GCs, one, none, some, or all students in the group may earn reinforcement; however, each student is responsible for their own performance. Dependent GCs identify a student or small group of students who are responsible for the performance of the entire group (e.g., "If these three students (Kimberly, Eric, Jordan) get 90% or higher on their spelling test, everyone in the classroom gets a sticker). Under dependent GCs, either all students in the group earn reinforcement or none of them do and the performance of one or a few students determines whether the criterion for reinforcement is met. Interdependent GCs set a criterion for reinforcement that the entire group must work together to achieve (e.g., "If the whole class averages 90% or above on their spelling test everyone gets a sticker"). Under interdependent GCs, either all students in the group earn reinforcement or none of them do but the effort required to achieve the criterion is equally distributed across all students.

Although all three types of GCs have been used to improve classroom behavior (e.g., Brantley & Webster, 1993; Heering & Wilder, 2006; Popkin & Skinner, 2003) and all three are effective in doing so (Gresham & Gresham, 1982), interdependent GCs have emerged as the most popular type due to their efficiency (compared to independent GCs) and lower likelihood in encouraging negative peer interactions (compared to dependent GCs). One of the most well-researched and versatile interdependent GCs is the Good Behavior Game (GBG; Barrish, Saunders, & Wolf, 1969). The fundamentals of the GBG are simple. Students within a classroom are divided into two or more teams, provided with a set of expectations, and earn a point for their team whenever they exhibit behavior consistent with those expectations. The team with the most points at the end of the game period is declared the winner and those students receive access to reinforcement. The GBG has been used to improve classroom behavior across a wide variety of settings, populations, and cultures (Nolan, Houlihan, Wanzek, & Jenson, 2014) Furthermore, because of its noted positive impact on distal outcomes such as high school completion (Bradshaw, Zmuda, Kellam, & Ialongo, 2009) and reduced drug use (Furr-Holden, Ialongo, Anthony, Petras, & Kellam, 2004; Storr, Ialongo, Kellam, & Anthony, 2002), the GBG has been described as a "universal behavioral vaccine" (Embry, 2002, p. 273). Thus, the focus of this chapter is on the GBG as a classroom management strategy. The following case study provides an example of how the GBG is typically implemented within a classroom and illustrates how common barriers to sustained implementation are addressed.

Case Study

Background Information and Description of the Problem Behavior

Ms. Jones is a second-year teacher in a fourth-grade general education classroom at a rural public elementary school (i.e., Longleaf Elementary School). She teaches all academic subjects to the 24 students in her classroom. Five of Ms. Jones' students receive special education services under the classification of

Specific Learning Disability (4) and Other Health Impairment (1) to address symptoms of Attention Deficit Hyperactivity Disorder (ADHD). To manage the behavior of her classroom, Ms. Jones uses both behavior specific praise and verbal reprimands to provide feedback to students on their behavior. Ms. Jones also reports using active supervision as appropriate, moving around the classroom during instruction to ensure students are meeting expectations.

Additionally, Longleaf Elementary uses a school-wide positive behavior intervention and supports (SW-PBIS) framework to address student behavior, meaning that all students within the school are expected to Be Responsible, Be Respectful, and Be Safe. These expectations were taught to students at a whole school assembly at the beginning of the year and students are able to earn "Leaf Bucks" when teachers and school staff members notice that they are meeting these expectations. Students are able to exchange "Leaf Bucks" for rewards at the end of each week at the front office.

Ms. Jones reports that these strategies work well during the morning lessons; however, she has identified one particular instructional period during which she has difficulty managing the behavior of her students. Specifically, Ms. Jones reports that her mathematics instruction occurs immediately after lunch and recess, from 1:15 p.m. to 2:10 p.m. each day. During the transition from recess to mathematics, Ms. Jones reports that the students are "full of energy," "unfocused," and "disruptive." Specifically, she reports that students are not prepared for math by the time the bell rings, frequently leave their seat during the lesson, yell and talk over each other, and do not attend to instruction or complete independent seatwork when it is assigned. She indicates that these behaviors persist through most of the mathematics lesson and appear to be a class-wide issue, making instruction extremely difficult. Furthermore, her usual behavior management strategies do not seem to have any effect. Due to these issues, Ms. Jones has reached out to the school psychologist to express her concerns and develop an additional classroom management strategy to implement during mathematics instruction. Her goal for her classroom is to streamline the transition between recess and math and increase academic engagement during instruction.

Problem Analysis

After speaking to Ms. Jones to gather this information, Ms. Williams, the school psychologist, thought it would be a good idea to collect some additional information about the students' behavior during mathematics instruction to confirm that the reported concerns are valid and to begin developing an intervention plan. To do this, Ms. Williams decided to observe the classroom during the first 50 minutes of their mathematics lesson (i.e., 1:15–2:05) on Monday, Wednesday, and Friday the week of February 10. She arrived to the classroom at 1:10 p.m., five minutes before the students transitioned in from the playground, and positioned herself in an unobtrusive location to prepare for the observation. Ms. Williams used a Planned Activity Check (PAC; Dart, Radley, Briesch, Furlow, & Cavell, 2016) with 5-minute intervals to estimate the percentage of time all students in the classroom were academically engaged (see Appendix A).

Additionally, Ms. Williams has asked Ms. Jones to complete a Direct Behavior Rating (DBR; Christ, Riley-Tillman, & Chafouleas, 2009) of the students' academically engaged behavior (AEB) in order to incorporate both of their perspectives into the problem analysis process. AEB was defined as either a) active engagement in which a student was exhibiting vocal or motor behavior that is relevant to an ongoing academic task or b) passive engagement in which a student's head was oriented toward academically relevant stimuli without exhibiting any vocal or motor behavior. Examples of active engagement included writing, answering questions aloud, raising hand, or talking to a peer or teacher about an academic task when allowed to do so. Examples of passive engagement included listening to instruction and silently reading. Nonexamples of academic engagement included sleeping, orienting towards academically irrelevant stimuli (e.g., wall), leaving assigned seat without permission, and talking to peers without permission. Ms. Jones was asked to estimate the extent to which her entire class was academically engaged throughout the entire mathematics lesson for each school day during the week of February 10. After collecting these data, Ms. Williams assembled them in a line graph with each day being plotted on the X axis and percentage of AEB plotted on the Y axis (Figure 15.1). Through visual inspection of the data, Ms. Williams noted that Ms. Jones' DBR ratings averaged 31% for the week and were trending downward. Her own PAC observations corroborated these data, revealing a decreasing trend of AEB, averaging 37.5% over the three days.

Finally, Ms. Williams took anecdotal notes during her observations and confirmed that Ms. Jones' report of her class' behavior was accurate. Many students appeared boisterous as they entered the classroom, took a long time to get their

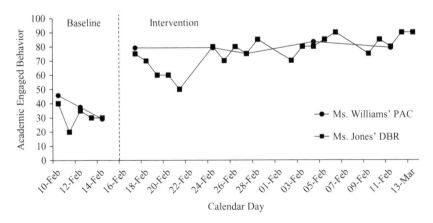

FIGURE 15.1 Academic engagement during baseline and intervention phases as measured by Planned Activity Checks (PAC) and Daily Behavior Ratings (DBR)

mathematics materials out, were frequently out of their seats during instruction or fell out of them while tilting them backwards, and spent much of the lesson talking to each other instead of completing their seatwork. In addition, she also made the following observations about Ms. Jones' classroom: (1) expectations for transition from the playground to math instruction were not made clear to students; (2) Ms. Jones appeared to rely more on reprimands instead of behavior specific praise; (3) once instruction began the verbal feedback from Ms. Jones decreased substantially; and (4) there were no contingencies in place for math seatwork completion. Given all of these pieces of data, Ms. Williams thought that the GBG would be an appropriate strategy to implement during Ms. Jones' math class.

Intervention Goals

Given that Ms. Jones reported that her students were "unfocused" and "disruptive" during mathematics and systematic data collection supported low levels of AEB during the period, an increase in AEB was identified as the primary intervention goal. Although disruptive behavior was initially identified as the behavior of concern by Ms. Jones, a decrease in disruptive behavior was not selected as the primary intervention goal as decreases in disruptive behavior do not necessarily result in an increase in desirable classroom behaviors (i.e., AEB). AEB is also considered an enabler of academic achievement (e.g., Greenwood, Horton, & Utley, 2002) further highlighting its importance as an intervention target.

Measurement of Target Behavior, Data Collection Strategies and Progress Monitoring

Systematic direct observation (SDO) has been recognized as the gold standard of behavior assessment in schools (Riley-Tillman, Chafouleas, Sassu, Chanese, & Glazer, 2008). Given the high levels of accuracy documented for PAC as a method for assessing AEB (Dart et al., 2016), it was included as a means of assessing student behavior and monitoring progress over time. The use of PAC also allows for the simultaneous and independent evaluation of treatment fidelity—a critical component to determination of a functional relation between an intervention and observed outcomes (Gresham, MacMillan, Beebe-Frankenberger, & Bocian, 2000). Despite the aforementioned benefits, the use of PAC requires a dedicated observer. Given the myriad of responsibilities of Ms. Williams within the school, it is unlikely that she would be able to be present for each intervention of the GBG. As such, a class-wide DBR and a self-report fidelity checklist were identified as the primary means of measuring student behavior and monitoring progress.

In developing a data collection plan, Ms. Williams and Ms. Jones collaborated to identify a class-wide DBR as a feasible means of daily data collection. Further,

Ms. Jones agreed to complete a daily self-report fidelity checklist. Ms. Williams suggested that the class-wide DBR and self-report fidelity checklist be completed immediately following the identified intervention period. Ms. Williams planned to complete SDO during at least 20% of implementation sessions—a commonly accepted standard for evaluation of data reliability (Kratochwill et al., 2010). Utilizing both daily teacher-collected data and the less-frequently collected SDO data from Ms. Williams, the effect of the intervention on student behavior was monitored over time. Additionally, these data also served to inform Ms. Williams regarding the need for performance feedback and retraining in intervention procedures should a lapse in intervention fidelity be observed.

Intervention Plan

After completing the problem analysis process, Ms. Williams met with Ms. Jones on Friday, February 15 to discuss the idea of implementing the GBG during mathematics. After a brief description of the intervention, Ms. Williams agreed to give it a try and the two worked together to develop the plan. First, because the GBG is a team-based intervention, Ms. Williams asked Ms. Jones to think about how the teams in her classroom will be formed. Ms. Jones already arranges the desks in her classroom into four groups of six students each and decided she would like to form teams that way. The two discussed any of the six groupings that may contain more active or difficult students and decided to switch the desks of two students to make the teams more even. Next, Ms. Williams and Ms. Jones developed three rules for the GBG that will provide behavioral expectations to students as well as let them know which behaviors will earn points for their team. Ms. Jones decided to align the rules with the SW-PBIS initiatives already in place at Longleaf Elementary and decided on the following three behaviors:

1) Be Responsible—enter the classroom quietly, go straight to your assigned seat, get out your math materials, and wait for instruction to begin; complete assigned work
2) Be Respectful—raise your hand to ask for permission before leaving your seat or beginning a conversation
3) Be Safe—keep your hands and your feet to yourself during instruction, keep all four legs of your chair on the ground

They decided that each of these behaviors would be written on a large poster board and hung near the front of the classroom so that all students would be reminded of them throughout the mathematics class.

Next, Ms. Jones needed to determine a goal for the GBG and how many teams would be able to win. Ms. Williams suggested that she consider trying to give at least one point every 2–3 minutes to teams meeting the expectations, so they decided to set the initial GBG point goal at 20. Also, Ms. Jones did not want students to become discouraged or frustrated if they were behind in the point total so decided to allow any team with 20 or more points to win the game. She thought that doing this might also reduce competitive behavior or taunting between the teams. Ms. Jones marked each point using tally marks on the dry erase board at the front of the classroom so that all students could see their team's standing. Finally, Ms. Jones had to decide what the winning team or teams would earn for their reward. She was already encouraged to provide students with "Leaf Bucks" when they met expectations as part of the SW-PBIS initiative so chose to give each student on a winning team 5 "Leaf Bucks." This was also an attractive option because it didn't cost Ms. Jones anything.

Now that the details of the GBG were set, Ms. Williams provided Ms. Jones a brief training on how to implement the intervention. She provided Ms. Jones with a checklist that included all seven steps of the GBG (see Appendix B) and asked her to indicate whether each step was completed each day. Ms. Williams showed Ms. Jones a nearly identical form (see Appendix C) and indicated that she would be completing it on some weekdays to make sure the GBG was being implemented appropriately and to provide feedback about implementation.

First, Ms. Jones announced to students that the GBG was beginning. Ms. Jones decided to do this in the hallway outside the classroom as students were lining up from recess and about to come inside. Second, Ms. Jones reminded students of the three rules (i.e., Be Responsible, Be Respectful, Be Safe) and explained the specific behaviors she would be looking for as signs those rules were being followed. Third, Ms. Jones reminded students they could earn points for their team by following these rules and that teams needed 20 points to win the game. Fourth, Ms. Jones reminded students that if their team won, every member of the team would earn 5 "Leaf Bucks." Fifth, Ms. Jones scanned the classroom during mathematics instruction and award points to the team of individual students who were following the rules, making a tally mark on the dry erase board accordingly. Ms. Williams encouraged Ms. Jones to also provide BSP whenever a point was awarded (e.g., "Kate earned a point for her team because she is keeping all four of her chair's feet on the ground and is completing her worksheet, great job, Kate!") to increase the effectiveness of the GBG. Finally, at the end of the mathematics period, Ms. Jones totaled each team's points and distributed the "Leaf Bucks" to all winning students.

After this planning meeting, all Ms. Jones had to do before implementing the GBG was make and hang the poster board with the game rules. She did this over the weekend and was prepared to implement the GBG on Monday, February 17.

Intervention Fidelity and Interobserver Agreement

Ms. Williams planned to observe the first day of implementation to provide support if issues arose. She was also present to conduct a PAC observation of student behavior and Ms. Jones' implementation of the GBG. The morning of the 17, Ms. Jones provided her students with a brief training on the GBG before they dismissed from science to lunch. She described that they would be playing a game for good behavior and that students could earn "Leaf Bucks" for meeting behavioral expectations. She also reviewed the expectations and all of the game rules so that students were prepared when making their transition from recess to math that afternoon. At 1:15 p.m., the first day of implementation went on without a hitch and it appeared to be extremely effective! Ms. Jones reported implementing 100% of GBG components and her DBR of student behavior suggested that students were on-task for 75% of the mathematics period. Although she didn't collect formal data on their transition behavior she noted fantastic improvements in the students' preparedness. Ms. Williams' data were similar, with her PAC observation of student behavior indicating 79.2% AEB and her observation of Ms. Jones' indicating 100% of components implemented. With such good data, Ms. Williams was comfortable letting Ms. Jones implement the GBG independently for the rest of the week.

Unfortunately, by Thursday of that week Ms. Jones contacted Ms. Williams concerned that the GBG was no longer effective. Together they reviewed the data. Ms. Jones indicated she was implementing 100% of GBG components each day but her DBR data suggested a clear decreasing trend of AEB, ending at 60% on Thursday. Ms. Williams decided to come by the next day, Friday, February 21 to observe implementation again. At the end of math instruction on the 21st, Ms. Jones and Ms. Williams met again to look at the data. Ms. Jones' data were even more concerning, student AEB had dropped to 50% according to her DBR despite perfect implementation. Ms. Williams' data told a slightly different story. Her PAC observation of student behavior did reveal low AEB (i.e., 57.1%); however, her observation of Ms. Williams' implementation revealed that one component was being left out: Delivery of the "Leaf Bucks" to students. When this was brought to Ms. Jones' attention, she reported that she had run out of printed "Leaf Bucks" and so had created an IOU for the winning students. She currently owed 15 "Leaf Bucks" to one team, 10 to another two teams, and 5 to the last team. The students were no longer motivated to meet the behavioral expectations because they were not receiving their reward for doing so. Ms. Williams emphasized the importance of delivering the reward every day it was earned to keep student motivation to perform high.

With this issue resolved, implementation continued for the next three weeks with only two additional lapses in reward delivery. Ms. Williams made sure to bring plenty of printed "Leaf Bucks" to Ms. Jones after the second week! Ms. Williams faded her presence during implementation to once per week after consistent implementation and improvement in student behavior was evident. Ms. Jones' DBR data and Ms. Williams' PAC observations agreed, student AEB increased to an average around 80% engaged, much higher than before the GBG. Ms. Jones reported that the GBG was feasible to implement concurrently with math instruction, especially in the later weeks when it had become part of the math period routine.

Intervention Outcome Data and Summary of Intervention Effects

Data reflecting student AEB and implementation of the GBG are graphed in Figures 15.1 and 15.2. As previously described, initial intervention data collected by Ms. Jones via class-wide DBR indicated a decreasing trend in AEB. Although the fidelity self-report form indicated adherence to all intervention steps, SDO revealed a lapse adherence. Following retraining, levels of AEB increased and remained high throughout the remainder of the intervention. Although some variability in student AEB was noted, the levels of AEB observed were generally high and represented a substantial improvement over baseline levels. The high levels of AEB corresponded with high fidelity of implementation as measured by both self-report and independent observation. Overall, the intervention was determined to be effective and sufficient in addressing concerns initially expressed by Ms. Jones. As such, Ms. Jones and Ms. Williams collaboratively developed a plan for the intervention to be implemented during the remainder of the year.

Intervention Acceptability

As previously stated, Ms. Jones found implementation of the GBG to be feasible during math instruction. Ms. Williams was also careful to assess other factors related to social validity of intervention procedures; namely, effectiveness and acceptability. During initial implementation of the intervention, Ms. Jones reported that the GBG had lost effectiveness. Following troubleshooting and retraining, DBR data collected by Ms. Jones indicated teacher perceptions of improved student AEB. During routine meetings, Ms. Jones also expressed to Ms. Williams that the intervention was successful and that student disruptive

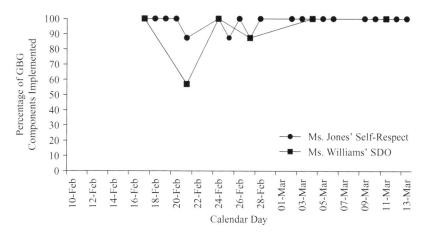

FIGURE 15.2 Good Behavior Game fidelity data

behavior was no longer a primary concern during math instruction. Ms. Jones also expressed that the GBG appeared to be an appropriate procedure for the observed concerns and indicated that she had recommended use of the GBG to other teachers. She also indicated a willingness to continue implementing the intervention over the remainder of the year—highlighting the acceptability of the procedure.

Intervention Considerations

Over the remainder of the academic year, Ms. Jones encountered a few implementation issues that required additional problem solving. First, one student, Charles, appeared to get pleasure from spoiling the game for his team. He would irritate his teammates, provoke them to leave their seats, and take their work materials. At the end of the math period Charles would smile as his team failed to meet the 20-point goal and his teammates expressed their frustrations. To solve this problem, Ms. Williams suggested that Charles be put on a fifth team, by himself. Within two days Charles asked Ms. Jones to be put back on his original team, which she agreed to under the condition that he no longer attempted to sabotage their performance.

Second, after playing the GBG for several weeks, students appeared unexcited if their team won the 5 "Leaf Buck" prize. Ms. Jones determined that students were earning so many "Leaf Bucks" playing the GBG that they were losing their value as reinforcers. To address this, she conducted an informal preference assessment to determine what other rewards students might like to earn. Ms. Jones developed a list of other rewards that were free or cost effective that she was able to provide to students each day. She distributed this list to the students and asked them to rank order their top three most preferred rewards. After doing this, she averaged the reward rankings across students and the top two selections (i.e., 5-minute of free time at the end of math; new pencil) were identified as new rewards. Ms. Jones chose to alternate between these two rewards each day.

Third, and related to the second issue, Ms. Jones found that some teams were only motivated on free time days while others were only motivated on pencil days. This created a situation where approximately half of the students were engaged and meeting expectations while the other half were not. To address this issue, Ms. Jones consulted with Ms. Williams who suggested that she keep the reward a secret to students until it was time to end the game. To do this, Ms. Jones filled a jar with slips of paper, some said "Free Time" and some said "Pencil." At the end of each math class, she drew a slip from the jar and winning students received whatever was written on the slip. The element of surprise increased students' motivation to perform under the GBG.

Finally, Ms. Jones noticed that some students on each team were not engaging in appropriate behavior and instead were allowing their teammates to earn their team enough points to receive the daily reward. After consultation with Ms. Williams, Ms. Jones decided to modify the GBG so that only one student from each team was able to earn points for their team each day. To ensure all students continued to meet behavioral expectations, Ms. Jones kept the selected student a mystery from the class. At the beginning of each math period she mentally noted which student from each team would be eligible to earn points but did not announce this to the class. She informed all the students that a "team hero" had been selected from each team and only that student could earn points for the day. Of course, all students wondered whether they were the "team hero" and modified their behavior accordingly. Ms. Jones reduced the goal to 5 points to account for the lower number of students contributing points to their team. She also did not provide behavior specific praise when points were earned but instead made more general praise statements (e.g., "Great job team hero on Team 1, you earned a point for Being Respectful!).

Conclusion

The GBG is one of the most well-researched interventions used to address student behavior within the classroom. Not only is it almost universally effective, it is also feasible for teachers to implement concurrently during instruction. Furthermore, as the case example illustrates, the GBG can be easily modified to address a number of concerns that may arise during implementation. Nearly every component of the GBG can be modified to suit specific needs or challenges within the implementation setting, making it an appealing classroom management strategy when more basic strategies have been ineffective.

References

Barrish, H. H., Saunders, M., & Wolf, M. M. (1969). Good Behavior Game: Effects of individual contingencies for group consequences on disruptive behavior in a classroom. *Journal of Applied Behavior Analysis*, *2*, 119–124.

Bradshaw, C. P., Zmuda, J. H., Kellam, S. G., & Ialongo, N. S. (2009). Longitudinal impact of two universal preventive interventions in first grade on educational outcomes in high school. *Journal of Educational Psychology*, *101*, 926–937. doi:10.1037/a0016586

Brantley, D. C., & Webster, R. E. (1993). Use of an independent group contingency management system in a regular classroom setting. *Psychology in the Schools*, *30*, 60–66. doi:10.1002/1520-6807(199301)30:1<60::AID-PITS2310300110>3.0.CO;2-X

Christ, T. J., Riley-Tillman, T. C., & Chafouleas, S. M. (2009). Foundation for the development and use of direct behavior rating (DBR) to assess and evaluate student behavior. *Assessment for Effective Intervention*, *34*, 201–213. doi:10.1177/1534508409340390

Dart, E. H., Radley, K. C., Briesch, A. M., Furlow, C. M., & Cavell, H. J. (2016). Assessing the accuracy of classwide direct observation methods: Two analyses using simulated and naturalistic data. *Behavioral Disorders*, *41*, 148–160. doi:10.17988/BD-15-49.1

Dufrene, B. A., Parker, K., Menousek, K., Zhou, Q., Harpole, L. L., & Olmi, D. J. (2012). Direct behavioral consultation in head start to increase teacher use of praise and effective instruction delivery. *Journal of Educational and Psychological Consultation, 22,* 159–186. doi:10.1080/10474412.2011.620817

Embry, D. D. (2002). The Good Behavior Game: A best practice candidate as a universal behavioral vaccine. *Clinical Child and Family Psychology Review, 5,* 273–297. doi:10.1023/A:1020977107086

Furr-Holden, C. D. M., Ialongo, N. S., Anthony, J. C., Petras, H., & Kellam, S. G. (2004). Developmentally inspired drug prevention: Middle school outcomes in a school-based randomized prevention trial. *Drug and Alcohol Dependence, 73,* 149–158. doi:10.1016/j.drugalcdep.2003.10.002

Greenwood, C. R., Horton, B. T., & Utley, C. A. (2002). Academic engagement: Current perspectives in research and practice. *School Psychology Review, 31,* 328–349.

Gresham, F. M., & Gresham, G. N. (1982). Interdependent, dependent, and independent group contingencies for controlling disruptive behavior. *The Journal of Special Education, 16,* 101–110. doi:10.1177/002246698201600110

Gresham, F. M., MacMillan, D. L., Beebe-Frankenberger, M. E., & Bocian, K. M. (2000). Treatment integrity in learning disabilities intervention research: Do we really know how treatments are implemented? *Learning Disabilities Research and Practice, 15,* 198–205. doi:10.1207/SLDRP1504_4

Haydon, T., & Musti-Rao, S. (2011). Effective use of behavior-specific praise: A middle school case study. *Beyond Behavior, 20,* 31–39.

Heering, P. W., & Wilder, D. A. (2006). The use of dependent group contingencies to increase on-task behavior in two general education classrooms. *Education and Treatment of Children, 29,* 459–468.

Kern, L., & Clemens, N. H. (2007). Antecedent strategies to promote appropriate classroom behavior. *Psychology in the Schools, 44,* 65–75.

Kratochwill, T. R., Hitchcock, J., Horner, R. H., Levin, J. R., Odom, S. L., Rindskopf, D., & Shadish, W. R. M. (2010). *Single case designs technical documentation.* Retrieved from http://ies.ed.gov/ncee/wwc/pdf/wwc_scd.pdf

Nolan, J. D., Houlihan, D., Wanzek, M., & Jenson, W. R. (2014). The Good Behavior Game: A classroom-behavior intervention effective across cultures. *School Psychology International, 35,* 191–205. doi:10.1177/0143034312471473

Popkin, J., & Skinner, C. H. (2003). Enhancing academic performance in a classroom serving students with serious emotional disturbance: Interdependent group contingencies with randomly selected components. *School Psychology Review, 32,* 282–295.

Riley-Tillman, T. C., Chafouleas, S. M., Sassu, K. A., Chanese, J. A., & Glazer, A. D. (2008). Examining the agreement of direct behavior ratings and systematic direct observation data for on-task and disruptive behavior. *Journal of Positive Behavior Interventions, 10,* 136–143.

Storr, C. L., Ialongo, N. S., Kellam, S. G., & Anthony, J. C. (2002). A randomized controlled trial of two primary school intervention strategies to prevent early onset tobacco smoking. *Drug and Alcohol Dependence, 66,* 51–60. doi:10.1016/S0376-8716(01)00184-3

Sutherland, K. S., Alder, N., & Gunter, P. L. (2003). The effect of varying rates of opportunities to respond to academic requests on the classroom behavior of students with EBD. *Journal of Emotional and Behavioral Disorders, 11,* 239–248. doi:10.1177/10634266030110040501

Appendix A: Planned Activity Check Form

Planned Activity Check

Target Behavior: Academically Engaged Behavior

Operational Definition: Academically Engaged Behavior is defined as either a) active engagement in which a student is exhibiting vocal or motor behavior that is relevant to an ongoing academic task or b) passive engagement in which a student's head is oriented toward academically relevant stimuli without exhibiting any vocal or motor behavior. Examples of active engagement include writing, answering questions aloud, raising hand, or talking to a peer or teacher about an academic task when allowed to do so. Examples of passive engagement include listening to instruction and silently reading. Nonexamples of academic engagement include sleeping, orienting towards academically irrelevant stimuli (e.g., wall), leaving assigned seat without permission, and talking to peers without permission.

Interval Length: 5 minutes

Observation Length: 50 minutes (11:00am — 11:50am)

Directions: Start a timer. At the end of each 5-minute interval, record two numbers. First, count the number of students that are currently engaged in the target behavior and write that number in the Count box. Second, count the total number of students present in the classroom and write that number in the Total box. Repeat this process for each interval. At the end of the observation, compute the percentage of students engaged in the target behavior for each interval and average that number for your total score.

Interval	*Count*	*Total*	*Percentage*
1			
2			
3			
4			
5			
6			
7			
8			
9			
10			
Sum values in Percentage column and divide by total number of intervals to obtain estimate of target behavior during observation			

Appendix B: Good Behavior Game Self-Report Fidelity Checklist

Good Behavior Game Teacher Self-Report Form

Directions: Please mark **Yes** or **No** for each step you completed today in the Good Behavior Game.

1. I stated that the Good Behavior Game is beginning.	Yes	No
2. I reviewed the target behaviors for today.	Yes	No
3. I stated the goal for the day.	Yes	No
4. I stated the prize available for the winning team.	Yes	No
5. I made tally marks for each instance of inappropriate behavior.	Yes	No
6. I stated group scores at the end of the game and announced the results.	Yes	No
7. I provided rewards to the winning team.	Yes	No

Appendix C: Good Behavior Game Direct Observation Fidelity Checklist

Good Behavior Game Direct Observation Form

Directions: Please mark **Yes** or **No** for each step you completed today in the Good Behavior Game.

1. Teacher stated that the Good Behavior Game is beginning.	Yes	No
2. Teacher reviewed the target behaviors for today.	Yes	No
3. Teacher stated the goal for the day.	Yes	No
4. Teacher stated the prize available for the winning team.	Yes	No
5. Teacher made tally marks for each instance of appropriate behavior.	Yes	No
6. Teacher stated group scores at the end of the game and announced the results.	Yes	No
7. Teacher provided rewards to the winning team.	Yes	No

16
TIMELY TRANSITIONS GAME

Elizabeth McCallum, Ara J. Schmitt, and Brittany Evans

Introduction

Transitions are open blocks of time when students are not engaged in academic instruction or traditional learning practices. These periods of time involve students moving from one activity to another (i.e., finishing up an activity, preparing themselves, and beginning another activity). Given the number of transitions students and teachers experience during a typical school day, teacher management of student behavior is particularly vulnerable during these periods of transitioning (Arlin, 1979). Additionally, teachers spend a lot of time waiting for students to engage in appropriate behavior in order to begin transitioning. One study demonstrated that by reducing transition times, teachers could cut this time spent waiting by almost two hours over the course of a five-day school week, increasing time devoted to instruction and other productive activities (Campbell & Skinner, 2004). Additionally, other researchers have concluded that children may engage in increased levels of challenging behavior when they do not understand transition-related expectations (McIntosh, Herman, Sanford, McGraw, & Florence, 2004).

Specifically during hallway transitions, inappropriate behaviors often include touching each other (i.e., kicking, hitting, pushing), talking to each other, and failing to follow directions. These inappropriate behaviors may occur more frequently in school hallways because students are in closer physical proximity to each other, making it more difficult for teachers to supervise and manage their behavior. Additionally, there are fewer chances for students to gain reinforcers for appropriate behavior in the hallway. Transitioning from one room to another takes time, and this process is prolonged when students engage in inappropriate behaviors (Campbell & Skinner, 2004).

The Timely Transitions Game (TTG), an intervention designed to speed up room-to-room transitions and reduce challenging behaviors during transitions, involves the application of explicit timing and interdependent group contingencies. It is based on the premise that effective management of room-to-room transitions allows teachers to devote more time to teaching and allows students to spend more time engaged in academic instruction. The explicit timing procedure involves the teacher using a stopwatch to overtly measure the amount of time that passes between the teacher prompting the students to transition to the next activity and the students having appropriately arrived at their subsequent location. General procedures might include (1) indicating it is time to transition using a physical cue such as the flick of a light switch (this cue would also prompt the teacher to start the stopwatch), (2) waiting for the students to be quietly seated at their desks, (3) verbally prompting the students to line up at the door one row at a time, and (4) waiting for a forward-facing, silent line before allowing them to file out of the classroom, (5) reminding students of the rules as they quietly move through the hall to their next location. The transition is considered complete when the final student walks into the designated classroom and follows the instructions of the new setting appropriately. Subsequently, all students in the class earn a reward if the transition is completed in fewer seconds than a randomly selected criterion (i.e., 130 seconds; Campbell & Skinner, 2004).

Reviews of the research suggest that there is strong evidence in support of the use of interdependent group contingencies as an intervention in school settings to improve student behavior, as they foster cooperation by providing positive contingencies and also require minimal teacher effort for implementation. Interdependent group contingencies increase pro-social behavior and do not point out individuals in the classroom who do or do not meet the criterion (Maggin, Johnson, Chafouleas, Ruberto, & Berggren, 2012). Research also indicates that this intervention can improve the behavior of middle and high school students with emotional and behavioral disorders in alternative educational settings, with the main benefit including the amount of instructional time recuperated by improving upon the transition behavior of the students (Hawkins, Haydon, Denune, Larkin, & Fite, 2015; Hawkins, Haydon, McCoy, & Howard, 2017).

Case Study

Background Information

Mr. Abbott is a computer lab teacher at Lincoln Elementary School who instructs 25 students in his 10:00 a.m. lab session. He sought the consultation services of the school psychologist, Ms. Jennings, because his class had difficulty transitioning from the computer lab back to their fourth grade homeroom classroom. In fact, the homeroom teacher, Mrs. Scott, had become increasingly frustrated with not only the class for arriving late to the next class period, but also with Mr. Abbott for not trying different strategies to decrease the transition time of the class. Mr. Abbott argued there were varied reasons for their late arrival. Some students were engrossed in computer activities and had difficulty disengaging from their work, while other students were simply noncompliant in the face of instructions. He also explained that the class must walk a notable distance, proceed past a kindergarten class that often proves intriguing to the students, and walk up a flight of stairs with multiple handrails that often result in students swinging on them. Each of these, he argued, posed an obstacle to timely transition.

Lincoln Elementary had an established system of Positive Behavioral Intervention and Supports (PBIS) in place. In brief, the school used "caught being good" tickets from the Tough Kid Toolbox (Jenson, Rhode, & Reavis, 2009) as a secondary reinforcer for the students to exchange at the school store for a reward (primary reinforcer). Teachers found this reinforcement system reasonably addressed most school-based problem behaviors. Mr. Abbott tried to use this system by reinforcing students for timely transition behavior, but the procedure did not result in reduction in transition time. This is not of great surprise as the approach only reinforced students who were already displaying expected behaviors, while the strategy did not reach the students who were engaging in problem behaviors.

Description of the Problem Behavior

The school psychologist conducted a problem-identification interview seeking to understand what is expected of the class during the transition period and the hypothesized reasons why the class was not timely. Mr. Abbott explained to Ms. Jennings that his classroom context was unique in its challenges. Unlike other classroom situations, each of his students must engage in different steps to finish their work and get ready to transition. For example, some must find a place to stop working and save their product, while others must also print their work at a crowded printing station. He characterized these students as engaging in expected behaviors, but not completing them in a timely manner. Mr. Abbott estimated that there are probably five students who have this difficulty. On the other hand, he suggested that there are two students who are generally noncompliant. The two students Mr. Abbott identified do not follow instructions to stand quietly at their respective computer station to transition, but also stop to look in the kindergarten classroom on the way to homeroom and invariably swing on the stairwell handrails despite daily redirection.

This account prompted Ms. Jennings to ask Mr. Abbott to imagine a video recording of his class engaging in appropriate transition behavior and to report what she would see on that video regarding both teachers' time expectations.

He reported that once given a prompt to begin the transition process, he believed that all students should be able to save their work, print if needed, and quietly stand by their desks within three minutes. From that time point, Mr. Abbott indicated that he would ask students to line up at the door. Then, he would expect students to file out of the room without talking and continue to walk in a straight line without talking, touching each other, stopping, or swinging on the handrails. He estimated it should take no more than two minutes to make it to homeroom from the computer lab. Ms. Jennings asked approximately how many days of the week the class transitions consistent with this expectation and he responded, zero days.

Problem Analysis

In order to gather data to understand the nature of the problem and inform intervention selection, Ms. Jennings arranged a day to observe the transition period between the computer lab and homeroom. Mr. Abbott gave the school psychologist freedom to choose the day of the observation, as the problem occurs every school day. Ms. Jennings decided that it would be best to conduct a latency recording of the time between (a) the end of Mr. Abbott's instructions to prepare to transition to homeroom and (b) the moment all students were standing quietly at their computer station and ready to leave the room. She also measured the time between when (c) the last student left the computer lab and (d) the time when the last student entered the homeroom classroom. Consistent with the referral for consultation, student transition time exceeded expected limits. Specifically, it took 355 seconds for students to stand quietly at their computer stations after directed, and 361 seconds for students to travel between the two classrooms. This is nearly double the time expected for students to transition and thus served as a data-based illustration of the teachers' frustration.

Because understanding why students were having difficulty during the transition period may inform intervention selection, the school psychologist also kept anecdotal notes of reasons why individual students were delayed. Ms. Jennings found that Mr. Abbott was an accurate reporter of reasons why students had difficulty transitioning. On that day, there were four students who had difficulty finding a stopping point once directed to finish their work. Three of these students quietly continued to type and one proceeded to type while also pleading with Mr. Abbott to allow him more time to complete his work. On the other hand, two students did not follow teacher prompts to save their work and stand quietly. These students instead talked and poked each other in their chairs, even after other students quietly stood. These same two students were guilty of stopping the line of students in hallways to look in classrooms and make faces at the students and swing on the handrails.

Intervention Goals

Ms. Jennings and the computer lab teacher discussed goals for the intervention. Mr. Abbott reported he simply wanted the class to make it back to homeroom by 11:00 a.m. without compromising his computer lab time. He understood well that he could simply move up the time that he prompted students to prepare to leave the computer lab, but that would compromise his valuable class time. Mr. Abbott was interested in implementing an intervention that maximized his time with students while also reducing transition time. Conjointly, the consultant and consultee decided that a target transition time of five minutes from the moment Mr. Abbott gave a transition cue to the time the students returned to their classroom was reasonable.

Measurement of Target Behaviors, Data Collection Strategies, and Progress Monitoring

The primary target behavior measured was transition time in seconds, which was defined as the time between a transition cue and the time all students exhibited *appropriate line behavior*. Appropriate line behavior was defined as standing between the student ahead of and behind oneself, facing forward, keeping hands and feet to oneself, and being quiet. Additional time was added during hallway transitions for inappropriate behaviors as described below. During baseline phases, Mr. Abbott used his typical request for the students to line up as the transition cue, and during intervention phases, the cue "time to unplug" was used. Once a cue was given, the teacher and/or observer recorded the time (start time), and then subsequently recorded the time (stop time) when all students met criteria for appropriate line behavior, indicating they were ready to transition. Then, if inappropriate line behavior occurred during the transition, Mr. Abbott would stop the students and resume timing until appropriate line behavior resumed. The transition was considered complete once the final student crossed the threshold into the destination classroom. Although Mr. Abbott provided transition warnings in both baseline and intervention phases (i.e., "you have two minutes before it's time to go back to your classroom"), the transition times did not include the duration of these countdowns in either condition. Data were recorded using iPhone timers and then inputted into an Excel spreadsheet.

Intervention Plan

Four "phases" or conditions were implemented across the case study in an ABAB single case design. An initial three-day baseline condition was followed by the first TTG condition, which lasted five days. A second two-day baseline condition was then implemented, followed by a final TTG condition, which lasted six days.

The team initially intended to implement the second baseline condition for three days, but Mr. Abbott requested reinstating the TTG intervention procedures after two days in the second baseline condition because of the substantial increase in the transition time that occurred during this phase.

Baseline Procedures

Baseline conditions mirrored procedures already being implemented by Mr. Abbott in terms of transitioning instructions. In the computer lab, students were seated in rows, each working independently at a computer station. When it was almost time to transition, Mr. Abbott gave students the following warning: "you have two minutes before it's time to go back to your classroom." After the two minutes had elapsed, Mr. Abbott told the students that it was time to go back to their classroom and discreetly started a timer on his iPhone. He then instructed the students to line up inside the entrance of the computer lab and waited until they had done so, providing reminders and redirections as he typically did. Once the students were exhibiting appropriate line behavior, he stopped the timer. He then led them through the hall and up the stairs, stopping them to remind and redirect them as usual. During transitions when students misbehaved, Mr. Abbott stopped the class and started the timer. When they were once again engaging in appropriate line behavior, he stopped the timer and continued the transition. The transition was over when the last student entered the classroom.

Intervention Procedures

After the initial baseline data were collected, Mr. Abbott and Ms. Jennings described and demonstrated behaviors that would indicate that the students were ready to transition. These included saving their work on the computers, logging out of the program, standing up, pushing in their chairs, and standing quietly at their stations. Upon prompting, all students successfully demonstrated these ready-to-transition behaviors. Next, appropriate line behavior was discussed and demonstrated. These included standing between the student ahead of and behind oneself, facing forward, keeping hands and feet to oneself, and being quiet. Upon prompting, all students successfully demonstrated these appropriate line behaviors.

Next, Mr. Abbott and Ms. Jennings introduced the Timely Transitions Game (TTG) to the students. First, the explicit timing component was taught in conjunction with the cue "time to unplug." Students were instructed that they would be warned two minutes before the cue was given, and then once Mr. Abbott gave the cue "time to unplug," he would start a timer. At that time, students should begin exhibiting ready-to-transition behaviors (save work, log off, stand up, etc.). Once all students exhibited ready-to-transition behaviors, Mr. Abbott would dismiss them row-by-row to line up near the door. Once all students exhibited appropriate line behavior, the timer would be stopped. If any inappropriate line behavior occurred while transitioning between classrooms in the hallways or on the stairs, Mr. Abbott would instruct the students to stop and he would resume timing until appropriate line behavior was restored. The explicit timing procedure was practiced in two mock transitions to and from the computer lab to the homeroom classroom.

After it was clear that the students understood the explicit timing procedures, Ms. Jennings explained the group contingency procedures. Students were shown a container with the word *Criteria* on it that would remain on Mrs. Scott's desk. Each day, the date and the transition time in seconds would be recorded on the whiteboard in large print in the students' homeroom classroom. Immediately following each transition during the intervention phases, Ms. Jennings would randomly select a criterion time from the container and compare it to the students' actual transition time that day. Mr. Abbott and Ms. Jennings decided it would be reasonable to set five required criterion times to range between 60 and 180 seconds below the average baseline transition time, at 30-second increments. For instance, if the average baseline transition time was 500 seconds, the criterion times would be 440, 410, 380, 350, and 320 seconds. After a criterion time was drawn from the container, it was placed back into the container and could be drawn again the next day.

When the actual transition time was less than the selected criterion time, the students would earn a reward for that day. Ms. Jennings, in conjunction with Mr. Abbott and the classroom teacher, had previously decided upon the reinforcements that would be offered. On days when a reinforcer was earned, the class earned a letter towards spelling a longer word (e.g., *P* in *P-A-R-T-Y*). When the word was completely spelled, the entire class would receive access to the reward (e.g., a pizza party). On days when the actual transition time was greater than the criterion time drawn, the class would not earn a letter. After explaining the TTG procedures to the students, Ms. Jennings and Mr. Abbott answered any questions that the students had regarding either the explicit timing or group contingency procedures.

TTG Implementation

On the first TTG session day, Mr. Abbott reminded the students of the procedures and informed them that they would be working toward earning a pajama party when they spelled out the word *P-A-R-T-Y.* Mr. Abbott implemented the TTG intervention using the explicit timing procedures described and Ms. Jennings recorded the transition time and date on the whiteboard in the students' homeroom classroom. Upon the transition's end, Ms. Jennings drew a random criterion from the container on Mrs. Scott's desk and compared it to the actual transition time. Because the actual transition time was less than the selected time, the students earned the *P* in *P-A-R-T-Y*. This was recorded on a special class-created chart which was publicly posted in the classroom. Once all letters in P-A-R-T-Y were earned, the next reward worked toward in this case study was R-E-C-E-S-S (extra 15-minute recess period).

Intervention Fidelity and Interobserver Agreement

During 36% of TTG sessions, an observer recorded the number of steps Mr. Abbott and/or Ms. Jennings completed on a procedural checklist (Figure 16.1), and intervention fidelity was calculated by dividing the number of

Step	Procedure	Completed (circle one)
1.	Provide transition warning two minutes prior to transition cue ("Two minutes until it's time to unplug.").	Yes No
2.	Provide transition cue, "time to unplug" and start timer.	Yes No
3.	As soon as all students are exhibiting *ready to transition behavior*, dismiss them row by row to line up.	Yes No
4.	As soon as all students are exhibiting *appropriate line behavior*, stop timer and lead students into hallway.	Yes No
5.	If inappropriate line behavior occurs during transition, stop students and resume timing. When *appropriate line behavior* resumes, stop timing and continue with transition.	Yes No N/A
6.	Continue transition until final student enters classroom and transition is complete	Yes No
7.	Write date and transition time on whiteboard.	Yes No
8.	Draw random transition criterion from container.	Yes No
9.	If actual transition time is less than criterion time, provide reward in form of written letter on posted chart in classroom.	Yes No N/A
10.	If students earned final letter in reward word, provide information on how and when reward will be provided.	Yes No N/A

FIGURE 16.1 Timely Transitions Game procedural checklist

steps implemented by the total number of steps possible. This number was then multiplied by 100. Intervention steps were found to have been implemented with a mean of 93% accuracy.

Mr. Abbott recorded transition time each baseline and intervention session using an iPhone. Additionally, an observer also recorded transition times and interobserver agreement (IOA) was assessed for 31% of all sessions (two baseline and three intervention sessions). To establish IOA, the smaller number of seconds recorded was divided by the larger number of seconds recorded and the results were multiplied by 100. Interobserver agreement ranged from 86% to 97% with a mean of 92%.

Intervention Outcome Data

Figure 16.2 displays the daily transition times across baseline and intervention phases. During the initial baseline phase, transition times ranged between 322 and 408 seconds, with an average of 370 seconds. Following the implementation of the intervention, the transition time immediately decreased and remained substantially reduced throughout the first intervention phase. During this intervention phase, transition times ranged between 96 and 158 seconds with an average of 119 seconds.

Following five consecutive TTG sessions, the intervention was withdrawn and baseline conditions were reinstated for two sessions. During the first of these two sessions, the transition time immediately increased to 267 seconds. The next of these sessions, the transition time increased again to 390 seconds, similar to pre-intervention levels. At this time, TTG procedures were reintroduced, and the students showed a substantial decline in transition times once again.

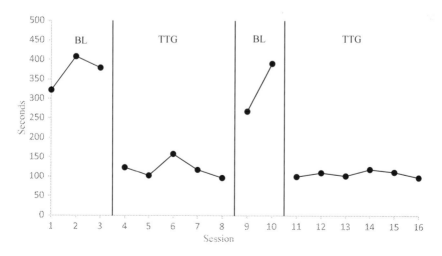

FIGURE 16.2 Transition time in seconds across baseline (BL) and intervention (TTG or Timely Transitions Game) phases

During this second TTG phase, transition times remained stable and ranged from 97 to 118 seconds with an average of 106 seconds. Overall, transition times averaged 353 seconds between the two baseline phases, compared to 112 between the two intervention phases, an average reduction of 241 seconds, or approximately four minutes, between conditions.

Summary of Intervention Effects

By implementing effective and efficient room-to-room transitions, teachers can reduce problem behaviors and gain valuable instructional time. The purpose of the current case study was to use the TTG to decrease the amount of time a class of fourth grade elementary students spent transitioning daily from the computer lab back to their homeroom classroom. In this case study, by applying the TTG to one transition per day, transitions times were reduced by an average of four minutes. Thus, over a five day school week, transition time was reduced by approximately 20 minutes. Taken altogether, Mr. Abbott and Ms. Jennings decided all intervention goals were met sufficiently. A single-case experimental design (i.e., ABAB) was used to demonstrate the effects of the TTG intervention on transition time and demonstrate a functional relationship between the intervention and observed changes in transition time. Given the visually analyzed data (Figure 16.2) and the high levels of intervention fidelity and IOA, Mr. Abbott and Ms. Jennings concluded that the TTG intervention was effective in reducing transition times.

Intervention Acceptability

In order to determine the treatment acceptability of the TTG intervention, Mr. Abbott was asked to complete an intervention feedback questionnaire after the final TTG session (see Appendix A). Mr. Abbott endorsed all items in the *agree* to *strongly agree* range, indicating that he found the intervention acceptable. Additional anecdotal evidence of social acceptability came from Mr. Abbott's request to return to the intervention condition one day sooner than originally planned to follow the second baseline condition.

Intervention Considerations

This case study demonstrated how TTG can be used to decrease transition time during daily room-to-room transitions within an elementary school. The class consisted of 25 general education students with varying degrees of problem behaviors. Mr. Abbott consulted with the school psychologist to identify an easy-to-implement and acceptable intervention that would quickly and effectively reduce the lengthy transition times, thereby decreasing challenging behaviors occurring during transitions and increasing instructional time.

Within a response to intervention (RTI) framework, the TTG intervention can best be categorized as a Tier 1 intervention. This intervention can be used as part of a teacher's classroom management system with students in both general and special education. Moreover, TTG can be combined with other evidence-based interventions, as occurred in this case study. For example, Mr. Abbott and Ms. Jennings used TTG concurrently with the existing PBIS system already in place at Lincoln Elementary. Adding an interdependent group contingency to an individual reinforcement system can be a powerful way of reducing problem behaviors by creating an environment in which students must depend on one another's appropriate behaviors in order to earn access to group rewards.

Additionally, the methodology used to evaluate the effectiveness of the TTG intervention should be discussed. The ABAB design allowed for three potential demonstrations of a functional relationship between the TTG intervention and transition times, one upon each change from one phase to another. Visual analysis of the data revealed clear and predicable changes in the transition times upon each phase change, providing robust evidence of a causal relationship between the TTG intervention and the reductions in transition time. Although controlled experimental designs allowing the demonstration of functional relationships between interventions and target behaviors are often not practitioners' first priority, they add persuasive evidence to teams' hypotheses regarding interventions' effectiveness and should be considered carefully when making intervention decisions. In the current case study, the initial ABAB design plan was modified slightly after consultation between Mr. Abbott and Ms. Jennings following the second A phase. Originally, three sessions in this phase were planned to fully establish the return-to-baseline condition data stability. However, after two sessions of transition time data revealed high transition times, Mr. Abbott requested reinstating the intervention (the second B phase) due to reports of the students' increase in inappropriate behaviors, their requests to bring back the TTG, and his desire to restore treatment effects. After reviewing the data, it was clear that an intervention effect had occurred and the return-to-baseline phase had reversed the effect, even with only two data points in the second baseline condition. The team decided that benefits in terms of classroom morale and intervention effects would outweigh any potential experimental design limitations of reducing the planned return-to-baseline phase by one session.

The TTG intervention can also be used across the school day to decrease transition time of multiple transitions. For example, Campbell and Skinner (2004) applied TTG to all transitions across the school day using an additional randomized component. In addition to randomizing the time criterion as in the current case study, they also randomized the particular transition that would be used to earn the reinforcer (e.g., recess-to-homeroom, lunch-to-recess). By applying TTG to multiple transitions across the school day, Campbell and Skinner (2004) were able to decrease overall transition times by approximately 1.5 hours per week.

The TTG intervention has also been used to decrease time transitioning between classroom activities (Hine, Ardoin, & Foster, 2015). In this study, researchers demonstrated that an automated version of TTG reduced students' transition times between activities, as well as increased their academic engagement, substantially increased teachers' instructional time, and decreased the frequency of teachers' prompting. In the current case study, specific data regarding disruptive behavior and teacher prompting were not collected. However, because during TTG the students exhibited ready-to-transition behaviors more quickly, and Mr. Abbott spent less time stopping the students in the hallways, it can be inferred that these measures were also reduced. Additionally, academic engaged time was not measured explicitly, but because transition times were substantially reduced, additional instructional time was available for Mr. Abbott to devote to his lessons.

Conclusion

The TTG intervention is an effective, easy-to-implement means of reducing transition times of groups of students, thereby increasing the time teachers have to devote to more productive endeavors. This chapter's case study demonstrates an application of TTG used to decrease the transition time of a fourth grade class of students transitioning between the computer lab and homeroom classroom daily. Combining explicit timing procedures with an interdependent group contingency, the teacher was able to regain an average of four minutes per day, or 20 minutes per week.

References

Arlin, M. (1979). Teacher transitions can disrupt time flow in classrooms. *American Educational Research Journal*, *16*(1), 42–56. doi:10.3102/00028312016001042

Campbell, S., & Skinner, C. (2004). Combining explicit timing with an interdependent group contingency program to decrease transition times: An investigation of the timely transitions game. *Journal of Applied School Psychology*, *20*(2), 11–27. doi:10.1300/J370v20n02_02

Hawkins, R. O., Haydon, T., Denune, H., Larkin, W., & Fite, N. (2015). Improving the transition behavior of high school students with emotional behavioral disorders using a randomized interdependent group contingency. *School Psychology Review*, *44*(2), 208–223. doi:10.17105/spr-14-0020.1

Hawkins, R. O., Haydon, T., McCoy, D., & Howard, A. (2017). Effects of an interdependent group contingency on the transition behavior of middle school students with emotional and behavioral disorders. *School Psychology Quarterly*, *32*(2), 282–289. doi:10.1037/spq0000202

Hine, J. F., Ardoin, S. P., & Foster, T. E. (2015). Decreasing transition times in elementary school classrooms: Using computer-assisted instruction to automate intervention components. *Journal of Applied Behavior Analysis*, *48*(3), 495–510. doi:10.1002/jaba.233

Jenson, W. R., Rhode, G., & Reavis, H. (2009). *The tough kid toolbox* (2nd ed.). Eugene, OR: Ancora Publishing.

Maggin, D. M., Johnson, A. H., Chafouleas, S. M., Ruberto, L. M., & Berggren, M. (2012). A systematic evidence review of school-based group contingency interventions for students with challenging behavior. *Journal of School Psychology, 50,* 625–654. doi:10.1016/j.jsp.2012.06.001

McIntosh, K., Herman, K., Sanford, A., McGraw, K., & Florence, K. (2004). Teaching transitions. *Teaching Exceptional Children, 37*(1), 32–38. doi:10.1177/004005990403700104

Appendix A: Intervention Feedback Survey

In order to obtain feedback regarding your impressions of the Timely Transitions Game, please complete this brief survey. The information you provide will help us plan, develop, and refine future behavioral interventions.

The Timely Transitions Game was easy to implement.	Strongly Agree	Agree	Neutral	Disagree	Strongly Disagree
The data collection process for the Timely Transitions Game was easy to implement.	Strongly Agree	Agree	Neutral	Disagree	Strongly Disagree
I was satisfied with the overall outcome of the Timely Transitions Game.	Strongly Agree	Agree	Neutral	Disagree	Strongly Disagree
The Timely Transitions Game improved students' transition behavior.	Strongly Agree	Agree	Neutral	Disagree	Strongly Disagree
The Timely Transitions Game decreased students' transition time.	Strongly Agree	Agree	Neutral	Disagree	Strongly Disagree
I would consider using the Timely Transitions Game with other students exhibiting similar behavior problems.	Strongly Agree	Agree	Neutral	Disagree	Strongly Disagree

The Timely Transitions Game did not result in any negative side effects for the students.	Strongly Agree	Agree	Neutral	Disagree	Strongly Disagree
I would recommend the Timely Transitions Game to colleagues as a strategy to improve students' transitions behavior.	Strongly Agree	Agree	Neutral	Disagree	Strongly Disagree
I would recommend the Timely Transitions Game to colleagues as a strategy to decrease students' transitions time.	Strongly Agree	Agree	Neutral	Disagree	Strongly Disagree

17
POSITIVE PEER REPORTING

Christine E. Neddenriep

Introduction

During elementary school, children begin establishing relationships with their peers and are actively involved in various groups. Forming these positive peer relationships promotes children's development socially, emotionally, and academically. More specifically, positive peer relationships provide children with emotional support, opportunities to practice social skills, and a sense of belonging in the classroom, which is positively related to academic motivation (Audley-Piotrowski, Singer, & Patterson, 2015). Not all children, however, successfully establish positive peer relationships. Some children experience rejection and isolation from their peers (Killen, Mulvey, & Hitti, 2013). Regrettably, peer rejection and isolation are common, persistent experiences that predict negative child outcomes academically, socially, and emotionally including lower self-esteem, greater academic struggles, and fewer pro-social behaviors (Mulvey, Boswell, & Zheng, 2017). School psychologists can collaborate with teachers to influence children's peer interactions and social acceptance in the classroom.

Positive Peer Reporting (PPR; Ervin, Miller, & Friman, 1996; Jones, Young, & Friman, 2000; Moroz & Jones, 2002) is an intervention initially designed to increase the social acceptance of children who experience rejection or isolation from their peers. This positive behavioral intervention employs the power of peers' social attention to increase positive social interactions between students, decrease disruptive behaviors, and increase social acceptance of peers in the classroom (Ervin, Johnston, & Friman, 1998; Jones et al., 2000; Morrison & Jones, 2007). Teachers can use the intervention to support individual students or groups of students ranging in age from preschool to middle school, although researchers have implemented the majority of PPR interventions in small, general education, elementary school classrooms (Murphy & Zlomke, 2014). Given the benefits of the intervention for all students, researchers have recommended the use of PPR with the whole group, rather than using it only to address the needs of a specific student. With regard to the length of the intervention, studies of the PPR intervention have varied in length from two days to four months, with researchers reporting positive change even in short-term interventions with especially positive outcomes at the onset of the intervention (Cashwell, Skinner, & Smith, 2001; Murphy & Zlomke, 2014). As well, teachers have consistently rated the PPR intervention as both effective and doable within classrooms, demonstrating the acceptability of the PPR intervention (Ervin et al., 1998; Jones et al., 2000).

How does the intervention work? Teachers explain to their students that over the course of several weeks, they will identify randomly selected students as "Star Students" daily. The teachers instruct their students to pay attention to the positive behavior of the star students and to share their positive observations with the students during a five- to 10-minute period typically at the end of the day. Prior to sharing their observations, teachers instruct their students in how to deliver praise statements by modeling with example statements that are specific, direct, and genuine. When students compliment the star students, teachers provide feedback about the appropriateness of their peers' comments. Students earn points towards a group reward for verbally praising the star students' pro-social behaviors. The teacher selects in advance the students who will be stars each day. The teacher also selects in advance the group rewards and determines how many points are required to earn the group reward such that the contingency is both realistic and ambitious for the group to attain (Ervin et al., 1998; Skinner, Neddenriep, Robinson, Ervin, & Jones, 2002).

What makes the intervention effective? The reinforcement contingencies within the intervention are effective in influencing both the star students' behaviors as well as the behaviors of their peers. The star students are encouraged to interact with their peers more positively to increase the likelihood of receiving their praise comments. Similarly, peers are encouraged to attend to the positive behaviors displayed by the star students so they can report these positive observations and earn points for the group, while ignoring any negative behaviors (Ervin et al., 1996).

With regard to implementation recommendations in the general education classroom, researchers recommend applying PPR to the whole group, rather than singling out an individual student(s). Whereas teachers may choose this intervention because they are concerned about a specific student who is rejected or isolated from peers, encouraging them to rotate the star students daily in a classwide PPR reduces the chance of further isolating rejected youth. Second, researchers have also shown that treatment fidelity is essential to ensuring positive treatment effects. School psychologists working with teachers should provide them with a treatment integrity checklist and should train them in accurately implementing each step by showing them, watching them, and then providing praise and corrective feedback regarding the completion of each step. In addition, school psychologists should be available to support in the classroom to ensure teachers are implementing PPR with integrity and to provide more training as needed. Third, when using a group reward, school psychologists may encourage teachers to allow students to make suggestions of rewards so that they are sure that the reward is actually reinforcing to the students. School psychologists may also encourage teachers to develop a visual display showing progress toward the goal. Visual posting of progress is generally helpful to students in maintaining motivation for achieving their goal and earning the corresponding reward. Finally, the effectiveness of the PPR contingency may fade over time, especially after the group has earned their reward. To ensure high levels of participation and praise, teachers may consider randomly selecting the star students at the end of the day such that they are "mystery stars." In doing so, the star students are unknown during the day, and students have to consistently attend to all students' positive behavior in order to increase the likelihood of their being able to provide positive comments about the selected students (Burns, Riley-Tillman, & Rathvon, 2017; Murphy & Zlomke, 2014; Skinner, Williams, & Neddenriep, 2004).

Case Study

Background Information

Mrs. Brown, a second-grade teacher, referred Meagan, a seven-year-old girl, to the school psychologist. Mrs. Brown had become increasingly concerned about Meagan's reluctance to interact with the other children in the class and her isolation from peers. During recess, Meagan frequently played alone, wandering around the playground and looking uncomfortable. In the classroom, she rarely initiated conversation with other children and was reticent to respond when approached by another child. Mrs. Brown reported that she did not have a friend in the classroom.

A review of Meagan's cumulative record indicated that her prior teachers noted her discomfort in interactions and her isolation from peers beginning in kindergarten. Her teachers in kindergarten and first grade had commented on her report card that she was withdrawn and uncomfortable with other children. Her mother indicated that her behavior at home was quite different, behaving in a warm and outgoing manner with her family in contrast to the withdrawn and isolated child observed by her teachers and peers. Tier 1 instruction in the classroom included implementation of the Second Step curriculum by the school counselor weekly and the implementation of Positive Behavioral Interventions and Supports (PBIS) school-wide since kindergarten, in which the classroom teachers taught and reinforced behavioral expectations and routines. In first grade, Meagan successfully completed a six-week, Tier 2 social skills group lead by the school psychologist. Meagan demonstrated fluent skills in initiating conversation, asking questions, taking turns in conversation, listening, and closing a conversation. Mrs. Brown affirmed that in spite of Meagan possessing sufficient social skills, she was noticeably uncomfortable and withdrawn. She also indicated that Meagan was an average student academically in all subject areas.

Mrs. Brown was in her third year as a second-grade teacher. She had experience in implementing individual and group contingencies to support students behaviorally but had not had experience with interventions to support students' social inclusion. The elementary school included approximately 300 students in kindergarten through fifth grade, with three classrooms per grade. Mrs. Brown's classroom included 15 students – seven female students and eight male students.

Description of the Problem Behavior

The school psychologist conducted a problem-identification interview with Mrs. Brown focusing on Meagan's withdrawn and isolated behavior in social interactions. The replacement behavior or alternative behavior Mrs. Brown desired to increase was Meagan's social involvement both at recess and during small-group activities in the classroom. Adapting the definition used by Moroz and Jones (2002, p. 237), social involvement was defined as engagement or participation in peer interactions during small-group activities in the classroom or unstructured recess activities. Social engagement was defined as any positive verbal or nonverbal interaction with a peer, such as talking, listening with eyes on the speaker, responding to a question, asking a question, holding hands while walking, or playing together on playground equipment. Participation was defined as involvement in a classroom activity or a game with structure or rules. Social involvement did not include playing or working alone, talking with an adult, parallel play, or negative interactions (e.g., fighting, arguing, being disruptive). Mrs. Brown indicated that small-group work time occurred daily for 20 minutes during social studies or science periods, which alternated daily. Recess occurred daily following lunch for 20 minutes. Therefore, the behavior of social withdrawal occurred in both structured and unstructured social situations.

The school psychologist observed Meagan and a comparison female peer in the classroom during small-group work in science and at recess. The school psychologist used a 15-second partial interval recording system to record the occurrence of social involvement, alternating between Meagan and the comparison peer every 15 seconds (see Appendix A). During the small-group activity in science, Meagan was observed to display social involvement during 20% of the intervals observed while her peer was observed to display social involvement during 75% of the intervals observed. The school psychologist noted that Meagan displayed social engagement by looking and listening to peers when they were talking; however, she did not respond to questions asked of the group members, and she wrote her responses to the questions independently of others. Her peers did not ask her any questions directly. During recess, Meagan was observed to display social involvement 17.5% of the intervals observed while her peer was observed to display social involvement 80% of the intervals observed.

The school psychologist noted that Meagan spent the majority of the time playing by herself climbing on the playground equipment, rather than joining into a game with others (e.g., four square). She did slide down the slide with others and returned a ball to a group of children who were playing four square nearby. Her peers did not ask her to play.

To gain an understanding of Meagan's perspective regarding her level of social involvement, the school psychologist met and talked with her. During the interview, Meagan noted that she likes school, especially her teacher, Mrs. Brown. When asked what her favorite subject was in school, she said reading, because reading allows her to learn about and experience new places and things. When asked about her relationship with her peers, she said that she frequently keeps to herself and believes that others think negatively of her: "If I keep to myself, I won't say or do something wrong." When asked what her teacher could do to help, she said she would prefer to have the option in class to work alone instead of with others.

Problem Analysis

Based on the information collected and observed, Meagan's level of social involvement in both small-group activities within the classroom and at recess was less than 30% of the involvement of her peer. The school psychologist hypothesized that Meagan's withdrawn and socially isolated behaviors did not reflect a skill deficit. She had successfully completed social skills training and conversed readily with adults at school and at home. Her social withdrawal from peers was hypothesized to be maintained by negative reinforcement, as playing or working alone allowed her to avoid the possibility of experiencing negative comments from her peers as she had indicated in her interview. In consulting with Mrs. Brown, the school psychologist suggested that implementing an intervention class-wide to systematically encourage and reinforce compliments by peers might increase Meagan's social involvement and inclusion in the classroom by increasing her experience of positive evaluations from her peers. Mrs. Brown and the school psychologist hypothesized that a class-wide approach might also increase positive peer interactions for all students.

Intervention Goals

Based on the initial observations of Meagan's social involvement in comparison to her peer, Mrs. Brown and the school psychologist collaborated to set goals. The school psychologist observed Meagan for two additional days to establish a reliable baseline from which to set a goal. With regard to the primary target behavior of increasing social involvement, Meagan was expected to increase her involvement from a median of 20%-50% of intervals observed within the first two weeks of intervention implementation and to 75% after four weeks of intervention. Attaining this goal would result in her social involvement being more comparable to her peer's involvement (median = 80%).

To set a goal to increase positive peer interactions for the class as a whole, the school psychologist asked Mrs. Brown to complete a Direct Behavior Rating (DBR; Chafouleas, Riley-Tillman, & Christ, 2009) form to measure the percentage of time positive peer interactions occurred during small-group work in science or social studies for three days. Positive peer interactions were defined as polite behavior when interacting with peers including working cooperatively, giving or offering assistance, talking or listening in a polite manner, or any other friendly or helpful interaction (see Appendix B). Mrs. Brown observed the class to engage in positive peer interactions a median of 60% of the time. Mrs. Brown suggested working towards the goal of increasing the class' positive peer interactions to 80% of the time after four weeks of intervention would be both realistic and ambitious for the class.

Measurement of Target Behaviors, Data Collection Strategies, and Progress Monitoring

Social Involvement

The School Psychologist continued to observe Meagan's social involvement daily and that of a comparison student using a 15-second partial interval recording, alternating between Meagan and her female peer. The school psychologist used this measure across a total of five days to establish a baseline and to measure progress relative to the intervention. She consistently used the same definition of social involvement adapted from Moroz and Jones (2002), which was included on the recording form (see Appendix A, for a completed example). The 20-minute observations occurred during small-group work in social studies or science and during recess.

Positive Peer Interactions

Mrs. Brown continued to complete a DBR form to measure the percentage of time positive peer interactions occurred class-wide during small-group work in science or social studies daily for a total of five days. Mrs. Brown used this measure to establish a baseline and to measure progress relative to the intervention. The definition of positive peer interactions was included on the form (see Appendix B, for a completed example). Mrs. Brown completed the rating daily at the end of the 20-minute period each day.

Intervention Plan

Mrs. Brown and the school psychologist collaborated to select an intervention to support both Meagan's social involvement in the classroom as well as increase positive peer interactions classwide. Consistent with the identified goals of the intervention, they selected PPR to implement daily in the classroom over a period of four weeks. Mrs. Brown specifically requested that the intervention be implemented class-wide so that Meagan did not feel singled out from her peers. Prior to implementation, the school psychologist supported Mrs. Brown in introducing the intervention using the following explanation adapted from Burns et al. (2017, p. 251):

> Over the next several weeks, we are going to participate in a new activity called the "Positive Peer Reporting Game" where we will practice reporting friendly and helpful behavior we notice in other students. Each day, I will randomly select three students to be the class' "mystery stars," and everyone will have a chance to praise the stars' friendly and helpful behaviors that have made the classroom a nice place to learn and have fun. You will also have the opportunity to earn a group reward for your positive peer reports.

The school psychologist then assisted Mrs. Brown in providing a 20-minute training for the students on how to give compliments to their peers using a four-step process: (1) Look at the person; (2) Smile; (3) Describe what they said or did; (4) Say something positive such as, "Good job!" or "Way to go!" (Moroz & Jones, 2002, p. 239). Mrs. Brown listed these four steps on a poster board along with examples such as, "Jane helped explain the directions to me when I didn't understand what to do." The school psychologist assisted Mrs. Brown in providing additional examples as well as non-examples (e.g., "Jane is a good person."). The students then provided their own examples and the school psychologist and Mrs. Brown offered praise and corrective feedback as needed. Mrs. Brown displayed the compliments chart in the front of the classroom.

The school psychologist also supported Mrs. Brown in explaining the daily PPR procedure to the class, identifying group rewards, and identifying a criterion for the class to meet to earn their group reward. Mrs. Brown explained that when the class plays the Positive Peer Reporting game, she will randomly select the three "mystery stars" for the day from the "Star Box" and invite other students to raise their hands to offer compliments about each of those students. Each student's name was listed on an index card in the box to be drawn – three students per day across five days so that every student in the class would be a star during the week. Mrs. Brown also explained to the students that because the students would not be selected until the end of the day, the students would have to pay attention to the friendly and helpful behavior of all students so that they could provide compliments. Mrs. Brown further explained that students would earn a point toward a group reward for each compliment offered. Finally, Mrs. Brown explained that a group reward would be randomly selected from the "Rewards Box" once the group met the criteria of 50 points. Mrs. Brown set the criterion such that rewards would be earned approximately once per week given three to four compliments per student. To ensure that the students would be motivated to earn the group reward, Mrs. Brown asked the class for suggestions of activity rewards, which they submitted to the "Suggestion Box." She explained that suggested rewards must take little time away from instruction, be age appropriate, consistent with school rules, and cost little money. Rewards that met these criteria were included in the "Rewards Box" and announced to the class. Examples of rewards included extra recess time, a joke party, a crazy hat day, a class homework pass, and a game of "Heads Up 7-Up." Mrs. Brown also make a "points chart" to display the number of points students accumulated toward the goal.

The school psychologist also supported Mrs. Brown on the first day of PPR implementation. At the beginning of the day, she reminded students that they would be playing the Positive Reporting Game. During the last 10 minutes of the day students would have the opportunity to earn points toward the group reward selected for giving compliments to the randomly selected mystery star students. She reminded the students to pay attention to the friendly and helpful behavior of all students so that they could provide compliments. At the end of the day, Mrs. Brown randomly selected three students' names from the "Star Box." She ensured that Meagan's name was included in the first three names drawn. She then announced the names and wrote the names in alphabetical order on the chalkboard. Finally, she asked students to raise their hands if they had an appropriate compliment for the first student on the list. She provided corrective feedback or asked clarifying questions if the compliment was vague. Once the first student had received three to four appropriate compliments, she moved to the next name on the list. After all three stars had received compliments, she tallied the number of appropriate compliments and added that number of points to the point chart. She reminded the students that a reward would be drawn from the "Reward Box" once the class earned 50 points as a group.

Intervention Fidelity and Interobserver Agreement

Mrs. Brown self-assessed intervention fidelity daily using the Classwide PPR Treatment Integrity Checklist (see Appendix C). The school psychologist independently assessed intervention fidelity during one intervention session per week, or 20% of the time, using the same checklist. Percentage agreement was calculated by dividing agreements by agreements plus disagreements and multiplying by 100. Treatment integrity was 96% during the observed sessions. In addition, Mrs. Brown indicated the intervention was implemented every day school was in session. Therefore, Mrs. Brown and the school psychologist concluded the intervention was implemented as intended with integrity.

Interobserver agreement (IOA) for the assessment of social involvement and positive peer interactions was evaluated by the practicum school psychologist, who was in the building two days per week. She independently observed the collection of each measure once per week during baseline and intervention phases, or 20% of the time, using the same data collection form as the primary observer (i.e., interval recording form and DBR). Percentage of agreement (i.e., IOA) was calculated by dividing agreements by agreements plus disagreements and multiplying by 100. Interobserver agreement for social involvement during small-group time was 90-92% during recess. IOA for positive peer interactions observed class-wide during small-group time was 90%, suggesting the data were reliably collected across measures.

Intervention Outcome Data

The results of the class-wide PPR intervention on Meagan's social involvement during small-group work and recess are displayed in Figures 17.1 and 17.2, respectively. Her peer's social involvement data are included on the same graphs for comparison. During baseline, Meagan's level of social involvement was relatively stable with no apparent increase or decrease in trend (average = 20% across small-group work and recess). Her peer's level of social involvement was stable as well, although higher (average = 75% during small-group and average = 82% during recess). When the PPR intervention was implemented Meagan's level of social involvement increased (average = 45% during small-group and average = 37% during recess), while her peer's social involvement increased as well (average = 82% during small-group and average = 91% during recess). After two weeks of intervention, Meagan had met or exceeded the goal of 50% of intervals observed on 4 of 10 days during small-group work, and she had met her goal once during recess. When the PPR intervention was removed, Meagan's level of social involvement returned to her initial level (average = 21% during small-group

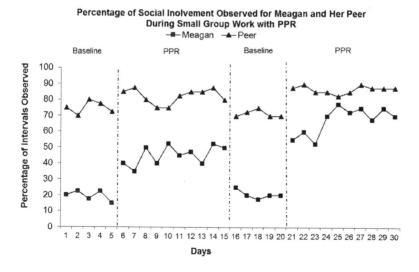

FIGURE 17.1 Effects of PPR on Meagan's level of social involvement during small-group work with peer comparison

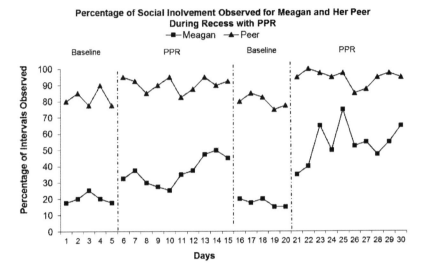

FIGURE 17.2 Effects of PPR on Meagan's level of social involvement during recess with peer comparison

and average = 18% during recess), while her peer's social involvement decreased as well (average = 72% during small-group and average = 80% during recess). When the PPR intervention was implemented a second time, Meagan's level of social involvement again increased to a higher level than previously (average = 68% during small-group and average = 54% during recess), while her peer's social involvement increased as well (average = 87% during small-group and average = 95% during recess). Over the course of two additional weeks of intervention, Meagan had met or exceeded the goal of 75% of intervals observed on 3 of 10 days during small group work, and she had met her goal once during recess. The PPR intervention had been very effective for Meagan with 100% of the intervention points exceeding her highest baseline data point during small-group work (PND = 100%) and 95% of the intervention points exceeding her highest baseline point during recess (PND = 95%). Her level of social involvement had become less discrepant from and more similar to that of her peer.

The results of the classwide PPR intervention on the class' display of positive peer interactions are displayed in Figure 17.3. During baseline, Mrs. Brown observed the class engaging in positive peer interactions an average of 60% of the time. When the PPR intervention was implemented, Mrs. Brown observed an increase in the frequency of the class' positive peer interactions, noting positive interactions an average of 81% of the time. When the PPR intervention was removed, Mrs. Brown noted a decrease in their positive peer interactions to a level similar to their initial level (average = 60%). When the PPR intervention was implemented a second time, Mrs. Brown again observed an increase in the

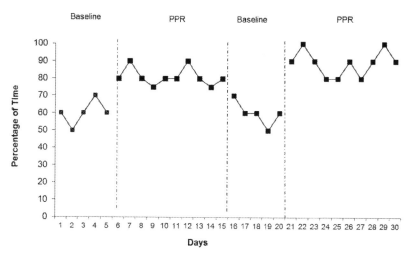

FIGURE 17.3 Effects of PPR on class-wide direct behavior rating of positive peer interactions during small-group work

frequency of the class' positive peer interactions, noting positive peer interactions an average of 89% of the time. Over the course of four weeks of intervention, the class had met or exceeded their goal of 80% on 18 out of 20 days. The PPR intervention had been very effective for the class, with 100% of the intervention points exceeding their highest baseline data point.

Summary of Intervention Effects

Using an ABAB experimental design, a functional relationship was established between the implementation of PPR and increases in Meagan's level of social involvement during small-group work in the classroom and at recess. Similarly, a functional relationship was established between the implementation of PPR and observed increases in positive peer interactions class-wide. The reinforcement contingency along with the structured provision of compliments benefitted both Meagan and her peers. Meagan's level of involvement became more similar to her peers, increasing by 182% on average from baseline to intervention during small-group work and increasing by 142% during recess. These results also support the hypothesis that Meagan's deficit in social involvement was a performance deficit. With the reinforcement of positive peer interactions classwide, Meagan was rewarded for interacting with her peers and experienced positive evaluations from her peers. As a result, she no longer had a need to avoid the experience of potentially negative peer evaluations.

Intervention Acceptability

At the conclusion of the intervention, the school psychologist met with Mrs. Brown to evaluate the effectiveness of the intervention and to determine her degree of satisfaction with the intervention. Mrs. Brown had collected feedback from her students regarding their satisfaction with PPR using an intervention acceptability survey. The survey form as well as the results are included in Appendix D. The results indicated that all participants said that that liked having a reward as a group; 14 out of 15 felt PPR was helpful to the class; 13 out of 15 liked giving compliments to others; 12 out of 15 felt PPR was helpful to them; and 12 out of 15 enjoyed being the mystery star student. Mrs. Brown agreed that the students enjoyed playing PPR and that using PPR was effective in supporting Meagan as well as all of the students in creating a more cooperative atmosphere in the classroom. She further indicated that the intervention was easy to use and that she would continue to use it, as the students had requested.

Intervention Considerations

This case study used PPR to increase the social involvement of an isolated student as well as increase positive peer interactions class-wide. When using PPR, several considerations are important to keep in mind and are illustrated within this case study. First, PPR is an effective intervention for students who possess the skills necessary to engage in appropriate behaviors, but need reinforcement to do so consistently (Burns et al., 2017). Meagan and her peers did possess the necessary skills. The reinforcement contingency rewarded them for demonstrating these skills consistently and for providing positive evaluations of others. Meagan, therefore, experienced peer attention as a reinforcer, rather than a punishment to avoid.

Second, whereas PPR can be used to support a single student, implementing PPR with the whole group is recommended (Murphy & Zlomke, 2014). In this case study, the intervention was used class-wide so that Meagan was not further isolated, and the "star students" were randomly selected daily without replacement so that all students were included as stars throughout the week.

Third, intervention fidelity is essential to ensuring positive treatment effects. In this case study, the school psychologist supported Mrs. Brown in introducing the intervention and in training the students to implement PPR. She also provided Mrs. Brown with a treatment integrity checklist to follow daily and observed implementation once a week. As a result, Mrs. Brown successfully implemented the intervention with fidelity.

Fourth, the effectiveness of the reinforcement contingency may fade over time (Murphy & Zlomke, 2014). To ensure consistent participation with high levels of reinforcement, Mrs. Brown incorporated an interdependent group contingency with a cumulative criterion and two randomized contingency components. An interdependent group contingency is one in which all the students or none of the students earn access to the reinforcer based on the performance of the group (Skinner et al., 2004). Therefore, each person's compliment earned the group a point and got the group closer to their goal. As a result, students were motivated to offer more compliments to earn access to the reinforcer more quickly. Mrs. Brown used two randomized components – a randomized reward and randomized target students. Mrs. Brown set up the randomized reward using a "rewards box." She allowed the students to make suggestions of possible rewards and included suggested rewards in the "rewards box." As a result, the students knew the range of reinforcers available but did not know in advance which reinforcer they were working towards, as Mrs. Brown did not select the reinforcer until the students had met the goal. Mrs. Brown also randomized the target students. She did so by randomly selecting three mystery star students from the "star box" at the end of the day. In doing so, the star students were unknown during the day, and students had to attend to all students' positive behavior in order to increase the likelihood of their being able to provide positive comments about the selected students.

Conclusion

When children are rejected or isolated from their peers, our first instinct may be to ask, "What is wrong with the child?" This typical response serves to reinforce the idea that the problem is within the child and may further isolate the child from their peers. An alternative question we may ask is, "How can we structure the classroom environment to encourage positive peer interactions of all students?" PPR is an intervention in which students are encouraged to monitor and report the positive behaviors of their peers. Researchers have demonstrated the effectiveness of PPR in increasing the quantity of positive peer interactions and improving the status of socially rejected and isolated peers in schools. As illustrated in this case study, PPR is an effective and an efficient intervention that can be used class-wide to benefit all students. In supporting teachers' use of the intervention, school psychologists may suggest using randomized contingency components within the intervention. Doing so may decrease the likelihood of the reinforcement contingency fading over time and ensure a consistently higher level of participation throughout the intervention.

References

Audley-Piotrowski, S., Singer, A., & Patterson, M. (2015). The role of the teacher in children's peer relations: Making the invisible hand intentional. *Translational Issues in Psychological Science, 1,* 192–200. doi:10.1037/tps0000038

Burns, M. K., Riley-Tillman, T. C., & Rathvon, N. (2017). Positive peer reporting. In *Effective school interventions: Evidence-based strategies for improving student outcomes* (3rd ed., pp. 249–252). New York, NY: Guilford.

Cashwell, T. H., Skinner, C. H., & Smith, E. S. (2001). Increasing second-grade students' reports of peers' prosocial behaviors via direct instruction, group reinforcement, and

progress feedback: A replication and extension. *Education and Treatment of Children, 24*(2), 161–175.
Chafouleas, S. M., Riley-Tillman, T. C., & Christ, T. J. (2009). Direct behavior rating (DBR): An emerging method for assessing social behavior within a tiered intervention system. *Assessment for Effective Intervention, 34*, 195–200. doi:10.1177/1534508409340391
Ervin, R. A., Miller, P. M., & Friman, P. C. (1996). Feed the hungry bee: Using positive peer reports to improve the social interactions and acceptance of a socially rejected girl in residential care. *Journal of Applied Behavior Analysis, 29*, 251–253. doi:10.1901/jaba.1996.29-251
Ervin, R. A., Johnston, E. S., & Friman, P. C. (1998). Positive peer reporting to improve the social interactions of a socially rejected girl. *Proven Practice: Prevention and Remediation Solutions for School Problems, 1*, 17–21.
Jones, K. M., Young, M. M., & Friman, P. C. (2000). Increasing peer praise of socially rejected delinquent youth: Effects on cooperation and acceptance. *School Psychology Quarterly, 15*, 30–39. doi:10.1037/h0088776
Killen, M., Mulvey, K. L., & Hitti, A. (2013). Social exclusion: A developmental intergroup perspective. *Child Development, 84*, 772–790. doi:10.1111/cdev.12012
Moroz, K. B., & Jones, K. M. (2002). The effects of positive peer reporting on children's social involvement. *School Psychology Review, 31*, 235–245.
Morrison, J. Q., & Jones, K. M. (2007). The effects of positive peer reporting as a class-wide positive behavior support. *Journal of Behavioral Education, 16*, 111–124. doi:10.1007/s10864-006-9005-y
Mulvey, L. K., Boswell, C., & Zheng, J. (2017). Causes and consequences of social exclusion and peer rejection among children and adolescents. *Report on Emotional & Behavioral Disorders in Youth, 17*, 71–75.
Murphy, J., & Zlomke, K. (2014). Positive peer reporting in the classroom: A review of intervention procedures. *Behavior Analysis in Practice, 7*, 126–137. doi:10.1007/s40617-014-0025-0
Skinner, C. H., Neddenriep, C. E., Robinson, S. L., Ervin, R., & Jones, K. (2002). Altering educational environments through positive peer reporting: Prevention and remediation of social problems associated with behavior disorders. *Psychology in the Schools, 39*, 191–202. doi:10.1002/pits.10030
Skinner, C. H., Williams, R. L., & Neddenriep, C. E. (2004). Using interdependent group-oriented reinforcement to enhance academic performance in general education classrooms. *School Psychology Review, 33*, 384–397.

Appendix A: Partial Interval Recording Form of Social Involvement

Student Observed: Meagan
Teacher: Mrs. Brown   *Grade:* Second
Date: Oct. 12   *Activity Observed:* Small-Group Science
Time Begin: 1:30   *Time End:* 1:50

Target Behavior(s) & Definition(s): Engagement or participation in peer interactions during small-group activities in the classroom or unstructured recess activities. Social engagement includes any positive verbal or nonverbal interaction with a peer, such as talking, listening with eyes on the speaker, responding to a question, asking a question, holding hands while walking, or playing together on playground equipment. Participation includes involvement in a classroom activity or a game with structure or rules. Social involvement does not include playing or working alone, talking with an adult, parallel play, or negative interactions (e.g., fighting, arguing, being disruptive).

Recording Instructions: Record a + if the behavior is observed at any time during the interval. Record a 0 if it is not. Total the number of +'s recorded and divide by 40 and multiply by 100 to determine the percentage of intervals observed.

Time/Interval	Student (+/0)	Time/Interval	Peer (+/0)
0:00–0:15	+	0:16–0:30	0
0:31–0:45	+	0:46–1:00	0
1:01–1:15	0	1:16–1:30	+
1:31–1:45	0	1:46–2:00	+
2:01–2:15	0	2:16–2:30	+
2:31–2:45	+	2:46–3:00	+
3:01–3:15	+	3:16–3:30	+
3:31–3:45	0	3:46–4:00	0
4:01–4:15	0	4:16–4:30	+
4:31–4:45	0	4:46–5:00	+
5:01–5:15	0	5:16–5:30	+
5:31–5:45	+	5:46–6:00	0
6:01–6:15	0	6:16–6:30	+
6:31–6:45	0	6:46–7:00	+
7:01–7:15	0	7:16–7:30	+
7:31–7:45	0	7:46–8:00	0
8:01–8:15	0	8:16–8:30	+
8:31–8:45	0	8:46–9:00	+
9:01–9:15	0	9:16–9:30	+
9:31–9:45	0	9:46–10:00	+
10:01–10:15	0	10:16–10:30	0
10:31–10:45	+	10:46–11:00	+
11:01–11:15	+	11:16–11:30	0
11:31–11:45	0	11:46–12:00	+
12:01–12:15	0	12:16–12:30	+
12:31–12:45	0	12:46–13:00	+
13:01–13:15	0	13:16–13:30	+
13:31–13:45	0	13:46–14:00	+
14:01–14:15	0	14:16–14:30	0
14:31–14:45	0	14:46–15:00	+
15:01–15:15	0	15:16–15:30	0

15:31–15:45	0	15:46–16:00	0
16:01–16:15	0	16:16–16:30	+
16:31–16:45	0	16:46–17:00	+
17:01–17:15	0	17:16–17:30	+
17:31–17:45	0	17:46–18:00	+
18:01–18:15	0	18:16–18:30	+
18:31–18:45	0	18:46–19:00	+
19:01–19:15	+	19:16–19:30	+
19:31–19:45	0	19:46–20:00	+
Total	8/40*100 = 20%	**Total**	30/40*100 = 75%

Appendix B: Classroom Direct Behavior Rating of Positive Peer Interactions

Date: 10/13
M T W Th F
Observation Time: 1:30–1:50 p.m.

Rater: Mrs. Brown
Activity: Social Studies
Behavior Description: Positive peer interactions were defined as polite behavior when interacting with peers including working cooperatively, giving or offering assistance, talking or listening in a polite manner, or any other friendly or helpful interaction.

Directions: Place a mark along the line that best reflects the percentage of total time the students exhibited the target behaviors.

Positive Peer Interactions

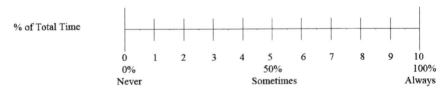

Appendix C: Treatment Integrity Checklist

Class-Wide Positive Peer Reporting with Mystery Star Students and Randomized Reward

Introduction and Training

1. ____ Tell the students that they are going to have an opportunity to help create a friendlier classroom and earn group rewards by participating in a new activity called the "Positive Peer Reporting Game." Each day, three students will be randomly selected to be the class "stars," and everyone will have a chance to praise the stars' friendly and helpful behavior.

2. ____ Using the compliment chart, conduct a 20-minute training session in which you teach students how to give compliments. Provide examples and non-examples of compliments, have students offer their own examples, and give praise and corrective feedback as needed. For example, if students give a vague compliment ("Maggie was nice today"), ask, "What nice things did you see Maggie do?"
3. ____ Tell students that during the last 10 minutes of the day, you will randomly select the three "mystery stars" for the day from the "Star Box" and invite other students to raise their hands to offer compliments about each of those students.
4. ____ Explain to the students that because you will not select the students until the end of the day, the students will have to pay attention to the friendly and helpful behavior of all students so that they can provide compliments.
5. ____ Explain that if you call on a student and he or she is able to offer an appropriate compliment about one of the class stars, the class will earn a point toward a group reward.
6. ____Explain that a group reward will be randomly selected from the "Rewards Box" once the group meets the criteria for the reward.
7. ____Have the class suggest possible activity rewards and submit their suggestions to the "Suggestion Box." Remind them that reward must take little time away from instruction, be age appropriate, consistent with school rules, and cost little money.
8. ____Inform the students that you will approve rewards and announce those rewards which are included in the "Rewards Box."
9. ____Show the students the "Suggestion Box" for including additional reward suggestions.

Implementation

1. ____ At the beginning of the day remind students that we will be playing the Positive Reporting Game today. During the last 10 minutes of the day, students will have the opportunity to earn points towards the group reward selected for giving compliments to the randomly selected mystery star students.
2. ____ Remind the students to pay attention to the friendly and helpful behavior of all students so that they can provide compliments.
3. ____ At the end of the day, randomly select three students' names from the "Star Box." Make sure that the target student's name is included in the first three drawn. Announce the names and write the names in alphabetical order on the chalkboard.
4. ____ Ask students to raise their hands if they have an appropriate compliment for the first student on the list. Use group rather than individual prompts to encourage praise statements – for example: "Would anyone else like to say anything?", not "Does anyone else have a compliment for Maria?"

5. ____ Once the first student has received three to four appropriate compliments, move to the next name on the list.
6. ____ After all three stars have received compliments, tally the number of appropriate compliments and add that number of points to the point chart.
7. ____ Randomly draw a reward from the "Reward Box" when the criterion has been reached. Praise the students for their positive and cooperative behavior and begin a new points chart.

(Adapted from Burns et al., 2017, pp. 251–252)

Appendix D: Intervention Acceptability Survey and Results for Students

Read each statement and circle the picture that best describes how you feel about it.

Intervention Acceptability Survey and Results for Students

Read each statement and circle the picture which best describes how you feel about it.

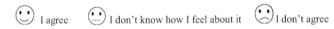

1. I think that the Positive Peer Reporting Game was helpful to me.

N=12   N=3   N=0

2. I think the Positive Peer Reporting Game was helpful to the class.

N=14   N=1   N=0

3. I enjoyed being the mystery star student.

N=12   N=3   N=0

4. I enjoyed giving compliments to others.

N=13   N=2   N=0

5. I liked have a reward as a group.

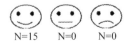

N=15   N=0   N=0

18
COLOR WHEEL

Kathleen Aspiranti

Introduction

Most teachers implement classroom management strategies, but the chosen strategies are often ineffective, unorganized, confusing, or not evidence-based. Many teachers feel unprepared to address student classroom behaviors, particularly if there are challenging behaviors from multiple students (Flower, McKenna, & Haring, 2017). High levels of disruptive or inappropriate behaviors within the classroom increases the amount of time teachers spend reacting to the behaviors, therefore decreasing instruction time. When transitioning from one activity to another, teachers may spend up to one to two hours per day waiting for students to stop one task, put items away, move to a new location, and be ready to begin the next task. Most teachers display a list of classroom rules to identify student behavioral expectations such as "be respectful," "no talking," and "ready to learn." However, these rules are often unclear, with students not necessarily understanding what these terms mean. Additionally, rules like "no talking" may not be applicable in all situations.

The Color Wheel System (CWS) uses three sets of rules corresponding to a color (Red, Yellow, and Green) that are designed for different types of classroom activities (Skinner, Scala, Dendas, & Lentz, 2007). Red rules are designed for short periods of time when the teacher needs undivided attention, such as when delivering instructions. Yellow rules are for academic tasks (e.g., large-group instruction, tests, independent seatwork), and Green rules are for free time or group activities. A paper wheel with colored wedges is rotated to show which set of rules is in effect, with the rules clearly displayed on colored posters on the wall. Each rule set includes three to five rules specifically designed for a certain type of classroom task, as student rules during group work (i.e., Green rules) are different than rules during large-group teacher-led instruction (i.e., Yellow rules). As the teacher moves between activities, the wheel is turned to display the behavioral expectations of the next activity. The CWS provides standardized procedures not only for classroom activities but also for transitions. Temporal warnings are provided to indicate there will be a transition. The warnings allow students time to finish a task, put materials away, and move to the next rules within the allotted time. Typically, the teacher will move to Red, provide instructions for the next task, and then turn the wheel to Yellow or Green to answer questions and begin the next activity.

Evidence for the CWS has shown that it is effective in decreasing inappropriate vocalizations, decreasing out of seat behavior, and increasing on-task behavior (Blondin, Skinner, Parkhurst, Wood, & Snyder, 2012; Fudge et al., 2008; Watson et al., 2016). For example, Watson et al. (2016) decreased inappropriate vocalizations across three kindergarten classrooms using CWS. Fudge et al. (2008) increased on-task behavior in every student in a second-grade classroom by implementing the CWS, with disruptive behaviors returning when the CWS was removed. Although the CWS has typically been implemented within general education classrooms, Aspiranti, Bebech, Ruffo, and Skinner (2019) successfully used the CWS within three self-contained classrooms for students with autism.

Case Study

Background Information

Ms. Matthews was a first grade teacher at Eaglecrest Elementary School. This was her third year teaching first grade, and the first time she reported having difficulties with behavior in her classroom. Eaglecrest did not have a School-Wide Positive Behavior Intervention and Supports (SWPBIS) system in place but encouraged teachers to use classroom management to prevent unwanted behaviors. The previous year, the first grade teachers at Eaglecrest came up with several classroom management strategies to use across all four first grade classrooms. The strategies included: a clip system where students moved their named clothespin on a chart based on their individual behavior; Class Dojo, an electronic point-collecting system where students would earn or lose points based on their individual behavior; the daily schedule posted on the front white board; and a list of classroom rules posted on the wall. The first-grade team decided the classroom rules were: be kind and respectful, be ready to learn, follow directions, work quietly, and raise your hand. Ms. Matthews reported that last year she did not have any notable problems when using the implemented strategies.

This year, Ms. Matthews had 24 students in her first grade class, although classes at Eaglecrest were typically capped at 20 students. An educational assistant (Ms. Lucas) spent one hour daily providing additional support in Ms. Matthews classroom. The classroom was organized with a group space at the front of the room including a rug and smart board and student desks clustered in groups of four, allowing for group work. Ms. Matthews reported frustration with her class this year, saying that she had too many students in the class and the students' behavior was out of control. Several of the students were always on 'red' on the clip chart, and sometimes no students earned Dojo points. She had taken away recess four of the last five days and was at a loss as to how to get her students to pay attention during class.

Description of the Problem Behavior

A problem-identification interview was conducted by the school psychologist to determine what difficulties Ms. Matthews was experiencing in her classroom. Ms. Matthews reported the students were not paying attention, talking constantly, out of their seats, and not following her directions. She repeated directions several times before the class would respond, and some students would talk instead of completing work. After further discussion, Ms. Matthews decided that students talking to each other during instruction was the most continuously disruptive behavior. The problem was identified as 'inappropriate noises' and was defined as talking or making noises without permission. Examples of inappropriate noises included talking while the teacher was talking, humming during independent seatwork, calling out an answer, or talking about Pokémon during a small-group activity. Non-examples of included answering a question after being called on, talking quietly during small-group work about the assignment, or participating in choral responding.

When asked when the behaviors occur, Ms. Matthews stated that the students engaged in inappropriate noises during all activities and transitions, but the behavior occurred most often in reading and math lessons, particularly during independent seatwork and transitions. She noted that it was difficult to get the students back on task after transitioning because they were all talking. When students engaged in inappropriate noises, as a consequence Ms. Matthews would reprimand them, take away Dojo points, have students move their clip down, take away recess, send them to the office, or have them sit in the back of the classroom away from other students.

The school psychologist observed in the classroom during one hour of reading instruction for three days. Data collection included keeping a tally of inappropriate noises, indicating which students were making noises, and recording antecedents and consequences of inappropriate noises in a chart. During the observations, there was an almost continuous stream of inappropriate noises. Every student engaged in inappropriate noises at least one time during the observation, and the behavior was more pronounced when students were sitting near each other. Many students did not complete the expected work because they were talking to their neighbor. Transitioning from one task to another took up large amounts of instructional time because of students talking to one another and not following teacher instructions. In one instance, it took the students six minutes to transition from the large-group area on the floor to their seats, and another eight minutes for all students to get out a pencil and turn their reading book to page 54. Transition time was defined as the amount of time between the end of one task and when all students were ready to begin the next task. Ms. Matthews ignored most instances of inappropriate noises, but across the three one-hour observation sessions reprimanded the class 37 times, took away Dojo points 19 times, and had eight students move their clip down. She did not add any Dojo points or have any student move their clip up.

Problem Analysis

Based on the data collected and the problem-identification interview, the school psychologist found that inappropriate noises occurred when students were presented with academic instruction/activities or when they were transitioning between activities. The excessive amounts of inappropriate noises prevented students from completing assignments, distracted other students from completing assignments, and created lengthy transitions from one activity to another. The behaviors were maintained through avoidance of academic work, peer attention, and teacher attention (via reprimands). The behaviors were not centered around any specific child but were pervasive. Therefore, Ms. Matthews and the school psychologist decided to implement the Color Wheel System (CWS), a classwide intervention that targets decreasing inappropriate noises and decreasing transition times.

To determine the percentage of time during the reading class that students engaged in inappropriate noises, the school psychologist observed for three more days during reading class using partial-interval recording procedures. The 60-minute reading session was split into 20-second intervals. Using an iPad, the school psychologist recorded the presence of inappropriate noises from any student during each interval. The percentage of intervals with inappropriate noises was then calculated for each day: day 1 had 77% of intervals with inappropriate noises, day 2 had 92%, and day 3 had 84%. The average transition time from the end of one activity to the beginning of the next activity was nine minutes.

Intervention Goals

Based on the problem analysis and preliminary data collection, the school psychologist and Ms. Matthews decided that the primary goal was to decrease the amount of inappropriate noises during reading class to 40% of intervals using partial-interval recording procedures. The secondary goal was to decrease transition time between activities to four minutes.

Measurement of Target Behaviors, Data Collection Strategies, and Progress Monitoring

The percentage of inappropriate noises was measured through partial-interval recording procedures, as described above. Additionally, the amount of time spent during transitions was calculated. Ms. Lucas and another educational assistant (Mr. Peterson) were trained on data collection procedures and alternated daily data collection during 30 minutes of reading class. The observers were also trained alongside Ms. Matthews on the CWS and collected data on intervention fidelity to help the school psychologist determine whether the CWS was being implemented correctly and to allow for teacher feedback (see Appendix A for a sample data collection sheet).

Intervention Plan

The CWS was implemented in seven stages: material development, baseline, teacher training, student training, CWS, return to baseline, return to CWS. First, CWS materials were developed. The CWS separates classroom rules into three categories. Ms. Matthews was hesitant to use the typical CWS Red, Yellow, and Green colors for the rules since she was already using those colors for her clip system and red was considered the 'bad' color. Instead, the school psychologist suggested using Blue, Grey, and White rules, which corresponded to the school spirit colors. Ms. Matthews was also uncertain about moving away from the rule set implemented in the other first grade classrooms. The school psychologist and Ms. Matthews discussed how her current rules could be used to form the CWS rules for each situation. For example, the first grade rule of "be kind and respectful" was not descriptive, so what does being kind and respectful look like? Table 18.1 provides the rules that were decided upon for specific classroom settings. The Color Wheel was made with posterboard using a circle with three pie-shaped wedges. A white circle with a wedge cut-out was set on top the first circle

TABLE 18.1 CWS Color Rules and Situations for Each Color Use

Color	Blue	Grey	White
Use	Quick periods of teacher directions or instructions that require undivided attention	Extended teacher instruction or independent seatwork	Group work or free time
Rules	Eyes on teacher In seat No talking Desk ready	Raise hand and wait to speak Hands and feet to self Eyes on teacher or work Follow directions	Hands and feet to self Inside voices Follow directions

to cover up the colors not in use and attached at the center using a brad. Both circles were laminated and magnets attached to the back of the wheel. Colored poster boards (Blue, Grey, and White) were created for each rule set and had a picture of a child following each rule beside the written rule.

During three days of baseline data collection, Ms. Matthews was instructed to use her typical classroom management strategies. The observers used the data collection sheets in Appendix A (ignoring the fidelity portion of the sheet) during 30 minutes of reading class from 9:15a.m. to 9:45a.m. daily to measure inappropriate noises and length of transitions. The time was chosen because it was in the middle of the lesson and included a transition. After school on the last day of baseline, the school psychologist provided a one-hour training for Ms. Matthews, Ms. Lucas, and Mr. Peterson on the CWS procedures using direct teaching, demonstrations, and role-playing exercises. This training followed the guidelines described by Skinner et al. (2007). The rules and the situations associated with each set of rules were first described. The students must first understand the rules for each situation, so the teacher should review the rules often and refer students to the poster boards to refresh their knowledge of the rules. When moving from one activity to another, first give a two-minute warning and then a 30-second warning (e.g., "In 30 seconds, I am going to turn the wheel to Blue!"). Even if the students do not know how to tell time, they understand the urgency and immediacy of the warning. The students should use that time to get ready for Blue rules by putting belongings away, returning to their seat, having their desk clear, and not talking to others. After the time has elapsed, turn the wheel to Blue and determine if the students are following the Blue rules.

The goal of the CWS is to allow students opportunities to be successful. The teacher should always go to Blue before switching to another color to provide students a stopping point before moving on to another activity. Blue should be used for quick instructions (e.g., "We are going to do some guided reading now. Please take out your reading books and turn to page 32.") and not for lengthy instruction because the number of acceptable behaviors on Blue is very limited. When in Blue, students cannot talk, raise hands, put things away, rummage through the desk, or go to the bathroom. Do not use Blue as a punishment, but praise the class for following rules and provide individual reminders to those students who are not following the rules. Blue should be used frequently but should quickly be followed with either Grey or White to respond to students concerns (i.e., answering a question or letting a student go to the bathroom).

Once the teachers were instructed on the CWS procedures and understood the rationale for each procedure, role-plays were used to practice switching the wheel, responding to correct and incorrect behavior on each color, and using the transitions to and from Blue for maximum effect. The day after the teacher training session, student training occurred in the classroom. The Color Wheel and posters were displayed at the front of the room. The students were introduced to the CWS and practiced transitioning from each color. At first, each time the wheel was switched to a new color, the teacher reminded the students of the rules, prompted students to repeat the rules, and asked the students to show her good rule-following. For the first two days, the school psychologist observed in the classroom for an hour in the morning and an hour in the afternoon, providing feedback to the teacher regarding CWS procedures. Data were not collected during these days. Ms. Matthews expressed comfort using the CWS after the two student training days and was making very few procedural errors at the end of the second day.

The next day, the intervention stage began with data collection of student inappropriate noises and transition times similar to baseline data collection procedures. The observers also collected data on implementation fidelity during each session by indicating if the transition procedures were followed during each transition. Although data were only collected during a 30-minute reading lesson, the CWS was implemented across the entire school day. Ms. Matthews was instructed not to change her other classroom management techniques and continued to use the clip system and give Dojo points during the CWS intervention.

After several days of CWS implementation, Ms. Matthews agreed to return to baseline conditions for three days. The Color Wheel and posters were removed, and Ms. Matthews returned to just using classroom management procedures similar to that of the other first grade classrooms. Data collection identical to baseline conditions was used, and when the students asked about "that color wheel thing," Ms. Matthews simply stated, "We aren't doing that right now." After three days without the CWS, the school psychologist asked Ms. Matthews if she could reinstate the CWS. The CWS was put back into place with the same data collection procedures as the first implementation phase.

Implementation Fidelity and Interobserver Agreement

Every third day, the school psychologist simultaneously and independently collected data. Interobserver agreement (IOA) of inappropriate noises and time in transition were determined by calculating the number of intervals in which the two observers agreed, dividing that by the total number of intervals, and then multiplying by 100. Average daily IOA for inappropriate noises was 96% and agreement for intervals in transition was 92%. As stated earlier, the observers collected data for intervention fidelity during each CWS observation and noted deviations on the data collection sheet. Procedural deviations were noted if the Color Wheel was on the wrong color during any interval and if during a transition there was no two-minute warning, no 30-second warning, or the wheel was not turned to Blue before moving to another color. The Color Wheel was turned to the correct color 98% of the time, a two-minute warning was given 82% of the time, a 30-second warning given 92% of the time, and Blue was used before a transition 94% of the time. The school psychologist also collected fidelity data during the interobserver days; agreement of fidelity steps was 100% and agreement of correct color for each interval was 97%.

Intervention Outcome Data

Data on inappropriate noises were graphed across each day with results displayed in Figure 18.1. During the initial baseline, intervals with inappropriate noises ranged from 77% to 89% ($M = 84.3\%$) with an increasing trend. When the CWS was implemented, a large immediate decrease in inappropriate noises occurred, with a difference of 57% from the last baseline point to the first intervention point. Percentages of intervals with inappropriate noises ranged from 22% to 44% ($M = 31.7\%$) with a slightly decreasing trend overall. All CWS points were much lower than any session of the initial baseline phase. Immediately after the CWS was withdrawn, inappropriate noises increased dramatically ($M = 88.6\%$, range 87%-92%) and mirrored initial baseline levels. When the CWS was reapplied, once again a large and immediate decrease in inappropriate noises occurred. Data during the second CWS phase showed a decreasing trendline with percentages ranging from 12% to 44% ($M = 25.6\%$).

The number of intervals in which transitions occurred is displayed in Figure 18.2. Data collected during the problem-analysis phase were not displayed on the graph because transition times were not consistently collected during those one-hour observations. During the first baseline phase, students were in transition between 36% and 47% ($M = 41\%$) of the half-hour observation

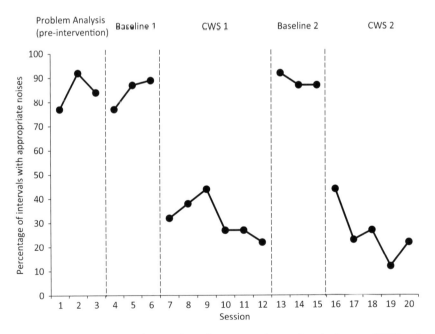

FIGURE 18.1 Percentage of intervals with inappropriate noises during no-CWS and CWS phases

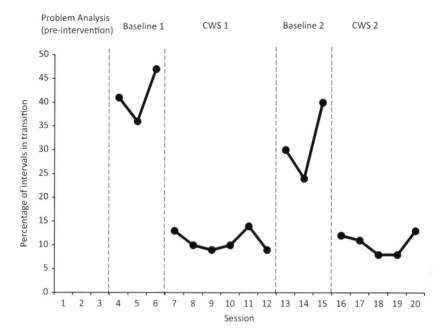

FIGURE 18.2 Percentage of intervals in transition time during no-CWS and CWS phases. Note: data were not systematically collected during the problem-analysis phase

session, which translated to between 10:40 and 14:00 minutes of transition time. This immediately and substantially decreased during the first CWS phase with between 9% and 14% ($M = 11\%$) of intervals in transition, or between 2:40 and 4:20 minutes. When the CWS was removed transition times increased, but not to the level of the first baseline phase ($M = 31\%$, range 24–40%). When the CWS was reapplied, transition times again decreased and remained relatively stable, ranging from 8% to 12% ($M = 10\%$) of the intervals, or 2:20 and 4:00 minutes.

Summary of Intervention Effects

The percentage of intervals during data collection in which there were inappropriate noises decreased dramatically when the CWS was applied in the classroom. The goal was for inappropriate noises to decrease to 40% of the intervals, and all but two intervention days met that goal. There was no overlap between intervention data and baseline data, with large differences between baseline and intervention means. When examining transition times, the goal was to decrease the time a transition takes to four minutes, which is 13% of the 30-minute observation time. During the CWS intervals, transition times ranged from 2:20 to 4:20, with all but one day meeting the goal of under four minutes. The goals for decreasing inappropriate noises and time in transition were both met. Furthermore, the high levels of IOA and treatment integrity suggest that the changes were because of the CWS intervention and the teacher was implementing the intervention correctly. The ABAB single-case design provided evidence of three phase changes, all of which showed large and sustained differences in behavior. Therefore, the school psychologist determined the CWS was effective in creating behavioral change in Ms. Matthews' class.

Intervention Acceptability

Ms. Matthews completed an intervention acceptability form that has been previously used in Color Wheel research (Appendix B; Aspiranti et al., 2019; Watson et al., 2016). She rated all items as 'strongly agree' except item 2, which she rated 'agree.' During a follow-up interview with the school psychologist, Ms. Matthews indicated that the CWS helped not just with talking but with other inappropriate behaviors such as students out of seats. It reduced the number of times she had to repeat directions and allowed for much shorter transitions, thereby increasing instructional time. She noted that other teachers noticed a difference in student behavior when visiting her classroom, particularly for the students who were the most disruptive and who continued disruptive behaviors in other class settings (e.g., specials, lunchroom, pull-out intervention classroom). There was also a notable difference in the number of completed assignments, with the amount of papers in students' 'incomplete' folders reduced by about half during the CWS days. Ms. Matthews said she would like to continue the CWS but would prefer Ms. Lucas assist with other classroom activities during that time.

The students were also given a CWS acceptability measure. They circled either Yes, Maybe, or No in response to the following items: I like using the Color Wheel; the Color Wheel helps me know what to do in class; the Color Wheel helps me behave in class; I want to keep using the Color Wheel; and I think my friends would like using the Color Wheel. All students circled Yes to all items.

Intervention Considerations

Visual analysis of time-series graphs provides evidence of the effectiveness of the CWS in this example for decreasing inappropriate noises and transition times in a first grade classroom. Research on the CWS has provided evidence of its efficacy in kindergarten through fifth grade classrooms (Saecker et al., 2008; Watson et al., 2016), but there has been no research conducted that has implemented the CWS in middle school or high school classrooms. Regardless, the components of the CWS such as setting-specific classroom rules, providing notification before switching tasks, and having a stopping point where the teacher is given undivided attention to deliver directions are applicable in the upper-level grades, suggesting that the CWS could be appropriate for older students. Additionally, the CWS has not been successfully implemented in the preschool setting. In order to follow the CWS rules students must be able to identify or at least match colors, which may be a skill some preschool-aged children have not yet developed. The same can be said for students in special education rooms; the success of the CWS depends on students being able to recognize that the color on the wheel corresponds to the color of the rule poster board. When the CWS was implemented in classrooms with students with autism (Aspiranti et al., 2019), the researcher first determined that the students could identify colors and introduced the CWS with a social story that included color pictures.

Although previous research on the CWS has focused on implementation in one classroom or a set of three classrooms, it could be a useful addition to a SWPBIS initiative. The CWS can be implemented as a Tier 1 SWPBIS intervention as part of a preventative strategy to establish, teach, and reinforce clear and consistent school-wide behavioral expectations (Bradshaw, Mitchell, & Leaf, 2010). The CWS rule sets can be matched to SWPBIS expectations, with perhaps additional colored CWS rule-sets (i.e., orange, purple) corresponding to other settings, such as the hallway.

The CWS can be used in conjunction with other classroom management strategies and reinforcement/punishment procedures. In the case study, ClassDojo was paired with the CWS so that students could earn Dojo points for correct behavior. Group rewards should be used for good rule-following behavior, as this reinforces the idea that the purpose of the CWS is to manage behavior of the entire class (Skinner et al., 2007). Extra recess, playing a classroom game, movement breaks, lunch in the classroom, or extra time on White are all ideas of class-wide rewards that could be used with the CWS. Rule-breaking can be addressed several ways. Using group prompts (e.g., "Class, remember we are on Blue, so that means there is no talking") instead of individual reprimands (e.g., "Mike, you should not be talking"), for occasional rule-breaking reminds all students of the rules and does not provide unwanted reinforcing attention to the rule-breaker. However, if a student continuously breaks the rules, individual consequences may be needed. The CWS should not supersede a student's individual behavior plan, but rather provide a classroom behavioral management framework within which a student can succeed. The class should not be punished for an individual classmate's behavior; therefore, group punishment is not encouraged. Likewise, time on Blue should not be used as a punishment because the teacher does not want Blue to have a negative connotation, even though the rules are most stringent on Blue.

An aspect of the case study that may be of consideration to teachers is the data collection procedures. The daily time-sampling procedures used in the case study took valuable time from the classroom assistant, and Ms. Matthews noted that she needed Ms. Lucas in other capacities during that time. Although the observations were divided between Ms. Lucas and Mr. Peterson, the half-hour of observation required undivided attention from the observer. An option to circumvent this obstacle may be to video the session and collect data based on the video. Another consideration is the implementation of an ABAB reversal design within the school setting. Although a design that provides at least three opportunities to show treatment effects is preferable, once an intervention is effective, many teachers do not want to revert to the baseline procedures. Therefore, within practical settings, decisions are often made using data from AB designs. If a rigorous design is desired without a reversal to baseline, practitioners may decide to implement a multiple-baseline design across classrooms (see Watson et al., 2016). With this method there is no return to baseline, but each class begins using the CWS in a stairstep approach.

There are several possible undesired side effects of the CWS. First, the rule-sets may not always fit the situation. For example, the wheel may be on Grey while the teacher is providing whole-group instruction, but she would like the students to engage in a think-pair-share activity. She may say, "The wheel is on Grey, but we are going to think-pair-share. When you pair up you can talk quietly to your partner. When you share, you need to raise your hand to speak, though." The teacher exception will supersede the Grey rule of "raise hand and wait to speak." Initially, the CWS may increase students tattling on peers who are not following the rules. Interdependent group rewards can be implemented to help decrease tattling. Students are less likely to point out peer inappropriate behavior with interdependent group rewards because that would reduce the likelihood of receiving the group reward. Although not necessarily a side effect, some teachers have complained that they do not like having to walk to the front of the room each time to turn the wheel to a new color. This could be avoided by using a portable wheel, such as the portable traffic light used in Aspiranti et al. (2019). However, a portable item may have the tendency to be misplaced, left in a different part of the room, or not be visible to all students.

Conclusion

The CWS has successfully been implemented within both general education and special education classrooms to reduce disruptive behaviors and increase on-task behaviors (e.g., Aspiranti et al., 2019; Fudge et al., 2008; Watson et al., 2016). This case study exemplifies using the CWS in response to high amounts of disruptive behavior across students. In the case study, the CWS procedures and rules were able to successfully reduce the amount of student talking as well as the amount of time in transition, therefore increasing instructional time and the amount of work completed.

References

Aspiranti, K. B., Bebech, A., Ruffo, B., & Skinner, C. H. (2019). Classroom management in self-contained classrooms for children with autism: Extending research on the color wheel system. *Behavior Analysis in Practice, 12,* 143–153. doi:10.1007/s40617-018-0264-6

Blondin, C., Skinner, C. H., Parkhurst, J., Wood, A., & Snyder, J. (2012). Enhancing on-task behavior in fourth-grade students using a modified color wheel system. *Journal of Applied School Psychology, 28,* 37–58. doi:10.1080/15377903.2012.643756

Bradshaw, C. P., Mitchell, M. M., & Leaf, P. J. (2010). Examining the effects of schoolwide positive behavioral interventions and supports on student outcomes: Results from a randomized controlled effectiveness trial in elementary schools. *Journal of Positive Behavior Interventions, 12,* 133–148.

Flower, A., McKenna, J. W., & Haring, C. D. (2017). Behavior and classroom management: Are teacher preparation programs really preparing out teachers? *Preventing School Failure, 61,* 163–169.

Fudge, D. L., Skinner, C. H., Williams, J. L., Cowden, D., Clark, J., & Bliss, S. L. (2008). Increasing on-task behavior in every student in a second-grade classroom during transitions: Validating the color wheel system. *Journal of School Psychology, 46,* 575–592. doi:10.1016/j.jsp.2008.06.003

Saecker, L., Sager, K., Skinner, C. H., Williams, J. L., Luna, E., & Spurgeon, S. (2008). Decreasing a fifth-grade teacher's repeated directions and students' inappropriate talking by using color wheel procedures. *Journal of Evidence-Based Practices for Schools, 9,* 18–32.

Skinner, C. H., Scala, G., Dendas, D., & Lentz, F. E. (2007). The color wheel: Implementation guidelines. *Journal of Evidence-Based Practices for Schools, 8,* 134–140.

Watson, T. L., Skinner, C. H., Skinner, A. L., Cazzell, S., Aspiranti, K. B., Moore, T., & Coleman, M. (2016). Preventing disruptive behavior via classroom management: Validating the color wheel system in kindergarten classrooms. *Behavior Modification, 40,* 518–540.

Appendix A: Color Wheel Data Collection

Observer: *Date:*
Observation Time:

Target behavior: Inappropriate noise – talking or making noises without permission from teacher

Fidelity	Time	0:20	0:40	1:00	1:20	1:40	2:00	2:20	2:40	3:00
2-minute warning	Data									
	Time	3:20	3:40	4:00	4:20	4:40	5:00	5:20	5:40	6:00
	Data									
30-second warning	Time	6:20	6:40	7:00	7:20	7:40	8:00	8:20	8:40	9:00
	Data									
	Time	9:20	9:40	10:00	10:20	10:40	11:00	11:20	11:40	12:00
	Data									
Blue before transition	Time	12:20	12:40	13:00	13:20	13:40	14:00	14:20	14:40	15:00
	Data									
Fidelity code: x-correct o-incorrect	Time	15:20	15:40	16:00	16:20	16:40	17:00	17:20	17:40	18:00
	Data									
	Time	18:20	18:40	19:00	19:20	19:40	20:00	20:20	20:40	21:00
	Data									
	Time	21:20	21:40	22:00	22:20	22:40	23:00	23:20	23:40	24:00
Observer Notes	Data									
	Time	24:20	24:40	25:00	25:20	25:40	26:00	26:20	26:40	27:00
	Data									
	Time	27:20	27:40	28:00	28:20	28:40	29:00	29:20	29:40	30:00
	Data									

Coding: x = inappropriate noise during interval; T = Transition; C = wrong color

Appendix B: Teacher Acceptability Form

Item	Strongly Disagree	Disagree	Slightly Disagree	Slightly Agree	Agree	Strongly Agree
1. The CWS was a good intervention						
2. Most teachers would find the CWS appropriate to deal with classroom behavior						
3. The CWS helped me stay consistent						
4. I noticed students' behavior improve when the CWS was used						
5. Transitions were easier when I used the CWS						
6. I spent less time disciplining students when using the CWS						
7. The CWS quickly improved students' behavior						
8. I will use the CWS for the remainder of the year						
9. I will use the CWS with future classes						
10. C would recommend the CWS to other teachers						

19

CHECK-IN CHECK-OUT/BEHAVIOR REPORT CARD

Daniel D. Drevon, Michael D. Hixson, Amy Campbell, Allison M. Brown, and Alexander M. Rigney

Introduction

In multi-tiered systems of support (MTSS), Tier 2 interventions provide targeted support to about 15% of students who are unresponsive to Tier 1 supports (i.e., School-Wide Positive Behavior Interventions and Supports [SWPBIS]). Tier 2 interventions are characterized by explicit teaching, increased structure, and increased feedback. Further, they are efficient and cost-effective (Campbell, Rodriguez, & Schrauben, 2019). Check-in check-out (CICO), also known as the Behavior Education Program (BEP), is probably the most commonly used and well-researched Tier 2 behavior intervention within MTSS (Crone, Hawken, & Horner, 2010).

CICO is a multicomponent behavior intervention that leverages several more basic behavioral principles and interventions (e.g., reinforcement, token economy). CICO contains five core elements. First, upon arriving at school, a student checks in with their CICO coordinator or mentor. Second, the CICO coordinator or mentor reviews the daily behavioral expectations and goals tied to a behavior report card (BRC; also known as a Daily Progress Report or Daily Point Card). Third, teachers assign points on the BRC and provide verbal feedback throughout the day. Fourth, the student checks out with their CICO coordinator or mentor at the end of the day, receiving an incentive if they meet daily behavioral expectations and goals. Finally, students take home the BRC for parent review and signature. Students return the BRC to their CICO coordinator or mentor for the following school day's check in.

CICO has nearly two decades worth of empirical support for improving student outcomes across different school settings for a diverse range of students.

A recent meta-analysis of 32 studies (31 single-case experimental designs and one between-groups experiment) found that CICO improved student outcomes (i.e., academically engaged behavior [AEB], percent of points on a BRC, disruptive behavior, office disciplines referrals) on average by over one standard deviation compared to baseline or control conditions (Drevon, Hixson, Wyse, & Rigney, 2019). Most research on CICO has been conducted in elementary schools, but there have also been studies conducted in secondary schools and alternative settings. Participants in the studies included in this meta-analysis averaged at 10 years old. Participants were about three-quarters male, and over half were racial/ethnic minorities. About one-third of participants were students with disabilities (Drevon et al., 2019).

This chapter will use case study material to illustrate how CICO can be integrated into a problem-solving framework addressing AEB and disruptive behavior for a student who is not responding to SWPBIS. Following this, considerations for the use of CICO will be discussed including (a) options for fading CICO for students who have met their terminal goal on the BRC, (b) flexibility of implementation of CICO, and (c) school resources and training needed to implement CICO.

Case Study

Background Information

Timothy is an 11-year-old boy in the sixth grade at Clarke Middle School. He was referred to the MTSS team due to persistent off-task and disruptive behavior in the classroom since the beginning of the school year. His problem behaviors in the classroom had not improved despite exposure to a Tier 1 behavioral intervention. Timothy's school utilized SWPBIS, and at the Tier 1 level, behavioral expectations were modeled and taught to all students and appropriate behavior verbally was praised by school staff. School-wide data showed a majority of the students demonstrated appropriate behavior and seemed to respond to the intervention in place at the Tier 1 level. However, Timothy's behavioral data indicated he was not responding in a similar manner.

Timothy rotated between five classrooms and teachers throughout the school day for his subjects: science, math, art, social studies, and language arts. School records showed Timothy had met academic performance benchmarks in previous years based on district and state testing, and the most recent school-wide fall benchmarking data indicated he was meeting grade-level benchmarks in reading and math. However, his teachers were concerned Timothy's problem behaviors would begin to impact his academic achievement if not reduced. In fact, he only just met the cut off for the fall benchmark in reading and math. Furthermore, Timothy's consistent disruptive behaviors impacted his teachers' ability to teach other students effectively and therefore impacted classroom learning as a whole. Timothy occasionally received office discipline referrals due to his behavior in the classroom and was frequently redirected by his teachers for not being academically engaged. Timothy's disruptive behaviors would occur regardless of the type of classroom activity and would not abate upon being told he would need to leave the room. Unless his teachers were in constant close proximity to Timothy, there was a low likelihood Timothy would be actively engaged in the required academic activity. Timothy did not have an Individualized Education Program (IEP) and he received all his instruction in general education classrooms.

Description of the Problem Behavior

Based on behavioral descriptions from his core academic teachers and a review of Timothy's office discipline referrals, AEB and disruptive behavior were identified as the two target behaviors. Subsequently, operational definitions of target behaviors were collaboratively developed with his teachers. AEB means that Timothy is actively or passively engaged in academic expectations. Examples include reading, writing, talking about academic material, and orienting towards others talking about academic material. Non-examples include looking out the window, walking around the room, and talking about an unrelated topic with others. Disruptive behavior means that Timothy is engaging in behavior disruptive to his learning and the learning of others. Examples include talking when the teacher is talking, poking other students, singing, shouting out answers, and tapping a pencil on the desk during worktime. Non-examples include listening to the teacher, raising hand to answer question, working quietly, keeping hands to self, and talking to the teacher or other students about the assignment when appropriate.

Problem Analysis

In an effort to try to determine why the problem behaviors were occurring, the school psychologist reviewed his discipline records, conducted teacher and student interviews, and observed him in his classrooms. Timothy had been sent to the office six times over the current school year for being disruptive in class. He was never reported to be aggressive, but he would sometimes repeatedly make inappropriate comments or jokes, resulting in a referral to the office. Most of his teachers reported generally good relationships with him, but said that he was often off-task or talking too much in class. They also said that the quality of his work and test performance were good, but that he often failed to complete assignments. Teachers indicated that he was most off-task during independent writing assignments and that he was most disruptive during group projects.

The observations generally confirmed the teachers' reports. Timothy was observed to frequently be talking to other students and sometimes yelled out answers. He also was frequently out of his seat and would make comments to other students while wandering (e.g., he told one student he was getting fat). Timothy did sometimes raise his hand to get help from teachers, but he did not spend a lot of time on his assignments. Teachers usually ignored his minor disruptions and off-task behavior, but repeated disruptions usually resulted in a warning from the teacher. Timothy always immediately complied with teachers' redirections. When the school psychologist interviewed Timothy, he acknowledged that he did often talk out of turn and he was mostly accurate in describing the classroom expectations for behavior. He also said he liked most of his classes, except for social studies because "it is boring." The results of this basic problem analysis did not identify a specific function for his disruptive behavior and low AEB, but the results suggest that escape from academic work and reinforcement from peer reactions may play a role. Also, the fact that he appears capable of doing the classwork indicates that an intervention to improve academic skills is probably not needed.

Intervention Goals

The goal of the intervention was to increase academic engagement and reduce disruptive behavior as measured by tracking of incompatible behaviors on a daily BRC. Timothy's initial goal was to achieve 60% of the possible points on the BRC each day, which was about 20 percentage points higher than his baseline performance. Timothy's goal was increased by 10 percentage points each time he met his goal for five consecutive days. Conversely, his goal would have been reduced by 10 percentage points after four consecutive days of not meeting his goal. Timothy's terminal goal was to achieve 80% of the possible points on the BRC.

Measurement of Target Behaviors, Data Collection Strategies, and Progress Monitoring

The BRC (see Appendix A) that was used as part of the intervention for CICO was also the primary source of data for monitoring the effectiveness of the intervention. The BRC listed four behaviors (Be Safe, Be Productive, Be Responsible, and Be Kind) that the school used as part of their SWPBIS. These four behaviors served as good incompatible behaviors to the disruptive behavior and low AEB Timothy exhibited. All students in the school were taught definitions of these behaviors and provided examples and non-examples of them. To obtain baseline data, Timothy's teachers completed BRCs for five days prior to the implementation of CICO. The teachers continued to complete the BRCs daily throughout the time period of the intervention. The percentage of points earned each day served as the dependent variable for progress monitoring.

Intervention Plan

Timothy's CICO plan included a daily check-in with Mr. Greenman, the school's CICO coordinator; feedback in the form of points for each expectation during each class period; a daily check-out with Mr. Greenman; daily feedback to his parents; and a token economy (TE) system based on points earned.

Prior to beginning the CICO program, Timothy met with the school's CICO coordinator, Mr. Greenman, for an orientation. Mr. Greenman, the special education teacher for the building, reviewed the school-wide behavior expectations (Safe, Productive, Respectful, and Kind), and further defined expectations related to Timothy's identified behaviors of concern (AEB and disruptive behavior). In addition, they reviewed the expectations for the program and completed a preference assessment to identify potential reinforcers that Timothy may earn with points.

Each morning, Timothy checked in with Mr. Greenman before first period. During this brief meeting, Timothy would return the previous day's BRC and Mr. Greenman would provide him with a new BRC and review specific behavior expectations. For example, Mr. Greenman might say, "Remember to focus on completing at least 75% of your independent math problems during class time today." He would also ensure that Timothy was prepared for the day (e.g., had his pencil and planner) and provide Timothy with the appropriate number of points during the check-in period.

Timothy's daily BRC included opportunities to earn points for each of the four school-wide expectations during each class period. After the class ended, Timothy brought the BRC to his teacher to complete. The classroom teacher provided feedback on Timothy's behavior in the form of points. A score of "2" indicated that he met expectations, a score of "1" indicated he partially met expectations, and a score of "0" indicated he did not meet expectations. Each teacher provided specific praise or feedback related to the assigned point value (e.g., "I rated you as a 2 for productive because you were working independently the entire class").

At the end of the day, Timothy checked out with Mr. Greenman. Timothy turned in his BRC and briefly discussed whether he met his goal. If he met his goal, Mr. Greenman would provide specific verbal praise. If he did not, Mr. Greenman would discuss strategies for improvement with Timothy (e.g., "What would help you remember to get your planner signed at night? Should we put a note on the cover as a reminder?"). Mr. Greenman then recorded the number of points he earned into Timothy's CICO record (see Appendix B). Timothy took home his BRC each day and obtained a parent signature. He then returned the signed copy the following day.

Timothy had the opportunity to earn a reward daily or to save and trade in his points for various items and social privileges once per week. The incentives ranged in point value and included food items, school supplies, school sporting event tickets, one-day extensions for homework assignments, and a pass that allowed him to go to lunch five minutes early.

Intervention Fidelity and Interobserver Agreement

The school psychologist evaluated fidelity of implementation once per week using a fidelity checklist (see Appendix C). An observation was conducted during the check-in period, at least one class period, and the check-out period. Upon observing each session, the checklist was completed. If items were scored as not occurring, the school psychologist problem-solved with the CICO coordinator to determine steps for improvement. In addition to the checklist, the CICO coordinator reviewed permanent products (e.g., the CICO record) to determine if Timothy was consistently checking in and out, obtaining feedback from the classroom teachers, and returning the signed BRC.

Intervention Outcome Data

Figure 19.1 depicts Timothy's BRC points across the baseline and intervention phases. During baseline, he earned an average of 38% of points on the BRC (range: 30%–50%) each day. On the first day that CICO was implemented, Timothy did not meet the original goal of earning 60% of points on the BRC, but he met or exceeded this threshold for the next five days. Across these first six days of the intervention, his BRC points increased significantly from baseline, with Timothy earning an average of 68% of BRC points (range: 55%–80%) each day. Hence, the goal was increased by 10 percentage points, making Timothy's new goal earning 70% of BRC points. Over the next five school days, Timothy met or exceeded this goal each day, with an average of 76% of points on the BRC (range: 70%–80%). The goal was again increased by 10 percentage points, making his new goal earning 80% of BRC points. Timothy's score fell short of

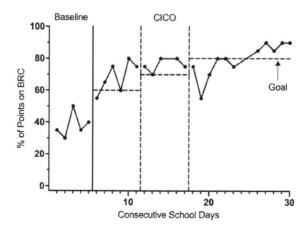

FIGURE 19.1 Percent of points earned on the BRC across consecutive school days for Timothy

this goal for the next three days, but his percentage of BRC points on the fourth and fifth days met the goal of 80%, so the decision rule was not met. Afterwards, Timothy had one more day below this 80% threshold, but he was then able to surpass the goal for five consecutive sessions. At this point, Timothy met the terminal goal of 80% of points on the BRC, so the intervention was faded. Ultimately, he ended up earning an average of 80% of points per day (range: 55%-90%), which is significantly higher than his average of 38% of points on the BRC during baseline.

Summary of Intervention Effects

According to the information above, Timothy's percentage of points earned on the BRC increased significantly during the intervention phase compared to the baseline phase. Further, his percentage of BRC points continued to increase as CICO was implemented across additional school days and his goal was increased. This suggests that Timothy was more academically engaged and had fewer instances of disruptive behavior as the intervention progressed and the goal was raised. Based on these results, the MTSS team determined that CICO was effective in increasing Timothy's AEB and decreasing his disruptive behavior. Ultimately, the team concluded that Timothy met the goals of the intervention.

Intervention Acceptability

To assess the acceptability of the intervention, Timothy's teachers completed the Behavior Education Program Acceptability Questionnaire-Teacher Version (Crone et al., 2010). Timothy completed the student version and his parents completed the parent version. Items on these questionnaires are rated on a six-point Likert scale, with one denoting Strongly Disagree and six denoting Strongly Agree. Overall, scores across the completed questionnaires indicated high levels of acceptability ($M = 5.4$, $SD = 0.49$).

Intervention Considerations

This section addresses considerations for implementing CICO including (a) options for fading CICO for students who have met their terminal goal on the BRC, (b) flexibility of implementation of CICO, and (c) school resources and training needed to implement CICO.

Fading CICO

Students should not participate in CICO in perpetuity. Once students have met their terminal goal on the BRC and have maintained performance for a period of time (e.g., four weeks) set by the MTSS team, systematic strategies for fading

CICO can be introduced. Fading may be implemented in a number of ways, but all require continued progress-monitoring of student behavior to determine whether performance is maintained.

The simplest fading method, after students meet their performance goals with CICO, is to systematically reduce the number of times teachers provide feedback throughout the day until no feedback is given (Campbell & Anderson, 2011). A second method of fading is to replace teacher feedback with student self-monitoring (Miller, Dufrene, Sterling, Olmi, & Bachmayer, 2015a). After students meet their performance goals with CICO, they can be taught to rate their own behavior on the BRC. This should be implemented in a gradual manner with teachers continuing to rate students on the BRC and their ratings used to determine whether students earned their reward. If and when there is high agreement between the teacher and student ratings, the teacher ratings may be discontinued and the student ratings used to determine whether rewards are earned.

Changing aspects of teacher feedback is not the only practicable strategy for fading CICO. After students meet their performance goals with CICO, a Mystery Motivator can be used to thin the schedule of reinforcement tied to meeting daily goals on the BRC (Miller, Dufrene, Sterling, Olmi, & Bachmayer, 2015b). This procedure involves students drawing a slip of paper from an envelope indicating whether they earned a reward that day, contingent upon meeting the daily goal on the BRC. When in effect, not all of the slips of paper indicate students earned a reward. Thus, students will not always earn a reward contingent on meeting their daily goal on the BRC when a Mystery Motivator is in effect.

Coupled with logistical guidance from Crone et al. (2010), it may be helpful to consider systematically fading or replacing teacher feedback and/or thinning the schedule of reinforcement associated with daily goals on the BRC to fade CICO for students who have met their terminal goals on the BRC and/or have maintained performance for a period of time (e.g., four weeks) set by the MTSS team.

Flexibility of CICO

CICO is typically implemented for students whose behavioral difficulties are maintained at least in part by adult attention. However, CICO has proven to be adaptable in addressing a wide range of behavioral difficulties evoked and maintained by a wide range of circumstances. Crone et al. (2010) devote a chapter to discussing modifying CICO to support students whose behavioral difficulties are maintained by peer attention or escape or avoidance of academic tasks. They also discuss adding academic supports to CICO for students struggling with organizing and completing academic tasks. Many of their recommendations have subsequently been investigated empirically.

Several studies have examined function-modified versions of CICO (Klingbeil, Dart, & Schramm, 2019). For students whose behavioral difficulties are evoked by academic tasks and maintained by escape and avoidance of academic tasks as well as peer attention, function-based modifications to CICO might include allowing students to request breaks or help during academic tasks (Boyd & Anderson, 2013). This might involve allowing students to take a predetermined number of breaks during the day for a short time (e.g., two minutes) during appropriate instructional activities and after asking their teacher.

CICO can also be modified for students struggling with organizing and completing academic tasks, including homework (Turtura, Anderson, & Boyd, 2014). For students demonstrating behavioral difficulties maintained by escape from academic tasks, CICO can be modified to included additions to check-in, the BRC, and range of rewards. Regarding check-in, students might show the coordinator they have the necessary materials for class (e.g., pencils, notebooks). If not, they can be required to obtain them. Further, the coordinator can check to see if students completed the previous day's homework. If not, they can be given homework passes to complete it during nonacademic periods of the school day. In addition to the usual behavioral expectations, the BRC can contain bonus points for having necessary materials, completing the previous day's homework, and recording homework assignments on a homework tracker attached to the BRC. In this modification to CICO, the range of usual rewards can be expanded to include homework passes and break cards.

School Resources

Implementation of CICO requires a carefully planned commitment of school resources. Crone et al. (2010) thoroughly discuss (a) initial adoption of CICO and (b) roles, responsibilities, and training needs of critical team members (i.e., CICO coordinator, MTSS team, administrators, teachers, parents, and students). Readers are encouraged to access this resource if they are interested in implementing CICO in their building(s).

Regarding initial adoption of CICO, both Crone et al. (2010) and Filter (2019) discuss the importance of assessing readiness. It is important to note CICO should be situated in the context of SWPBIS because it cannot effectively address the behavioral difficulties of more than 15% of students. School personnel should also consider whether administrators and staff are committed to implementing CICO. Prior to initial adoption, the MTSS team needs to meticulously lay important groundwork related to personnel (e.g., identifying a CICO coordinator), space, rewards, a referral system, data management, fading CICO, and a budget (Crone et al., 2010). After laying this groundwork, schools must address the training needs of the CICO coordinator, the MTSS team, administrators, teachers, parents, and students. Each of these roles has several responsibilities and training needs.

Conclusion

CICO is a commonly used multicomponent behavior intervention in the context of MTSS. Its daily implementation cycle contains check-in, a BRC, systematic feedback from teachers on the BRC, check-out, and home communication. CICO has nearly two decades worth of empirical support for improving student outcomes across different school settings for a diverse range of students. This chapter illustrated how CICO can be integrated within a problem-solving framework to address AEB and disruptive behavior for a student unresponsive to Tier 1 supports (i.e., SWPBIS). Following this, considerations for the use of CICO were discussed including (a) options for fading CICO for students who have met their terminal goal on the BRC, (b) flexibility of implementation of CICO, and (c) school resources and training needed to implement CICO.

References

Boyd, R. J., & Anderson, C. M. (2013). Breaks are better: A Tier II social behavior intervention. *Journal of Behavioral Education, 22*, 348–365. doi:10.1007s10864-013-9184-2

Campbell, A., & Anderson, C. M. (2011). Check-in/check-out: A systematic evaluation and component analysis. *Journal of Applied Behavior Analysis, 44*, 315–326. doi:10.1901/jaba.2011.44-315

Campbell, A., Rodriguez, B. J., & Schrauben, K. (2019). Tier two basics. In K. C. Radley & E. H. Dart (Eds.), *Handbook of behavioral interventions in schools: Multi-tiered systems of supports* (pp. 308–324). New York, NY: Oxford University Press. doi:10.1093/med-psych/9780190843229.003.0016

Crone, D. A., Hawken, L. S., & Horner, R. H. (2010). *Responding to problem behavior in schools: The behavior education program* (2nd ed.). New York, NY: Guilford.

Drevon, D. D., Hixson, M. D., Wyse, R. D., & Rigney, A. M. (2019). A meta-analytic review of the evidence for check-in check-out. *Psychology in the Schools, 56*, 393–412. doi:10.1002/pits.22195

Filter, K. J. (2019). Check-in/check-out. In K. C. Radley & E. H. Dart (Eds.), *Handbook of behavioral interventions in schools: Multi-tiered systems of supports* (pp. 335–348). New York, NY: Oxford University Press. doi:10.1093/med-psych/9780190843229.003.0017

Klingbeil, D. A., Dart, E. H., & Schramm, A. L. (2019). A systematic review of function modified check in/check-out. *Journal of Positive Behavior Interventions, 21*, 77–92. doi:10.1177/1098300718778032

Miller, L. M., Dufrene, B. A., Olmi, J. D., Tingstrom, D., & Filce, H. (2015a). Self-monitoring as a viable fading option in check-in/check-out. *Journal of School Psychology, 53*, 121–135. doi:10.1016/j.jsp.2014.12.004

Miller, L. M., Dufrene, B. A., Sterling, H. E., Olmi, J. D., & Bachmayer, E. (2015b). The effects of check-in/check-out on problem behavior and academic engagement in elementary school students. *Journal of Positive Behavior Interventions, 17*, 28–38. doi:10.1177/1098300713517141

Turtura, J. E., Anderson, C. M., & Boyd, R. J. (2014). Addressing task avoidance in middle school students: Academic behavior check-in/check-out. *Journal of Positive Behavior Interventions, 16*, 159–167. doi:10.1177/1098300713484063

Appendix A: Behavior Report Card: Clarke Middle School

Name: _____ Date: _____
Goal: 60% 70% 80% Percentage of Points Earned: _____

	Be Safe			Be Productive			Be Responsible			Be Kind			Teacher Initials
Period 1	0	1	2	0	1	2	0	1	2	0	1	2	
Period 2	0	1	2	0	1	2	0	1	2	0	1	2	
Period 3	0	1	2	0	1	2	0	1	2	0	1	2	
Period 4	0	1	2	0	1	2	0	1	2	0	1	2	
Period 5	0	1	2	0	1	2	0	1	2	0	1	2	

Parent/Guardian Signature: _____

0 = No
1 = Somewhat
2 = Yes

Appendix B: CICO Form: Clarke Middle School

Student Name: _____ CICO Coordinator: _____

Date	Returned Previous BRC	Checked-In	Delivered New BRC	Goal	% of BRC Points Earned	Delivered Reward
10/14/19	NA	Yes	Yes	60%	55%	No
10/15/19	Yes	Yes	Yes	60%	65%	Yes
10/16/19	Yes	Yes	Yes	60%	75%	Yes
10/17/19	No	Yes	Yes	60%	60%	Yes
10/18/19	Yes	Yes	Yes	60%	80%	Yes
10/21/19	No	Yes	Yes	60%	75%	Yes

Appendix C: CICO Fidelity Form: Clarke Middle School

Name: _____   Date: _____

	Area			
Check in	Student checked in with adult	Yes	No	NA
	Staff member provided daily BRC	Yes	No	NA
	Staff member provided a prompt for the student to be successful that day	Yes	No	NA
Classroom	Student turned in home report	Yes	No	NA
	Student approached teacher to receive feedback	Yes	No	NA
	Teacher assigned points to student	Yes	No	NA
	Teacher provided verbal feedback regarding the student's behavior	Yes	No	NA
Check out	Student checked out with adult	Yes	No	NA
	Student presented complete card to adult	Yes	No	NA
	Staff member added up total points and recorded	Yes	No	NA
	Staff member provided verbal feedback regarding student's behavior	Yes	No	NA
	Staff member delivered reward, if appropriate	Yes	No	NA
	Staff member handed BRC back to student	Yes	No	NA

Number of Yes / Number of Yes + No = _____
Note. horizontal lines in the intervention phase reflect Timothy's daily goal.

20
SOCIAL STORIES™

Frank J. Sansosti

Introduction

Social Stories™ (hereafter referred to Social Story or Social Stories) are individualized short stories that describe a social context, skill, or concept according to 10 defining criteria (currently Social Stories™ 10.2; see www.carolgraysocialstories.com). When created appropriately, Social Stories can be used to assist students with autism spectrum disorder (ASD) in interpreting and understanding challenging or confusing social situations (Howley & Arnold, 2005; Gray, 2015). The objective of a Social Story is to describe social situations in which a student might have difficulty identifying relevant social cues or expected behaviors, and provide strategies for negotiating those situations effectively through visual support and textual sequencing (McGill, Baker, & Busse, 2015). Specifically, a Social Story: (1) describes targeted situations, concepts, or skills by answering relevant "wh-" questions (where, when, who, how, and why); (2) describes how to think about or problem-solve the targeted situation; and (3) creates connections between past, present, and future experiences by having the students make logical guesses about what may happen using prior knowledge. In this sense, a Social Story provides a "how-to" guide for understanding, responding, and engaging within a difficult social situation or context (Sansosti, Powell-Smith, & Kincaid, 2004).

Over the past several decades, clinical support for the use of Social Stories in homes, schools, and community settings has been strong (Reynhout & Carter, 2009). In fact, many clinicians, advocates, and various school-based student support personnel (e.g., school psychologists, speech-language pathologists, behavior analysts) report anecdotally the benefits of using Social Stories within educational contexts. Moreover, a host of single-case research investigating the effects of Social Stories have demonstrated successful outcomes for reducing aggression and inappropriate behaviors (e.g., Benish & Bramlett, 2011; Reynhout & Carter, 2007), increasing appropriate play (Barry & Burlew, 2004), and improving social interactions (e.g., White, Caniglia, McLaughlin, & Bianco, 2018). As a result, the National Autism Standards recently has recognized Social Stories as an evidence-based procedure (National Autism Center, 2015). Despite their widespread use and perceived effectiveness, many researchers conducting systematic and meta-analytic reviews of the extant literature have revealed limitations or limited over-all effectiveness, leading authors to question the true efficacy of Social Stories as an evidence-based practice (e.g., Leaf et al., 2015; McGill et al., 2015; Sansosti et al., 2004)

Developing a Social Story is similar in scope to other approaches to creating individualized student supports. That is, a teacher or parent identifies a specific target behavior or a difficult social situation. Once a target situation or behavior is identified, the next step involves identifying the salient features of the context or setting. For example, information should be gathered on where the situation occurs, who is involved, how long it lasts, how it begins and ends, and what occurs. These steps are similar in scope to completing a functional behavior assessment (FBA). Finally, the information gleaned through this assessment is used to write the content of a Social Story.

Social Stories are composed of a combination of multiple *Descriptive Sentences* and one or two *Coaching Sentences* (Gray, 2015). *Descriptive Sentences* are the primary mechanism for delivering information within a Social Story and include objective statements of fact that, most often, describe observable features of a specific social situation. In addition, they describe or refer to feelings, thoughts, beliefs, attitudes, and opinion of others. Depending on the nature of the story, *Descriptive Sentences* also may be used to enhance meaning by stating commonly shared cultural beliefs. *Coaching Sentences* identify appropriate responses for the reader and guide behavior through descriptions of others or self-coaching. It is necessary for school-based personnel and parents to understand the specific guidelines for the creation of Social Stories.

School-based personnel are encouraged to engage in a variety of professional development activities that will ensure that Social Stories are being created accurately (currently Social Stories™ 10.2). Perhaps the most successful way for educators to gain the necessary skills is to attend workshops or trainings provided by Carol Gray. Educators may wish to engage in their own learning through a variety of training materials that are available through Carol Gray Social Stories (interested readers are encouraged to visit www.carolgraysocialstories.com). For the purposes of this chapter, a summary of the criteria, as outlined by Gray (2015), are provided:

- ***Criteria 1: Establish a Goal.*** The intent of <u>ANY</u> Social Story is to share information by describing underlying causes of challenging situations. A Social Story does not provide a list of steps for the child to engage in

(similar to a task analysis), but, rather, provides information for more effective responses to the challenging situation(s).
- ***Criteria 2: Gather Information.*** Essential to the creation of an effective Social Story is a clear understanding of the student in relation to a particularly difficult situation, skill, or concept. As such, it is critical for school-based teams to gather information about events in the student's environment that are contributing to or maintaining the occurrence of specific behaviors; develop hypotheses about such variables; and collect data to either support or reject those hypotheses. In addition, information is gathered regarding the child's strengths and weaknesses, as well as his or her perspective on the targeted situation (Gray, 2015). One of the most effective approaches to gather such information is conducting a thorough FBA, which, ultimately, allow practitioners to understand behavior and develop effective positive-behavior support plans. Strategies for the collection of data include, but are not limited to, interviews with teachers/caregivers and direct observations linked to information obtained during the interview process. Readers interested in the process of information/data collection specific to students with ASD are encouraged to use the steps and forms described by Sansosti, Powell-Smith, and Cowan (2010). Educators should make every effort to gather information <u>BEFORE</u> developing the content of the Social Story.
- ***Criteria 3: Create a Title and Basic Format.*** An appropriately created Social Story is written just like any other story. That is, each Social Story contains a title, introduction, central theme, and a conclusion. The title should bring the reader into the world of the story, capture his or her attention, and set up what's coming (e.g., "*What is Sharing?*"). An introduction, within the context of a Social Story, is brief, consisting of typically one sentence that indicates very clearly the topic (e.g., "*Sometimes I am asked to share.*"). Following the introductory sentence, further description and explanation are provided within the body of the Social Story. The body of the Social Story adds details that are intended to increase awareness and understanding of the what, when, who, and why of social situations/contexts (e.g., "*Knowing what sharing means and why my friends do it may make it easier to share.*"). The conclusion of a Social Story provides a summary and emphasizes the importance of achieving new behaviors to the reader (e.g., "*Sharing is a nice thing to do and helps me make friends.*"). Taken together, the basic format of a Social Story affords the reader the ability to gain perspective and apply such information to his or her own experience (Gray, 2015).
- ***Criteria 4: Individualize Content and Format.*** As with many other disabilities, the characteristics of ASD are highly variable and range in severity. Thus, it is important to recognize each individual's unique differences and personal preferences when creating a Social Story. It goes without saying that a Social Story must be written with regard to the student's

comprehension level. For younger children, stories should be brief and direct. Gray (2015) generally recommends that Social Stories contain 3-12 sentences in order to maintain interest and understanding. At times, topics will require much more description within the context of the story than what this recommendation allows. Subsequently, Gray (2015) recommends breaking complex skill sets into two or more shorter stories called Social Story Sets. Most Social Stories include some illustration (i.e., pictures, photographs, videos, diagrams, charts, etc.) to enhance the content of the story. Whatever may be used, it is important to ensure that illustrations portray the meaning and intent of the text.

- *Criteria 5: Use Voice and Effective Vocabulary*. It is important that a Social Story not only is supportive of the student (focus on what the child can do), but also is presented in such a way as to ease understanding. As such, language should be devoid of metaphors, idioms, or other abstract concepts that may confuse the reader, who is more literal. Vocabulary should be direct and as free as possible from any additional, double, or unintended meaning. Typically, the Social Story will be written from the perspective of the student (first-person) and in the present tense.

- *Criteria 6: Create Meaning within the Social Story*. Essential to creating an effective Social Story is to think of every step possible within a certain event or skill and include each step (including the 'hidden' implied steps we take for granted) within the context of the story itself. Gray (2015) recommends using basic "wh-" questions (who, what, when, where, why, and how) to remind authors to include essential information within the context of the story. Specifically, each Social Story should provide: (a) a description of the relevant social situation/context (where); (b) the relevant people involved (who); (c) time-related information (when); (d) contextual cues (what); (e) expected or suggested behaviors (how); and (f) rationale for engaging in new or confusing behavior (why). By answering such questions, educators will be able to create meaning within the Social Story.

- *Criterion 7: Use Specific Sentence Types*. As indicated previously, Social Stories are composed of a combination of *Descriptive Sentences* and *Coaching Sentences* (Gray, 2015). *Descriptive Sentences* are the only 'required' sentences in a Social Story, and they are used to describe the contextual cues and relevant facts of a situation or skill (e.g., "*The fire alarm is a loud bell that rings when there is a fire or when we need to practice getting out of the classroom.*"). In addition to describing information, *Descriptive Sentences* may be used to bolster understanding by referencing the thoughts, feelings, beliefs, moods, and/or opinions of the student or others (e.g., "*Fire alarms do not bother all people.*"; "*My teachers may not understand how much the fire alarm bothers me.*"). A *Coaching Sentence* guides (or directs) the student to a preferred behavior or an appropriate response. They state, in very positive terms, what is expected as a response to a given situation (e.g., "*I will try to remain calm when the fire alarm rings.*"). It is important to begin *Coaching Sentences* with "I can try…" or "I will work on…" so as to stress the importance of effort rather than outcome (Howley & Arnold, 2005).

- **Criteria 8: Review Sentence Ratios.** Because the goal of a Social Story is to describe more than to direct, it is necessary to have at least twice as many *Descriptive Sentences* as *Coaching Sentences* (Gray, 2015). While a Social Story can have an unlimited number of *Descriptive Sentences*, the number of *Coaching Sentences* should be limited to only one or two. When constructing a Social Story, educators should ensure that sentences adhere to the Social Story Formula (Gray, 2015):

    $$\text{Descriptive Sentences} / \text{Coaching Sentences} \geq 2$$

- **Criteria 9: Review and Modify Prior to Implementation.** After the Social Story has been created, educators should take time to review and revise. This may include distributing the Social Story to the educational team and/or caregiver(s) for their feedback. The objective is to provide an opportunity to hear from others (i.e., those responsible for educating the student) and find out if any barriers exist that may hinder the student's understanding of the story, or if the student may need additional resources or preparation to use the Social Story effectively.

- **Criteria 10: Implement and Monitor.** Following the revisions, school-based personnel should consider the manner in which the Social Story will be presented to the child. Selection of the most appropriate technique is dependent upon the individual abilities and needs of the student (i.e., if reading is an area of difficulty, use video-based approaches). A Social Story can be (a) read either independently or by others (e.g., White et al., 2018); (b) presented auditorily or through song (e.g., Fees, Kaff, Holmberg, Teagarden, & Delreal, 2014); (c) paired with video (e.g., Sansosti & Powell-Smith, 2008); or (d) presented via computer or mobile device (e.g., Kim, Blair, & Lim, 2014). Regardless of the implementation method, it is necessary for comprehension to be assessed (Gray, 2015). Comprehension may be assessed using checklists, open-ended questions, or through role-plays to demonstrate what he or she will do the next time the situation occurs. Once comprehension is assessed, it is suggested that an implementation schedule be created (Gray, 2015). Perhaps the most essential consideration when implementing a Social Story is monitoring of student progress once the Social Story has been introduced. Data should be collected to afford educational teams both formative and summative evaluation. Readers interested in the process of information/data collection specific to students with ASD are encouraged to use the data forms described by Sansosti et al. (2010).

Case Study

Background Information

Felipe was a fourth grade student who attended Ravello Pines Elementary School. A review of Felipe's records revealed a history of language, social, and behavioral difficulties at an early age. At the age of four, Felipe was diagnosed with ASD as a result of language delays, poor socialization skills, and temper tantrums. Subsequently, Felipe received early-intervention services through a full-day public preschool program for students with autism. At the age of six, Felipe was considered to be academically and socially prepared for regular kindergarten. Since that time, Felipe has been instructed in the general education classroom and has received passing marks in all academic subjects. A review of prior evaluations demonstrated that Felipe possessed average cognitive and academic abilities. Despite his positive academic progression, Felipe's teacher, Mrs. Caputo, referred Felipe because of concerns associated with following instructions and completing academic work.

Description of the Problem Behavior

The school psychologist conducted a problem-identification interview with Mrs. Caputo. She indicated that her primary concern for Felipe was his difficulty completing work and, at times, refusal to comply with teacher-led instruction. It was jointly determined that following instructions was likely the key behavior of focus for Felipe. Following instructions was defined as instances when Felipe would physically respond to a one- or two-step direction within 10 seconds and complete the request within 15 seconds. Examples of following instructions included engaging in the requested command or asking a question related to the instruction. Non-examples included making utterances that were not focused on the lesson, walking away from a lesson, or verbal refusal. Mrs. Caputo noted that if Felipe doesn't know the point of something, he often does not follow through with the assignment, and that he appears to demonstrate the most difficulty during reading activities.

Following the interview with Mrs. Caputo, the school psychologist conducted several classroom observations. These observations occurred during independent seatwork, large-group reading instruction, and large-group math instruction, respectively. For these observations, the school psychologist used the A-B-C Checklist from Sansosti et al. (2010) to aid in identifying response patterns in Felipe's behavior. A qualitative synopsis of the data gathered revealed that when a demand or request was made, Felipe would either not engage in the activity or, a few times, refuse to participate. When Mrs. Caputo would verbally or physically redirect Felipe, he engaged 80% of the time. However, when Mrs. Caputo ignored his behavior, Felipe would escalate (talk, stomp feet at desk) until Mrs. Caputo would redirect. During one occurrence, Felipe threw his book towards the back of the room, resulting in loss of privileges for preferred computer time.

In addition to A-B-C data collection, a school psychology intern separately collected data on the frequency of Felipe's on-task and off-task behavior compared with his peers using the Behavioral Observation of Students in Schools (BOSS) App for iPhone (Pearson Education, Inc., 2016). The BOSS observation was collected during small-group reading instruction and was approximately 15 minutes long (divided into 50 to 15-second intervals). Analysis of this observation revealed that Felipe was actively engaged at a level less frequent than his peers, and he engaged in high rates of off-task behaviors including playing with items in his desk, looking around the room, and paging throughout his book without reading. It was noted that this observation was conducted during an activity that was less structured than traditional instruction and may have contributed to Felipe's higher rates of off-task behaviors.

Problem Analysis

Information gathered validated previous descriptions of Felipe's behavior. Specifically, Felipe demonstrated difficulty following directions, which led to assignments not being completed and, at times, problematic behavior, especially during reading instruction. Analysis of available data led the educational team to hypothesize that Felipe's behaviors were maintained by adult attention/ assistance. Analysis of A-B-C data demonstrated that during the majority of instances when Felipe did not follow directions, he would receive direct one-on-one support from Mrs. Caputo either through verbal or physical redirection. Once Mrs. Caputo assisted him and redirected his behavior, Felipe often would remain engaged and on-task at rates similar to that of his peers. Relatedly, it was posited that Felipe may need to be repeatedly reminded of expectations and rules of the classroom.

Intervention Goals

The school psychologist and Mrs. Caputo reviewed the gathered data and hypotheses to find common agreement. Both parties established that while Felipe is capable of performing the academic tasks within the classroom, he must learn to focus his attention to following directions when given the first time. Given the highly fluid nature of the classroom, Mrs. Caputo asked that the intervention be something that did not require significant time for implementation or could be used by Felipe independently during certain periods of the school day. Because Felipe possessed sufficient reading skills, it was determined that a story describing the importance of following directions may be part of an effective solution.

Measurement of Target Behaviors, Data Collection Strategies, and Progress Monitoring

A basic, nonexperimental (AB) design was used to evaluate the overall utility of the intervention. Although this type of data collection would not be adequate for scientific purposes, it was deemed sufficient for demonstrating student improvement during a brief period of time. A baseline (A) period occurred for a period of two weeks. During the baseline phase, Felipe's teachers gathered data using the Behavior Recording Form and the school psychology intern conducted a minimum of four observations (two per week) using the BOSS App for iPhone. No intervention occurred during this period.

An intervention period (B) was implemented following baseline data collection and lasted six weeks. Prior to the initiation of the intervention, Mrs. Caputo and the classroom paraprofessional reviewed the Social Story and the procedures for implementation with the school psychologist. The school psychologist also met with Felipe to review the Social Story and assess understanding. Specifically, the school psychologist asked Felipe questions related to the story to assess comprehension of content. Once implemented, Felipe reviewed his Social Story each morning. Felipe's teacher or the classroom paraprofessional continued to collect data using the Behavior Recording Form and the school psychology intern conducted academic engaged time (AET) observations three times per week. The intervention phase lasted six weeks.

The effect of the Social Story intervention was assessed in two ways. First, a Behavior Recording Form (see Appendix A) was created for the teachers to record times that Felipe was not following directions and/or was noncompliant at any time during the day. This form was completed by either Mrs. Caputo or the classroom paraprofessional. Its purpose was to provide a basic frequency count of the times Felipe was not following directions and served as ongoing formative information to identify possible triggers (i.e., were there certain subjects that triggered noncompliance?). Second, the percentage of AET was used as an overall outcome variable and was defined as any time Felipe was engaged, either actively or passively, in class. Examples included periods of time when Felipe was engaged in assigned work such as reaching, writing, or talking to a teacher or a classmate about the assigned materials, as well as those times when Felipe was engaged passively by listening to his teachers, looking at an assignment, or looking at the teacher during instruction. AET data were collected by the school psychology intern using the BOSS App for iPhone and presented as percentages of time that Felipe was engaged both actively and passively. Observation of Felipe's behavior was conducted during structured reading activities that included teacher-led instruction. If any of Felipe's targeted behaviors occurred during the 15-second interval, the observer recorded the appropriate response (e.g., active). Data were collected two times per week and were, on average, 15 minutes in length.

TABLE 20.1 Following Directions Social Story (each bullet corresponded with a page)

Page 1:
  Following directions

Page 2:
  When I am at school, my teacher gives me directions.

Page 3:
  Sometimes it seems like my teacher is telling me a lot of things at once. It can feel like my teacher is being mean. I can feel angry or upset.

Page 4:
  My teacher gives me directions to help me learn and grow into a good student. My teacher's directions can be to line up, what to do next, how to finish my work, and what my choices are. I try to remember that my teacher is trying to help me.

Page 5:
  It is expected that I listen to the teacher's directions. When I hear a direction, I will do my best to do what the teacher asked as quickly as I can. If I am confused, I can raise my hand and my teacher will help me understand what to do.

Page 6:
  I know I make my teacher proud when I follow directions. I will try to follow directions the FIRST time and make my teacher proud.

Page 7:
  If I follow directions, my teacher will allow me free time to play on the iPad before dismissal.

Intervention Plan

A *"Following Directions"* Social Story was created by the school psychologist and school psychology intern (see Table 20.1 for sentences included in story). This story was developed using Gray's (2015) recommendations and was constructed using Microsoft PowerPoint. Each slide was black with a white box centered on the slide. Each page of the story contained one or two sentences typed in 14-point Times New Roman font printed near the bottom of the page—this allowed for pictures to be used. The Social Story was presented using a classroom iPad. Felipe reviewed the Social Story each morning during independent seatwork (morning bell work). Mrs. Caputo or the classroom paraprofessional were responsible for confirming that Felipe reviewed the story each day during morning work. It was expected that Felipe would follow instructions the first time given 80% of the time by the end of six weeks.

Intervention Fidelity and Interobserver Agreement

Fidelity of the intervention was assessed using the My Social Story Journal form (see Appendix B). This form was completed by Felipe each time that he reviewed the Social Story in class. This was selected because it was possible that Felipe reviewed the Social Story more than once during the intervention specific time. Fidelity was computed as a percentage by dividing the number of days Felipe reviewed the Social Story by the total number of days in the intervention phase, multiplied by 100. School holidays (e.g., Spring Break) were not included in this calculation. Mrs. Caputo indicated that the intervention was implemented on most days, although some mornings were difficult due to schedule changes. Overall, treatment fidelity was calculated to be 94%; and, consequently, viewed as being implemented effectively.

Interobserver agreement (IOA) for measures of AET were evaluated by the school psychologist during 25% of the intervention conditions. The school psychologist used the same BOSS App for iPhone and observed at the same time with the school psychology intern. IOA was calculated by dividing the number of rater agreements by the number of agreements plus disagreements and then multiplying by 100. Throughout the intervention phase, IOA was consistently above 80%, suggesting the data were reliable.

Intervention Outcome Data and Summary of Intervention Effects

Following Directions

The mean rate of instances Felipe was following directions during baseline and intervention phases are presented in Table 20.2. Before intervention, Felipe frequently failed to follow teacher directions and required redirection/attention to engage with the academic content. In particular, Felipe demonstrated an average of 4.3 instances of following directions and several instances of inappropriate behavior (e.g., stomping feet, throwing books on the floor). After implementation of the intervention, Felipe's mean rate of following directions increased to a

TABLE 20.2 Mean Rates of Felipe's Following Instructions and Inappropriate Behaviors Across Phases

Variable	Following Instructions				Inappropriate Behaviors			
	M	Min.	Max.	% Change in behavior	M	Min.	Max.	% Change in behavior
Baseline	4.3	2	8	—	2.3	0	6	—
Intervention	13.71	5	20	218.83	0.42	0	3	−81.74

mean of 13.71 instances. In addition, inappropriate behaviors reduced during the six-week intervention period.

Academic Engaged Time

The results of the Social Story intervention on increasing Felipe's time spent engaged in class are displayed in Figure 20.1. Before the intervention, Felipe displayed relatively consistent low rates of AET. Upon implementation of the intervention, a steady increase in engagement emerged. Examining the overall change in mean levels across phases demonstrated improvement in Felipe's behavior. During baseline, Felipe's overall mean of AET was 3.4 minutes during a 12-minute interval. Throughout the intervention phase, his level of performance increased to an average of 7.1 minutes during a 12-minute interval, a percentage change of 108%. These data suggest that Felipe demonstrated enhanced functioning during the intervention phase.

Intervention Acceptability

Acceptability of the intervention was assessed at the conclusion of the intervention phase. Specifically, Mrs. Caputo completed a questionnaire that was created to obtain information regarding acceptance of the intervention (see Appendix C). Overall, Mrs. Caputo agreed strongly that the intervention was beneficial for the child. Of particular notice, Mrs. Caputo strongly agreed that this intervention was consistent with those used in classroom settings and agreed that most teachers would find this intervention appropriate.

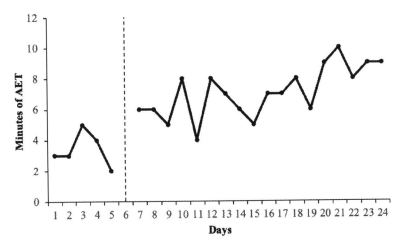

FIGURE 20.1 Minutes of time engaged (Academic Engaged Time) during selected instructional activity

Intervention Considerations

The case study presented within this chapter demonstrated the clinical utility of a Social Story for improving the academic engagement of a student with ASD. Despite the positive findings, this intervention did not demonstrate experimental control, and it is important not to assume that the Social Story was responsible for the majority of the behavior change observed. However, it is important to note that the observed behavior change that occurred was meaningful to the educational staff and appeared to help Felipe in understanding the importance of following directions and staying on-task. Therefore, this case study can serve as an exemplar of how school staff can work collaboratively to improve student performance.

Social Stories are used most often with students with ASD. However, they need not be regulated to only this population. Because the main focus of a Social Story is to teach expectations, it stands to reason that a majority of students would find the approach appealing. As such, Social Stories may be used at both an individual and at a systemic level for assisting all students. Educators can incorporate Social Stories into a systemic, multi-tiered approach for teaching a variety of skills (i.e., social, behavioral, academic). For example, the lesson focused within the context of this case study, following instructions, is a skill that is essential for students to master. However, how often do educators comment that their students "don't listen" or "don't do what I ask them to do?" Perhaps such observations are the results of a failure to teach classroom expectations. Just like other skills, classroom behaviors (i.e., following instructions) may be introduced through a class-wide Social Story with large-group instruction. For those students who may require additional supports, small-groups can be organized to review and model the Social Story content. Finally, a more detailed and individualized Social Story (such as was described in this case study) may be developed and used to provide some students with specific and more direct behavioral instruction for understanding and responding to a complex social world.

Conclusion

Social Stories have been heralded as an effective approach for assisting students with ASD (National Autism Center, 2015). While systematic research continues to examine the true efficacy of Social Stories, their use within schools is readily accepted by teachers, parents, advocates, and students. This chapter's case study is a demonstration of how a Social Story can be used to facilitate knowledge and learning for a student with ASD, as well as decrease rates of inappropriate classroom behavior. The results of this case report support previous research with regard to the use of Social Stories and demonstrate the application of research to practice. It is envisioned that this case analysis may serve as a foundation for the development of similar interventions.

References

Barry, L., & Burlew, S. (2004). Using social stories to teach choice and play skills to children with autism. *Focus on Autism and Other Developmental Disabilities, 19*, 45–51. doi:10.1177/10883576040190010601

Benish, T. M., & Bramlett, R. K. (2011). Using social stories to decrease aggression and increase positive peer interactions in normally developing pre-school children. *Educational Psychology in Practice, 27*, 1–17. doi:10.1080/02667363.2011.549350

Fees, B. S., Kaff, M., Holmberg, T., Teagarden, J., & Delreal, D. (2014). Children's responses to a social story in three inclusive preschool classrooms: A pilot study. *Music Therapy Perspectives, 32*, 71–77. doi:10.1093/mtp/miu007

Gray, C. (2015). *The new social story book: Revised and expanded*. Arlington, TX: Future Horizons.

Howley, M., & Arnold, E. (2005). *Revealing the hidden social code*. London: Jessica Kingsley.

Kim, M., Blair, K. C., & Lim, K. (2014). Using table assisted Social Stories™ to improve classroom behavior for adolescents with intellectual disabilities. *Research in Developmental Disabilities, 35*, 2241. doi:10.1016/j.ridd.2014.05.011

Leaf, J. B., Oppenheim-Leaf, M. L., Leaf, R. B., Taubman, M., McEachin, J., Parker, T., … & Mountjoy, T. (2015). What is the proof? A methodological review of studies that have utilized social stories. *Education and Training in Autism and Developmental Disabilities, 50*, 127–141.

McGill, R. J., Baker, D., & Busse, R. T. (2015). Social Story™ interventions for decreasing challenging behaviours: A single-case meta-analysis 1995–2012. *Educational Psychology in Practice, 31*, 21–42. doi:10.1080/02667363.2014.975785

National Autism Center. (2015). *Findings and conclusions: National standards project phase 2*.

Pearson Education. (2016). *BOSS™ – Behavioral observation of students in schools* (Version 1.2.0) [Mobile application software]

Reynhout, G., & Carter, M. (2009). The use of social stories by teachers and their perceived efficacy. *Research in Autism Spectrum Disorders, 3*, 232–251. doi:10.1016/j.rasd.2008.06.003

Reynhout, G., & Carter, M (2007). Social story efficacy with a child with autism spectrum disorder and moderate intellectual disability. *Focus on Autism and Other Developmental Disabilities, 22*, 173–182. doi:10.1177/10883576070220030401

Sansosti, F. J., & Powell-Smith, K. A. (2008). Using computer-presented social stories and video models to increase the social communication skills of children with high-functioning autism spectrum disorders. *Journal of Positive Behavior Interventions, 10*, 162–178. doi:10.1177/1098300708316259

Sansosti, F. J., Powell-Smith, K. A., & Cowan, R. J. (2010). *High functioning autism/Asperger syndrome in schools: Assessment and intervention*. New York, NY: Guilford.

Sansosti, F. J., Powell-Smith, K. A., Kincaid, D. (2004). A research synthesis of Social Story interventions for children with autism spectrum disorders. *Focus on Autism and Other Developmental Disabilities, 19*, 194–204. doi:10.1177/10883576040190040101

White, J., Caniglia, C., McLaughlin, T. F., & Bianco, L. (2018). The effects of social stories and a token economy on decreasing inappropriate peer interactions with a middle school student. *Learning Disabilities: A Contemporary Journal, 16*, 75–86.

Appendix A: Behavior Recording Form

Student:	Date:
Observer:	Time Started:
Activity:	Time Ended:

Did the student follow teacher-led instruction the FIRST time?	Yes	No
If No, what redirection was provided?		
After redirection, did the student follow the instruction?	Yes	No

Did the student engage in any inappropriate behavior?	Yes	No
What was the inappropriate behavior (describe in active terms)?		

Episode	Behavior Started	Behavior Ended	Duration
Total Duration of Inappropriate Behavior			
Percent of Time Target Displayed Inappropriate Behavior (Duration/Total Time)			

Adapted from *High-functioning autism/Asperger syndrome in schools: Assessment and intervention*, by F. J., Sansosti, K. A. Powell-Smith, and R. J. Cowan, 2010, p. 223.

Appendix B: Felipe's Social Story Journal

Today's Date: _____   *Time:* _____
I read my story called: _____

I read it:				
At Home	In the Bus/Car	On Playground	At Lunch	Other:
I read it with:				
A friend	Just me	An adult	Other:	
The A story makes me:				
Happy	Sad	Mad	Confused	

Appendix C: Intervention Acceptability Questionnaire

The purpose of this questionnaire is to obtain information regarding your acceptance of the intervention. Such information will aid in future selection of classroom interventions for students. Please circle the number the best describes your agreement or disagreement with each statement using the scale below.

	1 Strongly Agree	2 Agree	3 Slightly Agree	4 Slightly Disagree	5 Disagree	6 Strongly Disagree
This was an acceptable intervention for the student's difficulties	1	2	3	4	5	6
I liked the procedures used in this intervention	1	2	3	4	5	6
The intervention was a good way to handle the student's difficulties	1	2	3	4	5	6
This intervention was consistent with those I have used in classroom settings	1	2	3	4	5	6
The intervention improved the student's behavior in my classroom	1	2	3	4	5	6
I was satisfied with the overall effect of the intervention	1	2	3	4	5	6
Most teachers would find this intervention suitable to use in their classroom	1	2	3	4	5	6
I would suggest the use of this intervention to others	1	2	3	4	5	6

Comments:

21
FUNCTIONAL ANALYSIS

Ajamu Nkosi and Michael M. Mueller

Introduction

Conducted within the larger framework of a functional behavioral assessment (FBA), functional analysis is a behavioral assessment procedure utilized for the purpose of identifying a specific reinforcer for a targeted problematic behavior (Mueller, 2004). By presenting carefully arranged test and control conditions that mimic real-world antecedents and consequences from the referral environment, the functional analysis is the only FBA methodology that allows the assessor to make *causal* (i.e., as opposed to *correlational*) claims about whether a particular variable is functioning as a reinforcer (Lerman & Iwata, 1993).

Even severe and destructive behaviors are reinforced by a very small number of variables that include access to attention from adults or peers, access to preferred tangible items or activities, escaping or avoiding demands, and, for some behaviors, sensory/automatic reinforcement (Mueller, Nkosi, & Hine, 2011). Any one of these variables can reinforce disruptive or dangerous behavior. The goal of the FBA is to identify which of these is functioning as a reinforcer. However, when conducting an FBA in a classroom, it is possible that multiple potential reinforcers (e.g., attention, escape, etc.) occur simultaneously following the behavior. Because multiple different potential reinforcers are occurring simultaneously, and any of those could be individually reinforcing the behavior, descriptive assessment methods (e.g., direct observations, teacher reports, A-B-C data collection, etc.) cannot determine which of the potential reinforcers is actually a reinforcer. Functional analysis can.

The logic and general methodology of a functional analysis is to present different environmental arrangements, called "conditions," in a controlled manner, one at a time, that only allows the effects of one reinforcer to be observed. These conditions create an ideal opportunity for the target behavior to occur if the behavior is reinforced by the particular variable being tested. For example, if the hypothesis was that a student's self-injury was reinforced by access to tangibles, you would create a situation where the student has a preferred tangible. You would then restrict the tangible and therefore create motivation for the behavior to be demonstrated if the self-injury was reinforced by access. If self-injury occurs, the item is returned. In this condition, no attention would be delivered; no task demands would be placed on the student. Only the effects of the removal and subsequent return of the item would be observed on the self-injury. Conditions are created for any possible individual reinforcer to ensure the effects of only one variable at a time is observed. To test whether the reinforcer might be attention from staff, staff would restrict and then completely withhold attention, creating a prime opportunity for behaviors reinforced by attention to be demonstrated. Upon demonstration of the target behavior, staff would briefly deliver attention and then once again withhold it. No tangible items would be delivered. To analyze whether escape is the reinforcer, difficult or non-preferred demands would be placed on the student, creating the motivation for behaviors reinforced by getting out of non-preferred tasks to be demonstrated. If the target behavior occurred, the student would be given a small break from the demands. No attention and no tangibles would be delivered.

The logic to creating functional analysis conditions is to create a situation that would only motivate the behavior if it is reinforced by one specific variable. In the previous example of restricting a student's preferred item, this would not evoke behaviors reinforced by escaping work or by gaining attention. Restricting access to items would only motivate behaviors that lead to getting items. Withholding attention does not evoke behaviors that allow students to avoid work or gain access to preferred things. Presenting a student with difficult task demands does not set the occasion for gaining attention. It only sets the occasion for behaviors that are functional for escaping those demands. Each individual condition is designed to only evoke behavior by a single reinforcer (see Mueller, Moore, & Sterling-Turner, 2005; Sarno et al., 2011, for examples of multi-stimulus variables tested in functional analysis).

For each test condition, there must be a control condition. A control condition is one in which the potential reinforcer being tested is provided non-contingently (Fahmie, Iwata, Querim, & Harper, 2013). A control condition for attention would be a condition where attention is provided freely throughout the session. For tangibles, the control condition has the preferred item available for the duration of the session. For escape, no demands are placed in the session. In a functional analysis in which attention and tangibles are each being tested, a control condition would provide the tangible item and attention throughout the condition. The logic is twofold. First, if the reinforcer is staff attention, and staff attention is being delivered throughout the control condition, there would be no motivation for the target behavior to be demonstrated to access the attention as it is already present. The target behavior becomes nonfunctional if the reinforcer is available. Second, in the test conditions, the target behavior is the only way to access the reinforcer. If the only way to access the reinforcer is to demonstrate the target behavior, the target behavior is demonstrated.

Within a functional analysis, test and control conditions are presented in short sessions, typically 5–10 minutes (Wallace & Iwata, 1999) in some random or semi-random order. Each is presented before any condition is repeated. A minimum of two sessions of each condition type is required when using the multi-element design (Kazdin, 2011). Sessions are presented in this manner until there is clear separation between any test and control conditions. The level of target behavior in each of these different conditions is compared to the level of the target behavior in the other test conditions and to the control condition.

Basic Methods for Common Functional Analysis Conditions

Attention

The attention condition tests the hypothesis that the target behavior is positively reinforced by attention. This condition creates a situation where the only time the student can access attention is to engage in the target behavior. Prior to the start of the condition, the therapist provides attention though light conversation and interactive play. To start the session, the therapist delivers instructions such as, "You can do whatever you like; I have some work to do over here." The therapist then turns away so as not to be looking directly at the student and does something silently such as pretending to do paperwork or read a book. No verbal attention is provided for anything that occurs in the session unless the target behavior is demonstrated. For each instance of target behavior, the therapist delivers a brief reprimand (e.g., "Don't hit me. Nice hands please.", etc.) After the attention is delivered, the therapist again turns away.

Escape from Academic Demands

The escape condition tests the hypothesis that a target behavior is negatively reinforced by escaping or avoiding academic tasks. This condition creates a situation where breaks from academic tasks are only possible through the demonstration of the target behavior. The therapist engages the student with a high level of demands in a task that is difficult or non-preferred. A three-step prompting procedure is typically used that includes verbal, gestural, and physical prompts at five-second intervals to ensure compliance. Demonstration of target behavior leads to a 10-second break from task demands. Following the 10-second break, the therapist delivers another task demand using the three-step prompting procedure and the process repeats.

Tangibles

The tangibles condition tests the hypothesis that the target behavior is positively reinforced by access to preferred items or activities. This condition creates a situation where access to a preferred item or activity that was restricted can only be returned through the demonstration of the target behavior. Prior to starting this condition, the student is given access to a highly preferred item or activity for two minutes. The therapist then restricts the item to start the session. The therapist returns the item for 10 seconds following the target behavior. The item is restricted after the end of the 10-second access period and the process repeats.

Control

The control condition serves as an experimental control and counterbalance for all of the reinforcers in the test conditions. During this condition, the student has access to all of the reinforcers present in the other conditions. No programmed consequences are delivered for target behaviors.

Functional Analysis Logic

The aforementioned conditions are the most common in practice. However, the logic allows any positive or negative reinforcer to be tested. For any positive reinforcer, the reinforcer is provided before the session starts. The session starts when that reinforcer is withheld or restricted. Upon the occurrence of the target behavior, the reinforcer is very briefly delivered and then again restricted or withheld. To test any negative reinforcer, the purported aversive or unwanted variable is applied (e.g., a certain person's proximity, noise, visuals, academic demands, nonacademic demands, etc.) and that variable is only briefly removed upon the occurrence of the target behavior. You simply present whatever you think the student might be escaping, and only allow the escape if the target behavior is demonstrated.

In this chapter, we present a case study that describes the implementation of functional analysis in a public-school setting along with the evaluation of a function-based treatment based upon results of such an analysis. While the focus of this chapter is on functional analysis, it is important to note these analyses are always conducted as part of a larger consultative process and as part of a broader FBA. The consultative model followed is the Behavior Analytic Consultation to Schools (BACS) model, of which functional analysis is but one of eight steps (Mueller & Nkosi, 2007, 2009). The consultative steps and descriptive portions of the FBA that occur prior to the functional analysis inform decisions made regarding the functional analysis. Those that follow the functional analysis inform behavioral intervention selection, teacher training, and evaluations of effectiveness.

Case Study

Background Information

Cody was a nine-year-old male who was referred for a FBA of physical aggression towards school staff and peers. Cody was diagnosed with Down syndrome, a speech/language impairment, and was currently being served in a self-contained special education classroom for the majority of the school day. Due to the severity of his physical aggression towards school staff and peers, Cody was only receiving 9.5 hours per week of co-taught instruction in general education classrooms despite having the cognitive ability to be fully included in general education classrooms. Cody engaged in severe physical aggression towards staff and peers in the form of hitting, kicking, and biting. At the time of referral, Cody's target behaviors were increasing in frequency and intensity.

Description of the Problem Behavior

The various forms of physical aggression that were observed were defined as follows: hitting, making contact with any part of the therapist's body with an open or closed hand from a distance of six inches or more; kicking, making contact with the therapist's body using a foot from a distance of six inches or more; and biting, or any occurrence of opening and closing the jaw with upper and/or lower teeth making contact with any portion of the therapist's body. Prior to conducting a functional analysis on Cody's aggression, indirect and direct FBA methods were used (see Asmus, Vollmer, & Borrero, 2002). These methods consisted of record reviews (e.g., Individualized Education Programs [IEPs], teacher-collected behavioral data from the classroom, psychological assessments), teacher interviews (i.e., The Functional Assessment Informant Record for Teachers; Doggett, Mueller, & Moore, 2002; Edwards, 2002), and direct classroom observations (i.e., A-B-C observations; Bijou, Peterson, & Ault, 1968) to generate hypotheses regarding the environmental variables that were possibly maintaining Cody's aggression. The information obtained from these methods also allowed us to create functional analysis conditions in an ecologically valid manner to ensure the testing environment resembled the referral environment to the extent possible.

The interview with Cody's teacher resulted in the identification of several potential reinforcers. For example, it was reported that while sitting at his desk, if Cody's teacher made a request for him to complete a math worksheet, he would often respond by slapping her arm. The consequence for such behavior led to his teacher reprimanding him and removing the math worksheet. In this example, simultaneous with Cody escaping from the task, his teacher delivered attention by making statements such as, "Don't hit me," and, "Nice hands please." During such behavioral sequences, either variable (i.e., escape or attention) could have been reinforcing Cody's aggression.

TABLE 21.1 A-B-C Observation Results for Cody

A-B-C Observations

Antecedent	Problem Behavior	Consequence
Task Demand	Slaps teacher's arm	Attention/Escape
Task Demand	Kicks teacher and throws pencil	Attention/Escape
Task Demand	Says "no" while hitting teacher with closed fist	Attention/Escape
Task Demand	Slaps teacher's arm	Escape/Tangible
Task Demand	Throws keyboard	Attention
Task Demand	Kicks peer sitting next to him	Escape
Ignore	Yells "I want my stuff"	Attention/Tangible
Task Demand	Punches teacher with closed fist	Attention/Escape
Task Demand	Shoves everything off teacher's desk	Attention/Escape

Antecedent-Behavior-Consequence (A-B-C) observations were completed as part of Cody's descriptive FBA procedures. The goal of the A-B-C recording technique was to identify the specific antecedent events that preceded Cody's aggressive behavior as well as the events that followed as consequences of those behaviors. The A-B-C observations allowed us to identify and record the events occurring directly prior to and following Cody's aggressive behaviors in real time in his natural classroom environment. A sample of the results of the A-B-C observations is depicted in Table 21.1.

The A-B-C observations revealed that high levels of teacher attention followed Cody's problem behaviors. The observations also revealed that Cody's aggression often led to him escaping task demands and occasionally gaining access to preferred tangibles.

Problem Analysis

Based on the FBA data collected, reinforcers for Cody's aggression could be access to attention, escape from task demands, or access to preferred tangibles. No matter how many times situations are observed in which multiple potential reinforcers simultaneously follow a target behavior, no additional information about which of those events (i.e., attention, escape, access) might be reinforcing can be gained. Keep in mind that these three potential reinforcers encompass each class of social reinforcers that can possibly reinforce a behavior. Because the FBA process is intended to narrow down the possibilities and ultimately identify a single reinforcer, the results for Cody's FBA, as is common in descriptive FBAs, failed to help identify which of the three potential reinforcers was maintaining his aggression. Following the A-B-C observations, there was a need to conduct a functional analysis to determine why Cody was being aggressive towards his teacher and peers.

Functional Analysis Methods

A functional analysis was conducted on Cody's aggression using methods originally described by Iwata, Dorsey, Slifer, Bauman, and Richman (1982/1994) and described previously in this chapter. Based on the results of the indirect and descriptive portions of Cody's FBA, access to attention, escape from demands, and access to preferred tangibles were each hypotheses that required testing. All conditions were presented in an unused classroom located inside Cody's school. The data recorder used a rate of physical aggression per minute recording system. All sessions were five minutes in duration, with each session divided into 30 10-second intervals. The "rate of aggression per minute" was obtained by dividing the total number of instances of aggression by the length of the session and multiplying by 100. Consequences during the functional analysis of Cody's aggression were delivered for the following topographies of problem behavior: hitting, kicking, and biting. A behavior analyst from our consultation firm served as the therapist for all conditions during the analysis. This is the person who presents or withholds antecedent variables in each condition (e.g., present demands, withhold attention, restrict access to tangibles, etc.) and delivers the consequences specific to each condition (e.g., remove work, deliver attention or tangibles, etc.). The conditions used in Cody's functional analysis were attention, tangibles, escape from academic demands, and control.

Functional Analysis Results

Figure 21.1 depicts the functional analysis results for Cody. As can be seen, aggression occurred only during the escape sessions, demonstrating that his aggression was negatively reinforced by the removal of task demands. Zero levels of aggression occurred during all other test and control sessions.

Intervention Goals

Prior to conducting the functional analysis, we collaborated with Cody's teacher to determine her expected behavioral goals related to his target behavior. For the primary target behavior of aggression, the expectation was that it be reduced by at least 50% of the rate at which occurred during the condition in which it was highest during the functional analysis. It was the teacher's belief that such a reduction in the rate of Cody's aggression would lead to a situation where his behaviors would be more manageable in the classroom.

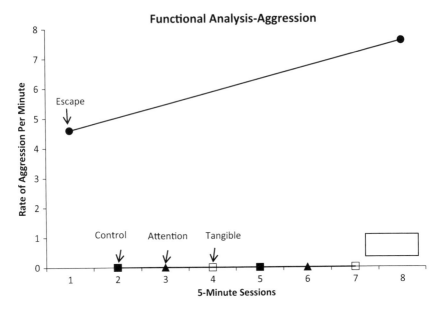

FIGURE 21.1 Functional analysis results for Cody

Intervention Plan

One strategy for addressing escape-maintained behavior is functional communication training (FCT). During FCT, the reinforcer identified via functional analysis as maintaining the problem behavior is delivered contingent upon an alternative communicative response while the problem behavior is placed on extinction (Geiger, Carr, & Leblanc, 2010). For Cody, the selection of FCT was deemed a highly preferred behavioral intervention by both his teacher and speech therapist because it sought to decrease his problem behavior and simultaneously teach him a more appropriate alternative communicative response for escaping from difficult task demands.

Following the functional analysis, a treatment evaluation employing the use of FCT was evaluated via an ABAB (reversal) design. Similar to the functional analysis, all sessions were conducted in an unused classroom at Cody's school. All sessions were conducted across two days, and a five-minute break occurred between each five-minute session. During the first day, a baseline phase was followed by FCT training trials and a treatment phase. On the second day, a return to baseline and a subsequent return to the treatment phase was conducted.

Baseline

The baseline condition was similar to the escape condition of the functional analysis. Cody was presented with a high level of demands on a task that his teacher reported as being difficult for him to perform. During this condition, the therapist utilized a three-step prompting procedure that included verbal, gestural, and physical prompts at five-second intervals to ensure compliance. Demonstration of problem behavior led to a 10-second break from task demands. Following the 10-second break, the therapist delivered another task demand using the three-step prompting procedure and the process was repeated.

Functional Communication Training Trails

Following baseline but prior to beginning the treatment phase, training trials were conducted to teach Cody an alternative communicative response that would produce an escape from task demands. The alternative behavior for Cody was the verbal response of saying, "break please." This communicative response was selected based on Cody's expressive language ability and based upon input from his teacher and speech therapist. Five-minute training sessions were conducted with Cody to teach the alternative communicative response. During the first three training sessions, the therapist verbally prompted Cody to emit the communicative phrase to request a break from work every 20 seconds, and physical aggression no longer led to a break or escape from task demands. Cody independently requested a break from task demands throughout the last two training sessions.

Functional Communication Training

The FCT phase was similar to the baseline phase but with the following exception. If Cody emitted the alternative response (i.e., "break please"), the therapist provided him a 10-second break from task demands. If Cody engaged in problem behavior, no consequence was provided (i.e., extinction). During the FCT sessions, a data collector recorded the occurrence of each communicative response on a five-minute data sheet consisting of 30 10-second intervals.

Intervention Fidelity and Interobserver Agreement

Using a checklist of the steps involved in FCT, the therapist recorded intervention fidelity for all sessions at 100%. A second observer recorded data on aggression and communication for 4 of the 17 sessions, with 100% agreement for both rates of aggression and communicative reponses during each session.

Intervention Outcome Data

The results of the treatment evaluation are presented in Figure 21.2. Cody engaged in a high rate of problem behavior in the first treatment baseline condition ($M = 5.7$ responses per minute), similar to that observed in the escape

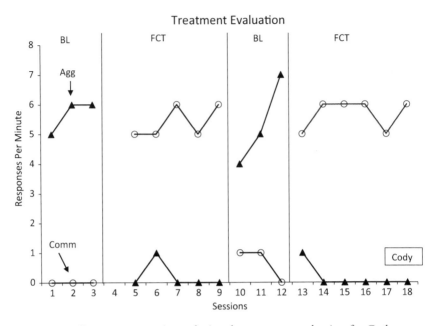

FIGURE 21.2 Responses per minute during the treatment evaluation for Cody

condition of the functional analysis, and did not emit any alternative communicative responses. However, following the FCT training trials, a significant reduction in Cody's problem behavior was observed during the first implementation of FCT ($M = 0.2$ responses per minute) and was accompanied by a significant increase in his use of the alternative communicative response ($M = 5.4$). A return to baseline resulted in a slightly lower rate of problem behavior ($M = 5.3$) relative to the initial treatment baseline, but still with a high rate of problem behavior and low rate of the alternative communicative response ($M = 0.7$). However, the reintroduction of FCT resulted in an overall decrease in problem behavior from baseline ($M = 0.2$) and increase of the alternative communicative response ($M = 5.7$).

Summary of Intervention Effects

Based on the results of treatment evaluation discussed above, Cody's rate of aggression decreased significantly during the implementation of FCT. There was also a simultaneous increase in Cody's use of an alternative communicative response during both FCT treatment phases, which allowed him to escape from difficult task demands by more appropriate means. The successful identification and implementation of an effective intervention for treating Cody's aggression was all made possible by a pretreatment functional analysis. The functional analysis revealed that Cody's aggression was maintained by a negative reinforcement contingency in the form of escaping from task demands. Armed with this knowledge, we were able to employ FCT to not only decrease his problem behavior but also to increase his use of a more appropriate communicative response. Our overall approach from functional analysis and treatment selection to treatment evaluation was very well received by Cody's teacher and speech therapist. A function-based approach for the assessment of Cody's problem behavior along with its treatment demonstrated the ease with which his problem behaviors could be decreased while simultaneously increasing his ability to more appropriately communicate in his needs in the presence of difficult task demands.

Intervention Acceptability

Following the treatment analysis, Cody's teacher was presented with behavioral graphs depicting the results of both the functional analysis and the treatment analysis. When asked to provide her feedback specifically concerning her satisfaction with the results of treatment analysis, she indicated that she was highly impressed with the results and would like for the same type of systematic analysis to be conducted on all students who engage in problem behaviors in her classroom as well as in those of her colleagues. Cody's teacher indicated that the treatment intervention was highly acceptable.

Intervention Considerations

These results highlight three important points related to FBAs. First, had we relied only on the descriptive information, a behavioral intervention would have required components to address each suggested reinforcer – access to attention, access to preferred tangibles, and escape from demands. The intervention would have been unnecessarily robust and included several irrelevant features to address concerns that were not valid. Second, a variable is not necessarily a reinforcer simply because it follows a behavior. As in Cody's case, many variables that regularly followed his aggression, such as attention and accessing more preferred items, were neutral with respect to increasing his aggression. That is, those variables followed his aggression but did not have any behavior-increasing effects in the way that reinforcers do. Third, because some variables were ruled out as reinforcers based on the results of the functional analysis, those variables could actually be used in the behavioral intervention. For instance, if attention was reinforcing Cody's aggression, using attention in some way following his aggression would be contraindicated as this would make the aggression worse, not better. Knowing from the functional analysis results that attention does not have a reinforcing effect on Cody's aggression brought verbal strategies into consideration when designing his behavioral intervention plan (BIP) and led to the FCT intervention plan.

Conclusion

FBA, including functional analysis, provides critical information to problem-solving teams to inform effective intervention planning. By developing intervention plans that are based on hypothesized or verified functions, teams increase the likelihood that selected interventions will have the desired effects. In doing so, teams may also increase the efficiency of problem-solving and prevent the development of overcomplicated intervention plans that may include components that are not linked to the problem behavior.

References

Asmus, J. M., Vollmer, T. R., & Borrero, J. C. (2002). Functional behavioral assessment: A school-based model. *Education and Treatment of Children*, 25, 67–90.

Bijou, S. W., Peterson, R. F., & Ault, M. H. (1968). A method to integrate descriptive and experimental field studies at the level of data and empirical concepts. *Journal of Applied Behavior Analysis*, 1, 175–191. doi:10.1901/jaba.1968.1-175

Doggett, R. A., Mueller, M. M., & Moore, J. W. (2002). Functional assessment informant record: Creation evaluation and future research. *Proven Practice: Prevention and Remediation Strategies for Schools*, 4, 25–30.

Edwards, R. P. (2002). Functional assessment informant record for teachers. *Proven Practice: Prevention and Remediation Solutions for Schools*, 4, 15–24.

Fahmie, T. A., Iwata, B. A., Querim, A. C. and Harper, J. M. (2013), Test-specific control conditions for functional analysis. *Journal of Applied Behavior Analysis*, 46, 61–70. doi:10.1002/jaba.9

Geiger, K. B., Carr, J. E., & Leblanc, L. A. (2010). Function-based treatments for escape-maintained problem behavior: A treatment-selection model for practicing behavior analysts. *Behavior Analysis in Practice*, 3, 22–32. doi:10.1007/BF03391755

Iwata, B. A., Dorsey, M. F., Slifer, K. J., Bauman, K. E., & Richman, G. S. (1994). Toward the functional analysis of self-injury. *Journal of Applied Behavior Analysis*, 27, 197–209. (Reprinted from *Analysis and Intervention in Developmental Disabilities*, 2, 3–20, 1982). doi:10.1901/jaba.1994.27-197

Kazdin, A. E. (2011). *Single-case research designs: Methods for clinical and applied settings* (2nd ed.). New York: Oxford University Press.

Lerman, D. C., & Iwata, B. A. (1993). Descriptive and experimental analyses of variables maintaining self-injurious behavior. *Journal of Applied Behavior Analysis*, 26, 293–319. doi:10.1901/jaba.1993.26-293

Mueller, M. M. & Nkosi, A. (2007). State of the science in the assessment and management of severe behavior problems in school settings: Behavior analytic consultation to schools. *The International Journal of Behavioral and Consultation Therapy*, 3, 176–202.

Mueller, M. M. (2004). Functional analysis. In T. S. Watson & C. S. Skinner (Eds.). *The comprehensive encyclopedia of school psychology* (pp. 121–125). New York: Klewer/Plenum.

Mueller, M. M., Moore, J. W., & Sterling-Turner, H. E. (2005). Towards developing a classroom-based functional analysis condition to assess escape-to-attention as a variable maintaining problem behavior. *School Psychology Review*, 34, 425–431.

Mueller, M. M., Nkosi, A., & Hine, J. F. (2011). Functional analysis in public school settings: A review of 90 functional analyses. *Journal of Applied Behavior Analysis*, 44, 807–818.

Mueller, M. M., & Nkosi, A. (2009) *Behavior analytic consultation to schools*. Marietta, GA: Stimulus Publications.

Sarno, J. M., Sterling-Turner, H. E., Mueller, M. M., Dufrene, B., Tingstrom, D. H., & Olmi, D. J. (2011). Escape-to-attention as a potential variable for maintaining problem behavior in the school setting. *School Psychology Review*, *40*, 57–71.

Wallace, M. D., & Iwata, B. A. (1999). Effects of session duration on functional analysis outcomes. *Journal of Applied Behavior Analysis*, *32*(2), 175–183. doi:10.1901/jaba.1999.32-175

INDEX

Page numbers in *italic* indicate figures. Page numbers in **bold** indicate tables.

A

academic engagement 15, 163–164, 231–232, *232*, 241, 254, 293, 313
acquisition deficit(s) 79–80, 87, 94, 98, 109
activity scheduling 176, 215, 221–222
aggression 49, 111, 125, 132–133, 175, 302, 327; physical 30, 33, 58, 116, 321; sibling 58; verbal 113, 116
aggressive behavior(s) 34, 50–52, 132, 322
antecedent 123, 215
anxiety 88, 175, 198–199, 208–210, 214–215; hierarchy 177, **180**, 202
assessment 218; conditions 5; interventions 16, 229; variables 2
assignment completion 143, 151–153
attention deficit/hyperactivity disorder (ADHD) 58, 63, 163, 175, 231
autism 31, 63, 78, 88, 132, 163, 276, 285, 302
avoidance 7, 65, 182, 198–199, 208–209, 215, 297–298; cycle 216; school 177–179, 186–187, 193, 201–202

B

behavioral activation (BA) 214–215, **216**, 226–227; contracting 7; momentum (BM) 111–112, 122; skills training 93–94, *96*, 98

behavior report card (BRC) 10, 45, 290–291, 296–299

C

challenging behavior(s) 30, 48, 63, 74, 129, 143, 244, 252, 275
Check-In/Check-Out (CICO) 32, 112, 290–291, 296–299
Class Pass intervention 16–17, 25–26, 28–29
classroom management 154; program 50; strategies/techniques 30, 113, 229–230, 239, 275, 285; system 122, 253
classroom rules 275, 279, 284
class-wide intervention(s) 142, 147
cognitive behavioral therapy (CBT) 175–176, 192–193, 198, 214, 227
cognitive restructuring 176, 184, 193, 198, 214
contingency contract 112
cueing 40, 77; *see also* prompting
culturally relevant 8; components 22; intervention 19, 21

D

depression 88, 177–179, 203, 214–215, 226–227
direct behavior rating (DBR) 19, 23, 30, 101, 164, 232, 262

direct observation(s) 9, 50, 304, 317; methods 187; *see also* systematic direct observation(s)
disruptive behavior 15, 30, 41, 62, 100, 109, 111, 163, 233, 277, 291

E

ethical consideration 58
executive functioning 64, 161
exposure 176, 186, 193, 198, 208–210, 215; therapy 198–199

F

fear hierarchy 198–200, 202
following directions 308–310, 313
functional: analysis 317–320, 327–328; assessment(s) 177, 187, 215, 218; behavioral assessment 317
functional communication: skills 56, 132; training 132, 324–325

G

Goal Attainment Scale (GAS) 116
goal-setting 8, 215, 221
Good Behavior Game (GBG) 230, 238–239
group contingency 249, 253–254, 268

H

habituation 199, 209
high-probability behavior 62–63
high-probability command 117; sequence (HPCS) 111
home-school connection 23; *see also* school-home communication

I

inappropriate behavior(s) 2, 16, 21, 23, 97, 130–132, 143, 275, 286, 303
instructional time 15, 17, 252, 254, 278

L

low-probability behavior 62–63

M

mood monitoring 214–216

multi-tiered systems of support (MTSS) 1, 30–31, 48, 200, 290
Mystery Motivator 143, 156, 297

N

noncompliance 30, 62, 111, 122, 124–125, 226

O

off-task behavior(s) 96, 103, 145, 293, 308
on-task behavior(s) 63, 96, 276, 286
overcorrection 97, 130–131, 138–139

P

peer attention 87, 114, 147, 268, 278, 297–298
performance deficit(s) 63, 73–74, 172, 276
positive behavioral interventions and supports (PBIS) 1, 48
Positive Peer Reporting (PPP) 257–259, 268–269
positive practice 93, 96–98, 109, 130–131
Premack's principle 62–63, 73–74
problem-solving: interview 78–80, 87; model 3–4; process 5, 9–10, 99; team(s) 9–11, 99, 135
prompting 40, 57, 77, 88–89, 172, 244, 319
prosocial behavior 144, 200
punishment 5, 16, 48, 97, 108, 130–132, 167, 268; positive 130

R

reinforcement 5, 7, 40, 124, 132, 179, 227, 290; automatic 317; -based strategies/interventions 48–49, 130; contingencies 2, 229, 258, 268–269; differential 16–17, 22–23; external 167, 170; menu 31; negative 179, 209, 215; positive 6, 48, 58, 73, 143, 179, 215; satiation 71; secondary 30; sensory 317; social 179; survey 31, 37
relaxation 164, 181, 196; training 199, 214
replacement behavior 34, 40, 57, 260; functionally equivalent replacement behavior 16–17, 96
reprimands 117, 278, 285; verbal 18, 231
request-response-reinforcement (RRR) trials 112

response cost 40, 132; intervention 143; Response Cost Raffle 143, 156
response effort 129–133, 138–139

S

school-home: communication 193; *see also* home–school connection; note 52, 54, 60
self-injurious behavior (SIB) 131–132, 318
self-injury *see* self-injurious behavior (SIB)
self-management; intervention 162; skills 94, **104**
self-monitoring 76, 89, 103, 297; form 10, *166*; intervention 161
self-regulation 161, 172; skills 96
social; involvement 217, 260–262, 268; isolation 215; withdrawal 88, 215, 260
social skills 1, 64, 76, 87–88, *96*, 257; deficit 6, 78–79, 87; instruction 41
Social Stories™ 302–303, 305, 313
systematic direct observation(s) 10, 233

T

therapeutic alliance 183, 187
Timely Transitions Game (TTG) 244, 248, 252–254
time-out 48–49, 53–54, 56–58
token economy (TE) 30, *36*, 40–42, 124, 290, 294

V

video modeling 76, 88–89; video self-modeling (VSM) 76–77
visual schedules 63, 69, 74

W

work completion 73, 147, 165; academic work completion 63, 122; homework completion 112, 227; time 63
work refusal 64–65

Printed in the United States
By Bookmasters